GOVERNMENT
OF DEVELOPMENT

GOVERNMENT
OF DEVELOPMENT

Peasants and Politicians in
Postcolonial Tanzania

Leander Schneider

Indiana University Press

Bloomington and Indianapolis

This book is a publication of

Indiana University Press
Office of Scholarly Publishing
Herman B Wells Library 350
1320 East 10th Street
Bloomington, Indiana 47405 USA

iupress.indiana.edu

Telephone   800-842-6796
Fax   812-855-7931

Manufactured in the United States of America

Library of Congress Cataloging-in-Publication Data

Schneider, Leander, author.
    Government of development : peasants and politicians in postcolonial
Tanzania / Leander Schneider.
      pages cm
    Includes bibliographical references and index.
    ISBN 978-0-253-01397-2 (cl : alk. paper) — ISBN 978-0-253-01399-6
(pb : alk. paper) — ISBN 978-0-253-01401-6 (eb) 1. Rural development—
Government policy—Tanzania. 2. Ujamaa villages—Tanzania—Ruvuma
Region. 3. Collective settlements—Tanzania. 4. Local government—
Tanzania. 5. Ruvuma Development Association. I. Title.
    HN797.Z9C6648 2014
    307.14120967—dc23

                                                          2014003264

1 2 3 4 5 19 18 17 16 15 14

Contents

Acknowledgments

W<small>HILE</small> I <small>HAVE</small> to assume full responsibility for this book's shortcomings, I cannot claim the same for whatever merits it may possess. Among the teachers who guided me through years of learning about Tanzania and how to think about politics, I want to thank three in particular. Tony Marx was an exceptionally patient and supportive advisor. Marcia Wright generously adopted this occasional refugee from political science. And Consuelo Cruz provided a crucial arena for exploring ways to think about politics and the state differently.

Had it not been for two chance encounters in Tanzania, this book would likely feature voids where there are now stories and angles of discussion that comprise its heart. David Edwards, our generation's world authority on the Ruvuma Development Association, generously allowed me to exploit his research, insights, and contacts. In research-land, prying a padlock off the door of the Songea document shed (archives?)—with official sanction, I hasten to add—surely must constitute *some* rite of passage: thank you for being a co-initiate. Even when research isn't that much fun, it is better and more productive when shared. Over many years now, Andy Ivaska has been a research companion, indispensible sounding board, colleague, and the source of much intellectual stimulation. He has read more drafts of various chapters and the entire manuscript than I want to remind him of. Always he has come back with incisive comments, suggestions, and critiques that have profoundly shaped the final product: this book owes much to him.

Many people gave their time to talk with me about the history recounted here. I owe a particular debt of gratitude to Griff Cunningham, Ralph Ibbott, the late Ntimbanjayo Millinga, Jørgen Rald, and the late Joan Wicken: they set aside many hours to answer questions, provided invaluable comments on my thinking, and gave me access to crucial sources.

John Saul and Colin Leys likewise were exceptionally generous with their time and support. At an especially crucial time, Yale's Agrarian Studies Program under Jim Scott and Eric Worby provided shelter and the community of my fellow Fellows, all under the expert care of Kay Mansfield. At Concordia University, I have been fortunate to be surrounded by colleagues who have read drafts and generally done more than anyone could expect to help make my work better. While being struck by the many parallels between what I write about in Tanzania and what she finds in China, Kimberley Manning has helped straighten out my version of the Tanzanian story. Amy Poteete and Ceren Belge have likewise greatly helped this book along with their incisive comments.

Other colleagues, too, have been generous with their time and insights. Kevin McMillan intervened early and helped to shape this book's foundation. Jim Brennan read the whole manuscript at two different stages and offered many valuable comments. Among the others who have commented on various drafts, Paul Bjerk, Andrew Burton, Hans-Martin Jaeger, Baz Lecoq, Joel Migdal, Jim Scott, Mark Williams, and Anya Zilberstein deserve special thanks. I am also grateful for the excellent research and technical support provided by Barbara Bottini-Havrillay, Eli Friedland, Shawn Katz, Kristjana Loptson, Dougal Monk, Luca Petryshyn, Patricia Schneider, and Adrienne Weber.

Several Tanzanian archivists went out of their way to aid a research project that frequently required materials outside of the most accessible channels. At the Tanzania National Archives Headquarters, Mwanahamisi Mtengula deserves special thanks. At the Party Archives in Dodoma, the late Said Ngwanga made possible within a few days what would have taken weeks in other archives. Herman Rwechungura was likewise exceptionally helpful at the Mwanza Branch of the National Archives.

I am grateful to Indiana University Press's team and my editor, Dee Mortensen, for patiently shepherding the book through to publication. Graduate funding from Columbia University, a grant from Concordia University's General Research Fund, and a *Nouveau Chercheur* grant from the *Fonds québécois de la recherche sur la société et la culture* (FQRSC) provided key financial support.

Significant parts of chapter 3 utilize material, in heavily revised form, from my article "Freedom and Unfreedom in Rural Development: Julius Nyerere, *Ujamaa Vijijini*, and Villagization," *Canadian Journal of African Studies* 38 (2004): 344–393. A small part of chapter 4 draws on my article "The Maasai's New Clothes: A Developmentalist Modernity and Its Exclusions," *Africa Today* 53 (2006): 100–131. Large parts of the remainder of the chapter rework my article "High on Modernity? Explaining the Failings of Tanzanian Villagization," *African Studies* 66 (2007): 9–38; © Taylor & Francis Group on behalf of the University of Witwaterstrand, used by permission.

Aspiring authors' absorption in their work and the anxieties that often come with it are no small burden on their partners. For far too long Heloisa has had to live with me living with this book. Its publication will thus bring at least one immediate reward. For all your patience and sacrifice: thank you.

GOVERNMENT
OF DEVELOPMENT

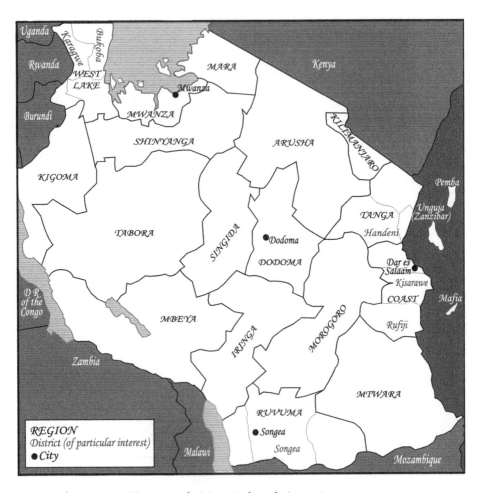

Introduction Map 1. Tanzania: administrative boundaries—1967.

Introduction

Remember, you farmers are the chickens and we are the mother hens. If you follow our example you will survive, but if you are not attentive you will perish.

—A Tanzanian agricultural extension officer in the late 1960s, quoted in H. U. E. Thoden van Velzen, "Staff, Kulaks and Peasants"

THIS BOOK IS about the practices of government that constituted state officials as a distinctive kind of authority over their peasant subjects in 1960s and 1970s Tanzania. Central to this configuration was their casting, vividly evoked in the epigraph's image of the mother hen and her chicks, as guardians whose duty it was to show their as-yet-incompetent charges the way into the future. The book offers a fine-grained analysis of this authority's effects and the various elements that went into constituting it in the arena of rural development in postcolonial Tanzania.

Firmly anchored as the book is in this discussion of a historically specific assemblage of practices of "developmental governing," its agenda extends beyond revisiting a long-ago history in a faraway place. Thematically, it seeks to elucidate the phenomenon, far from unique to Tanzania, of officials forcing often-enough-failing development projects on resisting "beneficiary" populations. This turn of Tanzanian history hinged on the ultimately self-contradictory resolution of tensions in a project of development that sought to elicit its subjects' "participation" in their own empowerment and liberation. Today, when such ideas are often hailed as the "new" panacea in development, this may be a largely forgotten history. But it is not, by any means, one that has therefore been transcended.

On a theoretical front, the account critiques and develops an alternative to the go-to paradigm for analyses of Tanzania's experience, which explains this history by pointing to political elites' pursuit of their own narrow interests. This theoretical agenda makes this a book not just about Tanzania or development, but much more broadly about politics and how to analyze it. The chapters to follow show that developmental governing in Tanzania must be understood as a complex field of discursive practices that far exceeded "interest-maximization." The analytical lens through which much of the political science literature approaches politics therefore stands to be fruitfully supplemented with, and perhaps profitably replaced by, the kind of thick analysis of discursive practices of government presented here.

Government of Development in Postcolonial Tanzania

That developmental governing took the authoritarian shape it did in postcolonial Tanzania was not what one might have expected. President Julius Nyerere's 1962 inaugural address had certainly promised a very different future for the newly independent East African nation of Tanganyika (united with Zanzibar and renamed Tanzania in 1964):

> My friends, let every one of us put all he has into the work of building a Tanganyika in which there will be no more distinctions and divisions. . . . Those of you who have capital . . . use it . . . like a trust fund in helping to build a prosperous Tanganyika in which there will be no more wide gaps between rich and poor. . . . And you, my friends, who have political power; do not make use of that power to oppress any of your fellow citizens . . . but use it to build a Tanganyika in which there will not be so much as one individual citizen who is made to feel that he is a second rate citizen. (Nyerere 1967, 181–182)

Nyerere, Tanzania's central political figure from the struggle against British colonial trusteeship in the 1950s until well into the 1980s, thus pledged to use the opportunity that the end of colonial rule presented to work toward Tanzanians' full liberation from both economic deprivation and political oppression. "Flag independence," he passionately argued, meant little if it was not put to use in the pursuit of a free, egalitarian, and more prosperous society.

Faithful to this agenda, Nyerere and the state apparatus under him would devote great efforts to improving the material condition of ordinary Tanzanians. Given the country's largely agrarian setting in which roughly 85 percent of the population lived as peasant farmers scattered over a vast and varied territory almost twice the size of France, this objective necessitated a focus on rural and agricultural development. From the second half of the 1960s, the promotion of so-called *ujamaa* villages, whose members were envisioned to engage in communal production and democratically govern their own affairs, was the central strategy for making advances on this count (the term "ujamaa," literally translated as "familyhood," broadly denotes Tanzania's particular brand of "African Socialism").

In making the case that bringing people together into such communities would improve their material position, Nyerere pointed to some conventional arguments. Especially in those areas of the country where people lived in a highly dispersed pattern of settlement, for instance, denser population clusters would allow for easier delivery of services such as safe water, dispensaries, and schools. Likewise, communal production, and more generally working cooperatively as village communities, would enable members to benefit from division of labor, economies of scale, and sharing of resources.

What made the ujamaa approach to rural development remarkable, however, was not these arguments but what it had to say about questions of government and authority in development. In his various writings and proclamations of the late 1960s, Nyerere made it out to be the very heart of the idea of ujamaa that the authority to choose and negotiate this path lay with ordinary Tanzanians themselves. Governing in development, in other words, was to rely on people's capacity to make their own free choices. In his 1968 paper "Freedom and Development," Nyerere (1973, 67) thus stipulated that "ujamaa villages . . . cannot be created from outside, nor governed from outside." Coercing people into them and dictating to their members how to run their affairs was anathema to the very notion of an ujamaa village, "for if these things happen . . . then it will no longer be an ujamaa village!"

On the one hand, the president offered an instrumental rationale for this stipulation. The effective functioning of ujamaa villages—particularly with respect to communal ventures and cooperative work—required that people were committed to this path, and being coerced onto it was certain to destroy any such commitment. In addition, top-down decision-making would undercut ujamaa communities' ability to develop locally appropriate solutions and dynamically expand local capacity by learning to do things themselves. In order to tap the full potential of ujamaa villages and secure the greater material wealth that would afford Tanzanians greater freedom from material deprivation, one therefore had to work through and not against people's freedom to make their own choices.

But, argued Nyerere, the connection between freedom and development also ran deeper than such instrumental rationales. Indeed, anticipating Amartya Sen's (1999) conceptualization of "development as freedom," Nyerere proclaimed in "Freedom and Development" that being in charge of directing one's own life was in fact *constitutive* of development: only by making their own decisions were people "develop[ing] themselves as dignified and confident human beings, in a way which is impossible if they simply take orders from someone else" (Nyerere 1973, 67). Freedom and development were connected not just as a means to an end: they were two sides of the same coin. On multiple levels, then, the idea of ujamaa villages crystallized the aspiration to build a society liberated from material deprivation and oppressive rule expressed in Nyerere's inaugural address.

Less than a decade after the president had set forth this inspiring vision of rural development, a letter from Mbezi village, Kisarawe District, reached the headquarters of Tanzania's ruling party. It offers a glimpse at how ujamaa had come to be implemented:

> On 23/9/1975 at eight in the morning we were startled to see seven government vehicles from Kisarawe District carrying 50 Police with fourteen (14) guns and two tear gas grenades [*mabomu za kutoa machozi*]. . . . They started to break down houses, tear down roofs and frames, break doors and windows, and spill the harvested rice. Food was spilled, we were moved out of the way, and some of our things were taken to be trashed out back in the bush. The things that stayed behind were strewn about outside out back where we too were scattered like insects, scattered outside, exposed to the sun, the rain. More than 250 chickens died because of this decree [to resettle] that we 250 villagers heard about on the radio. . . . We stayed where we were dumped

like insects only three days. We have returned to our village, Mbezi, and asked that an Officer come and measure out plots, but we don't get replies. . . . To conclude, *Ndugu* [brother, comrade] Secretary, we ask you, first, to come and see for yourself; also we ask you to call an official, face-to-face meeting between our leaders and those responsible for ujamaa villages and self-reliance so that we can know what our mistakes have been.[1]

Mbezi village had found itself caught up in a nationwide campaign to push rural Tanzanians into ujamaa villages by means of coercive and occasionally violent "villagization" drives, which, by the late 1970s, had corralled the vast majority of the population into approximately eight thousand officially designated villages. The result was a bitter disappointment of the promises of Nyerere's ujamaa vision on both the economic and the political front. On the former, ujamaa-turned-villagization generally failed to bring lasting material improvements in people's lives. Although assessing villagization's effects in absolute terms would require an intractable counterfactual (what would have prevailed absent this far-reaching intervention?), it is clear that great costs and efforts were expended for few positive and significant negative returns. Besides imposing immediate costs in terms of lost property, fields, and crops, the scheme generally failed to boost agricultural production in the longer term and likely significantly harmed it.

That the policy would thus turn into a "developmental failure" cannot, however, be understood without attending closely to the shape of the particular practices of "government" that came to constitute "rural development" in Nyerere's Tanzania. The mode of governing instantiated in villagization was, of course, a major contradiction of Nyerere's pronouncements regarding the constitutive role of freedom in development. But even vis-à-vis its material objectives, this was a modality of rule that proved deeply dysfunctional.

Viewed from one angle, its economic failings were a question of an overreach that had its roots in politicians and officials insisting that they and they alone held the key to Tanzania's development. A less expansive claim to authority may not have run up against the severe capacity constraints that prevented the state from effectively supporting rural production and created a host of problems with state-enforced resettlement—new villages that were often so large that there was too little agricultural land in close-enough proximity, for instance, and site selection that was problematic on basic counts such as the availability of water. But from another angle, one might also argue that the modality of governing manifest in villagization failed to produce more positive developmental outcomes because it squandered an opportunity. If ujamaa was indeed a path on which at least a significant part of the population may have been able to advance, the attempt to enforce it through villagization was inimical to the development of the community-based energies that had been envisioned to drive development in this approach. Had the state refrained from reaching for coercive means, there is at least a chance that ujamaa might have spread further than it did beyond a small group of villages in the country's south that had pioneered many aspects of the approach and provided the key inspiration for Nyerere's ideas.

Whether one is then interested in the economic outcomes of rural development in Tanzania or the increasingly authoritarian form of rule the country's rural population faced, the distinctive authority that Tanzanian politicians and state officials exercised over their peasant subjects is at the center of both these stories. This authority and the practices of government that centered on it are this book's main object of analysis.

That they took the shape they did, it is worth remembering, was not somehow a given. Against the backdrop of Nyerere's passionate argument that top-down and coercive governing in development would be contrary to ujamaa's emancipatory ideals and would fatally compromise the approach's ability to deliver advances on the economic front, it took *work*—of renegotiating and overriding these earlier programmatic proclamations—for ujamaa to merge onto the path of villagization. This book seeks to show how this work was done within a terrain of interlocking and subtly evolving discursive framings and practices that constituted politicians and state officials as authorities who were not just authorized but indeed obliged to direct the lives of their peasant charges, if need be by coercive means.

The analytical framework of governmentality, sketched by Michel Foucault, provides some focal points and a general theoretical orientation for this analysis. The objective of governmentality research is to analyze government—understood very broadly as "the way in which the conduct of individuals or of groups might be directed" (Foucault 2000, 341)—"on the basis of men's actual practice, on the basis of what they do and how they think," as Foucault (2007, 358) puts it.[2] Above all, this account seeks to heed this call for a deeply empirical engagement of a specific set of practices of government.[3] In so doing, it strives to elucidate in particular the "system of differentiation that permits one to act upon the actions of others" (Foucault 2007, 358) that underlay developmental governing in Nyerere's Tanzania: how, in other words, was authority produced within a particular field of governmental discourses and practices? What was its shape? And what were its effects in terms of the modality of government that was constituted around it?

In order to answer these questions it is crucial to examine how officials thought about progress, modernity, and the future—and Tanzania's, the peasantry's, and their own situation within such broader framings. Observing not just their explicitly articulated claims to authority but everyday ways of talking about development, the peasantry, and the country reveals a thick narrative that drew on multiple framings, tropes, and discourses in constituting officials as authorities over peasants. District Development Director Juma Mwapachu's (1979, 116) glossing of Nyerere's thinking on villagization, in the implementation of which he was intimately involved in the mid-1970s, provides a glimpse of several dimensions of this narrative at work:

Tanzania could not sit back and watch the majority of its people leading a "life of death." The State had, therefore, to take the role of the "father" in ensuring that its peoples chose a better and more prosperous life for themselves.

Tanzania was in search of a "better and more prosperous life," indeed, an escape from a "life of death." This urgent, developmental framing of the country's situation and objectives opened up quite a particular project of government in which, as this statement crucially suggests, not everybody was a fully competent agent. Thus, the "State" was to ensure that the people made the right choices for a more prosperous life. After all, the peasants would—as another official, quoted in this chapter's epigraph, insisted— "perish" if they failed to follow their "mother hens" in the guise of state officials.

The specific elaboration of this "developmental" framing of state officials' authority was also shaded in by broader discourses of authority and legitimation with which it dovetailed in a mutually constitutive way. Thus, Mwapachu invokes a generational/ patriarchal order that simultaneously authorizes and obligates "the father" (or "mother hens") vis-à-vis his (her) charges. Tapping into what Michael Schatzberg (2001) has argued is a broad moral matrix of middle African political life revolving around the figure of the father, this trope was ubiquitous in Tanzania. Nyerere, for instance, was known to his compatriots not in the first place as "the president" but much more commonly as *Baba wa Taifa,* "Father of the Nation," or *Mwalimu,* "the Teacher." Mwapachu's remark also treats as equivalent "Tanzania," the unitary nation, and "the State." Implicit in this equivalence is the claim that the state's officials acted in the name and for the good of all, hinting at certain "hidden normative theories of governance," a subject that Crawford Young (1994, 283) has urged attention to.

Such discursive framings were a constitutive dimension of the distinctive kind of authority that would eventually declare itself in the *Daily News'* November 7, 1973, headline, "To Live in Villages Is an Order—Mwalimu." I pay close attention to such framings and discourse because, as Joseph Rouse (2007, 675) has put it, the "finely-grained articulation that language makes possible transforms everything else we do." This does not mean, however, that state officials' authority over their peasant charges was constituted in a purely textual or mental realm.[4] Indeed, Rouse continues, because "language is itself a social practice that integrally involves a rich practical and perceptual engagement with our surroundings . . . the discursive and the non-discursive are inseparable."[5] When Tanzanian officials then gave speeches that harangued peasants to follow their advice, for instance, this was a *practice* that *did* and *consisted of* more than simply conveying meaning.[6] Giving such speeches was a thick and in part material performance that as such produced officials as authoritative figures dispensing advice and guidance to their audience. That officials so acutely resented occasional role reversal between speakers (officials) and audience (peasants) is a good indication that there was indeed more to such practices than their semantic contents: the distribution of roles— i.e., a nontextual aspect of lecturing—was a crucial dimension in the production of this practice's authority-effects. Or to take another example: drawing up plans for the new ujamaa villages was likewise a practice whose crucial effect of positioning "planning officials" as authorities over peasants did not hinge on any propositional contents such plans carried; rather, the activity of planning as such produced this effect as it staged officials as conductors of the peasantry's journey into the future. It was in the thick performance of planning in its materiality—of planning documents, official meetings, and the use of paraphernalia such as survey lines—that the difference was marked between those "expertly" in charge of making plans and those properly subject to them.[7]

This book then seeks to understand the shape, workings, and effects of the field of developmental government in Nyerere's Tanzania and officials' distinctive authority on which it centered from the ground of their constitutive discursive practices up. In developing this approach in explicit contrast with several more conventional ways of analyzing questions of "developmental failures" and "authoritarian rule" in Africa and elsewhere, the book's broader agenda is to develop a paradigmatic study that points beyond the particular place, time, and subject matter under discussion.

Discourse, Structure/Agency, and Explanation

The literature that has analyzed development as a discourse is a central point of departure for this account. In his seminal study of development as an "anti-politics machine," James Ferguson (1994, 18) captures well the central point of paying attention to development's discursive dimensions:

> The thoughts and actions of "development" bureaucrats are powerfully shaped by the world of acceptable statements and utterances within which they live; and what they do and do not do is a product not only of the interests of various nations, classes, or international agencies, but also, and at the same time, of the working out of this complex structure of knowledge.

Precisely how I aim to think with discourse (better, perhaps: "discursive practices") may, however, be contrasted on a number of counts with how this analytical concept has often been deployed in that literature. What a discursive-theoretical approach often amounts to especially in some earlier contributions is essentially an analysis of key terms in the vocabulary of development (e.g., "poverty" or "scarcity"). In these textualist treatments, "the" discourse of development emerges as a fixed, structural cause behind developmental practice, which, on a high level of abstraction, is largely glossed as the encounter between the "West/North" and the developing world.[8]

Paying attention to discourse does not, however, commit one to such a structuralist treatment. Indeed, Foucault, whose work is often invoked as the central theoretical inspiration in this literature, insists that "each moment of discourse must be welcomed in its irruption as an event" and "treated in the play of its immediacy" (1998, 306). Theorized thus, discourse, shaped only in the flow of its constitution in actual performances, becomes a constraining—but by the same token also enabling—field of *agentic possibilities*, not a fixed, determinative structure.[9] (Such a conceptualization of discourse closely parallels Foucault's [2000, 340] argument that power "exists only . . . when it is put into action" and always implies "a whole field of responses, reactions, results, and possible interventions."[10])

In terms of the role it can then be expected to play in explanation, an analysis of discourse, thus conceptualized in nonstructuralist terms, cannot aim to uncover structural determination. It is not, as Foucault (1998, 306) puts it, "a quest for . . . an origin that escapes all determination of origin." But if discourse does not supply such an ultimate origin/cause, what kind of an explanatory project does it serve? It fits with a mode of explanation, suggests Foucault (2007, 238–239), that does not aim at "assigning a cause that is always more or less a metaphor for the source" but at "establishing the intelligibility of . . . processes" by observing the always contingent "constitution or composition of effects" produced by "phenomena of coagulation, support, reciprocal reinforcement, cohesion, and integration."[11]

In such an explanatory project, discourse is not conceptualized as a text whose effects are already contained in its structure, but as a practice whose effects emerge with concrete and contingent performances. A key implication for empirical research is that such a perspective trains the analysis on closely observing the production of specific effects, as framings and practices act within particular contexts. The emphasis is on tracing *specific and contingent processes of generation* rather than on discovering the (structural) *causes of general determination.* Joel Migdal (2001, 23–24) has captured this idea nicely in thinking about the kind of explanatory goal an anthropological approach to studying the state (and politics?) might pursue. He suggests that such an approach aims at understanding processes of becoming rather than at discovering "hard causality" by way of a "search for what might be called *the moment of original sin*—the event or condition or crossroads that one can read back to from the present to see how the current state of affairs came to be" (emphasis original).

In contrast to treatments that turn discourse analysis into an examination of disembedded vocabularies and hypostatized "structures," a mode of analysis that is—in line with these theoretical considerations—attuned to "thick" contingency and agentic possibilities is also better equipped to recognize the variability and specificity of the effects produced.[12] On this count, structuralist accounts of "the" discourse of development have painted a rather generic and generically dystopian picture of its effects:[13] materially, spiritually, and politically, everywhere and always development has had the unidirectional effect of exploiting, alienating, and oppressing the "underdeveloped." Of course, such indictments do have a point: development has rarely fully lived up to its material or emancipatory aspirations. But even in terms of its material effects, it has produced a spectrum of outcomes that is not adequately described in terms of the binary of exploitation or its absence. (The old adage that the only thing worse than being exploited is not being exploited is cognizant of this reality.) Likewise, the binary freedom/oppression that such accounts at least implicitly reach for in their wholesale indictment of development discourse is of course only a rather rough shorthand: crucially, it ignores that agency never consists in some chimerical "total autonomy" (freedom) but is always embedded within a simultaneously enabling and constraining space of agentic possibilities. Instead of shoehorning power relations into a stark binary of oppression/freedom, analysis therefore ought to attend to the complex working out of power relations. For instance, as Frederick Cooper (1997) has argued, development discourse certainly contributed to shaping power relations and agentic possibilities in late colonial Africa, but not just by way of producing an ideological underpinning of colonial rule (oppression?): it also generated an opening and effective possibilities for demanding and realizing colonialism's end (freedom?).

The present account then seeks to steer away from a highly hypostatized and structuralist picture of "the" generic discourse of development to instead render a portrait of the complex field—in all its contingency and malleability—of discursive practices of development in the specific historical setting of 1960s and 1970s Tanzania. In so doing, it aims to pick up on possibilities and openings for arranging power relations, government, and authority in development—and observe how some of them were foreclosed while others were realized.

Recognizing the agentic possibilities that inhere in discursive practices is in the first place an antidote to a structuralist and deterministic reading of how discourse is implicated in the production of effects. However, at the same time the point is not to flip to the other extreme and work with a conception of "agency" that reduces the concept to the image of autonomous, instrumentally choosing agent-subjects. Agents—Tanzanian officials, for instance—do of course also act instrumentally (besides also acting in other modes). But even their instrumental choices are always deeply embedded in the specific agentic space—the ecology—that discursive practices constitute and make accessible to them. What they desire, how they go about realizing these desires, what repertoires of actions are open to them: all this is contingent on the world of practices within which they live. As Andreas Reckwitz (2002, 256) has put it: "Agents . . . 'consist in' the performances of practices," meaning that "they are neither autonomous nor . . . judgmental dopes. . . . They understand the world and themselves, and use know-how and motivational knowledge, according to the particular practice."

Making room for agency in this way is therefore not a question of reaching "behind" the practices in which agency is constituted—for some universally applicable "materialist" instrumentalism, for instance (see also below). This, however, is how the specter of agency in the end seems to make an (oblique) appearance in the generally structuralist treatments offered by discourse-theoretical accounts of development. The functionalist tenor of many such treatments—development discourse serves the rich and powerful, and it takes the shape it takes and does what it does precisely because it generates this effect—at least seems to steer perilously close to ignoring Ferguson's (1994, 17) warning against the kind of reductionism in which discourse is just "an ideological screen for other, concealed intentions: 'mere rhetoric.'"[14] Here, too rigidly structural a conception of discourse runs the risk of collapsing onto itself as it crashes into the hidden foundation of its functionalist argument: too disembedded and generic a notion of agents and their interests.

Sidestepping this problem requires a conception of the world that does not treat structure and agency as an either-or, but instead thinks of the two supposed opposites as mutually constitutive: there is nothing more to "structure" than the agentic performances that constitute it; at the same time, there is no "agency" outside the (discursive) practices that "structure" agentic spaces. The key implication for empirical research is to embrace the "thick imbroglio," to borrow Bruno Latour's (2005, 46) felicitous phrase, that is an actor and an action: rather than attempt to reduce these notions to some thin, parsimonious shell or bury them under "structure," we ought to engage the panoply of questions that quite naturally arise "if we accept to unfold the metaphor" of an "actor":

> As soon as the play starts . . . nothing is certain: Is this for real? Is it fake? Does the audience's reaction count? What about the lighting? What is the backstage crew doing? Is the playwright's message faithfully transported or hopelessly bungled? Is the character carried over? And if so, by what? What are the partners doing?

The Materialist-Utilitarian Perspective on Politics: The Failure of Rural Development Policy as Ploy

Is such a complex and "messy" way of approaching the Tanzanian experience really necessary? Can it not be explained far more parsimoniously? Treatments from what I call the materialist-utilitarian perspective on politics—on account of its focus on the maximization of material gain as the key logic driving the political game—would certainly seem to suggest that it can. My argument vis-à-vis such accounts, dominant in the literature on Tanzania as well as in discussions especially (but not only) of the politics of development more generally, is twofold: first, I show that their explanation of why and how Tanzanian development policy took the shape and produced the effects it did does not mesh with significant dimensions of the empirical record; secondly, I argue that this misreading of Tanzania's experience is the result of these accounts' perspective on actors and agency, which is far too narrow and limiting.

Materialist-utilitarian accounts of rural development in Nyerere's Tanzania come in two main guises. New Political Economy treatments couch their argument in the language of rational actors maximizing the satisfaction of their largely materially defined interests by way of instrumental choices. Robert Bates's *Markets and States in Tropical Africa* is a canonical treatment of African politics from this perspective. Featuring Tanzania as one of several cases treated in some depth, the book sets out to explain the general malaise afflicting the sub–Saharan African agricultural sector in the 1960s and 1970s. By the mid-1970s, this *explanandum*—and soon-to-be stereotypical, broader "African economic failures"—were registering in no uncertain terms: in Tanzania, as in the sub–Saharan African region as a whole, the growth of average income,

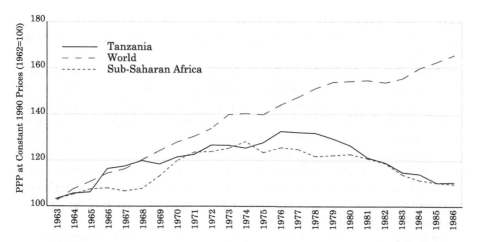

Introduction Figure 1. Development of Tanzania's GDP per capita in comparison (1962=100).

which had roughly kept pace with global trends for a good part of the 1960s, began lagging behind from the tail end of that decade and dramatically deteriorated in both absolute and relative terms from the mid-1970s.[15] Tanzania's agricultural sector, the main source of income and consumption for the vast majority of Tanzanians, showed similarly poor performance: although they must be taken with a large grain of salt,[16] the available figures suggest stagnant per capita production of food as well as other crops between 1965 and 1980 (Msambichaka, Ndulu, and Amanti 1983, 139).

Bates argues that national policies are the key culprit in this story. (Tanzania's and Africa's structural position in the global economy and other nonpolicy factors that shaped possibilities and performance generally receive less attention than they might in New Political Economy accounts.[17]) To Bates, the central question to ask about developmental failure is therefore, "Why should reasonable men adopt public policies that have harmful consequences for the societies they govern?" (1981, 3). His answer is straightforward: instead of pursuing public goals, agricultural policies were designed—or at least systematically bent and then persistently maintained—to serve the interests of political elites and their largely urban, well-connected clients.[18] Shaped to further these elites' material advancement and retention of power, it is little wonder that (therefore only putatively) "development policies" harmed the large, politically powerless, and poor majority of small agricultural producers and, by implication, the economy's performance as a whole. Michael Lofchie's more closely Tanzania-focused work similarly finds that the country's policies were afflicted by an "urban bias":[19] since politicians' "political and economic base was exclusively urban" (1989, 186), policy served the interests of these urban clients (and, by this route, politicians), not those of the rural majority; concludes Lofchie, "Tanzania's agricultural policies thus provide one of Africa's clearest examples of a system designed to transfer economic resources from the countryside to the city" (191).

Although its prescriptions and analytical vocabulary are starkly different, the large class-analytical literature on Nyerere's Tanzania explains the failure of interventions to deliver for the Tanzanian peasantry in remarkably similar terms. Thus, Issa Shivji's (1973) seminal essay "Tanzania: The Silent Class Struggle" interprets the state's actions in agriculture and elsewhere as the "bureaucratic bourgeoisie's" triumph in a class struggle in which the biggest loser is the peasantry. Both dedicated exposition of this "Dar Marxist" thesis[20] and several other key accounts that more loosely lean on a class-analytical framework[21] thus again explain the shape and eventual "failure" of development interventions mainly by reference to the material interests of the powerful that these policies are said to have served.[22]

In their essence, these analyses then share a common perspective on what drives politics, policies, and their outcomes: the pursuit of self-regarding economic interests—augmented, perhaps, by a desire for power for power's (or perhaps again Mammon's) sake. As the ubiquitous interlocking vocabulary describing politics as neopatrimonial, prebendal, kleptocratic, frequently predatory, and generally clientelist indicates, analyses especially of African politics have been dominated by this perspective:[23] these terms all indicate a framework of analysis that sees politics as driven by a logic "in which," as Nicolas van de Walle (2001, 52) has put it, "officeholders almost systematically appropriate public resources for their own uses and political authority is largely based on clientelist practices, including patronage, various forms of rent-seeking, and prebendalism." This framework sees the material interests of a narrow set of politically well-connected clients and the ruling class force a narrowing of the available "policy space" to effectively a single track.[24]

I argue that this storyline runs into significant problems when confronted with the Tanzanian empirical record. Neither in intent nor result was the main thrust of development policy about lining the pockets of politicians or—in a bid to buy political allegiance—those of a narrow elite of well-connected clients. While numerous interventions that specifically sought to close off channels of personal economic advancement to officials and the politically well-connected fly in the face of that storyline on a general level, the actual effects of rural development policy, which typically did not enrich officials or powerful constituents, likewise do not support the contention that policy failed to serve the rural majority to the extent to which—and because—it was a tool that officials used to help themselves.[25]

In thus challenging the account that materialist-utilitarian accounts give of Tanzania's experience, this book makes the broader point that this perspective cannot tell us all—or even most—that we need to know about (development) politics in all places and at all times.[26] Tanzania's experience must be understood as more than a tale of actors conceptualized as the bearers of generic, self-regarding material interests and producers of choices about which no more needs to be said than that they are instrumental to the pursuit of such interests. What various Tanzanian actors made out to be their interests—and more broadly their goals, obligations, and mission—and what repertoires of actions they turned to in the pursuit of such goals was varied, contingent, and constituted within thick webs of discursive practices: making sense of the Tanzanian experience requires that this complex reality not be shunted aside in favor of some conveniently parsimonious fictional universe.

The State and (Peasant) Society in Struggle

Thinking about actors and actions in this way does not just mark a departure from the materialist-utilitarian perspective. It helps fill a significant gap, too, in accounts— in which elites' self-regarding material interests may not be taken to be the driving force—that interpret historical experiences such as ujamaa and villagization in terms of a struggle between "state and society."

In Göran Hydén's (1980) *longue durée* portrait of the Tanzanian peasantry's encounter with the state, for instance, Tanzania's rulers, colonial and postcolonial alike, do not do their own bidding so much as that of "progress" in their largely unsuccessful attempts to "capture the peasantry."[27] This framing of the Tanzanian state and its project may be a serviceable general description of aspects of Tanzanian state elites' conception of their historical role. But how they came to assume this mantle and turn to the *particular* mode of governing the peasantry that would indeed lock "the state" in a struggle with "society" remains uninterrogated.

In Hydén's account, it appears to be the forces of historical materialism that assign this role to them: after all, claims Hydén (1980, 31), "development is inconceivable without a more effective subordination of the peasantry to the demands of the ruling classes. The peasants simply must be made more dependent on the other social classes if there is going to be social progress that benefits the society at large." But that Tanzanian political elites would make specifically this project their own was not entirely preordained. Indeed, at least in his initial pronouncements on ujamaa, Nyerere had clearly not conceptualized the peasantry as Marx's famous "sack of potatoes" that warranted being ruthlessly cleared out of the way. Instead, ujamaa promised to work with and through the peasantry—and not in order to consign it to the dustbin of history, but in order to improve its position and see it thrive. If this original vision of governing in and for development was therefore one of harmony between the state's developmental project and (peasant) society, how did the more antagonistic constellation arise that eventually indeed appeared to require the peasantry's coercive "subordination"?

Such questions regarding the genesis of always quite specific projects and modalities of government are likewise largely left unanswered in the broader literature on state-society relations, which tends to take it as a more or less generic given that "Third World" states battle to establish centralized political authority over domains of life within which a variety of societal organizations and institutions "still" exercise significant control. Migdal's (1988) canonical work, for instance, is less concerned with the particulars of states' quests for domination than with the generalizable obstacles and mechanics of such struggles. As does Hydén, he also ultimately grounds such projects of rule in a generic force—in his case the imperative to mobilize populations and resources imposed on states by the struggle to survive among competitors. But this imperative could likewise be argued to be far too generic to be able to explain how diverse projects of government take the always specific shapes they take.

The "laws" of historical materialism or state survival cannot explain the emergence and unfolding of ujamaa's and villagization's specific project and modality of government. Getting at this question requires attending to the "state" and "society" not as preconstituted, generic actors pitted against one another by some generic logic of history, but as contingent and specific entities emerging only through the practices that constitute them—practices that, in Nyerere's Tanzania for instance, *made up* the constellation of a "developmentalist state" pitted against a "reactionary peasant society" (to capture a complex picture by way of a shorthand).[28]

A Fresh Look at Ujamaa and Villagization

The empirical focus of this book's analysis, Tanzania's villagization drive, is perhaps the most famous case of ambitious economic and social engineering in post-independence Africa. As such, it continues to be a touchstone for analyses ranging from James Scott's (1998) discussion of "high modernism" to Mahmood Mamdani's (1996) treatment of authoritarianism in Africa. However, although the large existing literature—including the key accounts of Dean McHenry (1979), Michaela von Freyhold (1979), and Andrew Coulson (1982)—provides a good general picture of this chapter of Tanzanian history, our knowledge of certain key dimensions of it is in fact quite limited.

New Angles and a Note on Sources

With its distinctive focus on the constitution, workings, and effects of the particular authority Tanzanian politicians and officials exercised over peasants, this account seeks to fill in one such dimension of the Tanzanian story that has not received sustained attention in existing treatments.

Tanzanian newspapers are an especially important source for my discussion of these aspects of the story.[29] Besides yielding a plethora of factual information on events and activities in the country, the press opens a unique window on how policies and interventions were framed and situated within a broader casting of the role of political elites and Tanzania's situation and place in history. Broadly commenting on the Tanzanian press as a source, Andrew Ivaska (2011, 32–33) has made the point that "newspapers and the stories, opinions, arguments, gossip, and tales of the town they contained were a vital component of public culture in Dar es Salaam in the sixties." A similar, if somewhat narrower, argument pertinent to this book's interest in the framings of officials' political universe can be made in particular with respect to the party-owned and controlled *Nationalist,* on which I draw most heavily. On the one hand, the paper serves as something of an archive of politicians' activities, speeches, and statements to which its coverage was very attentive. But it was also an important site in the discursive construction of the political universe of government and party officials and the relatively small, largely urban, and English-speaking elite on which its readership centered.[30]

In this respect, the paper's tight link with the government and party enhances its value as a source. Emblematically, for instance, Benjamin Mkapa, later to become Tanzania's third president, attended meetings of the party's small and exclusive Central Committee in his capacity as the editor of the *Nationalist* (and its Swahili-language sister-paper, *Uhuru*). Little wonder, then, that editorials on crucial events in the country seemed to closely mirror the gloss they received in the minutes of Central Committee meetings.[31] Beyond such institutionalized ties, highly placed officials were also occasional contributors to the press: a December 9, 1969, retrospective of his ministry's history, organization, and mission penned by Peter Kisumo, minister of regional administration and rural development, is a good example.[32] In terms of his audience, Kisumo could expect officials in his ministry to be among his avid readers. Only a few weeks prior to his article's appearance, for instance, his principal secretary had reminded all divisional heads of the ministry by means of an official circular that they received the paper every morning "for it to be read before starting the day's work."[33] Although the party-press in particular generally provided a supportive gloss on government policy, occasionally critical and searching reporting, and quite an active culture of debate conducted through letters to the editor, also featured.[34] Overall, the papers present a rich source for tracing the contours of the particular "reality" of policy, politics, and society that was constituted in their pages.

Besides paying close attention to the constitution of officials' distinctive authority over peasants, this book also sheds new light on a number of straightforward factual questions. How, for instance, did the idea of ujamaa villages take shape and capture the national agenda in the first place? What kind of planning and preparation went into villagization campaigns? And what were the respective roles of the political center, technical staff, and various officials in the regions? The book draws extensively on previously untapped archival sources from the Tanzanian National Archives system (including its regional branches), government and party offices, and public and private collections, as well as interviews with participants in this history to answer these and related questions.

Chapter Overviews

Chapter 1 offers a close-up examination of the pivotal role in the history of rural development in Tanzania played by the Ruvuma Development Association (RDA), an independent organization of villages formed in the south of the country in the early 1960s. As Coulson (1982) has previously noted, much of what might look like utopian presidential daydreaming about ujamaa and rural development was in fact a point-by-point description of many of the RDA's practices. Besides documenting the channels through which the RDA shaped the direction of rural development in Tanzania, the chapter also closely examines its mode of operation. This analysis shows that the practices of authority and governing that evolved in the RDA were subtly but at the same time profoundly different from what would prevail in Tanzania when the RDA's model of rural development was supposedly being implemented through villagization.

If the RDA's practices were presented as a model in the president's writings, how did Tanzania arrive at villagization, in many ways the antithesis of what the association stood for? Chapter 2 seeks to find some answers in the RDA's own immediate experience. In late 1969, the association was destroyed by a decision of the ruling party's Central Committee. This dramatic reversal of fortunes transpired after a series of interactions between the association and key politicians. While some of the frictions that showed in these encounters had mundane sources—an apparent personal rivalry between a key association leader and Peter Kisumo, the aforementioned minister, for instance—they also reflected a deeper clash over what constituted a proper order of authority, in particular within the terrain of development. In this regard, the RDA's practices were at odds with how politicians, at a truly visceral level, expected this field—and authority in it—to be configured. They responded to the RDA's offense against this proper order by decreeing its destruction.

Chapter 3 traces the assemblage of the particular kind of authority that state officials asserted in the RDA's destruction on a nationwide scale as Nyerere's pronouncements about ujamaa turned into villagization. Given his sympathies with the RDA's approach and philosophy, Nyerere's role in this history presents a particular puzzle. How did the author of statements that described development and freedom as two sides of the same coin turn into a leader who, within a few years, would proclaim "To Live in Villages Is an Order"—setting off a national frenzy of compulsory resettlement? With a focus on the president, the chapter traces the shifting articulations of authority in development from the vision of ujamaa to the shape it took in villagization. Although the preponderance—in speeches and public statements in the late 1960s—of the image of state officials as patient teachers had already left little doubt about the ultimate locus of authority in development, frustration with the "stupidity" and "stubbornness" of the peasantry soon brought forth more forceful figures: the "teacher" became the "mobilizer," and, by 1972/1973, developmental authority had increasingly morphed into an "implementer" and "enforcer."

Chapter 4 takes a close look at "planning" in Tanzania and the distinctive developmentalist temporality in which such practices were embedded. In so doing, the chapter takes up a key theme of James Scott's account of villagization as an instance of "high-modernist" social engineering. In pondering the role of modernity, planning, and expertise in this history, Scott (1998, 228) portrays planning as an all-encompassing, disciplinarian practice that was shaped by normalizing "scientific" knowledge and/or an aesthetics of "high modernity." The failure of villagization, in his account, resulted from the effective imposition of a thus *substantively* "modern" (straight lines, science, machinery) straitjacket that impeded the functioning above all of agricultural systems of production. By contrast, the chapter shows that planning and plans in Tanzania did not exhibit the substantively modern traits (chiefly: "high-modernist" aesthetics) that Scott attributes to them; nor was planning ever efficacious enough in terms of specifically directing realities on the ground for plans of whatever shape to in fact discipline the physical reality of villagization in their image. Planning, therefore, did not contribute to villagization's failure through the mechanism and for the reasons Scott highlights. Nonetheless, it did have effects with deeply problematic consequences. These lay, the chapter argues, in planning's crucial role in staging politicians and officials as authorities over peasants. Planning functioned as an authorizing practice, as it positioned officials on the side of rationality, proactive agency, and modernity—juxtaposing them against an unenlightened, conservative, and backward peasantry. That planning was typically struggling—and failing—to catch up to villagization's realities on the ground, and was generally far too spotty and weak to effectively direct it, proved no impediment to its production of this authorizing effect.

Within the thick terrain of such practices and framings, people—for instance mid-level state functionaries in the regions and districts—maneuvered and positioned themselves. Chapter 5 explores their world and shows their motivations and repertoires of actions as varied, multidimensional, and embedded in a specific terrain of practices in which "development" featured very prominently. Even a perspective that views these actors as interest-maximizing agents must therefore examine the thick world within which they lived in order to make sense of what "interest maximization" might have meant in their specific setting. One key upshot of this chapter is just how nonmonolithic "the state" really was: the state apparatus's internal dynamics made its agents' motivations and modes of actions highly site-specific and often set different parts of the state at cross-purposes with one another.

Against the backdrop of this discussion of the embeddedness, contingency, and site-specificity even of such aspects of the story as can be told as a story of interest maximization, chapter 6 returns to a discussion of the materialist-utilitarian perspective on politics. A close examination of the empirical record shows that the tale told about Tanzania from this perspective, in which the main thrust and effects of rural development policies can be explained by reference to politicians' self-regarding pursuit of wealth and power, does not stand up under scrutiny. Why, then, is this such a common way of understanding development interventions (and the operations of politics more generally) in Tanzania and elsewhere? The chapter closely examines how Robert Bates's rational choice version of such arguments makes Tanzania a case in point. Based on this forensic exercise, I identify the strategy of "inferring" the interests that are said to lie behind the production of policy outcomes from a frequently tendentious reading of these very outcomes themselves as the move that is key to materialist-utilitarian accounts' turning complex and ambiguous history into seemingly confirming evidence. In critiquing the widespread practice of inquiry that is centered on this move, the chapter makes an argument for the different approach to analyzing politics that the preceding chapters flesh out.

The specific configuration of development, government, and authority this book traces in Nyerere's Tanzania was constituted in discursive practices of a particular time and place. Looking at the contemporary scene, neoliberal development and government make for a rather different constellation. In sketching this contrast, the epilogue asks what might be expected from this shift in terms of delivering on the still disappointed promises of development. In its 1960s and 1970s Tanzanian incarnation, development did not deliver on its promises in good part because at its heart was an authority that was (paternalistically) responsible *for*, but therefore not responsible *to*, the people. How and to what effect have multiparty democracy and "free" markets changed this constellation in the new millennium? Unlike in the 1970s, people today do seem safe from interventions like Tanzanian villagization. But it is questionable whether this is the result of their empowerment as "citizens" who are now truly in a position to demand responsible government. Too often, this greater freedom from authoritarian interventions seems but one side of a new bargain that also includes a significant abdication of the responsibility to care for the less advantaged: the state, less prone to intrude, has by the same token increasingly left the former subject-targets of developmental government to fend for themselves.

1 The Ruvuma Development Association
Tanzania's New Model Villages

> An ujamaa village is a voluntary association of people who decide of their own free
> will to live together and work together for their common good.
>
> —Julius Nyerere, "Freedom and Development"

Development and Its Varied Shapes

It is a shared problematic—roughly, improving the material well-being of populations—
that ties the set of discursive practices we recognize as "development" together as such.[1]
What precisely these practices make of this problematic and how they respond to it,
however, is a matter of both variation and contestation. This is true even with respect
to the object whose lack of development becomes the target of ameliorative actions.
Michael Cowen and Robert Shenton (1995) argue, for instance, that in nineteenth-century
Europe, to where they trace its rise, development found its object in the form of in-
dustrializing societies ravaged by uncontrolled change and the national economies of
late industrializers in need of "catching up." By the 1940s, however, development had
undergone a globalizing transposition: its primary object had become the former and
late colonial world, soon to be reconstituted as the "Third World." While in this basic
configuration of development, still largely intact today, the institutional apparatuses
of nation-states and international institutions such as the World Bank and the United
Nations Development Programme (UNDP) focus development at the level of national
economies, in this regard, too, there also exist other accents. The structuralist analysis
of the dependency school, in its heyday in the 1960s and 1970s, for instance diagnosed
the problem of development not as the *un*-development of individual national economies, but as the *under*-development of the "periphery" that resulted from the workings
of global capitalism. And while this systemic perspective in the main still bolstered the
rationale for industrialization strategies focused at the level of national economies, development has also found its object beneath that level in the form of particular populations whose material condition seems especially in need of improvement. Hence the
focus on their situation under the banner of poverty alleviation, the rise of which in
the World Bank Martha Finnemore (1997) has charted.

As development's object varies, so do its objectives and the strategies through which they are pursued. Thus, development has often been manifested as programs to boost the growth performance of that curious construct, the "national economy," making industrialization drives a centerpiece of what we recognize as development. But challenges to this way of approaching development have not lagged far behind. One key contention—that growth guarantees nothing about the condition of poor populations because it is silent on the distribution of its fruits—has been taken in a variety of directions. There is now a longstanding debate, and a variety of positions, on the question of how growth and distribution may be combined or traded off against one another (socialist development strategies, such as the Tanzanian, raised this question especially explicitly—not, however, to always answer it in the same fashion). Connected to this debate, there is also a well-established position that growth is but a not always necessary and never sufficient means to the material objectives—such as nutritional adequacy, education, and good health—that development really ought to be concerned with. Since 1990, the UNDP has for instance sought to capture such objectives in its Human Development Index, although such conceptions of development have much earlier precursors, including in 1960s Tanzania.[2] More radically still, development's entire economistic and materialist preoccupation has been challenged. Thus, while Amartya Sen's (1999) conception of "development as freedom" recognizes the material side of development as a crucial means to the achievement and realization of substantive freedoms, it also considerably expands development's objectives to encompass a broad catalogue of civic and political freedoms. "Post-development" critiques, on their part, have even called for an exorcising of the consumerism and materialism of "Western" culture to which they find development beholden.[3]

As actions targeting such varied objects and objectives are taken, development constitutes power relations and practices of governing and authority. Indeed, development has been a central dimension of what "government" and "the state" have meant in practice to many populations the world over.[4] This observation has been central to "post-development" critiques, which have argued that development's effects in this regard have often been violent and oppressive. Indeed, for these critiques this problem runs so deep that ameliorative moves—such as making development less "top-down" and more participatory—merely tinker at the margins.[5] Too inextricably enmeshed is development with the expansion of the scope of the state's repressive apparatus,[6] with imposing a Western ethnocentric *telos* on other societies and peoples who, by this maneuver, are positioned at the back of an ordering not of their own choosing.

There is no denying that development has often given rise to or undergirded authoritarian modes of government and that its project of improvement—as it takes shape in a relational context of comparison with already "developed" parts of the world and groups of people—is fertile ground for constituting or reinforcing hierarchical orderings of values: as "the West" marks a universal *telos*, "the rest" is inscribed into a scheme that defines it by what it is "not yet." Such concerns resonate especially acutely in Af-

rican contexts, where an enmeshment of development with colonial rule and a temporalizing casting of African society as savage and primitive had development dovetail
tightly with the old civilizing mission.[7] Yet, as Frederick Cooper (1997) has argued in
tracing how the late colonial project of modernizing "backward Africans" was turned
into an argument for the end of colonialism, even in this context the effects of development are more complex than just oppression (or, of course, simply emancipation).[8]
As they are worked out in complex processes, the power relations and practices of government and authority that development constitutes are contingent and rarely unidirectional in their effects. Centrally directed interventions explicitly targeting large-
scale change that are tied up with the typical "development regime" (Ludden 1992)—a
cognitive-*cum*-institutional field in which state officials and central planners feature as
essential protagonists and populations as passive recipient-targets—are of course one
prominent ingredient in these processes. But popular responses and appropriations of
such interventions, as well as popular engagements with the problematic of development, such as the ones James Smith (2008) has traced in postcolonial Kenya, that do
not necessarily take their primary cue from such state-practices, likewise figure into
working out what development is and becomes.

Development in Tanzania

The variety of ways in which Tanzanians have engaged with development—the broad
project of "making better futures," as well as the various programs conceived in the pursuit of this objective—bears testimony to this. Thus, Steven Feierman (1990) observes
peasant intellectuals working out an alternative constellation of authority and vision
to both the colonial and the nationalist state's development regimes in counterhege-
monic practices of "healing the land." Dorothy Hodgson (2001) shows how Tanzanian
Maasai have engaged state-directed development in ways that range from resistance,
to reworking, to embrace. Likewise, James Giblin's (2005) social history of Njombe in
southern Tanzania illustrates how colonial policies of cash crop development, for instance, became a resource in people's strategies for self-advancement. And David Edwards's (2003) work on Ruvuma offers a fine-grained portrait of how pioneer tobacco
cultivators seized similar opportunities in that Tanzanian periphery to fashion a whole
"cultural project" of both material progress and ethno-political emancipation.

Such popular engagements with development (*maendeleo* in Kiswahili: literally,
"moving ahead in a particular direction") are of course part of a broader matrix, significant aspects of which are indeed constituted by practices that subject target populations to coercive modes of government featuring state officials as developmental authorities. In colonial Tanganyika, rural populations, summarily glossed as "peasants,"
were the quintessential focus of such practices of development by which "modernizing
bureaucrats" sought to authoritatively redirect peasants' actions and indeed reform
what was perceived to be their "backward" subjectivity. Compulsory growing campaigns; strict regulation of trade in produce; the imposition of deeply resented agri-

cultural practices such as anti-erosion measures; and, occasionally, attempts to enlist (and thereby transform) Africans in tightly controlled schemes of "modern" agricultural production: these were the mainstays of colonial policy from at least the 1940s into independence in 1961.[9] Being a central dimension of the authoritarian practices of colonial government in the rural areas, many of these policies were a major popular grievance, and the key anticolonial organization, the Tanganyika African National Union (TANU) under the leadership of Julius Nyerere, seized on this as a rallying cry in the anticolonial struggle of the 1950s (Cliffe 1972).

Development had thus had a long history in the country when Nyerere declared that independence, won relatively swiftly and without a violent struggle, established an "opportunity" that "has now to be used, and our national pride has to be given to the basis of a healthy, educated, and prosperous people" (Tanganyika 1964, vii). Given its place in galvanizing opposition to colonialism, this was, moreover, a history that may have led one to expect not just renewed and expanded efforts devoted to improving the situation of ordinary Tanzanians, but also a reconfiguration of the modalities of government and constellations of authority through which this task would be tackled. Yet, at least in the immediate aftermath of independence, development's past proved more model than point of departure. In rural development in particular, the new nationalist government apparently still/again largely saw compelling the peasantry into appropriate actions through punishment or reforming peasant subjectivities in tightly woven disciplinary systems of spatially regulated production and dwelling as the path toward the better future that development promised.

The two most prominent types of interventions that, besides the regimentation of marketing processes and prices, constituted the mainstay of rural development policy immediately after independence slotted precisely into these modalities of governing. There was, first, the widespread use of agricultural bylaws, backed up by quite severe sanctions, covering anything from specific growing practices to the compulsory cultivation of certain crops. Despite having been a major source of anticolonial agitation in the rural areas, resort to such measures began almost immediately after independence and escalated into the second half of the 1960s.[10] Already at the first meeting of the newly constituted Tanga Regional Development Committee in early 1962, for instance, Lawi Sijaona, parliamentary secretary for the Ministry of Local Government and Administration, stated that "Government was quite prepared to use methods stronger than persuasion if persuasion failed. Local Authorities would be expected and even required to pass bye-laws [sic] which might be necessary to enforce increased agricultural production."[11] Rashidi Kawawa, prime minister of Tanganyika at the time, re-emphasized the same line a few weeks later when he told the same committee that "Local Authorities must pass by-laws to bring about increased production of food and cash crops; and these laws *must be enforced.* . . . Development was the over-riding task of today and *everyone* must be made fully aware of this."[12]

Such statements bring into sharp relief the framings underlying the mode of governing instantiated in such measures to compel. Governing for development was predicated on a clear-cut distinction between vanguard officials and their peasant subjects: officials' authority was grounded in their superior knowledge and appreciation of what development required. (As Crawford Young [2004, 29] has remarked about post-independence Africa more generally, "In the war against poverty, ignorance and disease to which African nationalism was committed, the state bore an historical mandate as manager of transformation, at once the architect of development and its primary theologian.") Governing peasants through compulsion was not just justified but necessary: only a vanguard could ensure that a population whose traits and inherent tendencies disposed it to act against the requirements of development would act in accordance with them. As the Handeni area commissioner's report to the Tanga Development Committee emphasized, "The main difficulty" in his district "was the laziness of the people, and there could be no increased production until they were made to see that Government was determined to enforce increased cultivation."[13] Like many of their similarly positioned counterparts around the globe, Tanzanian officials, in other words, saw themselves confronting what scholars at the time, too, were debating as the "peasant question":[14] what to do about a large section of the population and economy that had, since Marx, typically been seen as a reactionary "sack of potatoes" obstructing the wheels of history?

If compelling peasants' *actions* into conformity was one option in tackling the peasant problem, an attempt to reform peasant *subjectivities* wholesale through a tightly woven disciplinary regime was another. Drawing inspiration from various sources—including a 1961 World Bank strategy report for Tanzania's economy and two reports written by Israeli experts in the early 1960s—the nationalist government pursued this second strategy through what was aptly referred to as the "transformation approach" to rural development. The core idea was that so-called Village Settlement Schemes would, as Colin Leys (1969, 272) put it, sweep "away all the social and cultural constraints which barred the way to surmounting . . . simple technological hurdles." Under close supervision, the settlers on these government-controlled, heavily capitalized, and professionally managed state farms would be plucked out of their stymieing peasant context, spatially segregated from it, and transformed into disciplined, productive participants in the modern economy.[15] As the 1961 World Bank report had argued, "When people move to new areas, they are likely to be more prepared for and receptive of change than when they remain in their familiar surroundings" (quoted in Coulson 1977, 86). One of the Israeli reports was likewise looking to achieve an attitudinal transformation, surmising for instance—on the basis of a two-and-a-half-week visit to the country mostly spent in consultations with government officials—that "irrigation is also of supreme educational importance, as it trains the cultivator to be less fatalistic, less dependent upon the uncertainties of nature" (Yalan 1963, 15–16).

Such ideas, too, had a history in Tanzania: concentrating populations in supervisible spaces, one 1933 report on colonial sleeping-sickness-control measures had judged, would help with the disease, but it also had the potential side benefit of "changing a disease-ridden and backward horde of savages into a disciplined and prosperous community" (quoted in Kjekshus 1977, 169). There was also a physical inheritance: the initial core group of the "new" settlement schemes of the 1960s was made up of eight successors to the ill-fated post-WWII colonial venture in large-scale industrial farming known as the Groundnut Scheme.[16] Early visions for the expansion of the program were ambitious. Tanzania's 1964 Five-Year Plan foresaw the establishment under the newly created Village Settlement Agency of "over 69" such schemes by mid-1969 (Tanganyika 1964, 33); Nyerere envisioned one million people living and working on them by 1980—implying something on the order of one thousand such farms.[17]

Had Tanzania's story ended there, it would perhaps not be particularly remarkable: just another case of a polity that quickly fell into similar modalities of governing and development as it had experienced under colonialism. But the country's experience turns out to be more complicated than that. Most intriguingly, there was—at least for a significant moment—a palpable sense that Tanzania might spawn a different model of development, one that would not predominantly operate through a centrally administered disciplinary regime or compulsion. This model emerged out of the experience of an independent association of, at its peak in 1969, seventeen villages in the southern Ruvuma Region. Because President Nyerere began to promote the practices of this Ruvuma Development Association (RDA) as a model for the whole country, the RDA's experiment would have ramifications far beyond its member villages.

Nyerere's vision of *ujamaa vijijini* (literally: "familyhood/socialism in the villages") was distilled from the RDA's practices and principles. It had at its core an embrace of a model of governing that would work through the freedoms of peasant farmers: their conduct would be conducted not through compulsion and discipline imposed by the external authority of a developmentalist vanguard, but through their own capacities to make choices. One might call this a model of "liberal" governing, in which, as Mitchell Dean (2010, 82) has put it, "practices of government have come to rely on the agency of the governed themselves." To Nyerere, the experience of the RDA suggested that—besides being attractive in its own right—this modality of government was also a rationalized, effective way of achieving the material goals of development. Indeed, the association's practices of government had been integral to making its villages that rarest of exceptions, cooperative villages that, unlike the myriad of failed and unhappy experiments the world over, were economically successful and provided a highly attractive life to their members. This chapter traces the association's growth, its model of governing, and the role it played in the formulation of the policy of rural socialism.

What, though, became of this apparent opening for a new departure in development? As the next chapter shows, the practices of governing and culture of authority that had been built in the RDA ran fundamentally counter to what key segments of Tanzanian officialdom were accustomed to and demanded. The first victim of this clash was the RDA itself: in late 1969, it was destroyed by the Central Committee of the ruling party. But investigating the nature of this clash speaks not just to the RDA's immediate fate, but also to the broader trajectory of the country's experience in rural development. The kind of authority and attending practices of governing that are brought into sharp relief in the destruction of the RDA would fundamentally configure development in Tanzania over the ensuing decade. They drove the subtle but profoundly transformative morphing of a vision of rural development based on the experience of the association into the economically dysfunctional and oppressive attempt to reshape rural Tanzania through villagization.

The Ruvuma Development Association

A Sketch

In a bid to further the country's development—as well as tackle the perceived dual problem of "urban overcrowding" and a directionless youth—Nyerere had, already in the run-up to independence, called on the country's young people to develop the land.[18] Heeding this call, in November 1960 a group of around fifteen young men under the leadership of the Peramiho Branch TANU Youth League (TYL) secretary Ntimbanjayo Millinga embarked on starting a new farm on undeveloped land at Litowa near Songea town in Ruvuma Region.[19] Seemingly destined to go the way of the many other similar pioneer schemes that had sprung up around the country, the group—out of food before any crops could be harvested—gave up in February 1961.[20] However, with much organizational input and encouragement from a local agricultural field officer, a second group tried again in June 1961. Besides Millinga, only one other man from the first attempt returned, but the new group included a number of highly committed members—if their willingness to give up salaried positions in order to join is any indication. Four of them had for instance worked in various jobs at the Benedictine mission in Peramiho, a key hub of the local economy; Millinga, too, had attended school and worked at Peramiho, and he had also been employed as an agent for the Sisal and Plantation Workers Union for a short spell in 1959.[21]

External support was crucial in preventing a repeat of the prior attempt's failure. Encouragement from the local area commissioner was backed by a loan to Litowa from the District Council, and NGOMAT, the local tobacco processing cooperative union, donated food.[22] Millinga was key in building connections that would ensure the continuation of such support. In July 1961, he joined the first class of students for an eight-month course at Kivukoni College, the new adult education college in Dar es Salaam, which had close links with TANU and was from early on something of a stepping stone into a political career (in his absence, Ado Mgimba managed day-to-day operations at Litowa).[23] There, he met Ralph Ibbott, a British expatriate who was managing an agricultural scheme in Southern Rhodesia at the time.[24] Later that year, Ibbott visited Litowa, then consisting of two huts and approximately four acres of cleared land, and secured a small grant of one thousand Tanzanian shillings (TSh), then around fifty pounds, for crucial food supplies from a benefactor in London (Ibbott 1970, 29).[25] Mean-

Figure 1.1. Noreen Ibbott, Ado Mgimba, Ntimbanjayo Millinga, Ralph Ibbott, and the Ibbott children at Litowa, 1964. Courtesy of Ralph Ibbott.

while, Millinga went to work on recruiting Ibbott as a full-time advisor for Litowa and approached Oscar Kambona, the prominent Ruvuma politician and secretary general of TANU, for help: Kambona solicited a letter of invitation to Ibbott from Nyerere.[26] Following several more visits, Ibbott and his family moved to Litowa permanently in April 1963. The RDA would grow out of these beginnings.

In terms of Litowa's economic ventures, the focus was initially on developing private plots (Sanger 1969, 56). However, an early, 1962 constitution for Litowa, based on discussions in the village and put into writing by Millinga and Ibbott, already envisaged a communal farm.[27] Early discussions about internal management led to the establishment of an elected committee that would deal with the day-to-day business of communally decided work programs (Ibbott 1970, 127–129). But economic viability and making these arrangements work did not come easily. In mid-1963, the newly formed managers' committee was not working effectively and there was little effort going into accomplishing the various tasks that had been set: at a village meeting, Ibbott asked whether his advice was still wanted, as he should leave if it was not (132–133). In his telling, this intervention provided some new momentum, but the key to putting the day-to-day operations of the village on a firm footing came in early 1964: an impressive maize and tobacco harvest gave a major boost to Litowans' commitment and confidence in their venture, and the villages' management system and communal organization of production were firmly anchored from that point on.[28]

Soon, Litowa's activities began to draw the attention of several groups that had started under similar circumstances as Litowa in other parts of the region. With local officials facilitating such contacts, they began to seek out the Litowans' advice.[29] This had in fact been envisioned as early as 1962—when Millinga and Ibbott had drafted a constitution for a Songea Development Association (renamed RDA in 1963) that would advise other groups based on Litowa's experience (Ibbott 1970, 30–31, 36–37). This and related documents foresaw a growing number of associated villages gradually expand their agricultural activities beyond an initial focus on food crops, and engage in basic processing and manufacturing.[30] Despite initial skepticism among these groups—especially regarding communal cultivation (Sanger 1969, 56)—tangible results inspired confidence in Litowa's approach and leadership. After a period of informal contacts with such groups, several became formally associated. In August 1964, leaders from eight such groups met for a course in crop management at Litowa. Later that year, Millinga and Ibbott started discussions about instituting a group of leaders that would be freed from their duties in their home village to assist all associated villages: this Social and Economic Revolutionary Army (SERA) drew people from a number of RDA villages and began working in early 1965.[31] Together with other village leaders, SERA was instrumental in drafting a new 1965 constitution for the RDA that provided for a governing body entirely constituted from the villages and independent of the state apparatus (until then, the Ruvuma regional commissioner had, at least nominally, been the chair of the association, although successive incumbents of the post had not played an active role).[32]

Over the ensuing four years, the membership of the association gradually expanded as more groups drew into its orbit and passed through a one-year trial membership. While drawing on Litowa's and, later, other members' experience facilitated the newer groups' fairly rapid movement toward the kind of routines and communal production that had taken longer to establish at Litowa, one size was not forced on all. Whereas Litowa's members held weekly village assemblies, for instance, at Liweta, reports James Brain (Syracuse University 1966), twice-weekly communal meals-*cum*-assemblies served the same purpose of providing a forum for discussing work plans and, where necessary, bringing moral pressure or sanctions to bear on members who were felt not to be doing their part. Likewise, Liweta maintained individual plots in addition to some communal fields into 1965, deciding only in the middle of that year to switch entirely to communal production.[33]

At its peak in 1969, the Association comprised a network of seventeen villages with a total of approximately four hundred households.[34] By then, the association had facilitated a remarkable improvement in the material and social quality of life in its member villages. In material terms, the older member villages had attained self-sufficiency

Figure 1.2. Litowa's carpentry workshop, September 1968. Courtesy of Tanzania Information Service.

in food, and new members advanced to this point more and more rapidly due to the support and advice they received from the association.[35] The villages had also begun to diversify their agricultural production and move into processing and basic manufacturing. Litowa and Matetereka had started a vegetable and fruit garden. Matetereka kept sheep whose wool was fed into a budding spinning, knitting, and weaving business that had started earlier at Litowa.[36] Other ventures included brick making; carpentry (given a boost by the association's 1967 purchase of a sawmill in Songea town); and grain processing, which the association moved into with the acquisition in 1966 of a grain mill in Songea. Water supplies had been constructed in a number of villages, and by 1969 work had begun on improvements to a number of them. With the help of a British volunteer, the association had also trained a team of mechanics for a technical support center and ran a mobile workshop for repairs of the association's vehicles and machinery.[37]

In other spheres the villages were also thriving: a school had been established at Litowa in 1964; by 1969, it had expanded to include Standard VII (the seventh year of primary education) and served all villages as a boarding school. Emulating Litowa, several villages had started daytime nurseries.[38] There were dispensaries—Litowa's was run by a man whom the RDA had sent to the Songea hospital for training—and adult education classes. The health of the villagers and their children had improved dramatically, an achievement that was of particular importance to the villagers and a point of great

Figure 1.3. Weaving at Litowa, September 1968. Courtesy of Tanzania Information Service.

pride.[39] Compared to the surrounding areas, the life that was developing in the RDA villages apparently also implied major strides for women's equality; Ibbott (1970, 148) reports a Litowa man's reply to the question of whether he had beaten his wife that at least reflects an apparent expectation that the villages lived by a different set of rules than may have prevailed elsewhere: "No! It is not the custom here at Litowa to beat our wives."[40]

The success of the RDA and its villages can thus not be measured by looking at production figures alone: the association spawned communities that offered an attractive life and a hopeful future to their members. Perhaps the best testimony to this was the great enthusiasm with which the first group of thirty-six students who completed Standard VII at the RDA school in mid-1969 were planning further training to fit their future in their home villages and not, as was common for students at their level of educational attainment, in towns (Ibbott 1970, 187–189). This genuine developmental success was not lost on outside observers. Looking back, Brain (1977, 244), a member of a research mission that evaluated various settlement projects in Tanzania in 1965–1966, noted on his 1966 stay at Liweta, "The whole quality of life at the village was exciting and enjoyable, and I count the two weeks I spent there as some of the happiest of my life."

Authority and Government in the RDA

The RDA did not, it is then clear, operate with an especially alternative version of what a better, "developed" future for its members would encompass: a materially more prosperous life was, quite conventionally, central. Nor was the association attempting to refuse an (at least in the 1960s) equally conventional tight enmeshment of imagining and constructing better futures with "the state": Millinga's group was explicitly participating in the project of nation-building to which the nationalist leadership was rallying Tanzanians, and the association was also tied to the state's institutional matrix materially through aid and organizationally through its TYL connection.

The respect in which the RDA did generate an unusual and—compared to then-prevailing practices—perhaps even "alternative" practice of development was in how it addressed the question of government and authority. Centered on members as choosing agents, the philosophy, institutions, and practices of governing in the association exhibited key characteristics of what Dean (2010, 171) has described as "liberal governmentality" and its "emphasis on governing through freedom." Members joined the association by (reversible) choice, and governing the affairs of the villages and the association likewise centered on members' own decisions. Frequent assemblies at which village affairs were discussed and decided upon institutionalized this in mechanisms of direct, deliberative democracy; and where decision-making was delegated, democratically elected leaders were substantively accountable to members. But beyond such institutional arrangements, the association's practices of governing also much more generally enlisted its members as responsible and self-governing agents.

This does not mean, of course, that authority and power played no role in the association, that its members should be thought of as "autonomous subjects"—in the sense of their somehow not being interpolated in relations of authority and always particular fields of agentic possibilities that shaped their very subjectivities. Indeed, joining the scheme can be interpreted precisely as a decision to insert oneself into such relations of authority, as positioning oneself in such a simultaneously enabling and constraining field.

Millinga and the leaders of other groups that joined the RDA, for instance, stood in a long lineage of local leaders who, for decades before the advent of ujamaa, had been assembling groups of followers around visions of making a future in pioneer settlements in the region's frontier (Edwards 2003). Likewise, the particular subjectivities of these leaders did not somehow come out of nowhere. Calling to mind Comaroff and Comaroff's (1997) work on how strategic engagements with powerful outsiders, and in particular missionaries, have been an integral part of projects of fashioning selves in Africa, for instance, Millinga's and several other early RDA members' education at the Peramiho seminary and employment at the mission may be noted. (Consequential interpolation in such contexts of power does not imply wholesale subjection to them, of course: just particular subjectification. Influential as Millinga's contact with the mission likely was, for instance, the blind obedience of authority that was demanded there and some missionaries' unsympathetic stance toward nationalism led him to leave Peramiho in the run-up to independence. His decision, around the time of Litowa's founding, to switch his name from the baptismal John to Ntimbanjayo, "one who makes big strides,"[41] could be read to give symbolic expression to such a repositioning.)

In the immediate context of the RDA, it is Ibbott's presence that most prominently illustrates the association's embeddedness in wider circuits of power and authority. What RDA members had to say about throwing their lot in with the association gives some indication that they saw themselves as very much operating within such circuits— whether or not one takes their statements at face value or as strategic and well-rehearsed anticipations of what the white foreigners they were addressing might have wanted to hear. Thus, a 1966/1967 essay entitled "Why I Came to Litowa," written by one of the earliest members as an English composition exercise for the village's adult education classes, professed, "We thank to all of those who come and help and give their knowledge which we wanted. . . . We shall be very happy if they show the right way of living. For the schemes should begin following their teaching. . . . By steps we can understand" (reproduced in Wenner 1970, 78). In a similar vein, Ibbott (1970, 28) recounts, the village's pioneers welcomed him on his first visit to Litowa with a song about "how Ralph Ibbott had come to save them from their poverty."

Clearly, the RDA was not an authority-free zone: regular members had no pretensions otherwise, and neither did leaders. Ibbott's response to being welcomed as a savior—he reports making "a mental note of the need at an appropriate time to disabuse them of such an idea"—underlines this: he would certainly not shy away from "disabusing" people of *their* expectations regarding how he would fit into the association when *he* had other plans. Yet, in terms of its substance, his refusal to be enlisted as a savior also indicates that the authority he envisioned for himself was of a very particular kind. He and other leaders would not run things for others and short-circuit their decision-making. As Ibbott (1966, 16) would later write, "The ideal would be, if the people vitally affected by this type of development—the people in the villages—were themselves responsible for running the Association."

To get to that point, however, leaders' intervention—in what might be described as a particular kind of pedagogical mode—was required. "Here were people prepared to change and looking for a new way of life," Ibbott (1966, 29) felt, but there were "missing factors," chiefly "the lack of experience of the people and because of this a lack of confidence": it was leaders' role to help to overcome these deficiencies. They could only achieve this objective, however, if they worked through procedures and practices of governing that were commensurate with fostering members' capacity to govern themselves, as groups and individual subjects. Crucially, this implied clear limits on the authority of leaders. A programmatic vision along these lines speaks from several early RDA-related documents. Thus, a section entitled "To Gain People's Confidence: To Lead and Not Drive" of a 1964 document states, "There is a limit to the distance that people can be driven, but we believe that there is no limit to the distance people can be led" (reproduced in Ibbott 1970, 51).[42] This distinction was crucial: it meant that while leaders would advise and seek to guide, they would not be making decisions for members or work through compulsion: exercising that kind of authority through such modalities would be antithetical to the goal of expanding members' capacity to do and organize things for themselves.

This philosophy of leadership would find expression in the RDA's institutions, formal decision-making procedures, and practices of leadership. Ibbott (1970, 10–11) describes what this looked like in the context of the regular village assemblies:

> After those first months I never attended any complete organisational meeting of Litowa or of any other of the villages or of the Association. Many times before a meeting village or Association leaders would come and ask my views on particular topics which were to be discussed and sometimes during a meeting I would receive a message asking me to go along when I would be told of the topic of discussion, what had been said on it to that point and then asked my views. . . . Invariably at a certain stage I would be thanked for coming and told that I might go to get on with my work. . . . Ntimbanjayo [Millinga] understood the necessity of the villages having the power to make their own decisions. . . . He was most responsible for successfully developing organisations absolutely controlled by the villagers, generally described as controlled from below but I never quite see why this should be thought of as below.

> [Millinga] would talk easily at all levels feeding out ideas, while at meetings in the chairman's seat he could sit back and let the people decide. . . . He helped create a situation where people could express themselves and so they came. Toroka [the headmaster] in a similar way in the school was prepared to encourage and feed in ideas while the children learnt the management of their affairs. (278)

This way of running the association's affairs would deliver practical benefits familiar from discussions of participatory approaches to development: it was expected to ensure that undertakings were in touch with local needs, desires, and possibilities and would function to build members' commitment to their plans.[43] But these practices' biggest value was that they opened up arenas for dynamically developing skills, experience, confidence, and even dispositions that together would generate new capacities for agency among the association's members. With respect to building technical skills and experience, this longer-range objective is for instance articulated in Ibbott's insistence that although the turn-key provision by the government of a produce storage for Matetereka had certainly been a great deal more convenient, the way Litowa had come by its own storage was far preferable:

> They [people at Litowa] had a carpenter but no bricklayers, they had savings to buy certain necessary materials, but not enough for the roofing. . . . The villagers negotiated a loan to be able to buy the galvanized corrugated iron sheeting for the roof. They had to calculate how many bricks would be needed and make them. The whole process necessary for producing the building was in the hands of the village and this much increased village ability at many levels including the very important one of certain members beginning to learn various building skills. (Ibbott 1970, 205)

Beyond facilitating the acquisition of such technical skills, cultivating a particular kind of subjectivity—confident, responsible, "autonomous"—among the association's members also shines through in a number of commentaries by RDA leaders and closely connected observers as a key objective of running the association's affairs along participatory, deliberatively democratic lines. When, in later years, Nyerere was pushing the idea of building up ujamaa cadres through short training courses held at the RDA, Ibbott was skeptical for a very specific reason: a quick training course simple could not ensure that these cadres had "begun to build up the confidence which is gained through experience whilst taking responsibility" (113). Likewise, the "tendency" of Millinga's successor as RDA chairman "to take too much onto himself" was problematic because "what would be possible in the future depended so much on the number of people prepared to take responsibility and how much they had learnt about life through taking responsibility" (92). The same emphasis on fostering responsible selves also speaks from Emil Ndonde's (1975b, 367) discussion of how Litowa was handling the reality that "Ujamaa villages are not villages of angels" (a law graduate from the University of Dar es Salaam, Ndonde had joined Litowa in 1969). The village addressed this fact of life in two ways. On the one hand, members subjected themselves to the communally decided discipline of work plans: shirking could be sanctioned through public opprobrium in village assemblies and even through deductions from occasional monetary payouts that Litowa made to members.[44] But the more fundamental—and in the village's experience more effective—solution to the problem, Ndonde suggested, lay in "proper ideological guidance" (366) and "political education, criticism and self-criticism" (367). Likewise, Roger Lewin (1973, 192), reporting on his 1967/1968 observations, stressed how the people at Matetereka were able to "change themselves" by virtue of "their ideology and their social organization," and Brain (Syracuse University 1966) attributes Liweta's successes to "the moral atmosphere of the scheme" fostered in particular through long discussions at village assemblies.

Governing in the RDA thus involved multiple positionalities of authority. Leaders acted as representatives to whom decision-making was delegated, as experts who would advise and guide in technical matters, and even as pedagogues who sought to foster members' capacity to make decisions for themselves ("a particular kind of responsible subjectivity" might be a better way of putting the same point). These general figures of authority would make an appearance, too, in villagization. Yet there they took on a rather different shape, as they operated through different modalities. Whereas in the RDA authority's main thrust was to open up and support possibilities for action by its members (even if it of course was not "neutral" about what kind of actions and subjectivities it sought to elicit), the authority of state officials manifest in villagization largely operated through the deductive logic of seeking to compel and coerce by punishing what it deemed undesirable. Villagization operated essentially through driving, not just leading, as, in officials' eyes, peasants' choices increasingly added up to an overwhelming body of evidence that they were incapable of truly rational agency.

What kept governing in the RDA from sliding in a similar despotic direction? The obvious differentials in coercive capacity and means between a grassroots organization and a state apparatus explain that the state *could* exert a far more forceful authority. Likewise, effective democratic checks on the authority of leaders in the RDA—Liweta's early leader was replaced in 1965 "because he wanted to be too much of a boss," comments Brain (Syracuse University 1966), and the autocratic leanings of Millinga's successor as RDA chairman contributed to his removal in 1969[45]—generally had no parallel on the larger stage of Tanzania's "one-party democracy."[46] But that the state would make use of its coercive capacity, and that, conversely, mechanisms limiting the authority of leaders were put in place and actually allowed to function in the RDA, is indicative not just of different formal institutions and coercive capacities, but of different cultures and practices of authority in the national and the association's arenas.

A certain anti-authoritarian bent of the RDA's culture of authority certainly owed much to the commitments and styles of its key leaders. What Ibbott describes as his own, Millinga's, and the Litowa headmaster's practices of leadership (above), for instance, was not just or even in the first place a function of the constraints popular checks may have imposed on them. This particular set of leaders with their particular commitments and qualities may well have laid the groundwork and remained important pillars of this culture of authority. But this culture also solidified in practices and attendant expectations and norms of authority that drew all participants in them into their ambit. There would for instance have been few other places in the country where the suggestion, voiced by a Litowa resident in a 1974 village meeting with a visiting team of experts, to "keep quiet and let mtaalamu [the expert] tell us the answer, he is paid for that" would be shouted down by the village with a reminder "that if they were going to depend on the 'mtaalamu' they would never develop, for the 'mtaalamu' would not be there with them everyday. . . . The 'mtaalamu' is only there to help the villages help themselves" (Ndonde 1975a, 171). Likewise, Nyerere likely paid few visits to villages where a grade-school student would relentlessly quiz him on the meaning of his statements in a recent radio address (see chapter 2). This suggests that over time the RDA evolved a broadly shared culture of authority that had moved quite a distance from what had found expression in the song welcoming Ibbott in 1962. A fitting image of this journey is provided by Millinga's ruminations, reported by Ibbott (1970, 129), as he contemplated a hill near Litowa "rising from the level floor of the valley like an island in the sea": "When they [Litowans] had first discussed their plans, they had looked upon that hill as a possible site for the manager's house, imagining him as someone separate from the other members of the village." In the event, Litowa's leaders took their houses on a level with all others. Liweta, where "the first manager had his house built larger than and separate from the other villagers," soon swung onto the same path as well: such pretensions to a status "above" led to the manager's "removal from the position, and no-one occupying this larger house which slowly decayed."

Grassroots Development—within National and Global Circuits

While decision-making and management in the association were firmly in the hands of the villages themselves, outside support from within the country and abroad in the form of material aid, volunteers, encouragement, and political backing was crucial to its developmental success story. The RDA leadership was very conscious of this and adroitly built a network of supporters: as a 1962 "Appeal for Funds" newsletter, shrewdly invoking Nyerere's recruitment letter to Ibbott, put it: "We in the Association, as our leader Mr. Julius Nyerere wrote in a letter to Ralph Ibbott, are 'conscious of the fact that these (plans) will proceed more efficiently if they are able to draw on the experience elsewhere and assistance from outside.'"[47]

Connections to the very top of the leadership of the country were an especially critical part of the RDA's network of support. Oscar Kambona, secretary general of TANU, who was from the area and had secured Nyerere's help in recruiting Ibbott, was enlisted early on as the (ceremonial) president of the association.[48] At Kivukoni College, Millinga had met Griffith Cunningham, an instructor at the college since 1961 and, from 1963 until mid-1969, its third principal. Cunningham was in regular contact with Joan Wicken, Nyerere's personal assistant, who had been a driving force behind the establishment of the college; he facilitated Wicken's giving advice to Litowa on adult education.[49] Wicken subsequently stayed abreast of developments at the RDA and also kept Nyerere informed.[50] The president himself repeatedly intervened materially and politically on the association's behalf. In August 1965, he visited Litowa and approved the new RDA constitution (it had been stuck in the bureaucratic pipeline), granted the association an exemption from the general requirement to market maize through the cooperative system, and expressed his approval of the innovative educational experimentations at the Litowa School.[51] When the association later sought an official blessing of its educational approach and the expansion of the school into higher grades directly from the Ministry of Education—and over the heads of the antagonistic district educational authorities—it found an open ear: the president had instructed the principal secretary at the ministry to give Litowa all necessary assistance.[52] Similar instructions—to give support but remain in the background—had been given to the Ministry of Agriculture.[53] During a second visit to the association in January 1966, the president presented it with a check for ninety thousand shillings (around £4,500 at the time) toward the purchase of a grain mill and—because the village was still too small to qualify under government regulations—the exceptional installation of a water supply at Liweta (Ibbott 1966, 24; 1970, 202). Beyond material support, Nyerere's keen interest in the association—and the sense this inspired among its members that they were "his" pioneers, that their work was an important part of much bigger developments—also did much for the spirit and sense of purpose of the association.[54] Support also came from other quarters, including in 1964 from the regional commissioner and the NGOMAT tobacco union, in 1965 from the agricultural department and regional administrative headquarters, and in 1968–1969 from a number of government institutions.[55]

Several foreign development organizations and Ibbott's personal contacts also supported the RDA. In early 1963, War on Want financed a Peugeot station wagon, a tractor, a plough, a harrow, and support for the Ibbotts; other grants were to follow. During a 1967 trip to England, Ibbott secured most of the funds for the RDA's purchase of a sawmill in Songea. Swiss friends formed an organization that gave money toward the purchase of the association's grain mill in 1966. A mechanic from the UK-based Volunteer Services Overseas arrived in 1965 to train people for the RDA's mechanical workshop. A Swiss mechanic recruited through the Swiss Volunteer Corps replaced him in early 1967. The Harvard-based Volunteer Teachers for Africa sent a first volunteer in late 1965; two more followed in 1966, one of whom, Kate Wenner, wrote a book about her experience. The American Friends Service Committee also sent two volunteers on a two-year engagement in late 1966. Three agricultural extension experts and financing for livestock for Matetereka, Litowa, and Liweta came from the Swiss government's Department for Technical Cooperation (Ibbott 1970).

Oxfam (UK) became an especially important donor and supporter of the RDA from 1964. According to Michael Jennings (2008, 147–148), the organization's financial support between October 1964 and April 1968 totaled £22,399 and went toward the purchase of materials for Matetereka's and Litowa's water supplies; the acquisition of two tractors and several other vehicles; building projects; the purchase of a car and equipment for the RDA's mechanical workshop; and support for leadership training courses that the RDA was beginning to run for leaders from non-RDA villages in late 1966. As Jennings shows, Oxfam's support also went beyond material aid: in early 1968, Ibbott wrote to Jim Betts, Oxfam's field director in Tanzania, and alerted him to the RDA's increasing problems with the regional political establishment. Betts wrote to Joan Wicken to request a meeting with Nyerere.[56] In Betts's view, this intervention was instrumental in prompting the transfer of an antagonistic regional commissioner in April 1968 (Jennings 2008, 157).

While material support was clearly an important ingredient in the RDA's success, it had a lasting positive impact because of how it was used. Strategically deployed to facilitate locally appropriate projects, managed and conceived through a participatory and democratic organization, such support went far in the RDA villages where elsewhere it often ended up ineffective. Far greater material subventions did not, for instance, yield similar results in the very differently organized Village Settlement Schemes. Like most of them (see below), Mlale Pilot Village Settlement Scheme, started in 1963 not far from Litowa with big outlays, was an economic failure.[57] A mid-1965 assessment by Robert Myers (Syracuse University 1966) found that even under the most optimistic assumptions regarding yields and prices Mlale's settlers would have nothing to live on and would still not be able to meet even the scheme's recurrent costs. According to figures reported in the February 22, 1968, *Nationalist,* in 1966 the scheme did not even cover 10 percent of its recurrent costs through sales of its predominant crop, tobacco.[58] Despite the fact that settlers were apparently protected against the scheme's lack of economic viability (tobacco sales receipts appear to have been paid out to them without deducting costs),[59] Mlale still did not prove attractive to its settlers. Besides economic disappointments, the very unhealthy relations between settlers and the management likely contributed to "desertions," as the *Nationalist* put it, of almost three-quarters of the settlers between 1965 and 1966. That the scheme's manager's house—"only slightly less elaborate than the modest California ranch houses of some movie stars"—had "been dubbed 'Harty's Palace'" by the settlers may be read as broadly indicative of such problems (Ross, Worsley, and Clayton 1965, chap. 12).

The key factors that made for a very different trajectory in the RDA villages included: a membership that self-selected based on a commitment to working hard for the success of their project; a group of equally committed, locally present leaders and experts whose role was to advise and manage the villages' day-to-day affairs, the broader direction of which was democratically determined; and, more generally, a democratic and participatory system of running the villages' affairs that deliberately sought to lever opportunities for learning-by-doing in multiple spheres.

If one then sought to draw lessons from the RDA's experience, several would resonate with promising avenues in rural development that the literature has highlighted. For instance, the association's story underlines the potential of strong organizations at the local level, as well as the promises of a strategy of "assisted self-reliance" and a "learning process approach"; it is likewise a textbook demonstration of the synergistic potential generated by strong connections between relatively autonomous, democratically run local organizations and institutions at higher levels.[60] The crucial role in making the RDA a success that was played by the particular quality of social relations in the villages, on the other hand, is captured well by thinking of the association as a "social capital builder."[61] Finally, and on the most abstract level, the RDA's approach and philosophy calls to mind Sen's conceptualization of "development as freedom": indeed, the stress, in this formulation, on "both the *processes* that allow freedom of actions and decisions, and the actual *opportunities* that people have" (Sen 1999, 17; emphases original) could have been distilled directly from the RDA's documents.

Among these documents' avid readers was of course none other than President Nyerere. Soon, this would have broad ramifications for the whole country.

Tanzania's New Model Villages

An Opening

Since 1965, the Tanzanian government had been evaluating its approach to rural development, central elements of which had been inherited at independence. Besides working through directly prescribing or proscribing particular actions in agricultural production, the main strategy had been a planned massive expansion of heavily capitalized Village Settlement Schemes. But whereas Nyerere had envisioned one million people living and working on them by 1980, at its peak in 1965/1966 the whole program involved only around fifteen thousand people (URT 1966a, 10). Only seven new "pilot settlement schemes" had been added to eight Groundnut Scheme successor schemes inherited at independence and three cotton farms started under an Israeli program (Nellis 1972, 158). With more than ten million Tanzanians in the rural areas in the mid-1960s, the program could no longer realistically be expected to make a difference for more than a tiny fraction of the rural population—especially as foreign aid, which, it had been hoped, would fund the schemes, was not forthcoming in the amounts that had been expected. By early 1966, it had been determined that the strategy was not yielding satisfactory results, and the government was casting about for an alternative.

Any such alternative would have to remedy several problems with the settlement approach. A series of reviews conducted in 1965–1966 showed that the schemes were chronically unproductive, in terms of both hard economic returns and broader developmental goals.[62] Cost controls appeared to be absent—or at least routinely overruled— and capital expenditures smacked of equipment fetishism. The contrast with the kind of financial support the RDA received is instructive: probably the largest single source, Oxfam support to the association's villages, amounted to £22,399 over a four-and-a-half-year period. For the Settlement Schemes, the 1964 Development Plan had budgeted an initial "investment in economic and social overheads of about £150,000 per settlement" (Tanganyika 1964, 21). As this amount was likely far exceeded, large sums were wasted with little economic return: for instance, TSh 4.4 million (around £220,000) went into the Village Settlement Agency's Mobile Land Development Unit that would carry out mechanized land clearing. Due to breakdowns and equipment failures, this investment, on its own amounting to about 15 percent of budgeted overhead per new scheme, had to be completely written off within just two years (Myers 1973).

Among the farmers recruited to the schemes, there were grave incentive problems. Settlers appear to have perceived themselves as wage laborers, and morale, productivity, and relations with management were poor. The quality of management proved another major impediment, and it also pointed to serious skill shortages in the country: qualified managerial staff could not be found even for the schemes in operation, which numbered only around twenty.[63]

These assessments'—and the government's—conclusion was that Tanzania could neither afford nor staff a significant settlement program. But even absent these material constraints, continued investments in the program appeared of dubious merit: they would amount to feeding an approach with serious design flaws and an inbuilt tendency toward financial profligacy. The negative experience with the settlement program challenged the basic rationale that had underpinned it—that a heavy injection of capital and CEO-style expert management would be able to effect, to use the catchphrase of the 1961 World Bank Mission that had recommended the approach, the "transformation" of the rural areas and of the peasants that would work on the schemes.

During his January 1966 visit, reports Ibbott (1970, 66), Nyerere told Litowans that "many people came to him in Dar es Salaam and asked what Ujamaa meant. He wanted Litowa to be a practical example where he could send such questioners to see for themselves Ujamaa in practice. He asked three times whether the people would do this job for him and three times they said they would." Three months later, at a high-level April 1966 seminar on rural development, Second Vice President Rashidi Kawawa announced the decision to stop the Village Settlement Program.[64] This flung the door wide open to a different approach: it was to be the RDA's moment. One of the reports that fed into the decision to halt the Settlement Program had already made explicit comparisons with the RDA—and several of the researchers involved joined top state officials at the April seminar. Also in attendance were Cunningham of Kivukoni College and Betts, Oxfam's field director, both of whom had worked with the RDA for several years, as well as Millinga and Ibbott (Ibbott 1970, 80–81).

In comparison to the settlement schemes, the RDA was attractive most immediately because it demanded neither massive start-up capital nor scheme-style "management." But would the alternative model it offered of incrementally strengthening local expertise and capacity actually be able to deliver? Robert Myers's background report on the association (Syracuse University 1966) was skeptical:

> It is my opinion that both from a social and an economic development viewpoint this proposal has very little merit. It is not only based on some nieve [*sic*] (incorrect) notions of the reality of the needs for economic development, but it is also such a small scale proposal that it would be impossible to implement throughout the nation.

As Myers's points of criticism outlined in a nutshell the dimensions in regard to which the RDA presented an alternative to received practices in development and the type of authority that was instantiated through them, it is worth examining them in detail. By point of contrast to the RDA's model, his report insisted, in proper development "authority regarding the use of productive resources is entrusted to 'development experts.'" These were called upon to impose on their charges the necessary "anguish" of modernization. And their authority was founded on the superior vantage point they occupied by virtue of their access to "modern" techniques and "capital" as well as their understanding of "the development process." The urgency of their intervention, finally, was grounded in the conviction that their authority was indispensible if the necessary rapid and large-scale change was to be achieved. These would be recurrent themes in the unfolding history of villagization.

Other seminar participants saw virtue where Myers had seen defects, and some pinpointed as crucial precisely the different constellation of authority prevailing in the RDA. John Nellis's report (Syracuse University 1966), for instance, saw in Litowa "an existing alternative to the dubious mass-capital, closely supervised schemes now on the ground." In a report based on a long follow-up visit to the RDA after the conclusion of the seminar (Syracuse University 1966), Brain would be even more explicit. Drawing a contrast with the nearby Settlement Scheme at Mlale, he commented,

> We cannot expect the results of the Ruvuma schemes unless we are prepared to use their methods, which means there must be a spiritual change in both settlers and staff, between whom on pilot settlements there now exists what amounts to a class war. If we give up the principale [sic] of communal work at Mlal[e] because the people will not work cooperatively, and yet ten miles away the very same people are working with energy and enthusiasm in a communal fashion, it would appear that the fault lies not in the people, but in the way in which their affairs are run.

Unlike Myers, these commentators thus envisioned development not as an undertaking that was to be hierarchically organized by a vanguard, expert authority that would impose necessary "anguish," but as a project that would be directed and propelled by the people's own choices. This was a vision of governing through freedom—precisely what Nyerere would outline as the new approach to rural development based on the RDA's practices.

Ujamaa Vijijini, or: The RDA's Practices in Theory

During a visit to Litowa in 1966, Millinga recollects, Nyerere had told the RDA leaders that "the [TANU] National Executive Committee is going to come up with a resolution that will be a guide for the government in order to promote your type of activity."[65] In early 1967, said committee issued the Arusha Declaration, a document for which Tanzania would become famous.[66] Its key theme was that growing material inequalities—and in particular those between urban and rural areas—and "exploitation of man by man" ought to be combated.[67] In pursuit of this objective, it famously elevated ujamaa ("familyhood," "African Socialism") to the guiding principle for Tanzania's future trajectory.[68]

The declaration affected Tanzania's economic, political, and social trajectories in many respects, for instance in heralding the nationalization of many sectors of the economy. It can be argued, however, that its central and most innovative legacy lay in redirecting the focus of Tanzania's development efforts toward the rural areas. "Agriculture," it announced, "Is the Basis of Development" (Nyerere 1968, 243; capitalization original). What this meant—and how the declaration's broad principles would be translated in this and other specific issue areas—was the subject of Nyerere's "post-Arusha" writings. Especially key were the September 1967 "Socialism and Rural Development" or, in the Kiswahili original, "Ujamaa Vijijini" (literally: "Familyhood/Socialism in the Villages"), and the October 1968 "Freedom and Development." Both papers elaborated on the idea that ujamaa villages would form the central plank in Tanzania's development strategy. Here is the vision "Ujamaa Vijijini" sketched of how such communities would function:

It would be a meeting of the villagers which would elect the officers and the committee, and a meeting of the village which would decide whether or not to accept or
to amend any detailed proposals for work organization which the committee had
drawn up in the light of general directions given by earlier meetings. . . . These detailed proposals they would bring to the next village meeting, and once they had
been accepted it would be a job of the officers to ensure that all members carried out
the decisions. . . . As the village became more established and the need for a village
carpenter, a village nursery, or a village shop became more pressing, the committee
would work out proposals as to how these would be organized and run by a member
for the common benefit. The village officials would also be responsible for liaising
with other villages and with the general machinery of government. Thus they would
be responsible for making any requests for outside assistance about schooling, credit,
agricultural advice, and so on, which the village had decided it needed. . . . And in
co-operation with other nearby villages of the same kind, a system of locally based
small industries would be possible for the benefit of all involved. Thus a group of villages together could organize their own servicing station for agricultural implements
and farm vehicles; they could perhaps make their own cooking utensils and crock-
ery out of local materials, or they could organize the making of their own clothes
on a communal basis. (Nyerere 1968, 353–354)

That this "vision" was a point-by-point description of the RDA's activities and practices was of course no coincidence: the RDA was the well-studied and explicitly acknowledged inspiration behind it.[69]

The association's influence is especially unmistakable in Nyerere's pronouncements
on the questions of governing and authority in development. The vision he laid out of
democratic, local-level control and his strong proscriptions of coercive means are precisely how the RDA leadership and sympathizers thought about these issues. "The ujamaa village," the 1968 paper "Freedom and Development" would thus categorically state,

is a new conception, based on the post-Arusha Declaration understanding that we
need to develop people, not things, and that people can only develop themselves. . . .
Ujamaa villages are intended to be socialist organizations created by the people, and
governed by those who live and work in them. They cannot be created from outside,
nor governed from outside. No one can be forced into an ujamaa village, and no
official—at any level—can go and tell the members of an ujamaa village what they
should do together, and what they should continue to do as individual farmers. No
official of the Government or Party can go to an ujamaa village and tell the members
what they must grow. No non-member of the village can go and tell the members to
use a tractor, or not to use a tractor. For if these things happen—that is, if an out-
sider gives such instructions and enforces them—then it will no longer be an ujamaa
village! An ujamaa village is a voluntary association of people who decide of their
own free will to live together and work together for their common good. (Nyerere
1973, 67)

(Ibbott [1966, 7–8], writing in the Tanzanian journal *Mbioni* two years earlier, had put
it thus: "Such groups of people in order to build a successful community cannot be

Figure 1.4. Nyerere (in white) inspecting Litowa's 1968 corn harvest. Courtesy of Ralph Ibbott.

'planned' from outside. . . . The initiative must be from the people and this initial initiative must grow within the group.")

"Freedom and Development" offered several interrelated rationales for this emphatic endorsement of such a radically grassroots-democratic vision. On the one hand, Nyerere argued that autonomy over one's own life was an essential part of what development meant; after all, development was of "people, not things":

> The people will have begun to develop themselves as dignified and confident human beings, in a way which is impossible if they simply take orders from someone else. The fact that the orders of an "expert" may have led to greater output of a crop if they were fully carried out, does not affect this issue. By debating this matter and then deciding for themselves, the people will be doing real development of themselves. (Nyerere 1973, 69)

While people's ability to make free choices was thus a constitutive part of development and not just a means to an end, Nyerere also offered several instrumental rationales behind this endorsement of local decision-making and noncoercion. Chiefly, any approach founded on dictates, argued Nyerere, would undercut the people's understanding, commitment, and enthusiasm—all of which were essential if the kind of effective practices of communal cooperation he had seen at the RDA were to be realized:

> Unless the purpose and socialist ideology of an ujamaa village is understood by the members from the beginning—at least to some extent—it will not survive the early difficulties. . . . And the greater self-discipline which is necessary when working in a community will only be forthcoming if the people understand what they are doing and why. (Nyerere 1973, 68)

Coercing farmers into practices they did not themselves embrace had been counterproductive in the past, Nyerere warned in 1969, and such attempts had been thwarted by evasive maneuvers, foot-dragging, and outright defiance—the whole gamut of what James Scott (1985) would theorize as "the weapons of the weak":

> We make a big mistake if we try to force people to produce certain amounts or even to cultivate certain acreages of cash crops. Political officers who have tried this in the past find that the people cultivate the required area for the first year but that the crop is surprisingly small, and then when the second year comes along the peasants have moved further into the bush to get away from the officers of the Government! (Nyerere 1973, 94)

Irrespective of people's reaction to coercive measures, centralized authority also had inherent limitations: it could never be sufficiently cognizant of local particularities, and this implied that autonomous local decision-making was key. Thus, "it would be foolish for someone in Dar es Salaam to try to draw up a blueprint for the crop production and social organization which has to be applied to every corner of our large country" (Nyerere 1968, 348). Finally, the Settlement Scheme experience had also brought home the particular limitations the Tanzanian government faced in terms of resources and personnel:

> We would . . . be making a mistake if we think in terms of covering Tanzania with mechanized farms, using tractors and combine harvesters. Once again, we have neither the money nor the skilled manpower nor in this case the social organization which could make such investment possible and economic. (319–320)

> Government advice and help can only be of marginal importance; it must not be expected everywhere, for if all our two million families started such communities, it would clearly be impossible to help all their schemes at once. (358)

In the new approach, the key rationale that had previously underpinned physically concentrating people in villages—it would make for better entry points for government services and support—was thus relegated to a secondary role; now, closer settlement was important chiefly as a condition that would enable communal production, local self-government, and community growth.[70] In 1968, Nyerere thus drew an explicit contrast on this and the connected broader philosophical front with the thinking that had underlain the Settlement Schemes:

In effect, we said that capital equipment, or other forms of investment, would lead to increased output, and this would lead to a transformation in the lives of the people involved. The people were secondary; the first priority was the output. As a result, there have been very many cases where heavy capital investment has resulted in no increase in output—where the investment has been wasted. And in most of the officially sponsored or supported schemes, the majority of the people who went to settle lost their enthusiasm, and either left the scheme altogether, or failed to carry out the orders of the outsiders who were put in charge. . . . It is important, therefore, to realize that the policy of *Ujamaa Vijijini* is not intended to be merely a revival of the old settlement schemes under another name. (Nyerere 1973, 66–67)

Ujamaa vijijini, then, had new things to say about authority, organization, methods, and goals in development. Centrally, and in an explicit departure from the model of earlier approaches in which the set-apart authority of experts and officials would act on peasants through compulsion and disciplinary schemes, ujamaa vijijini projected a vision of development in which authority would be dispersed and vested in local communities, and governing would work through peasants' free decisions.

Becoming a Policy

The RDA's salience in the emergence of this vision was not confined to its inspirational role. Nyerere also increasingly drew on RDA leaders to promote the new policy. Thus, the *Nationalist* of July 22 and August 8, 1968, reported on the recent installation of Millinga as the head of a newly created Department of Ujamaa Vijijini at TANU headquarters. Cunningham, who had recommended both this institutional innovation and appointment, became a special presidential advisor on ujamaa villages a few months later.[71] Working mostly through a cadre school set up at Litowa in early 1969, Millinga's department attempted to train both village-level leaders and a group of young TANU cadres who would become roving ambassadors for the policy.[72] From early 1969, however, the most prominent function of Millinga's department became the organization of seminars to prepare the country's political leadership for ujamaa.

While Nyerere had already been pushing officials to familiarize themselves with the RDA, the department greatly expanded the scope of such efforts. Through its seminars, top officials heard about the RDA leadership's experience and philosophy. A number of them also experienced life in the RDA villages firsthand. This familiarization drive started at the top: in February 1969, the Central Committee of TANU met at Kivukoni College for a week-long seminar. Millinga, Ibbott, John Ngairo (who had replaced Millinga as RDA chairman), Suleman Toroka (the RDA school's principal), and Cunningham were all present. Following this seminar, the *Nationalist*'s extensive coverage noted on February 25 and March 3 and 7, 1969, the members of the Central Committee were scheduled to visit ujamaa villages, including those in Ruvuma. Additional seminars followed in quick succession. In June 1969, there was a three-month seminar for TANU district chairmen. A month-long seminar in Handeni in June and July again targeted the members of a newly expanded TANU Central Committee—and again featured several RDA speakers. On August 5, another seminar, with RDA speakers, commenced for all party regional chairmen and some ministers. Regional administrative secretaries, regional commissioners, and development officers were scheduled to attend a two-week seminar beginning on September 1 and regional development officers were to gather for another.[73] At least five more for lower-ranking officials were announced in September and October and more followed in early 1970.[74] Since early 1969, many similar, less formal gatherings and "ujamaa experiences" had also been organized for a wide variety of people.[75]

Nyerere's comments, reported in the *Nationalist* of August 6, 1969, to one of these seminars spell out the rationale behind this extremely broad-based offensive:

> Ujamaa villages were the most important pre-occupation of TANU at this point of national reconstruction because it was only through living in such socialist villages that the people would get progress. "That is why TANU is endeavoring in every way to educate the leaders on why and how they can mobilize the people into ujamaa villages throughout the country."

It was often RDA leaders who communicated the central message of these seminars—that their successful model of communal production was inextricably tied to the particular model of governing in development that the RDA villages had grown to exemplify.

What would become of this apparent opening toward a new departure in rural development in Tanzania? The RDA would remain at the center of this story, albeit not in the way Nyerere's elevation of it to a model for the country might lead one to expect.

2   Culture Clash
The Destruction of the Ruvuma Development Association

The shutting down of the Ruvuma Development Association (RDA) . . . is not a moment that finds much resonance in most writing about Tanzania. . . . I find the moment emblematic, although, to be honest, I'm not quite certain whether it marked a turning point in and of itself or instead merely epitomized clearly the limits of the vision—Nyerere's? TANU's?—that underpinned the *ujamaa* project in the first case. In any case, the incident does warrant a great deal of thinking.

—John Saul, *The Next Liberation Struggle*

From the second half of 1968, Nyerere had been orchestrating a big push to mobilize all levels of the state apparatus to promote what he had told the RDA leaders would be "their type of activity." In the institutional realm, this push was for instance reflected in the creation of a new Ministry of Regional Administration and Rural Development with an upgraded portfolio placed directly under the President's Office.[1] Because—in the estimation of the September 6, 1968, *Nationalist*—there was a "great need to bringing [*sic*] under the supervision and leadership of the Party people's endeavors in rural development particularly the establishment and construction of Ujamaa Villages," Peter Kisumo, the newly minted minister, was also appointed to the Central Committee (CC) of TANU. The mid-1969 further expansion of the CC—to include a representative from each of Tanzania's seventeen regions—would likewise help to facilitate nationwide coordination with respect to the policy.[2]

In parallel to such institutional maneuvers, officials at all levels were bombarded with a host of initiatives designed to educate and mobilize them for the implementation of Tanzania's new approach to rural development. The CC, for instance, had already been subjected to a week-long seminar on ujamaa in February 1969. In June 1969, Nyerere had the newly enlarged committee packed off to the rural Handeni District for a month-long seminar, again organized by Millinga's Department of Ujamaa Vijijini. There, various "peasants," the majority of whom came from RDA villages, lectured these high political functionaries on ujamaa. Besides officials' minds, the seminar also targeted the attendees' bodies. Noted the July 9, 1969, *Nationalist*'s caption under a picture (figure 2.1) splashed across its front page:

Figure 2.1. Central Committee members participating in night exercises at an ujamaa seminar in Handeni, July 4, 1969. Courtesy of Tanzania Information Service.

The rugged group above are not recruits to the defense forces, but members of the Tanu Central Committee and officials of the Party and the government attending a month-long seminar on Ujamaa villages at Handeni. Every morning Sergeant Major Shaban Esau from the Field Force Unit marches them at the double to prepare their bodies for life in an Ujamaa village.

Being granted but a short reprieve from such rigors, CC members were then scheduled to spend several weeks in the "most advanced" ujamaa villages in the country: Litowa, Liweta, and Matetereka—all RDA—as well as two others with RDA connections.[3]

On September 20, 1969, a few weeks after this experience, the CC met in Dar es Salaam. Members shared reports on their stays in the villages, following which, the sparse minutes record, "the Central Committee discussed at length and in a very calm manner [*kwa makini sana*] the question of leadership of some of the ujamaa villages under the Ruvuma Development Association." On September 24, the meeting produced a bombshell: it had, according to the minutes, "decided that now a good time had come for TANU itself to be in charge of the leadership of all ujamaa villages everywhere in the country in order for there to be uniformity in direction and development [*usawa wa maongozi na maendeleo*] in all parts of the country."[4] The next day, a high-powered delegation headed by Peter Kisumo arrived in Songea to inform local officials and the association of the decision: the RDA was to disband and be replaced by the state's machinery.[5]

Figure 2.2. Central Committee members undergoing military training at an ujamaa seminar in Handeni, July 29, 1969 (eyes to the right: Second Vice President Kawawa). Courtesy of Tanzania Information Service.

The Bureaucratic Bourgeoisie Strikes Back?

How to make sense of this decision? The most in-depth existing treatments have stressed material and programmatic ideological motives. Thus, for Bruno Musti de Gennaro (1979, 3), the "RDA represented an advanced form of peasant struggle, striving to regain control of the surplus product generated in the rural areas. Therefore it entered into open contradiction with the dominant trends existing within the State and after years of confrontation the Association was suppressed." Coulson (1984) likewise highlights the state apparatus's material interests, although he does not interpret the fact that the RDA denied local officials opportunities for graft as rising quite to the level of a class struggle over peasant surpluses.

This chapter shows that the RDA's destruction was not in the main a skirmish in such a struggle centered on surplus extraction. While within its local political economy the association's noncorrupt practices apparently did create some misgivings, such local frictions had little direct bearing on the national-level battle that ultimately sealed the association's fate. At that level, those "material interests" that likely did play into the decision did not take the shape of a struggle over surpluses and economic rewards; rather they appear to have centered on personal career ambitions, the most fitting interpretation of an apparent rivalry between Kisumo and Millinga.

But the RDA was also far more than a chip in a contest for position by some individual politicians. Far more broadly, it offended against a whole assemblage of practices, a particular culture, of authority. In this assemblage, framings of state officials as paternal/generational authorities dovetailed tightly with their casting as the spearhead of a unitary nation under attack from (neo)colonial enemies. These elements also meshed with a set of discursive practices that produced officials specifically as developmental authorities. The RDA directly clashed with this order on multiple levels.

Coulson (1984, 19) does point to this question of authority as being at the heart of the destruction of the RDA when he notes that the association represented "a working alternative to a model of central bureaucratic control" and therefore ran into opposition from both proponents of "a strong 'democratic socialist' party" and elements who disliked socialism and thus the RDA's model of communal production, but still favored "a strong 'parastatal' state."[6] However, this glossing does not do justice to the actual texture of the clash between the RDA and officials: observed close up, this clash was not a fight over divergent ideological visions in which officials calculated the programmatic implications (or material consequences for themselves) if the RDA were to become a model.[7] Rather than to such reasoning about consequences, the RDA fell victim to an act of vengeance taken in reaction to the visceral, affective offense it had given not against a political program or scheme but against a rather more ineffable culture of authority.

The Regional Scene

Within the local scene in Ruvuma, the RDA's anti-graft stance apparently did make it some enemies. For instance, Ibbott (1970, 104, 257–259) reports—and both Coulson and Musti de Gennaro highlight on this basis—that in the association's last year government contracts were taken away from its sawmill and its grain mill and given to more pliant partners. But this (ultimately minor) skirmish was confined to the local political economy, and as such did not pose a serious threat to the RDA's existence.

That the RDA's assets were "confiscated" upon its destruction—its grain mill, sawmill, and several of its vehicles were placed under the regional commissioner—has also been taken as something of a smoking gun for officials' avarice. While one may wonder why some of the most powerful political figures in the country would have bothered with the surely inferior opportunity for surplus appropriation that the association's assets presented, the bigger problem is that this evidence is in fact quite weak. For one, at least a number of these "confiscations" were temporary measures by way of which association property was turned over to individual villages. Thus, at least two of the RDA's tractors continued to operate at Litowa and Matetereka, and the sawmill too appears to have been turned over to Litowa.[8] Furthermore, the broader picture of the villages' treatment by the state shows that rather than extract surpluses from them, the state in fact pumped exceptionally large (compared to other villages in the region) material support into at least the larger ex-RDA villages almost from the moment of the association's destruction. Although some of this support arrived only after fierce lobbying on the part of a village,[9] there were for instance grants of livestock, a new tractor, a grain mill, water supplies, cattle dips, and other building projects.[10]

The one other episode that has been interpreted as evidence that the RDA was perceived as a threat to surplus appropriation involved tobacco, the area's predominant cash crop (Musti de Gennaro 1981, 131–132; Coulson 1984, 16, 19). While the RDA grew tobacco and was acknowledged to be an excellent producer, the villages did not find it very worthwhile: it was very work-intensive, required excellent soils or expensive fertilizers, and brought a low price (Ibbott 1970, 69–70). It was therefore not accorded the same high priority as food-crop production, a fact about which officials were not happy (86); at the same time, there is no evidence that this produced a serious clash with the political establishment—after all, the association did grow the crop.

Even if there were some misgivings about the association's less than desirable focus on the crop, jumping to the ready-made conclusion that this reveals that exploitative motives were behind officials' desire to see more tobacco grown in the region is a leap too far. The motivations of Edward Barongo, Ruvuma's chief promoter of tobacco and the regional commissioner from 1965 to 1968, for one, appear to have been a great deal more complex.[11] Raising tax revenues was certainly part of his motivation, but rather than signifying exploitation, larger revenues would for instance finally allow him to cover teachers' pay—a perennial problem given the nearly bankrupt Songea and Mbinga District Councils (Ibbott 1970, 247–248). According to David Edwards (2003, 143), Barongo was also concerned about the survival of the local tobacco processing plant, the only industry in the area; and farmers would of course also benefit directly from their tobacco, for which Barongo's lobbying had apparently secured a higher purchasing price from the marketing authority. As Ibbott (1970, 246) relates, "Towards the end of his time he [Barongo] produced and circulated a pamphlet with a picture of himself and an account of what he had done for the Region in which he claimed that later on people would look back and be thankful and say that they had Barongo in their pockets." (Edwards [2003, 143] reports that a third of a century later local tobacco growers recalled referring to their money in this way—albeit not without some irony.) In sum, in Barongo's eyes tobacco was the one steppingstone the region had out of its developmental backwardness.[12] If farmers needed a push to see the light, it was his job to provide it. Against this background, the regional commissioner appears not so much the peasantry's class enemy than a paternalistic developmentalist.

Although this was not because of the association's relative lack of interest in the crop, tobacco did in fact land the RDA in trouble with Barongo. Examining why this happened is revealing of the issues at stake in the RDA's difficult relations with officials in the region and more generally. The problem arose in the context of Barongo's 1965/1966 attempt to enforce minimum tobacco acreages in Ruvuma. Ibbott (1970, 244–245) relates how this campaign was implemented:

Before the planting season all regional and district officers as well as party leaders went out to all parts of the district telling people to grow tobacco. Several months later when the crop was nearly ready to harvest these same officers were again sent out to round up those who had failed to plant, turning in effect the whole of the administration into a temporary police force. . . . People who were caught might have been given a prison sentence or in other cases forced to work on roads. Many peasant farmers who had not grown tobacco disappeared for the time of these raids into the bush with their bed-rolls.

Millinga, for one, attempted to play a constructive role and spent several days advising new growers on tobacco because the agricultural department found itself overextended. But when Barongo was criticized for his campaign's coercive methods in Parliament, trouble arose: Millinga, who had been elected as the local MP in 1965, was absent on the day and hence failed to defend his commissioner (245–246). Adding insult to injury, he also attempted to get Barongo to release several people who had been locked up for neglect of their tobacco crop.[13] Barongo was reportedly very unhappy that the RDA's most prominent leader did not fall in behind him. With relations soured, he scratched Litowa from the itinerary of Nyerere's December 1966 visit to Ruvuma. When, upon Nyerere's insistence, the village was written back in, the president was fed negative stories about the association at a regional meeting—among others that the RDA ignored the Ministry of Agriculture's cultivation advice on tobacco and maize spacing (Ibbott 1970, 86).

However, the president appeared to be taking sides against the commissioner: in what Ibbott—in the context of the compulsory tobacco campaign—interprets as a direct slight against Barongo, Nyerere "opened the new [Ruvuma] Regional Administrative block with what must surely have been his shortest speech before hurriedly unveiling the plaque—'This building is meant for development not for ruling'" (271–272). At Litowa, the president then undertook to personally investigate the rumors about the association's agricultural practices. Kate Wenner (1970, 137–138), who served as a volunteer at the village, witnessed the scene: at Litowa's tobacco field, Nyerere

> reached into his pocket and pulled out a tape measure. . . . "One yard exactly," he said loudly. He repeated the measurement at another row of plants. . . . Nyerere turned to the agricultural officer beside him who now looked a little red in the face. "Seems as if the tobacco is just as it should be. I don't know what you were complaining about." It was easy to see where his sympathies were. . . . Now he had dealt with it, and the people of Litowa knew they had the President's backing.

Nyerere then publically lectured Barongo and his entourage on the importance of getting the balance right between tobacco and food crops, pointing to Litowa's early focus on food crops as crucial to its success (Ibbott 1970, 86).

The RDA's most significant troubles with Barongo therefore had very little to do with surpluses. The association posed a different sort of challenge and offended for different kinds of reasons. As a presidential appointee vulnerable to Nyerere's whims, Barongo could ill afford question marks over his performance, especially in the crucial matter of development. When a nationally visible leader of the association failed to defend his development campaign, even seeming to side with his accusers in asking for the release of prisoners, this was a serious problem. And when the association attracted the president's attention, it stole the limelight away from the commissioner. In short, the RDA's independence and its leaders' self-assured autonomy were constant irritants—and the president's intense interest and openly displayed favoritism only exacerbated this situation. Attempts to divert Nyerere's attention (scratching the Litowa visit), bad-mouth the association (rumors about improperly spaced crops), and generally treat it as a political competitor were the outgrowth of officials' navigating the complex political world that they co-inhabited with the RDA, not a struggle over surpluses.

Still: why plant a false rumor about improper crop spacing when it could so easily be disproved? Perhaps such incidents hint at something more than officials playing a calculated game to discredit a competitor. Perhaps such rumors were not deliberately invented falsehoods at all, but spiteful assumptions. For one: how could the association possibly be doing things right, when it "ignored" as it did officials and their advice in its stubbornly independent ways? Indeed, who were these people, to rebuff officials' developmentalist authority? Emil Ndonde (1975a, 171), who had been a teacher with the RDA, remarks on the self-assuredness he still encountered among Litowans in 1974: "Few officials would like this kind of peasant, for they challenge the officials' role as helper!" Hell hath no fury like a developer scorned.

The Central Committee and the RDA

Ultimately, skirmishes at the regional level did not break the association's back: in 1968, it was in fact Barongo who was transferred, quite likely at least in part because—upon Ibbott's request—Oxfam's Jim Betts reported to Nyerere that the commissioner was making life difficult for the RDA (Jennings 2008, 157). The association's encounter with the Central Committee, however, turned out to be a different matter.

As they had in the region, career ambitions, rather than a struggle over peasant surpluses, played into this encounter, too. An apparent rivalry between Millinga and Kisumo, from mid-1968 the minister for local administration and rural development and prominent member of the Central Committee, may have been the most fateful. In Millinga's assessment at least, Kisumo was the "brain behind the disbanding of the RDA" (quoted in Edwards 1998, 15). This contention is supported by anecdotal evidence that Ibbott reported in a long October 1969 letter to Nyerere. Kisumo apparently threw down an explicit challenge to Millinga and told him that he and the RDA would lose in their confrontation with Kisumo and the political establishment. A letter from Ibbott to Kisumo had likewise received such a hostile reply that Ibbott took it to be part of a design to get rid of him also.[14]

Millinga's star had been rising: in 1965, he accompanied Nyerere on his visit to China and was elected MP for Songea South. In late 1967, he became a presidentially appointed assistant secretary for Ujamaa at TANU Youth League headquarters in Dar es Salaam and, in mid-1968, the head of the new Department of Ujamaa Vijijini at TANU headquarters. Attesting to his growing influence, he made several successful recommendations of candidates for area commissioner (in charge at the district level), a matter that directly related to Kisumo's local administration portfolio.[15] Then, the creation of an Ujamaa Villages Division within Kisumo's ministry set up a direct institutional rival to Millinga's department.[16] If this was in fact the goal, the destruction of the RDA indeed dramatically diminished Millinga's role and that of his department, leaving Kisumo to assert a leading role in the promotion of ujamaa vijijini.

Besides this personal rivalry, Nyerere's apparent penchant for putting officials down by raising the RDA up generally contributed to disposing the CC against the RDA. Edwards (1998, 28) reports, "Millinga described how once he was in a large meeting in Tanga, when Nyerere said, 'Show me an ujamaa man here! None of you are ujamaa people except for that one! [pointing at Millinga].' Later he requested Nyerere to stop saying such things because it was giving him problems" (brackets original). Joan Wicken, Nyerere's personal assistant for many years, likewise recounts, "Gossip had it that the RDA people had said at the Seminar [for the Central Committee at Kivukoni in February 1969] that the only socialists in Tanzania were Mwalimu [Nyerere] and [they] themselves. Whether this was said or not, the attitudes clearly left the idea."[17] Whoever was responsible for rubbing the CC's nose in the RDA's superiority, the result was apparently widespread antagonism among officials.

Was there—besides such jockeying for positions and the president's approval—also an overt ideological clash over socialism and communal production that turned the CC against the RDA as a model? Certainly public statements give no inkling that the move against the RDA was in any way tied to such considerations. There were unanimous declarations that the association's socialist model would continue to be pursued, only now under the state's tutelage (the attempt to do so through the villagization campaigns of the ensuing years suggests that this was not mere rhetoric). Thus, the meeting that sealed the RDA's fate summarized its discussion by extending its "congratulations to the Ruvuma Development Association for the efforts that had been made by that organization to further and bring to fruition TANU's policy of ujamaa villages"—while at the same time declaring its intention to now have "TANU itself" be "in charge of the leadership of all ujamaa villages."[18] On September 26, 1969, two days after the meeting, a lengthy column in the government-controlled *Nationalist* newspaper explained the "decision by the Party to take charge of all Ujamaa villages" in similar terms: it had been a necessity because ujamaa villages were the "model of socialism in rural areas and the Party and its government ha[d] arrangements in hand for the development of these villages politically, socially and economically." The *Sunday News* of September 28 likewise presented the decision as a move against neither the RDA's villages nor their socialist approach, but simply as the substitution of the state's apparatus for the association: "The villages will still remain totally in the hands of the community. But instead of having some form of association as the guiding body, this in [the] future will be replaced by a TANU branch or sub-branch depending on the size of the community and it will be Tanu they will turn to for assistance and advice."

Such declarations of intent to faithfully further the very same socialist project the RDA had pioneered were apparently not a false pretense meant for public consumption. Like the investment campaign launched in its villages after the association's destruction, internal government reports from the region indicate that regional officials were not under the impression that they were expected to destroy the ex-RDA villages or their model of communal production—quite the contrary. The region's report on 1969 party activities, for instance, clearly pandered to a perceived expectation that officials ought to ensure the success of the ex-RDA villages as ujamaa communities, never mind that this required the fabrication of an alternative reality to the dire situation in the villages post-destruction (see below). Thus the report noted that "the Ujamaa villages in the region are developing well; especially after these villages have come from under the leadership of the RDA to be under the leadership of TANU they seem to be successes." Specifically on the situation at Litowa it could be reported that the "politics of this village have been developing very well from the time when the leadership changed hands from being with the RDA to TANU and the Government." Gone were the times when "some other people have refused to join an ujamaa village because they felt that the leadership of the RDA was corrupting the people": "Since all the reins should now be held fast by TANU and its Government the situation has changed and the enthusiasm to start ujamaa villages is increasingly pressing ahead."[19] All in all, the substitution of the state for the RDA was presented as a resounding success for the very socialist model of rural development that the association had pioneered. The only difference was that now the state was in charge.

Nyerere's decision to allow the association's destruction, which—given his obvious sympathies—appears very puzzling indeed, is perhaps less of a mystery in light of this reading of events. He may have seen the association as a necessary sacrifice in the struggle for the bigger prize, the implementation across the country of the model it had pioneered. This, in Millinga's recollection (he was present at the CC meeting), appears to have been Nyerere's reasoning when he acceded to the demands of the Central Committee: "I think you people want to disband the RDA without any reason. But because you are 'the power,' then let us disband it. But I want this kind of development for the country. If necessary, then, we will make TANU the controllers and implementers of this kind of development" (quoted in Edwards 1998, 17). Oxfam, a strong supporter of the RDA, apparently came to terms with its destruction in much the same fashion.[20] The RDA's destruction was not about a repudiation of its "model"—if by this one means "socialism" or "communal production."

However, personal rivalries and political jealousies were not the only issues that set the CC against the RDA. There was indeed a clash of "models"—albeit on a different terrain than explicit ideology or programmatic policy visions. What was at stake was the RDA's refusal to fit into a particular assemblage of practices of authority.

This was a constant issue during the CC members' stay in RDA villages in August 1969. Immediately upon their arrival, the members who had gone to Litowa complained that the village had not received them properly as nobody had returned from the fields to welcome them.[21] A brief background: in early 1964, Litowa had resolved that work in the fields would not be interrupted to welcome frequent visitors, as this was causing serious disruptions to the work schedule. Junior Minister for Labour Vincent Mponji, on the occasion of whose visit this decision had been instituted, is said to have appreciated the decision since he had not come to hinder Litowans' work (Ibbott 1970, 50). The CC evidently had other priorities. Indeed, in their eyes the offense was apparently serious enough to have made the rounds: "There was nobody making an effort to receive these delegates, nor welcome them," an essay by I. G. Binamu (1969, 55) in Kivukoni College's Swahili-language periodical *Ujamaa* would complain a few months after the visit. "Well, is this really ujamaa that we are building?"[22] The delegation then refused the accommodation Litowa offered and stayed in tents on the edge of the village. After Ibbott (1970, 120–121) had gone to introduce himself, he "was told the next day that they were saying that [he] treated them with disrespect. It was part of what we soon saw was to happen throughout their visit."

The association's school was a particular lightning rod in this regard.[23] Its innovative approach to education explicitly sought to foster "self-reliant" thinking in its students, for instance by involving them in the school's management.[24] During Nyerere's visit in 1966 the students' self-confidence and willingness to question authority were clearly on display. It was one of Litowa's children who was the first to ask a question when the president sat down with the villagers to discuss issues they wanted to talk about, and he did not relent until Nyerere had explained satisfactorily what he had meant in a recent radio broadcast when he said that one did not need money to build the nation (Wenner 1970, 139–141). Unlike the president's welcoming reception, however, other officials clearly found such behavior from primary school students unacceptable and disrespectful. Having been invited by the students to speak at the school, for instance, one of the CC members "stood and for five minutes harangued the children as being badly brought up and lacking in respect." Dispatching the school representatives to go after the visitors and ask for an explanation of their anger only aggravated things further. Comments Ibbott (1970, 190), "However much care he [the students' chairman] used and however much respect he showed he was fighting a losing battle. One's knowledge of the world tells one too well that the present Central Committee of the Party and the Litowa school children could not live side by side."

CC members had of course had occasion to be offended by their interactions with the RDA even prior to their visit. Two such occasions were the ujamaa seminars at

Figure 2.3. This is how you do it: a proper welcoming reception at Kideleko village, Handeni District, on the occasion of Nyerere's visit, July 1, 1969. Courtesy of Tanzania Information Service.

Kivukoni College in February 1969 and in Handeni in July 1969. In a radical role reversal of the usual ordering of authority, at both these events several "peasants"—as the July 5, 1969, *Nationalist* referred to them—from the RDA lectured the attending officials on ujamaa life. Joan Wicken comments specifically on the February seminar:

> The NEC [National Executive Committee] and Central Committee people were really annoyed by it. Making them sit down with these youngsters [of the RDA]! Remember that most of them [the officials] . . . had had very little education, and had risen up "through the ranks" of TANU and by now were "veterans" and looked up to in the same way as "The Elders" were traditionally regarded. . . . It could have been got over if the "teachers" were conscious of the problem, and had shown their great respect to them. But they did not realize the need—and were probably disinclined to do so anyway.[25]

Indeed, by the July Handeni seminar, some key players' minds seem to have been made up: arriving back from the seminar, the Litowa school's headmaster reported to the RDA that Second Vice President Kawawa had declared that the RDA had to stop.[26]

The RDA offended against the everyday practices in which officials' authority was constituted. This was not an ideological disagreement about alternative political or economic arrangements, but a clash that unfolded within a terrain of practices that made

Figure 2.4. Government and party leaders listening to a lecture at the Central Committee seminar on ujamaa in Handeni, July 1, 1969. Courtesy of Tanzania Information Service.

up a particular culture of authority. The visceral terms in which the CC articulated its case against the association reflected this, and they give an indication of how profoundly unsettling and threatening the encounter with the RDA had been to the CC's members. Edwards (1998, 16) records Millinga's recollection of the discussions at the CC meeting that sealed the RDA's fate, as repeated complaints about the disrespectful ways of the villagers culminated in the following exchange:[27]

> Those Committee members who had visited Litowa accused the villagers of planning to kill them, and they gave several examples to support their claim: apparently they tried to make a tree fall on top of one member while he was witnessing a demonstration of how to fell trees with a winch. Similarly they had apparently tried to roll a large rock onto another member while he was inspecting the village water supply construction project. A third attempt to kill the visitors involved a hostile bull. According to Millinga: "Mwalimu [Nyerere] was very annoyed with this (explanation): 'You people, are you serious! You have failed to convince me that there is any reason for disbanding the RDA. If you think they want to kill you with a rock, a tree and a bull, then you must be very stupid! How many people have been killed in this way?' Everyone in the meeting responded by saying that they wanted the RDA dead. Then someone stood up and said to Mwalimu, 'If you think the RDA should continue, then you should go and lead them on your own. They only respect you, anyway.'"

That anybody in the room would throw down the gauntlet to Nyerere in this way—surely a rare occurrence given his dominance of Tanzanian politics and his power to determine people's political fortunes—gives a sense of just how much must have seemed at stake.

It is worth, on this note, paying some attention to the specific idiom within which these accusations against the RDA were couched. Talk of assassination attempts might have seemed "stupid" to Nyerere, but it also indicates how deeply threatening the RDA was perceived to be.[28] Falling trees, rolling rocks, and a raging bull as weapons of choice also might harbor clues as to the nature of this perceived threat. In a context in which at least two RDA villages elsewhere found themselves explicitly subject to witchcraft accusations from state officials, it is not far-fetched to note such echoes here.[29] What to make of this? As Peter Geschiere (1997, 134) has argued, witchcraft accusations are a common feature of struggles over the "universal problems of power and inequality."[30] Like/as witchcraft accusations, which make actionable perceived threats from hidden forces suspected of being employed "to elaborate and realize transformative visions of the world" (West 2005, 6–7), these assassination stories concretized an ineffable menace. What this underlines is that the RDA was not an opponent in a programmatic policy debate, but an offender against a proper order of authority, the challenging of which was felt and negotiated at a visceral level.

An Offender against the Proper Order of Things

What were the contours of this order and what were its constitutive elements? The *Nationalist*'s gloss on the decision to dissolve the RDA provides a good starting point for answering this question. As this book's introduction argues, the party-run paper's coverage gives a good sense of "the official line" and the political establishment's framings of key events. In this specific context, it is very likely, for instance, that the announcement "TANU To Run All Ujamaa Villages" on the day after the RDA's destruction, as well as the next day's, September 26, 1969, editorial "Correct Guidance," commenting on the same event, were penned by Benjamin Mkapa, later to become Tanzania's third president, who attended Central Committee meetings in his capacity as the editor in charge of both the *Nationalist* and the Swahili-language *Uhuru*.[31] Here is the editorial's vision of properly configured authority:

> Ujamaa is Tanzanian Socialism, based on the principles acknowledged by all Tanzanians, for goals cherished by all Tanzanians. As an ideology it must evolve uniformly throughout the country as a condition of unity and correct development. And it is to the Party that one must look for direction and guidance. . . . Now before this analysis and detailing of the path which rural people should follow to socialism [in the Arusha Declaration and Nyerere's paper "Socialism and Rural Development"], some people had got together and set up communities on socialist lines. Through practice if not definition they were evolving their pockets of socialism in a wilderness still not impelled on to socialist transformation. The Party gave such associations its encouragement. It could not have done otherwise, for in their own

ways they were grappling with [the] idea of socialism. But the Party now has defined the idea of socialism and it's preparing the mechanism for implementing it in rural areas. The ujamaa village is a model of socialism in rural areas and the Party and its government has [sic] arrangements in hand for the development of these villages politically, socially and economically. There was thus clearly the danger that if matters continued as they were we would have a mushroom[ing] of "Ujamaa" villages representing at the most extreme, every shade of [the] idea of socialism. Already some regions were talking of starting their own Ujamaa village development associations. . . . But they can only prosper if they are TANU communities, inspired by its principles, politically guided by, and looking up to TANU for assistance. The decision by the Party to take charge of all Ujamaa villages was a correct, logical, political and ideological necessity.

The authority to set agendas, define models, and control mechanisms for implementation was vested exclusively in the party: the people were to find themselves "inspired" and "look up to TANU for assistance." This authority claim, which the CC reasserted in its fight with the RDA, was drawn together from a number of specific elements. Two are especially visible in this column. There is, first, a discourse of unitary movement-nationalism that undergirded the claim that the party acted for "all Tanzanians." Secondly, however, the editorial also firmly embeds this claim within the specific terrain of "development"—in which the party provided indispensible vanguard leadership as it authoritatively defined "the path which rural people should follow to socialism." The first framing—of the party as the only legitimate representative of all Tanzanians—made the RDA's independence and occasional outspokenness against officials much more than a mere nuisance: it raised deep suspicions and made the association anathema. The second framing—of the party as a necessary developmentalist vanguard—likewise raised concerns regarding the RDA's independence and inspired a sense that the association was depriving its villages of the superior leadership the party-state had to offer.

TANU Leaders' Monopoly on Legitimate Authority in Postcolonial Times

From the association's perspective, operating independently did not imply a rejection of the party but was a pragmatic choice that enabled it to effectively make day-to-day decisions.[32] The pioneering role Nyerere bestowed on the association—and Millinga's as well as Ibbott's quite extensive involvement with state institutions at the district, regional, and eventually national level—would seem to clearly indicate that there was no question of the association's "working against the party."[33] This, though, was precisely the accusation that would be repeatedly leveled against it, including by Peter Kisumo when he announced the association's destruction at Litowa (Ibbott 1970, 6, 122, 293).[34] The issue was the association's independence; comments Wicken, "Think about the way 'Nationalists' and TANU and Government might (and in practice did) think about such decisions. It appeared to be a rejection of Govt., and of TANU."[35]

It took a particular historical context for things to appear this way. In a January 1963 speech entitled "Democracy and the Party System," delivered to TANU's annual conference, Nyerere refuted the need for more than one party in Tanzania by drawing a contrast between European and African circumstances:

> Our own parties had a very different origin. They were not formed to challenge any ruling group of our own people; they were formed to challenge the foreigners who ruled over us. They were not, therefore, political "parties"—i.e., factions—but nationalist movements. And from the outset they represented the interests and aspirations of the whole nation. (Nyerere 1966, 198).

Having fought the colonial enemy of all Tanzanians, TANU continued to stand for the interests and aspirations of all after independence. This sentiment drove a swift conversion of TANU's de facto single-party status into a de jure monopoly position.[36]

A 1966 protest by students at the university in Dar es Salaam against a newly instated requirement that they complete two years of National Service yields a revealing illustration of the impact of such framings on everyday politics in the country. In an angry reaction against the students' "selfish" protests, Nyerere suspended the entire student body. A statement released by the party leadership and reported in the October 29, 1966, *Nationalist* explained why such a seemingly harsh reaction had been called for. It derided the notion that the students "could be against TANU, Afro-Shirazi Party [Zanzibar's ruling party], the Government and the President but not against the nation":

> From the inception of TANU and Afro-Shirazi the people have always rallied and supported the correct line of the leadership of these parties; and it was precisely due to the people's endorsement of the party's policies that opposition parties failed on the mainland before and after independence, this led to the establishment of a one Party State. . . . The faith of the people in the two parties has stood the test of time and goes much deeper than it can be imagined by our armchair philosophers on the Hill [the university] who have succumbed to be used as tools of neo-colonialism. . . . We wish to state clearly that we regard as enemy No. 1 any person who avertly [*sic*] or covertly tries to divide our ranks.

The underside of this assertion of the nationalist party's all-inclusiveness was that it created its delegitimized exclusions: only TANU politics and policies were legitimate; dissenters, even independent voices, quickly became "enemy No. 1" and—highlighting the salience of the legacy of TANU's anticolonial origins and the 1960s' particular historical and political context—"tools of neo-colonialism." This pattern of argumentation and accusation—and the resulting pervasive tendency toward intolerance and vilification of "opposition"—was ubiquitous in Tanzanian politics.

Against this backdrop, the RDA's independence raised suspicions bordering on paranoia. Wicken, for instance, recollects that the association was suspected of trying to set up an "independent State" and "introducing a local currency." (Ibbott surmises that this rumor might have been related to some discussions in the association about setting up a barter system among the villages.)[37] Despite the association's very close allegiance to Nyerere, there also appear to have been rumors that it was in cahoots with Oscar Kambona, by many estimates next to Nyerere the most powerful political figure in the country, who, in July 1967, had gone into self-imposed exile in Britain and turned into a vocal opponent of Nyerere by 1968.[38] The fact that activities at Litowa warranted being watched very closely underlines the intensity of the suspicions the RDA provoked: among the files of Central Committee member Rajabu Diwani at TANU headquarters, there is, for instance, an unidentified eyewitness report on the farewell Litowa had organized for the departing Ibbott family on October 3, 1969, following the association's destruction.[39]

The involvement of foreigners in the RDA only amplified suspicions of the association's independence. "The development of this country," Millinga (quoted in Edwards 1998, 15) recollects Second Vice President Kawawa erupting at the Handeni CC seminar in July 1969, "will be brought about by the people of this country, and no foreigners! The RDA will disband itself!" Wicken comments, "These (the 1960s and after) were highly political days. We were independent—and suspicious of the colonialists!"[40] In her assessment, concerns were heightened by the RDA's physical location close to the border with Mozambique; with FRELIMO fighters operating on the Tanzanian side, the presence of NATO citizens in the RDA villages became especially problematic. The February 1969 assassination of Eduardo Mondlane, FRELIMO's president, at the organization's headquarters in Dar es Salaam could only have underlined such concerns.[41] Already in mid-1968, travel documents for two Swiss technical volunteers had been long delayed,[42] and in 1969 Peter Kisumo's ministry blocked the RDA's request for new foreign volunteers. An official of the ministry also inquired with Millinga how he knew that Ibbott was not a spy (Ibbott 1970, 120, 249, 274).

Such "security" concerns mixed with more general nationalistic undertones and suspicions of foreigners that often implicitly or explicitly attached themselves to Tanzania's policy of "self-reliance," announced in the Arusha Declaration.[43] (In a clear indication of the broader prevalence of such invocations of the policy, Nyerere [1968, 386] quickly felt the need to clarify in an October 1967 speech: "Some of our people have spoken and acted as though it meant self-sufficiency in manpower and financial resources. It means nothing of the kind.") In its report on its November 1968 visit to Litowa, for instance, a group of teachers college principals

> questioned most strongly the advisability of employing expatriate staff to advise in any way the functioning of an Ujamaa village in Tanzania. These projects, it was felt, touched most fundamentally TANU's policy on the basis of rural development. As such, the party did not believe that there could be room for an Englishman or Frenchman in this kind of work. The fear was that, most of these expatriates might well end up writing books or thesis [sic] for higher degrees on the failures or successes of the endeavours of our people. (Reproduced in Ibbott 1970, 262–263)

Taking up the same issue, Binamu's (1969, 49) essay in Kivukoni College's journal that complained about the lack of a proper reception for the CC at Litowa was considerably more vitriolic. It accused an unidentified "foreign advisor" (Ibbott) of the association's villages—depicted in an accompanying cartoon smoking a pipe in a rocking chair while overlooking Africans toiling in the fields—of not doing "any work," "using our villages as a means to further his own ends," and misappropriating aid to feed his own bank account. The RDA's solicitation from Europe of secondhand clothing, referred to in the piece as "corpses' property" (*mali maiti*), was a capitalist ploy to make Tanzania and its policies look bad: "Do these advisors want to tell the world that our countrymen who live in ujamaa villages cannot get clothes to wear for themselves and their families?" (52). The villagers had been "drugged" (*wamepigwa kasumba*) (55–56) by their foreign advisors, and readers are warned to be on their guard "so that such sly operators [*wajanja*] shall not use our ujamaa policy to suck [*kuwanyonya*, i.e., to be a parasite on/exploit] those who are asleep" (49).

As James Brennan (2006, 2008) has shown, the trope of *kunyonya* (sucking/exploiting) in which these suspicions were couched was a central element in Tanzanian nationalist and anticolonial discourse and tapped into a rich local discourse about the workings of unseen, powerful forces.[44] In this idiom, the "exploiter" achieved his end by sucking his victims' blood, zombifying and thus gaining power over them. The accusations that people in the RDA had been dressed in "corpses' property" and "drugged" fit into the same discourse of forces operating in the dark and behind people's backs. Like the stories about assassination attempts against the Central Committee, this vocabulary again indicates an intense feeling that what was happening in the RDA was profoundly dangerous, deviant, and subversive.

The authority that the CC defended against the RDA's subversion was thus constituted within a number of quite specific, historically contingent framings revolving around nationalism and (neo)colonialism. Another prominent element in this assemblage was a discourse of paternal/generational authority. As Andrew Ivaska (2005) has argued, the conflation of state office and the position of an "elder" was quite pervasive in postcolonial Tanzania.[45] Indeed, Michael Schatzberg's (2001) work on the "idiom of the father" in the politics of middle Africa suggests that this conflation also tapped into a broader culture of authority that extended beyond Tanzania's borders. (To make this point, it should be added, is of course not to say that this was somehow an "essentially" African culture; rather, it was itself the product of a complex history that, among other elements, included colonial rule, which often—though not invariably—fortified the authority of older men materially and ideologically.[46]) As discussed in the introduction, in Tanzania, this culture was most prominently in evidence in how the president was typically referred to: only rarely was Nyerere "Nyerere" or "the president"; he was simply "Mwalimu" (the Teacher) or "*Baba wa Taifa*" (Father of the Nation). The 1966 National Service crisis at the university, referred to above, yields an especially vivid illustration of how authority and deference were negotiated through this idiom. Thus, after their expulsion, the university students apologized to Nyerere in a letter:

What happened recently between the students and the Government was a misunderstanding between father and son. It is clear that the son was wrong and so the son today apologises to the father. Kind father, pardon us your children. (Quoted in Carthew 1980, 545)

On this front, too, the RDA did not play along. At the Litowa school, of course, "badly brought up" students were perceived to show a lack of respect that politicians deserved quite literally as their elders. On the other hand, differences in age alone cannot explain the apparent offense caused by the role reversal between officials/teachers/elders and "peasants"/students/youngsters at RDA-run ujamaa seminars: this hints at a mutual permeation of cultures of authority rooted in generational hierarchies and claims to authority that were based in particular framings of postcolonial politics. As Wicken comments, "Making them sit down with these youngsters!" They "were 'veterans' and looked up to in the same way as 'The Elders' were traditionally regarded."[47]

Officials as Indispensible Authorities in Development

How development and authority in its field of practices were configured dovetailed and interacted with these elements in the assemblage of officials' authority in a mutually constitutive way. A "developmental" juxtaposition of childlike peasants and officials who were consequently required to chart a course into a better future for them, for instance, both fed off and reinforced a model of paternal authority. Likewise, the casting of the party-state as the defender of the welfare of all Tanzanians against neocolonial enemies underpinned a vesting of developmental authority exclusively in party and state officials. When the CC then asserted its authority over the RDA villages, this was a claim that was constituted in a multidimensional assemblage in which officials' casting specifically as developmental authority was one salient element.

The association's insufficient acknowledgment of this particular dimension of officials' authority not only bred resentment but also seems to have made it hard for officials to recognize the RDA's successes: achieved independently of their interventions, something always seemed amiss. There were, for instance, the accusations about improper crop spacing brought to the president's attention under Barongo's commissionership; the aforementioned report of the visiting group of teachers college principals noting "unfortunate signs of a class society developing" at Litowa (reproduced in Ibbott 1970, 262), a suspicion apparently based on the existence of old houses next to the new ones that the village's ongoing building program had constructed (why not count this as a sign of progress instead?); renewed complaints about the remaining old houses by the visiting CC members, whose report also understated Matetereka's coffee acreage by 70 percent;[48] and, finally, rumors that there was no progress in the villages, about which

Nyerere had confronted association representatives at the February 1969 CC seminar on ujamaa (Ibbott 1970, 257).

Finding and pointing out such deficiencies in the RDA may of course have been in part a question of badmouthing an organization that was disliked and perceived as a competitor. Thus, although, according to Ibbott (1970, 249), an official in Kisumo's ministry told Millinga after visiting the RDA with Kisumo "that the standard of agriculture in some of the villages was quite high, particularly at Liweta where it would, he said, 'be difficult for an agricultural officer to face the village Bwana Shamba [agricultural extension expert],'" Kisumo would list insufficient development as a key reason for the state's takeover of the villages when he announced the decision in Ruvuma.[49] But besides officials' instrumental reasons for rendering such assessments, there also appears to have been a genuine inability to recognize as "successful" anything that was not draped in the constitutive practices—drawing up "planning" documents, launching "operations"—of officials' developmental authority. As the *Nationalist* had protested, "Correct Guidance" in development had to come from the party and government: proper development was impossible without these, officials' distinctive modes of intervention.

That such practices seemed to be crucial in constituting what counted as (proper) development helps to explain the comparative assessments officials tended to make of the RDA and a series of "competing" initiatives. Such alternatives appear to have been generally deemed more promising not by virtue of better results, but insofar as they featured prominently the ritualistic "planning" practices through which officials' developmental authority was constituted. Unlike in the RDA, in these preferable initiatives production targets—three to five years at a time—were set; formal planning documents drawn up; exhortations issued to follow "scientific" and "modern" methods; and spectacular "operations" launched. This is what development looked like, and, as such, it required the kind of interventions that officials alone could provide. As a 1972 Morogoro Regional Development Committee meeting would proclaim, "It must be remembered that the peasants have never been planners and that is why they have not improved their standard of living for ages" (quoted in Mushi 1981, 154).

Njoomlole, a village founded in 1962/1963 and one of the early RDA members, eventually emerged as one such preferable alternative to the RDA. In 1965/1966, it had a serious falling out with the RDA over how its leader, Josephat Mhagama, elected to Parliament for Songea North in 1965, was directing the village's affairs. In particular, the association's leaders had criticized a development plan that Mhagama had drawn up for lacking concrete, practical ideas, setting unrealistic targets, and being premised on large amounts of aid (Ibbott 1970, 225–226).

If such planning documents failed to inspire the RDA, more receptive audiences existed elsewhere. Njoomlole's large and round numbers, multi-year production targets, income projections, and capital requirements apparently appealed at least to some of the national leaders who found themselves on Mhagama's mailing list.[50] The village's targets of 250 families and ten thousand acres under cultivation, outlined in its October 7, 1967, constitution, for instance, were exactly what Kisumo's ministry would adopt as its own targets for ujamaa villages about half a year later.[51] Kisumo's ministry and other government institutions would also circulate Njoomlole's constitution and documents closely modeled on it as examples to be emulated.[52] The press, too, latched onto Njoomlole's "planning"—its targets, projections, and budgets—in quite extensive coverage it devoted to the village.[53] Thus, on September 29, 1969, *Uhuru* devoted an enthusiastic front-page article overflowing with statistics to Njoomlole's budget and income projections; the next day, it followed up with an exhilarated opinion piece on the village, and a similar report was also broadcast on the radio (Ibbott 1970, 227). (Appearing within a week of the destruction of the RDA, this coverage can probably be counted as an illustration of the government-controlled media's use in making certain political points.)

In contrast to the RDA's approach, Njoomlole's was packaged in precisely the practices that made it recognizable as being engaged in (proper) development: this was the kind of project behind which key leaders could throw their full weight—as well as quite extraordinary financial subventions.[54] Of course, its inspiring plans were the products of techniques and practices that were constitutive of officials', not peasants', repertoire of actions. As such, they reflected a configuration of development at the village that elevated Mhagama as an authority over regular members to the point where his autocratic leadership style caused not just a rupture with the RDA but also a serious crisis in the village.[55]

To a series of officials, Mlale Pilot Scheme, started in 1963 near Songea as one of the heavily capitalized Village Settlement Schemes, was another paragon of development properly conducted that was therefore deemed a superior alternative to the RDA. With a land survey, plans, budgets, long-range targets, and a plush capital expense account, it too fit a configuration of development that centered on the techniques and practices that officials alone commanded—and that were taken to guarantee the scheme's success (quite mistakenly so, as chapter 1 discussed).[56] Thus, the commissioner for village settlement, having been told about the RDA in 1963, suggested to Ibbott and Millinga that they fold their operation and have Litowa's members sign up for Mlale. Peter Walwa, Ruvuma's regional commissioner from 1964 to 1965, would likewise push the scheme as an alternative to the RDA in 1965 (Ibbott 1970, 33, 241–242). These officials apparently shared the soon-to-be-sorely-disappointed expectation of the TANU area secretary who explained to Ibbott "that there would soon be many settlers at Mlale, as after a year or two, when the first settlers began to buy their cars, many more would want to join too" (62). And how could it be otherwise when the scheme enjoyed, for instance, the benefit of Kawawa's coordinating a flurry of renewed planning activities that climaxed in government planes completing an aerial survey of potential new sites for the scheme in 1965?[57] This, obviously, was a different kind of undertaking altogether from the literally more down-to-earth RDA.

In 1969, similarly inspiring scenes repeated themselves further to the east in Rufiji. With Kawawa again at the helm, a military-style "Operation Rescue" responded to a flood emergency around the Rufiji River: planes were dispatched to survey the area, army gunboats deployed, and rescue teams dispatched from Dar es Salaam—all creating a sense of excitement and radical action. Quickly, this emergency intervention morphed into the first large-scale, centrally initiated campaign to resettle rural populations into ujamaa villages.

Into the middle of all this arrived the TANU CC, having interrupted its September 1969 Dar es Salaam meeting that would soon seal the RDA's fate in order to participate in TANU's National Executive's meeting in Rufiji.[58] The trip provided an opportunity to witness firsthand what a government-led ujamaa/villagization program would be able to accomplish: this was how development would be achieved. At the center of it was the state's transformational agency instantiated in planning activities, target setting, and "operations." This, then, was the background when, a few days later, Kisumo pointed to Rufiji as a model when he delivered the news to Litowa that for development's sake all ujamaa activities would henceforth be firmly under the state's authority.[59]

Conclusion

Officials, jockeying for positions and Nyerere's approval, saw the association as a rival. But this was not the only reason behind the RDA's destruction. The CC's move against the association was also centrally an act of vengeance visited upon an offender against the proper order of authority. Key elements in this order's assemblage were a framing of political leaders as the embodiments of the unitary nation and a culture of generational authority that overlapped with and reinforced this construction of officials. But the destruction of the RDA shows that what the CC was defending against the RDA was also officials' positioning specifically as developmental authorities over peasants. The next two chapters pay close attention to the constitution of this particular element in officials' authority and the effects it produced.

The history of ujamaa in Ruvuma soon began to be written to render a world that, properly back under officials' tutelage, was finally governed well. While the *Daily News'* long January 24, 1975, article on "Ruvuma Ujamaa Villages" briefly mentions the RDA (now "defunct"), it strongly suggests that the proper purveyors of ujamaa and development were to be found elsewhere: "Of course, until the Arusha Declaration in 1967, these villages followed a haphazard pattern. But today, with a clear Ujamaa policy, the region boasts of villages like Litowa, Njoomlole and many others." The caption under a picture of an "Ujamaa farm" reads, "At least now there is some planning as opposed to the old system." Indeed, it had also only been "after the Arusha Declaration" that "these villages were transformed into Ujamaa villages including the Litowa Tanu Youth League Farmers Scheme": even Litowa's initial TANU Youth League association evidently had to be resurrected to make this chapter of rural development fit into a narrative of development steered by the vanguard authority of state officials.

Tragically for the RDA villages (as soon after for the rest of the country), this confident narrative protested too much. The post-RDA experience of its member villages was difficult. The association's destruction delivered a blow on several fronts: at least temporarily, the villages lost access to some of their resources; the expatriates quickly left the country and the teachers were posted elsewhere; finally, the CC's move was deeply demoralizing. As the "lead village," Litowa was especially hard-hit on this latter front; in late 1969 and early 1970, its members were apparently so demoralized that outsiders had to be brought in to harvest the village's crops.[60] Even among the generally self-congratulatory official reports emanating from the region—since the state had taken control of the RDA villages, things were finally looking up—one finds a note that lists Litowa and Liweta as two of only five villages in Songea District that had been struck by a food shortage in late 1969.[61]

After the initial shock, the more established villages apparently stabilized, although many of the smaller, newer villages swiftly collapsed.[62] The selection of Liweta in 1971 and Litowa in 1972 as the best village in the region could be read as an indication that at least these two were doing quite well. Alternatively, these awards perhaps also came suspiciously close on the heels of the major problems both villages experienced in 1969/1970 and could thus be interpreted as making a political point, besides being a self-congratulatory note on the government's quite extensive 1970/1971 investment campaign in the two villages.[63] Indeed, not all was well even after the initial blow of the association's destruction had had time to subside. At Litowa, for instance, relations between "ordinary villagers" and the new, government-appointed staff were bad, as typically autocratic "staff behavior" vis-à-vis "peasants" quickly reclaimed its territory at the village.[64] This apparently led to the erosion of key elements of the RDA's way of running its affairs that had underlain its success at facilitating an attractive life for its members. Thus, Ndonde (1975a, 175), who had originally joined Litowa in mid-1969 as a teacher and was observing the development of a cattle ranching project at the village in early 1974, comments that at that point "village organization was poor and the level of ujamaa commitment very low."

If this was an indication of the longer-range effects of the association's replacement by the state's developmental machinery, occasional bright spots, suggests Ndonde, still owed to what the RDA had built in its member villages. For instance, what, after an initially bleak outlook, apparently turned the cattle project around, he argues, was a broad soul-searching with many internal discussions about village discipline, organization, and leadership that drew on, and brought something of a revival of, the practices of authority and governing that had evolved at the village under the RDA. Thus, when one Litowan suggested in a village meeting to "keep quiet and let mtaalamu [the expert] tell us the answer, he is paid for that," "other villagers would shout him down and tell him that if they were going to depend on the 'mtaalamu' they would never develop, for the 'mtaalamu' would not be there with them everyday. Besides, there were several occasions when they themselves did things without the 'mtaalamu' being around. The 'mtaalamu' is only there to help the villages help themselves" (1975a, 171).

Edwards (1998) likewise argues that Matetereka village's emergence as the most sustained success story out of the association's destruction was a testimony to the RDA's legacy. Located far from the RDA's epicenter at Litowa, and hence somewhat out of the spotlight, Matetereka's leadership and internal structures remained largely intact. Explicitly informed by the RDA's principles, a key group at the village retained its strong sense of common purpose and persisted in its collective endeavors past the 1980s as "Tanzania's Last Ujamaa Village."[65]

However, at Litowa and Liweta, a massive influx of new settlers in 1974/1975, when large-scale villagization reached Ruvuma, finally appears to have broken the last remaining underpinnings of the successful ujamaa communities the villages had once been.[66] This suggests that—in an especially tragic twist—villagization not only failed to facilitate the growth of the kind of dynamic ujamaa communities it was meant to jump-start, but indeed threw up major problems for those that already existed.[67] During a visit to Litowa four decades after the RDA's destruction, facilities such as the school that have fallen into disuse or disrepair were reminders of a more prosperous and promising past. Taking stock of this reality in 1992, Suleman Toroka, former principal of the Litowa school, confided in Ibbott (2000, 88) "how in quiet moments he often thought, 'Where might we have been today if they had just left us alone.'"

3 Chronicle of a Failure Foretold

State Officials' Developmentalist Authority in Action

> One view is that the actions of the bureaucratic bourgeoisie do very closely mirror its class interest. Thus the most recent villagization operations are seen as a deliberate attempt to distort policy and to wreck socialism as represented by ujamaa. . . . This supposedly clear and self-interested attitude seems not to portray accurately the opinions of most bureaucrats on villagization. . . . The rather simplistic view cited above fails to take account of the self-mystification of the bureaucracy by its own ideology. In spite of the veneer of socialism, this has its roots so deep in modernization theory and the various suppositions which accompany operations within a bureaucratic hierarchy, that sane and intelligent men can really believe that the present compulsory villagization operation and the re-imposed colonial regulations, will achieve socialism and/or development. Nor can this false consciousness be considered entirely and directly self-serving since it is hard to see that the policy serves the economic interests of anyone in Tanzania, cutting as it does at the productive base which provides the entire surplus on which the class exists.
>
> —Philip Raikes, "Ujamaa and Rural Socialism"

In 1968, a special Working Group on the Machinery for Coordinated Rural Development was considering how to promote the new policy of ujamaa in the rural areas. A key question in its discussions was "spontaneous versus bureaucratic initiative,"[1] also glossed as "selective versus frontal attack."[2] RDA sympathizers in the working group repeatedly drew on its example to caution against pushing ujamaa too hard, too early, and too broadly; as one memorandum noted, "Many of those who enthusiastically support the R.D.A. for example, are skeptical regarding the possibility of the extension of its principle through a predominantly government initiative."[3]

Step by step, such concerns were written out of sequential drafts of the group's recommendations to be included in the 1969 Tanzania Second Five-Year Plan for Economic and Social Development. The group's first draft report of May 25, 1968, had been blunt: "It is not yet time for a mass campaign to organize ujamaa villages throughout the countryside." The second draft of June 13, 1968, had dropped this sentence, although it retained other cautionary remarks. When the discussion moved into its final stages, however, a mid-1968 confidential memorandum noted that "it seems likely that the selective approach, while it may have a place, will not be sufficient to ensure the required momentum. We should therefore discuss the possibility of a frontal attack in some detail."[4] The final decision came from higher up, passed down to the group from the Ministry of Development Planning.[5] The 1969 Five-Year Plan (URT 1969, 27) would unequivocally state, "The frontal, or broad-based, approach has been chosen because of the desire to mobilize the widest possible participation in socialist activity throughout the rural society." In his preamble to the plan, Nyerere explained, "We have rejected the idea that we should concentrate all Government assistance on the development of ujamaa villages in certain Regions or Districts, and have decided that we must make a wide-spread frontal attack on this problem" (xvii). Simply put, there should be no privileged access to the solution to the problem of rural development that he had discovered.

For the villages of the RDA, the Central Committee's expectation that the state would be a superior replacement for the association proved to be in vain. This was not a good omen for the broader drive to build ujamaa vijijini ("ujamaa in the villages") across the country under the state's vanguard authority. The state's "frontal attack" would eventually take the shape of coercive villagization campaigns intended to enforce what was seen as at least a "first step" toward ujamaa. This modality implied a radical departure from the RDA's noncoercive and patient building of commitment and nurturing of capacity through a process of learning-by-doing. But working through dictates and compulsion was no shortcut to the foundation of the RDA's success, the organization, commitment, and capacities that had taken years and careful nurturing to evolve and solidify. To the contrary: precisely as Nyerere had warned in his proclamations about development and freedom, cajoling and coercing people into "making a start" bred such resistance and antagonism to the project that it is doubtful whether constructive, capable, and patient nurturing of ujamaa communities would have found a receptive audience even if such support had been available.

Villagization never was the spark that ignited the growth of dynamic communities of the kind Nyerere had admired in Ruvuma. Without such communities as its driver, however, rural development would again have to fall back on material, technical, and organizational resources provided by the state. The success of the thousands of official villages in which villagization concentrated Tanzania's rural population, in other words, would hinge on the very inputs that had proven so woefully inadequate in the fewer than two-dozen Village Settlement Schemes of the early 1960s.

Thus, as ujamaa vijijini—born out of a clear recognition of the state's capacity constraints and eloquent arguments about the instrumental as well as intrinsic value of freedom in development—morphed into villagization, it would ignore the very lessons that had lain at its foundation. Why did Tanzania under Nyerere's leadership rush headlong into this failure that he himself had very much foretold? The process of renegotiating and overriding Nyerere's earlier programmatic proclamations of course had many faces and authors. For subordinate officials, for instance, ignoring his proscriptions of coercive means was often to a significant extent driven by the pressure they were under to deliver "results" on the ujamaa front as demanded above all by the president himself. For many officials, there might in fact not ever have been a question of renegotiating anything: if the attitudes that were reflected in the reinstitution of colonial-era compulsory cultivation in the immediate aftermath of independence are any indication, many never had had compunctions about "driving" peasants in the desired direction. But what about Nyerere himself, whose insistence on rapid progress on the policy, increasingly permissive stance toward coercion, and eventual call for compulsory resettlement were absolutely crucial in steering the state apparatus in the direction of villagization? He—and perhaps a not-insignificant number of other officials—really do seem to have made a journey from ujamaa to villagization.

Focusing to an extent on the president himself, this chapter traces the shifting articulations of authority in development that took him (and the country) from that original vision to a very different reality. An opening toward this shift had in fact already been present in tensions—more easily left unresolved in abstract philosophizing than in practice—in those early presidential pronouncements. While, on the one hand, they valorized the peasants' freedom to choose, they did not, on the other, betray much openness regarding what making the *right* choice for Tanzania's future might involve: Nyerere had discovered the way forward, and what was left for the peasantry to do was not to find its own path, but to merge onto Nyerere's—hopefully, of course, by the light of their own enlightened choice. What propelled the resolution of this tension between the peasantry's freedom to choose and the leadership's authority in favor of the latter was a hardening of a crucial distinction: a juxtaposed construction of peasants as ultimately incompetent to exercise authority over the broader direction of their own lives and a vanguard leadership that was thus obligated to make choices for them. This and the next chapter trace the texture of this distinction and examine the discursive framings and practices from which it was assembled.

The Tensions of Freedom in Development

Nyerere's message about ujamaa vijijini had seemed unequivocal enough (see chapter 1). The state's limitations in terms of resources and local knowledge made it impossible for it to ensure through its own agency improvements in the material well-being of Tanzanians. The necessary expansion of economic resources would have to be generated through the people's expanding capacities and the synergies that working together in ujamaa communities would release. This new engine for rural development would be fatally compromised, Nyerere had argued, if ujamaa communities were not democratically self-governing at the local level or if they were established through any means other than the free decision of their members.

But the centrality of freedom and noncoercion in this new approach to rural development was not just a matter of this, their instrumental value. In his October 16, 1968, paper "Freedom and Development" Nyerere reasoned that because "the purpose of development is the greater freedom and wellbeing of the people, it cannot result from force" (1973, 61). The freedom from material deprivation that increased output could buy was thus only one dimension of development, which more broadly required the "development *of people*" (60; emphasis original) as "dignified and confident human beings" (69).[6] The implication of this conception was that "development of a man can, in fact, only be effected by that man": "He develops himself by what he does; he develops himself by making his own decisions, by increasing his understanding of what he is doing, and why; by increasing his own knowledge and ability" (60).

Unacknowledged in these proclamations are the tensions inherent in the very idea that "freedom" ought to be not just an instrumental mode but also an end of development. If the particular subjectivity Nyerere here sketches as the hallmark of a truly free/developed person was a goal still to be striven for, it was also, by implication, as yet unattained. Development thus defined was therefore premised precisely on a *deficiency* in a "man's" "understanding of what he is doing, and why," his capacity to make "his own decisions." Whether these underdeveloped capacities could then be relied upon in the process of their own development was therefore very much in question: such an as-yet-deficient man, in other words, may be in need of a guardian.

This is the back door through which authoritarian modes of rule enter into Nyerere's conception of development through and for freedom. In this regard, Tanzania's story illustrates tensions—and the potential toward their ultimately self-contradictory resolution in favor of despotic rule—that Dean (2010, 171) detects in liberal forms of governmentality more generally: "The . . . emphasis on governing through freedom means that it always contains a division between those who are capable of bearing the responsibilities and freedoms of mature citizenship and those who are not. For the latter, this will often mean a despotic provision for their special needs with the aim of rendering them autonomous by fostering capacities of responsibility and self-governance." Indeed, one does not have to look hard to find John Stuart Mill in Nyerere.[7] Thus, in *On Liberty*, Mill argues that freedom both consisted in and was developed through the exercise of a distinctive set of faculties: "Reasoning and judgement to foresee, . . . discrimination to decide, and when he has decided, firmness and self-control to hold to his deliberate decision" (quoted in Cowen and Shenton 1995, 39). Mill, of course, found this kind of subjectivity so entirely lacking in India, note Cowen and Shenton (1995, 41), that he argued that—in the very name of freedom—"India needed to be governed despotically by an incorruptible imperial cadre who exercised trusteeship in order to create the conditions under which education, choice, individuality—in a word development—might occur."

Contemporary discourses and practices of development and government that stress "empowerment" must likewise negotiate this often unacknowledged tension: frequently enough they, too, do so in favor of more or less open versions of trusteeship. As Barbara Cruikshank (1999, 4) puts it in *The Will to Empower*, which examines government programs and empowerment movements in the United States, relations of empowerment always "shape . . . as well as enlist" "the autonomy, interest, and wills of citizens": "It is in those cases where individuals do not act in their own self-interest or appear indifferent to their own development as full-fledged citizens," where, in other words, their autonomy requires shaping before it can be enlisted, "that the limits of the liberal state at the threshold of individual rights, liberty, and pursuits must be crossed."

Witness, for instance, Majid Rahnema searching for liberating alternatives to what he characterizes as the oppressive *qua* culturally imperialist project of development. How may such an alternative be constructed? Relying on people's own judgment of what is "good and desirable," finds Rahnema (1997, 388), is complicated by the fact that this judgment is "often changing and confused." Confronted with this problem of false consciousness, one can for instance not rely on "a 'voting' process alone" to determine the good. Instead, one must turn to "vernacular societies" for a model of authority and governing structured around the belief "that the good of the community was better served by those of its members it considered to be the wisest, the most virtuous, and hence the most 'authoritative' and experienced persons of the group." Real liberation, a truly emancipatory alternative to development as usual, this comes within a hair's breadth of stating, requires submission to the authority of guardians.

The story of freedom and development in Tanzania, then, is the story of the negotiation of tensions that are perhaps inherent in liberal forms of government and liberational projects. Whereas in the RDA's practices the institutional limits of a grassroots organization, democratic accountability, and self-imposed restraints in the exercise of leadership added up to an effective safeguard against crossing onto the terrain of what one might call liberational despotism, in Nyerere's project of building a better future for Tanzanians through ujamaa such limitations were quickly eroded and overridden. This slide of a liberational project into self-contradiction hinged on the emergence of a distinction between those who (still) required trusteeship and an authority that could fulfill the role of a guardian.

Initially, Nyerere shied away from sharply drawing such a distinction and conjuring such an authority. In his January 21, 1968, ruminations on the "implementation of rural socialism" and the proper role of leaders in it, for instance, Nyerere (1973, 9–10) seemed to categorically refuse to countenance going against ordinary people's choices:

> Suppose a group of families have decided to start a co-operative farm and village, and are discussing where to build their houses. The problem is whether to build on a hill or down in the valley; and the argument is about the ease of getting water versus the danger of flooding. A good leader who is a member of this group may argue that it is better to build on the hill and face the drudgery of carrying the water until they can afford a pump and pipes; but let us suppose that despite all his efforts the general opinion is to build near the water's edge. What should he do? The answer is clear: he must play a very full part in the work of building the village in the valley.

Indeed, he insisted on this point:

> It may easily happen that a visiting political or government leader knows that the people are making a mistake which could prove fatal to their ambition, either in or-

ganization, in their selection of their leader, or in their methods. The temptation to intervene must surely be very great indeed under these circumstances; part of the visitor's job is to help these communities. Obviously he should explain his point, illustrate his argument by pointing to experience elsewhere, and discuss the whole question with the members. But suppose the members still insist on their own decisions and therefore their own mistakes. Only if we accept this are we really accepting the philosophy of Socialism and Rural Development. (8)

Yet, despite his seemingly unequivocal conclusions, the seeds of tension are already detectable in these hypothetical scenarios: always, the leader knew best; always, it was the villagers who were about to embark on a "fatal mistake." Confronted with situations framed thus, Nyerere (1973, 8) observed, the "temptation to intervene must surely be very great indeed." Indeed, if in practice the people's freedom largely actualized as the freedom to make their own *mistakes,* there was a strong suggestion that such freedom would ultimately have to be weighed against its costs. If the costs were too great, and if, moreover, the people's exercise of their freedom went to waste because they did not learn from their mistakes, the balance might be tipped. Then, Nyerere's worry about the "danger that enthusiastic TANU members, and others, might rush out and bully people into artificial communities which will collapse with the first breath of adversity" might be outweighed by what he felt was the opposing "danger that nothing will happen at all" (6).

This calculus was set in motion by the pernicious premise that the leader knew best: only then could no movement in the direction of his vision be considered a danger. Although Nyerere fairly consistently defended a degree of local autonomy in everyday decision-making in rural development, this calculus would lead him to embrace the necessity of exercising an increasingly forceful authority at least with respect to determining the broad direction of regular Tanzanians' lives. On this front, the costs of ignoring his wisdom were just too great—especially as hopes diminished that the people would freely and quickly learn the lesson Nyerere had to impart. Tanzania's slide from the tension-laden ideas of ujamaa vijijini to the "good despotism" of coercive villagization thus pivots on the increasing sharpening of the distinction between a leadership in possession of the right answers and peasants whose persistent failure to make the one *correct* choice only served to underline that they were not ready to make decisions for themselves. This and the next chapter trace the assemblage of this authorizing juxtaposition.

Freedom, Development, and Villagization in Rufiji, 1968–1969

A first test case for how these tensions would be negotiated arose in early 1968. An estimated forty thousand inhabitants of settlements in the Rufiji River plain had been engulfed by floodwaters. As the government initiated a rescue operation, the idea that this recurrent situation should be solved "once and for all" quickly took hold—and presented an opening for the first centrally directed campaign to establish ujamaa villages in the country. These, Nyerere and his government had decided, would have to be located on the river plateau: Nyerere's hence not entirely hypothetical January 1968 scenario in which a decision was required whether to locate a village in a river floodplain or on a plateau was playing out in real life.

Quickly, the president's premise that the leader knew best emerged and went to work in Rufiji—chipping away at his injunction, issued on paper, against dictating the right choice to the people in such a scenario. Whereas the May 9, 1968, *Nationalist* had still reported that "a village elder" had (quite reasonably) pointed out that "we like floods because after a period, the flooded area becomes our best fertile land," soon the peasants' reluctance to move could no longer have anything to do with such sensible arguments. Thus, a July 22, 1968, *Nationalist* report had a "Rufiji elder" put Rufiji peasants in their proper place; the paper has him declare to a visiting Nyerere that he had seen the light: "We are awake from the dead. We can no longer live on the myths of our great grandfathers, living up to the floods. We must move." Pre-campaign Rufiji was a land of the past's outdated myths, an image that, in the September 24, 1969, *Nationalist*'s telling, Nyerere echoed back when he told a mass rally in Rufiji, "If we want to develop, the way we lived years ago must come to an end and we must lead new lives based on hard work."

On the one hand, Rufiji thus featured the peasants' old lives of the past, akin to a state of death; on the other, there was a leader who knew which new lives everybody would have to lead. This basic constellation was never in question. Wrote Nyerere in his late 1968 paper "Freedom and Development," "When [not "if"] we have convinced the people that TANU's policies are good and sound, then we should be working with them to create a society in which exploiters will find no opportunities for their evil doing" (Nyerere 1973, 62). Within this framing, popular hesitations about Nyerere's solutions were almost automatically dismissed as a matter of the people's as-yet-inadequate appreciation of the promise of his plan (insufficiently rapid implementation on the part of officials was outright sabotage). As Philip Raikes (1972, 13) observed at the time, "The failure of peasants to respond positively to any given proposal leads not, as it should, to a detailed analysis of why it was rejected but to an automatic assumption that the cause is the ignorance, superstition and venality of the peasant."

This framing shaped the state's basic posture in the campaign. As long as there was still a hope that such efforts might rectify the problem of an unenlightened peasantry, "educating" people about the benefits of establishing ujamaa villages away from the floodplains was the appropriate response. On March 7, 1968, the *Nationalist* reported that leaflets asking Lenin's question—"People of Rufiji: What Is to Be Done?"—and informing their readers of the "benefits of living and working together" were being distributed. But this initiative—like the educational efforts by a flurry of visitors that included Nyerere, Kawawa, Kisumo, and a conference of regional commissioners—appear to have borne no fruits: despite promises of services such as piped water and schools, people were evidently reluctant to move.[8]

Prodding therefore became necessary for a population that was revealing itself to be mired in conservatism and its old ways. Regional Commissioner Songambele, the September 13 *Nationalist* reported, was soon issuing public warnings against "subversive activities which frustrate the implementation of ujamaa villages." As the regional surveyor at the time notes, this sharpened tone was echoed in calls for stronger measures than mere warnings: "Some, like the Regional Police Commander, wanted to resort to force to drive the reluctant villagers from the valley and destroy their houses. Then, he argued, the peasants would have no alternative but participate in the bush clearing necessary for the new villages." But Nyerere told the regional commissioner that this was not acceptable, and, in the end, only "a few persons were arrested, apparently for obstructing progress or for discouraging people from moving" (Turok 1975, 402). While Nyerere may thus have refrained from endorsing outright coercion, by early 1969 he too was sufficiently frustrated with the lack of progress to personally authorize making the receipt of famine relief conditional on residence in the around twenty-five designated new settlements away from the floodplains to get people to move (398). Then, the April 5, 1969, *Nationalist* reported, a "Government's deadline" was proclaimed "for . . . people to move of their own free will before any action is taken to save their lives and enable them to enjoy the better living conditions provided for by the Government in ujamaa villages."[9]

The creeping breach of Nyerere's own injunction against forcing people into ujamaa villages was thus not just a question of implementing officials subverting Nyerere's fine ideals. Already in Rufiji, Nyerere himself treated the line he had drawn as a wide gray zone; and his demands for decisive action ensured that his subordinates would do the same, as presidential pressure left them little choice but to resort to coercive means, even if the full extent of this was perhaps not quite officially sanctioned or intended. In February 1969, for instance, Kawawa called ministerial and regional representatives in for a meeting: he told them that since "the Ministries concerned had not seized this opportunity to start Ujamaa villages on a proper and planned scale," Nyerere "had made it clear that the Govt. cannot afford to fail." The Ministry of Agriculture's copy of the meeting's minutes bears the penciled-in remark, "This is important and I would like you to write to RD [regional director] Coast [Region] informing him that he must put his best officers to this work immediately."[10]

With the impediment to a quicker uptake of the leadership's plans identified as the peasants' conservatism and lack of enlightenment, compulsion did after all hold out a promise: at least it would ensure that peasants "made a start"; soon, the assumption was, their leaders' choice for them would become their own as its wisdom would reveal itself. A dosage of good despotism, in other words, was necessary to move a benighted peasantry along the path toward their new, enlightened selves and a better future. That this was the destination that the leadership's plans would lead them to was indisputable: "Ujamaa Villages Ensure Progress," an August 18, 1969, *Nationalist* headline summed up one of many similar speeches by Second Vice President Kawawa that he delivered just to the south of Rufiji:[11]

> Mr. Kawawa told a mass rally that TANU, Government and the people of Tanzania regarded the call for Ujamaa life as an answer for close co-operation among the people, their Party and Government for the country's development and the eradication of all sorts of exploitation. He pointed out that the obstacles of development were numerous and could not be tackled single-handed. The best way to forge ahead towards development was to unite and live together in Ujamaa Villages. Mr. Kawawa said that the call to start Ujamaa Villages had been going on for a long time now and it was time people in Nachingwea District started Ujamaa Villages without delay. He urged the people to embark on co-operative farming in Ujamaa Villages where ox-driven ploughs could be used. Tractors could be used later to ensure quick economic development.

One key consequence of the leadership's blind self-assuredness in its developmental authority that emerges from this and many similar exhortations was that frequently any consideration of details and serious probing of rationales was dispensed with. Not just in speeches but also in the practical conduct of government interventions, general exhortations were often all there was—as even "technical" planning exercises typically did not rise above the level of throwaway slogans and target-setting that was divorced from any practical reality.

What did development thus configured produce in Rufiji? Eventually, more or less mild forms of coercion herded large numbers of people into close proximity with one another, but this did not make for "ujamaa" communities committed to a common project. Resentment of being coerced and an apparent general unease about living in a "community" of strangers—reflected in Rufiji as in many other parts of the country in a rise in witchcraft fears—militated against any such development.[12] The predictable result was an almost complete failure of the attempt to introduce communal production and, more generally, build the kind of dynamic communities that ujamaa vijijini had envisioned. A confidential January 1971 TANU report on villagization in Rufiji, likely penned by Millinga in his function as the head of the Department of Ujamaa Vijijini at TANU headquarters, did not mince words in its diagnosis: "Farmers are not people who will trust a thing in a second, many times they have exercised caution about things they did not know. It is necessary that the leaders avoid breaking the spirit of the people."[13]

Rufiji also underlined the state's limited resources and technical capacity. Only a third of the new settlements had a working water supply about a year after their inception, for instance.[14] Other predictable problems with resettlement—and especially the loss or impairment of a successful cultivation system that utilized the annual floods for rice, maize, and cotton cultivation on the rich soils of the floodplains—were ignored to the detriment of Rufiji's agricultural productivity and food security.[15] In the upstream area in particular, recurring food shortages prior to villagization "turned into an almost chronic lack of food" after resettlement (Bantje 1980, 8). Perhaps the clearest symptom of the glaring "technical" inadequacies of the campaign was the sheer size of several of the new settlements. One of the collection points of the campaign, Ikwiriri "village," soon boasted sixteen thousand inhabitants. Such a size not only rendered the kind of internal organization practiced in the RDA villages practically impossible from the start; it also inevitably created problems in terms of access to sufficient arable land. Little wonder, then, that one report on the campaign found "loitering" to have been a key activity taken up by the majority of Ikwiriri's inhabitants.[16]

In the trenches, such practical problems with the campaign soon became apparent. The people at Kipugira village, for instance, quickly learned "that farming in the river plateau is as risky as farming in the flood plain, as all their rice was burnt by the sun in the infant stage. Now they want to go and farm in the flood plain again, not because of 'peasant conservatism' but because, after all, other opportunities were more costly" (Sandberg 1973, 13). Perhaps such realities were not readily apparent to national leaders and this is why the necessary lessons were not learned; but even for locally present officials aware of the on-the-ground situation, such problems did not apparently occasion a rethinking of the role they assumed as guardians over the people: "This threat by the peasant to 'go back' to the flood plain," Audun Sandberg continues, "is viewed with grave concern by the local authorities and agricultural extension workers. They feel that the peasant's defiance of all their efforts and all their investment in river plateau agriculture is a personal defeat" (13). While one may surmise that pressures from their superiors likely also weighed heavily on these officials' minds, they too, apparently, cast the central problem of their campaign as an issue of "defiance" on the part of the peasants. This was Rufiji through the lens of Nyerere's premise: since officials came bearing the right solutions, the problem was the peasants' stubborn insistence on continuing on their mistaken path.

If Rufiji should have underlined Nyerere's earlier prophetic warnings about limited state capacity and the detrimental effects of coercion, this message was lost: the key lesson was that peasants were stubborn and that any problems with the campaign came back to that basic fact. This "learning" pattern would be repeated elsewhere. For instance, in the context of what was, according to James de Vries and Louise Fortmann (1979, 134), a largely disastrous 1974 villagization campaign in Iringa Region, "government and party officials" would thus still/again be "convinced that a step towards the rapid development of the rural sector had been taken."

The Education of Mwalimu Nyerere

The pedagogical model that underlay the ubiquitous trope of "education" in officials' discourse about rural development was not overly sophisticated: it conceptualized students as the recipients of knowledge passed down from those possessing superior wisdom. The peasantry required education about their developmental needs as well as the appropriate course of action to address them. Noted Nyerere (1973, 61) in his 1968 paper "Freedom and Development": "There is only one way in which you can cause people to undertake their own development. That is by education and leadership. Through these means—and no other—people can be helped to understand both their own needs, and the things which they can do to satisfy these needs." Nyerere stressed that such enlightenment was to be delivered from a stance of benevolent sympathy: "Just as it was stupid to despise a child going to kindergarten simply because of his low level of schooling," the *Daily News* of August 12, 1972, had Mwalimu ("the Teacher") remind a TANU seminar for district chairmen, "so was it meaningless to despise the peasants who take the central stage of living together simply because at that low level they do not fulfill all conditions of socialist living." Other officials saw their function in similar, if even cruder, "educational" terms. Notes Cuthberg Omari (1976, 123) about local mobilizing meetings prior to Operation Kigoma in 1971, "The aim was not to discuss whether people liked it or not, but to inform people about the benefit of such living. In other words, to educate the masses on Ujamaa life."

Over time, subtle shifts in the coloring of the educator's authority and its mode of operation can be traced. As it had in Rufiji, progress toward establishing ujamaa villages proved wanting across the country, despite all educational efforts. By the time of his February 1970 "Survey of Socialist Progress" on the occasion of the third anniversary of the Arusha Declaration, Nyerere (1973, 155–156) had therefore learned a disappointing fact about the peasantry—and his patience was wearing thin:

> I must agree that it is not easy to change the ideas of peasants. But factories bring progress; a factory is a place where many people work together. . . . The working together is unavoidable. You cannot tell the workers in a shoe factory, or a textile factory, that they will be better off if each one of them has a back-yard factory in which he makes shoes or clothes. A factory like that would not be a factory at all; it is just stupidity, and no foundation for progress. . . . But unfortunately it is true that many peasants still think that the way to progress is for every individual to have his own little shamba [field]. But such shambas cannot bring progress.

With the overall agenda so clearly set out, and any alternative disqualified as "just stupidity," it is thus not clear in what regard leaders had to be "willing to learn from our peasants and workers" (158) as Nyerere also proclaimed. This philosophical demand seemed to be condemned to lose all practical relevance in a situation in which the path to Tanzania's better future had been authoritatively determined. Thus, "every Tanzanian must have the courage to *try*. He must take the initiative to suggest new ideas, and he must be courageous enough to accept new ideas from others. And especially, if the ideas are good, he must try to implement them" (158; emphasis original). The teacher was morphing into the figure of the mobilizer and implementer. As Nyerere declared, "Now we have entered the stage of planning. The stage of explaining and persuading (although that will continue for those who still need it) is really ending everywhere" (157).

Far off as that moment might have seemed, Nyerere had in fact already mused in his 1967 "Socialism and Rural Development" that education alone might eventually not suffice: "It may be possible—and sometimes necessary—to insist on all farmers in a given area growing a certain acreage of a particular crop until they realize that this brings them a more secure living, and then do not have to be forced to cultivate it" because "only experience will convince them, and experience can only be gained by beginning" (Nyerere 1968, 357). By 1970, he was apparently ready to thus prod the peasantry into going where mere talk was not succeeding in leading them.

This seemed effective for a while—at least in the kind of situations that were the typical targets of early campaigns. Thus, the restriction of famine relief to new settlements—which proved an effective "mobilizing" tool in post-flood Rufiji—was again employed in Dodoma Region, where people struck by a drought depended on it (Hill 1979, 110–111; Thiele 1982, 36–38). As a result, the May 26, 1971, *Nationalist* could again report, largely in reference to Dodoma, that "where a good degree of mobilization and politicization has been carried out, the people in the so-called less developed areas have overwhelmingly responded to Ujamaa living."

Less vulnerable populations, however, proved less likely to develop such enthusiasm. A general sense of disappointment and growing impatience with the peasantry took hold. In the opinion of Peter Kisumo, the December 16, 1970, *Nationalist* reported, "there were many peasants who spent their time idle in the villages": "If peasants in the rural areas spent their time wisely by engaging in economic and social development activities, the country's economic and social progress would have been easy progress." Nyerere, reported the paper on March 22, 1971, likewise diagnosed that "Tanzania is still under-developed and it is the peasants and workers who are to blame if no efforts are made to develop the nation." Headlines from the time bore witness to the leadership's frustration: "Get Down to Hard Work—Party Now Entering Most Difficult Phase—Nyerere" and "Morogoro RC [regional commissioner] Condemns Laziness—Progress Will Not Come Through Witchcraft" are two examples from July 8, 1971. On July 28 the paper followed up with "'Work longer and drink less'—Nyerere," a particular piece of advice he and others offered repeatedly.[17] The tirade continued in 1972: "Nyerere has bitterly condemned laziness, loitering," noted the *Daily News* on August 17, 1972; six days later, the paper reported that "Mwalimu deplores laziness" and that he had "said that part of the blame for certain failures in agricultural production must be borne by peasants."

Because the peasantry, despite years of preaching, obstinately refused to heed their leaders' sermon, "education and mobilization" began to backslide into old patterns of enforcement. Although Nyerere had perhaps never been quite immune to the temptation of such measures,[18] a more general abandonment of the positions espoused in ujamaa vijijini took several years to emerge. Eventually, though, the paternalistic presumption that Mwalimu knew best squarely put the blame for the problem of slow progress on the peasantry's "obstinacy"—and it had to be broken. Perhaps the state could not enforce "working together" if this was to take the shape it had in the RDA villages, Nyerere still conceded, but at least it could ensure "living together" as a first step: villagization first would be followed by full ujamaa later. Thus, reports Pius Msekwa (1977, 63–64), in mid-1972

> the President suggested to the NEC [National Executive Committee] . . . that it is possible to separate the aspect of 'living together' from that of 'working together on a communal farm,' and that these two could be tackled in different stages. He recommended that efforts should first of all be concentrated on getting people to live together, and once they live together they will themselves see the benefits of cooperation for their common good. The NEC discussed and accepted the President's submission, and directed that it should be implemented throughout the country.

With clear echoes of the thinking that had underlain the transformation approach of the Village Settlement Schemes, Nyerere put the matter thus to TANU's September 1973 Sixteenth Biennial Conference: "Development has its laws and one law is the gathering of people. If people have gathered in one place, they will be compelled into various things. It is necessary that this shall be done. Necessary!" (TANU 1973, 19). Noting the "eleven million of our people who were left behind still living scattered," he complained: "Eleven years—eleven years since we started making this noise about living together in villages. Now we do not have another Operation Dodoma [i.e., merely a regional campaign] . . . and the issue of living in villages is now an issue for the whole country" (21). Then he charged the delegates to implement this initiative. Dutifully, they resolved that "the question of living in these villages is now no longer a question of operations by single regions, but instead of the whole country" (48). In November 1973, Nyerere imposed a deadline for the completion of the settlement of Tanzania's entire rural population in villages: it was to be effected by 1976. *Uhuru*'s editorial of November 8 summed up the message: "Those who were reluctant to join Ujamaa villages have been given enough time and their fear can no longer be tolerated. . . . The issue of living in Ujamaa villages is now an ORDER of the party" (quoted and translated by McHenry 1979, 108).

The teacher, turned mobilizer, had finally become an enforcer. This metamorphosis had been forced on him by the peasantry's stubbornness and his obligation to his countrymen; like a physician facing a life-threatening disease, he had to take charge. Yes, he admitted, villagization had become

> partly compulsory . . . [but] so is vaccination. For 12 years we have been arguing, arguing. Now we have to deal with the problem of inertia (people refusing to move). We have said the government must provide services, but we have limited resources. So we have told the people "If you want these modern changes you must reorganize yourselves!"[19]

Many officials in Tanzania apparently followed this line of thinking effortlessly. Samuel Mushi (1981, 154) reports on the June 9, 1972, Morogoro Regional Development

Committee's reception of TANU's 1971 party guidelines *Mwongozo,* which, ironically, had centrally been concerned with elaborating why "for a Tanzanian leader it must be forbidden to be arrogant, extravagant, contemptuous and oppressive" (TANU 1972, 5):

> It was noted that *Mwongozo* was both good and necessary in the fight against bu-reaucratization, but that it had flattered the peasants by declaring that they were the true "experts"; one negative outcome being that the planners did not get the necessary cooperation from them. Thus, it was argued: "Although the peasants must be encouraged to participate more and more, it must be remembered that the peasants have never been planners and that is why they have not improved their standard of living for ages."

The justification for compulsory villagization offered by Juma Mwapachu (1979, 116), Shinyanga's district development director at the helm of villagization there in 1974, echoes this sentiment as it invokes the key markers of the peasants' and the politicians' positionalities: the peasants' "life of death" necessitated officials' exercising their indispensible, paternal authority:

> As Nyerere argued, the move had to be compulsory because Tanzania could not sit back and watch the majority of its people leading a "life of death." The State had, therefore, to take the role of the "father" in ensuring that its peoples chose a better and more prosperous life for themselves.

The development director himself was of course quite in tune with what he proffered as the president's view on the subject: "The people must continue to be led," he contended (122); "we must remember that the problems of the rural peasantry have been based fundamentally on their traditional outlook and unwillingness to accept change" (117); simply put, "The greater part of the rural peasantry is unaware" (122).

Such representations of the state's paternal intervention for the betterment of its benighted and backward charges were typical of officials' and official narrations of villagization.[20] The *Daily News* of August 23, 1974, for instance, put the following gloss on renewed and sometimes violent villagization efforts in Coast Region and Rufiji District:

> For Tanzanians living in ujamaa or planned villages . . . it sounds unbelievable to hear that some of their brothers in the Rufiji River valley have been refusing to move to higher ground to live in planned villages. . . . Those who have refused to move, they will now have to be taught a lesson. They will be made to hang their superstition and be moved compulsorily. . . . Those who think they can avoid living in such villages are deluding themselves. Those who try to resist going into such villages are also fighting a lost cause. Every Tanzanian peasant will have to move and live in such villages. Anyone who refuses will be taken there by force. On this, there will be no half-measures. Tanu will not force anyone to become a socialist. The Party will educate the people on the superiority of the socialist ideology over any other ideology. But Tanu will not allow any Tanzanian—big or small—to hinder progress.

Against the backdrop of such framings, it then comes as no surprise that force was palatable to villagization's implementers on the ground.[21] A secret 1974 TANU report on villagization in Coast Region, for instance, documents that destruction of property and physical violence were common there: it contains a list of 51 residents of Rufiji District who had been injured in various manners, including by whiplashes inflicted by the *kiboko,* a whip made from rhinoceros hide feared since colonial times; others—215 victims in Rufiji alone are listed by name—had their houses burned down and property destroyed.[22]

Despite the pressing need for decisive action, such measures finally did go too far in the eyes of the national leadership: the high-powered TANU delegation that had made these findings recommended the transfer of Rufiji District officials. But it also noted that, luckily, and in contrast to Rufiji District, "the state of leadership [was] good" in neighboring Kisarawe: likely just a few bad apples in Rufiji. Kisaraweans should have been so lucky. As Mbezi village's letter quoted in the opening pages of this book attests, Kisarawe saw very similar scenes, as houses and other possessions were destroyed and people forced to move at gunpoint.[23] In all this, Coast Region might well not even have seen the worst of villagization, as its proximity to Dar es Salaam, both physically and socially, likely acted as a check on the worst excesses.[24]

Nyerere's conviction (and subordinate officials sharing or accommodating themselves to it) that rural Tanzania's future indisputably lay in ujamaa villages eventually led to the attempt—blind to its contradictions and glaring inadequacies—to promote ujamaa vijijini through coercive villagization. In 1968, Nyerere had put allegorically the point that compulsion would not produce the desired results: "You can drive a donkey to water, but you cannot make it drink" (Nyerere 1973, 61). But of course it was also obvious that the stubborn animal had no real choice if it was to escape death by thirst. While one would try to talk to it calmly for a while, in the end, one owed it to the obstinate beast to force its nose into the water: surely then it would recognize its own salvation.

Developmentalist Authority: Some Constitutive Elements

The framing of the peasantry as benighted—juxtaposed against an enlightened leadership—sanctioned and energized an authority that, in claiming responsibility *for* Tanzania's rural population, would not be responsible *to* it. An almost Promethean framing of the moment in history at which Tanzania found itself was a key element in the assemblage of this constellation. The country's "new and revolutionary outlook," the July 13, 1971, *Nationalist* put it,

> proceeds clearly and unmistakably showing the dynamic role of man. . . . Who is mightier[,] MAN or NATURE? Here too great and mighty have been the triumphs and achievements of man for he alone has been able to master the art of Fire; he alone has learned to sail the seas and tamed animals and birds. Today he has begun the long

and arduous task of conquering space. He has so mastered nature that he can produce food of such abundance that he can relieve hunger of the entire mankind. . . .
Our producers have to be inculcated with the outlook that no problem known to
man is insuperable.

History's arc—from the mastery of fire, to the domestication of animals, to the exploration of space—pointed toward the deliverance of humankind. Yet such progress
depended on an enlightened vanguard: while the writer and the elite readership of
the English-language paper could be assumed to be already cognizant of this progressive unfolding of history, "our producers" would still have to be "inculcated" with the
same outlook.

Such framings enchanted the mundane. Here, for instance, is the July 19 *Nationalist*'s glossing of an ongoing villagization campaign in Dodoma:

> From their clusters isolated by miles of arid and hostile thorny bushland, the Wagogo
> [the predominant ethnic group in the area] are on the move—in their thousands—
> towards Ujamaa villages. . . . For too long the peasants of Dodoma have been the vic-
> tims of oppressive forces beyond their control. . . . In the continued warfare with the
> vicious trinity of poverty, ignorance and disease, they have realised the wisdom of
> President Nyerere that only in living together and working together for the benefit
> of all lies the salvation of this country. . . . The Wagogo have been among the most
> oppressed of our people. Nature too has been very cruel with them. But since the re-
> alisation of the need to form Ujamaa villages, they are becoming aware every pass-
> ing day of their own importance as motors of the revolution that will sweep away
> their misery.

Like the Rufiji elder who declared his people "awake from the dead," so the Wagogo,
long mired in "poverty, ignorance and disease," "were becoming aware" of the possibility of their "salvation" only under the tutelage of Nyerere. No mere villagization campaign, Operation Dodoma saw Nyerere parting the waters—or, in this case, the "thorny
bush"—as he led his people to the Promised Land.

This casting of the political leadership and officials as indispensible conductors of
Tanzania's journey into the future was a constant refrain in the echo chamber of top
leaders' pronouncements and official journalism. As he had been in the context of the
RDA's destruction, Peter Kisumo was an especially prominent carrier of this message.
"Development Committees of local authorities under the leadership of TANU will have
the overall supervision of the activities of the people in the field of production," he told
Parliament according to the June 29, 1968, *Nationalist*. The June 3, 1969, paper summed
up his speech to TANU's Bi-Annual National Conference conveying the same message:

> Activities of the Party and the Government "will be more closely co-ordinated at
> the regional, district, and village levels" in order to streamline development. . . . The
> Minister said that for the overall success of the plan, the people would have to be
> taught very, very thoroughly the policies of TANU and the Government on rural
> development.

The official press routinely picked up and amplified such framings. The *Nationalist*'s November 4, 1969, column "The Way Ahead" glossed Tanzania's situation thus:

> President Nyerere . . . called on the entire nation to put itself into GEAR. What he meant was that all our development endeavors . . . must be harmonized, balanced and synchronized. This means that in our practical implementation of the "follow-up" products of Arusha such as the current Five-Year Plan, there must be rythm [*sic*] everywhere. As Mwalimu pointed out, the leadership at all levels, in the Party, the organizations affiliated to the Party, in Government and in all national institutions has a duty to bring about this harmonization, balancing and synchronization of the nation's endeavours. . . . When this happens then the country can be said to be in GEAR—and when the country has thus become fully engaged in GEAR there is nothing else that follows except DEVELOPMENT as the crowning climax of the whole exercise.

A number of elements went into thus rendering state officials necessary vanguard authorities. The general conflation of a model of paternal/generational authority with political office already observed in the context of the RDA's destruction is again discernible in the pervasive imagery of "the father" and "the teacher" in the discourse around villagization. Likewise, a construction of the nation as unitary underlined the claim that the political leadership exercised the authority to conduct Tanzania's journey into the future for the good of all and hence legitimately. Already in 1968, Nyerere had thus demanded "discipline" in the implementation of national decisions on the basis of just this argument: "We have to accept that the people in authority in Tanzania now are the agents of the people of Tanzania. . . . They must be upheld while they are carrying out the law, or issuing orders which are in conformity with the law" (Nyerere 1973, 65). In the Tanzanian context of "one-party democracy," in which the law typically functioned as an (frequently dispensable) instrument of power rather than as a constraint on it, such proclamations of course amounted to a claim to a rather unchecked authority.[25]

Besides these discourses of paternal authority and the unitary nation, practices of "planning" and "expertise" were crucial in elevating officials as authorities over peasants' lives. Operation Dodoma, for instance, was characterized by constant talk of targets; incessant production and recitation of statistics; high-profile planning missions; and officials' self-positioning as purveyors of typically unspecified "modern" solutions. Here, for instance, is Kisumo explaining the rationale behind the operation to a regional meeting in the run-up to the campaign:

> The means to eradicate the scourge [*unyonge*] (the evil of famine) of Dodoma Region is to start new plans of modern development for all farmers in the Region. These are plans to cooperate in better and modern AGRICULTURE [*kilimo*] in Ujamaa villages where people will stay together to do work together, in a modern fashion, for the benefit of all.[26]

What any of this meant concretely, or how it would practically improve the fortunes of the region, was unclear. But given the fact that the campaign was on the side of "modernity" and brought the panacea of ujamaa villages, there could be little question that it would represent a major step forward.[27]

Representations of the campaign that invoked its "planned" nature imbued it with an aura of control, precision, and scientificity—underpinning this aura of infallibility. A veritable fetishization of (large) numbers and statistics in internal government reporting and the official press coverage was an important component of this casting.[28] On July 10, 1971, for instance, the *Nationalist* triumphantly reported that "nearly half a million men, women and children are on the move in the entire region with about 60 per cent in Dodoma District alone." By March 1973, an official report found, the target set in 1971 of 249,970 people to be resettled in Dodoma District had been met with an astonishing degree of 100 percent accuracy (even though this example of perfect plan-fulfillment would also have implied that fewer people had moved than the July 10, 1971, *Nationalist* had counted two years earlier).[29]

How practices and invocations of "planning" functioned to confirm officials' rightful authority and deflect any challenge to it is well illustrated by a spat over the assessment of Operation Dodoma that unfolded in the pages of the *Nationalist*. In late 1970, two lecturers from the University of Dar es Salaam, Walter Rodney and Grant Kamenju, had taken a group of students to Dodoma to gather firsthand impressions of the ongoing campaign. Their critical reports, published in the *Nationalist* on September 25 and October 5, 6, and 7, 1970, documented that Dodoma's new ujamaa villages were little more than hastily thrown-together population clusters with no signs of any strides toward the social and economic communities ujamaa villages had been envisioned to be. Already their initial, only mildly critical report drew a scornful repudiation in an October 3 letter to the editor from an M. S. Bokuzolwe:

> One of the villages in which they [the students and lecturers] stayed and presumably worked was Nkulabi Ujamaa village. In this particular village there is a dispensary, school, a fully equipped Government building field unit, an agricultural extension officer, a rural development assistant, a TANU Branch, a cattle dip, a Government constructed borehole for the supply of water. In addition, a Presidential Economic team of experts under the able leadership of a high-powered TANU leader has been to this village to help the peasants plan viable economic projects which they understand and are able and willing to implement, given the leadership, guidance, and supervision of Government technical workers.

Government provisions, "leadership, guidance, and supervision of Government technical workers," and especially a "Presidential Economic team of experts" under a "high-power TANU leader": wrapped in the garb of "planning" and "expertise," the very fact of officials' involvement seemed to put the village's future success beyond doubt.

In an astute diagnosis of this authorizing effect of "expertise," Kamenju's November 10 reply to Bokuzolwe's letter indicted "the self-centeredness of these 'experts' that explains their preoccupation with the projects and publicity of their activities which they consider to be more important than those of the masses" for producing "the DIS-DAIN as well as the Distrust which they betray towards the peasants."

As had been the case in Rufiji, in Dodoma, too, the authority conferred on officials through their self-positioning on the side of modernity, expertise, and planning turned out far more fallible than imagined. Nkulabi village's story was symptomatic in this respect. Despite having received an exceptional level of attention—the presidential team's five-year plan for the village referred to in Bokuzolwe's letter had for instance projected several hundred thousand shillings' worth of investments,[30] the village was to become one of the settlements where Graham Thiele (1982, 88) found in 1980 that "famine was no longer a singular occurrence, deriving from stochastic factors, lasting one or two years" but "a constant state."

To several contemporary observers such results came as no surprise: they had worried about the campaign's inattention to the crucial question of how a largely semipastoral society in an arid area with highly place-specific rainfall variability would benefit from being fixed in place in nucleated villages.[31] "From the Gogo point of view," noted Peter Rigby (1977, 96), the campaign "was an ecological, economic, and social impossibility, at least on a voluntary basis, as well as a potential disaster." But such concerns and the resulting popular reluctance could not be recognized as worthy of officials' careful consideration: they were simply more evidence of an attitudinal deficiency and ignorance, which called for remedial measures appropriate to *that* problem. In keeping with this interpretative grid, when a mix of exhortations and inducements—such as the withholding of famine relief—produced significant population movements into designated settlements, this was then celebrated as a victory in the battle for the enlightenment of Dodoma's benighted population: they had, as the *Nationalist* had put it, "realised the wisdom of President Nyerere."

The Villagization of Tanzania

How do campaigns such as the ones in Rufiji and Dodoma fit into the broader experience of villagization? While such summary statistics elide crucial differences in the kinds of entities recorded as well as their mode of establishment, figure 3.1 conveys a sense of villagization's overall unfolding in terms of the number of officially recorded villages and their population.[32]

Deconstructing an early count of 476 villages in the country, reported in the *Nationalist* on July 15, 1969, gives a sense of the heterogeneity of villagization. The 15 villages recorded in Ruvuma Region, for instance, included the villages of the Ruvuma Development Association. The 25 or so villages attributed to Coast Region were just being established in Operation Rufiji: in terms of their origin and character these centrally decreed and generally very large settlements were of course very different entities. The 19 much smaller villages in West Lake Region had a different history again—having been newly established in the course of a campaign discussed in chapters 4 and 5 that had been initiated and spearheaded by the regional commissioner. The majority of Tanga's 14 villages had been created in a campaign in Handeni that was similarly geographically confined, but which had seen much more central state involvement than the West Lake campaign. With 333 villages, Mtwara Region, finally, contributed by far

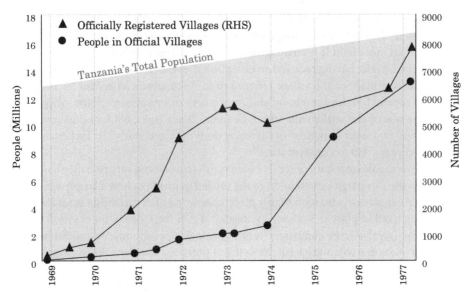

Figure 3.1. Villagization in numbers.

the largest number to the total.[33] This region's exceptional "achievement" was the work of an especially committed and effective campaigner, Regional Commissioner Wilbert Klerruu.[34] The suddenness of the appearance of these villages in the statistics and the absence of any records of a large-scale resettlement campaign indicate that the Mtwara numbers were largely achieved through the registration of existing settlements.[35] A hostile Portuguese colonial regime on Mtwara's southern border had made for a strong incentive to register and (at least pro forma) organize people for national defense.[36] These special circumstances made Mtwara's situation something of a special case, a fact that was reflected in Klerruu's March 1968 *Guide and Plan for the Implementation of the Arusha Declaration in Mtwara Region* (Klerruu 1968, 25), which added national defense as a key responsibility to Nyerere's familiar definition of ujamaa villages: "People will live together and do the work of guarding/defense [*kazi za ulinzi*] and production together for the benefit of all."[37]

Over the next three years, villagization largely followed two of the three trajectories that had led up to this 1969 baseline. While the grassroots-driven establishment of "authentic" ujamaa villages contributed to the numbers only marginally, Mtwara's route—what Raikes (1975, 43) aptly calls "Ujamaa through Signpainting," i.e., the registration of preexisting villages with neither significant movements of people nor a significant reorganization of the lives of their inhabitants—was apparently widely followed.[38] For local officials, but also ordinary people, sign painting was the easiest route through which they could live up to the top leadership's ever more urgent demands, backed by a variety of negative and positive sanctions, to establish "ujamaa villages." On the part of villagers, securing an official registration could also act as an insurance against future resettlement: it created a nominal but crucial reality that might prompt officials to move other people to such a registered site and protect its inhabitants from having to move themselves.[39] Such dynamics are well illustrated by events at Suwa in Handeni District, for instance. Four groups vied to have their hamlet selected as an official village site in a 1968/1969 villagization campaign in the district, but only one site was picked. Under intensifying pressure from local officials, two groups eventually moved to that site, but the fourth held out and even sent a delegation to Dar es Salaam to make its case; eventually, it was granted official permission to continue as a separate village.[40]

Official "operations" such as the ones in Rufiji and Dodoma represented the second trajectory. Typically, it involved physical relocation of populations to a far greater extent.[41] In addition to local campaigns in West Lake and Handeni, nationally decreed campaigns implemented at the level of districts or regions effected significant movements of people in Kigoma and Tabora Region, as well as Chunya District.[42]

Then, the announcement in late 1973 that all rural Tanzanians would have to live in villages by 1976 sparked a countrywide scramble; Rufiji's and Dodoma's experience became the model. In most parts of the country, this phase saw considerably more physical relocation of people than had been the case in earlier years. One indication is that the average number of registered members per village increased from roughly 350 to roughly 1,700 between 1972 and 1977 (see figure 3.1). Some of this "influx" was still a matter of expanding village boundaries or simply registering people as members of a village without moving them. This method appears to have predominated in high-density areas such as Kilimanjaro, Arusha, Rungwe, and Bukoba.[43] However, there were, especially between late 1973 and 1975, also massive relocations of rural Tanzanians. Overall, Ian Thomas (1985, 143) suggests, "13 million [people] villagized did not mean 13 million relocated; perhaps eight to nine million were actually moved."[44]

Beyond thus physically reordering rural Tanzania, what did villagization effect? Most immediately, large-scale resettlement disrupted agricultural production. This and the loss of houses, agricultural land, and infrastructure constituted a hit that was at least in part responsible for a mounting food crisis in the mid-1970s.[45] That many villages subsisted on famine aid for at least a number of years after their establishment is the most direct indication of the severity of the disruption that villagization wrought.[46]

Villagization also created persistent long-term problems. The concentration of large numbers of people in nucleated settlements increased pressure on the land and contributed to soil exhaustion in many areas. The long distances many people now often had to walk to get to their fields resulted in time—often hours—lost to commuting; in many places, it also precipitated crop losses, as remote fields could no longer be protected from animals at night.[47] Because of their ecology and production systems, some places were especially vulnerable to such effects of concentrating often large numbers of people in one place. In Dodoma, for instance, soils could no longer be rested over longer fallow periods because there was now a lack of rotational plots within acceptable distance of enlarged settlements; likewise, households' ability to apply manure to their fields was diminished, both because of increased distances between homesteads and fields and because concentrated settlements generally posed problems for cattle-keeping.[48] Finally, cases of bad site selection for new or greatly expanded villages—problems ranged from barren soils, to inadequate water supply, to flood proneness—were numerous enough to necessitate a special "Operation *Masahihisho/Marekebisho*" (Rectification) in Dodoma, Arusha, Shinyanga, Kigoma, Rukwa, Mbeya, Iringa, Morogoro, Tanga, Kilimanjaro, and possibly other areas to correct for mistakes that made many new settlements outright unviable.[49]

Villagization's failure to bring improvements in terms of agricultural techniques and organization of production is well documented.[50] In terms of organization and management at the village level, the situation was bleak. A 1979 survey of 514 villages—which, according to the Villages and Ujamaa Villages Act of 1975, were supposed to be functioning as cooperative producer societies—revealed that only around 10 percent of them kept all the required books and that only 10 percent of the books that were kept could be judged to be of a "good standard." About half of the surveyed villages had not even designated somebody to keep their books (URT 1980).[51] This situation prevailed despite the fact that a Village Management Programme, started in December 1975 with World Bank support and credit, had since 1977 focused particularly on training bookkeepers in the villages.[52] In an assessment that would be appropriate about Tanzania as a whole, John Moore (1979, 79) notes about villagization in Mwanza that, by late 1975, "disillusionment was commonly setting in . . . as it became apparent that positive support for the new development villages would not be forthcoming, and that there were no new ideas as to how the villages might help themselves."

Especially in its later incarnations, villagization brought very little movement toward effective communal production or the growth of the kind of dynamic, grassroots-democratic communities that the policy of ujamaa vijijini had originally envisioned. A 1974 report on Dodoma, for instance, concluded that there were almost no signs of communal production, "modern farming," or "political consciousness" in the region's ujamaa villages.[53] Indeed, even in places where a degree of communal production and organization had previously taken root, the influx of new settlers due to forced resettlement proved very damaging to such ujamaa features. From Iringa, de Vries and Fortmann (1979, 143) report that people resettled in 1974 were often very resentful toward established groups whom they blamed for being forced to move. Simeon Mesaki (1975) likewise found very poor relations between original settlers and new arrivals in the Kisarawe. Ndonde (1975a, 167–168) notes that villagization generally heralded the widespread destruction of existing ujamaa activities: ujamaa fields were parceled out to new settlers and forced resettlement did not spare practicing ujamaa groups either.[54] An overall indication of the lack of ujamaa in the wake of villagization is how few villages were ever even recorded in the two categories reserved for settlements with advanced communal ventures. In 1974, for instance, only around 400 out of the total of 7,000 official villages were registered as "producer cooperatives," indicating a relatively high degree of communal activity (Loxley and Seushi 1975, 542). In January 1978, a government statement stressed that *none* of Tanzania's 7,400 registered villages had been granted the status of "ujamaa village" under the criteria set out by the 1975 Villages and Ujamaa Villages Act (McHenry 1979, 100–102). Under the acute economic crisis conditions that Tanzania found itself in from 1979 on, even the attempt to promote cooperative production was finally dropped for all intents and purposes.[55]

As the use of force, intimidation, and destruction of property—most frequently directed at houses to prevent people from returning—proliferated in its last phase,[56] villagization bred a great deal of resentment and opposition. Already in the earliest villagization campaign, initiated in West Lake Region in 1968, one group of forcibly recruited settlers arrived at their designated village site singing "TANU breaks/destroys the nation" (*TANU yavunja nchi*) in a subversive take on the lyrics of the party anthem "TANU Builds the Nation" (*TANU yajenga nchi*): their "defection" from their new village followed suit.[57] In the same spirit, an August 1974 letter from Msanga village in Coast Region to the local member of Parliament proclaimed, "Therefore honourable M.P. I say and I am asking you to tell your bosses that Juma Mwenegoha and all my brothers in Msanga do not want socialism neither living together" (quoted in Mesaki 1975, 102–103). In some places, such resistance developed into a drawn-out battle: thus, by the time Mohoro village (Rufiji) took hostage several government officials who had come to shift the village in December 1980, it had already successfully resisted pressures to relocate during Operation Rufiji (1968/1969) and Operation Pwani (1973), and again after the damaging floods of 1979.[58]

Where it was not resisted outright, villagization was negotiated so as to limit its costs and secure available benefits. Especially from early 1971 on, particular stress was laid on the services that would be provided to those living in ujamaa villages: registration— whether with or without relocation—promised entitlements. "Live together and get water," "Ujamaa Makes for Quicker Amenities," "Live Together and Get Amenities— Nyerere," proclaimed headlines in the *Nationalist* on January 5, January 7, and May 19, 1971, respectively.[59] Besides formal subventions ranging from seeds and implements, to water supplies, to a school and a teacher, resettlement might also provide access to land occupied by larger farmers or set aside for conservation.[60]

While officials demanded that peasants do their part in national development and promised support in return, farmers elaborated occasionally quite intricate strategies of constructing and then calling in obligations from the state. Within months of its coercive establishment, Rugazi village in West Lake, for instance, petitioned a visiting Nyerere for permission to call itself Rugazi-Nyerere Ujamaa Village. This request was granted, and the story retold whenever officials came to visit.[61] Of course, the state was also supposed to keep up its end of the bargain and reciprocate in response to such devout behavior: the records contain an unceasing stream of letters from the village requesting everything from rifles for keeping intruding elephants at bay, to agricultural inputs and implements, to credit, to help with a poultry project—there were even repeated requests for two footballs.[62] Officials' self-representation as bringers of development was thus strategically echoed back in the form of claims on resources from the countryside. Although its situation was of course somewhat idiosyncratic, Matetereka's lobbying a reluctant regional commissioner for a grain mill, a water pump, and construction materials after the RDA's construction is another good illustration of these dynamics:[63] Lukas Mayemba, the longtime leader of the village, explained to Edwards (1998, 18–21) that he argued that the village was due these items as the RDA would have provided them had it not been destroyed by the state. Villagization thus tightly entangled peasants and officials in a web of claims and obligations.

However, even if state provisions had been sustainable over the long term, villagization's reliance on material inducement and largesse, perceptive observers worried already at the time, would prove to be problematic. This was not only because provisions were often wasteful, but also because, as Raikes (1975, 43) put it, "They may substitute for, rather than supplement any viable plan for how the village is to improve the level of living of its members through increased production." And while the provision of water supplies, dispensaries, and schools often was an initial boon, such services often proved a very temporary benefit.[64] As early as the late 1970s, many such amenities could not be maintained by a state severely overstretched in terms of staffing and finances. The soon-collapsed drive to expand safe water supplies illustrates especially well that the massive efforts expended in this area did not produce many lasting improvements.[65] Comments Gavin Kitching (1982, 121) on the general situation,

> In all the accounts of *ujamaa* one sees the same picture of inadequate resources stretched so thinly as to render them useless. Extension officers trying to cover several villages in a huge area. Not enough transport, not enough surveyors and natural resource analysts . . . and so on. Even a highly competent and motivated public service would have struggled under such circumstances, and the evidence is that Tanzania had no such thing.

Conclusion

Villagization manifested a modality of governing centered on a distinctive vanguard authority of state officials that had them claim responsibility for the peasantry's journey into a better future. They had to take on this guardianship role because the peasantry revealed itself not to be fully competent to make rational decisions itself. This constellation implied an openness to the adoption of compulsion and coercive means that, while easy to overlook in Nyerere's philosophical statements, quickly became apparent in the practice of developmental governing. As it turned out, this was a practice that was not only deeply inimical to its supposed liberational objectives, but also quite dysfunctional vis-à-vis its goal of effecting material improvements in people's lives. For one, resort to compulsion militated against any possibility that material progress in the rural areas would be won through the kind of processes and dynamics that had underlain the RDA's successes. As a result, an approach to rural development that had been explicitly conceived as an alternative to heavy reliance on the state's resources soon discovered that it had nothing else to fall back on. In many ways, the failure of rural development as it thus manifested itself had therefore been foretold.

The next chapter explores in greater depth two constitutive elements in the assemblage of officials' authority over peasants, which have already been sketched above: the particular temporality that opened up a space conducive to the constitution of this authority; and, within this context, the role of practices of "planning" in authorizing and staging officials as conductors of the peasants' journey into the future.

4 Planning the Future
A Practice and Its Authority-Effects

The supposed inability of certain societal actors—peasants, for example—to calculate their situation . . . provided the justification for an entire politics of social improvement, and for later programs of technical development.

—Timothy Mitchell, *Rule of Experts*

The practice of "rendering technical" confirms expertise and constitutes the boundary between those who are positioned as trustees, with the capacity to diagnose deficiencies in others, and those who are subject to expert direction. It is a boundary that has to be maintained and that can be challenged.

—Tania Li, *The Will to Improve*

DEVELOPMENTALIST TEMPORALITY OPENED up a space within which officials' vanguard authority over peasants could be plotted. This chapter opens with an illustration of this temporality's shape and effect drawn from a late-1960s Tanzanian campaign to "modernize" Maasai modes of dress. In this campaign, just as in villagization, the necessity of "bringing into the future" those who were described as leading lives of death and being stuck in the past authorized interventions over the objections of their putative beneficiaries. It was within this temporal framing that "planning" instantiated and reinforced the distinction between planning officials as developmentalist authorities and their rural subjects. The chapter traces this authorizing effect through a close-up study of planning in villagization.

The chapter's argument about the role of "modernity" and "planning" in villagization is developed in contrast with James Scott's (1998) treatment of these same subjects. In his telling, villagization failed because of its substantively "modern" characteristics—in the main, the high-modernist aesthetics of Cartesian orderliness that Scott argues governed the plans for villagization. These substantively modern traits were planning's and villagization's undoing because Tanzania's systems of agricultural production were strangulated in the Cartesian straitjacket that high-modernist planning forced them into. Essentially, villagization's failure was the failure of substantive aspects of "modernity," whose dysfunctionality and defects showed as Tanzania's physical realities were remade through its methods and in its image.

The reality of planning in villagization casts doubt on this argument on a number of counts. Crucially, the few plans that existed in Tanzania neither betrayed a "high-modernist" aesthetics nor were nearly efficacious enough in shaping the physical reality that villagization created on the ground to make plausible Scott's argument that they contributed to villagization's failure specifically by reshaping rural Tanzania in a distinctive, high-modernist image. This chapter argues that planning did have problematic effects—but for other reasons and through different mechanisms. Rather than by determinatively directing the physical reality of villagization, planning shaped this undertaking by undergirding the blanket authority of state officials as indispensible and unchallengeable conductors of Tanzania's journey into the future—as it conjured an aura of rationality and control around them. Though this aura very much flew in the face of the actual paucity and glaring "technical" weaknesses of planning in Tanzania, practices of planning were thus a central element in the staging of officials as imperial authorities over their peasant subjects. The autocratic nature of rule that they thereby underpinned was a problem in and of itself, but the fact that they wrapped officials in a largely illusionary garb of empty rituals that left them stark naked for most practical purposes added insult to that injury. In fact, significant aspects of the material problems that villagization created were precisely due to failures *to* plan rather than to some inherent dysfunctionalities or defects of planning *qua* its "modernity." With respect to the aesthetic aspects of this modernity, which Scott's account stresses, Tanzanian plans neither had the looks of a high-modernist uniform nor pressed the country's landscape into a modernist, orderly appearance. (Where "aesthetics" did figure, in the campaign to reform Maasai fashion and villagization's occasional attempt to replace "traditional" houses, for instance, they did so largely by way of undergirding a negative reaction against especially deviant forms of "tradition" rather than by way of supplying an elaborate, avant-gardist vision of a "high-modern" future. The focus was on eradicating images of "pastness"—flat-roofed houses and men's wearing garments other than trousers below the belt. But there was no futuristic elaboration of alternatives. Indeed, what was supposed to replace such "traditions" was typically highly conventional.)

Developmentalist Temporality

Villagization was explicitly inscribed into a temporality that juxtaposed the "traditional ways of the past" of the peasantry and a "future" of science and modernity whose construction conjured a horizon of great expectations. This developmentalist temporality underlay the urgency of Nyerere's call, reported by the September 24, 1969, *Nationalist,* that "the way we lived years ago must come to an end" and provided fertile ground for the emergence of a vanguard authority that would guide Tanzanians' journey into such a future.

The pages of the *Nationalist* open a useful window on the narration of the future that circulated among the political class and the paper's largely urban, educated readership. Frequent musings under headlines such as "Power Sources of the Future," "Schools of the Future," "Towns of the Future," "What Is the Future Like," and "Predictions for the Year 2000 AD" yielded prognoses of truly revolutionary change.[1] (In this, Tanzania was of course part of broader global currents; this is underlined by the fact that many of these *Nationalist* stories were picked up from foreign news services.) On November 8, 1969, for instance, "African Farms in 2000" predicted huge greenhouses, satellite- and computer-controlled climate, and fully automated harvesting. On August 1, 1969, "Towards a Superman?" speculated about new developments in genetics and psychology that pointed toward "the superman of the year 2000" and wondered about the coming of the "bionic age." A December 27, 1968, piece promised that "Man Will Soon End Droughts" through "mammoth rain making programmes." "When man finally inhabits the Moon, probably in the decade," speculated the paper on January 10, 1969, "his permanent settlements there will feed on fresh fruits and vegetables grown in plantations without soil and producing harvests far richer than yields expected from even the most profitable conventional farm on earth." There would also soon be "Cities on the Sea Floor," predicted a September 22, 1967, article; and if a December 15, 1969, feature was to be believed, seafloor farming would not be far behind.

Bridging the gap that divided Tanzania from such a future was an urgent matter—and it would require guidance from a leadership that, unlike especially rural Tanzanians, was cognizant of this future's promise and the path to its realization. A campaign that sought to "modernize" the Tanzanian Maasai's modes of dress and body care shows especially clearly how state officials' vanguard authority was thus deeply embedded in developmentalist temporality.[2]

Code-named "Operation Dress-Up," the campaign originated in a 1967 ban on Maasai applying red ochre (a clay-derived pigment) to their skin and wearing the "traditional" *lubega* (a kind of toga) that, according to the *Nationalist* of February 16 and 17, 1970, had been instituted by Arusha Regional Commissioner Mwakang'ata in concert with other politicians from the region, notably including Tanzania's most prominent Maasai politician, Edward Sokoine, member of Parliament and future prime minister.[3] Besides frequent exhortations by politicians, the campaign also resorted to a diverse set of more or less coercive sanctions to get Maasai to change in(to) the desired fashion as it attempted to face down noncompliance and open opposition.[4]

How was this motivated and justified? A casting—repeated in numerous statements by politicians, letters to the editor, and newspaper editorials—of Maasai modes of dress and body care as relics of the past with no place in the present was key. The problem of the Maasai was, as the February 25, 1968, *Sunday News* put it, that theirs was "a culture . . . seeking to survive in the wrong century." The same trope of the Maasai's "pastness" appears in Nyerere's remark that it was "1964 for everybody in the world, *including* the Masai, and the pressure for all to live in 1964, including the Masai, [was] fantastic" (quoted in Smith 1981, 12; emphasis original). Indeed, Maasai difference was almost entirely subsumed under this temporalizing framing:[5] as a February 22, 1968, letter to the editor of the *Nationalist* commented, "Every tribe has or had its customs more or less like those of the Masai. But since other tribes were quick to see the modernizing torch before them, they discarded them."

This positioning of Maasai in developmentalist temporality had important political effects. To borrow Johannes Fabian's (1983, 2) phrase, the "denial of coevalness" this positioning amounted to put time to an "oppressive use." Thus, developmentalist temporality set in motion the kind of "dynamic which negates the existing Other" that Reinhart Koselleck (1985, 165) analyzes in the construction of the binary Heathen/Christian: "Expressed temporally, the Heathen was 'not yet' a Christian. . . . Thus the eschatological horizon contained a processual moment in the arrangement of the counterconcepts which was capable of unleashing a greater dynamic than that inhering in the ancient counterconcepts" (182). In Tanzania, the eschatological horizon of modernity and development that opened up in developmentalist temporality likewise admitted no legitimate place for "traditional" Maasai practices in the contemporary world. As a February 10, 1968, *Nationalist* editorial put it,

> As we develop we must part with old ways and evolve new ideas, thereby creating new values, and new men—men of today and tomorrow and not men of yesterday and the day before. . . . Here in Tanzania, the Masai is a conscious revolutionary man of tomorrow. He has nothing to lose but exploitation and degradation. His inevitable victory is progress.

Maasai traditions thus belonged where the November 10, 1970, *Nationalist* saw them heading in its report from Kenya that conjured the potent image of a "number of young Masai" who "decided to cut off their red ochre daubed hair and send it to the museum." As B. B. Mbakileki of the University of Dar es Salaam warned in a letter to the editor published on February 17, 1968, Tanzania could not turn "any one section of our society into a museum of traditional culture. Museums are not made up of men." Maasai MP Sokoine, the paper had reported the previous day, could likewise "see no reason why 'I should accept my people as museum pieces of an extinct people.'"

Inscribed into developmentalist temporality, objections to the campaign were—when not outright denied or attributed to neoimperialist foreigners—merely a symptom of the very lack of enlightenment that Operation Dress-Up set out to remedy. This specific temporal casting of Maasai practices thus authorized—and indeed obliged—a vanguard to take action on their behalf. "We are trying," explained an administrator of the Masailand Ranching Association in the April 6, 1968, *Nationalist*, "to take the Masai from the Stone Age to the Atomic Age." The imperative to thus take responsibility for Maasai was a matter of honoring their equal entitlement to the benefits of development and modernity. The campaign, which after all sought to coercively eradicate popular Maasai choices, mused Mbakileki's February 17, 1968, letter to the editor, was furthering "our avowed goals of human equality (in any sense you take it), human dignity and respect for all men." The speaker of the Kenyan House of Parliament, the

March 2, 1968, *Nationalist* reported, defended the Tanzanian campaign in similar terms: "The Masai must be developed and not be left as museum pieces. They are human beings and are fully entitled to development like any other tribe in Kenya. . . . 'The government must up-hold the principles of democracy at whatever cost.'"

Developmentalist temporality was a key element in the assemblage of the paternalistic authority of officials far beyond the confines of Operation Dress-Up. In this assemblage, officials' authority-conferring positioning on the side of "the future" was instantiated in two practices in particular. One was the constant issuance of formulaic exhortations for Tanzanians to adopt "modern" and "scientific" ways: vacuous as much of this talk often was, it nonetheless rendered officials as champions of science, modernity, the future.[6] A long March 1, 1972, *Nationalist* feature entitled "Science: A Necessary Weapon" rendered this positioning in a nutshell: "To raise production we must employ technology and equip the people with useful scientific knowledge." Planning was a second set of practices that produced officials as purveyors of the future and, by this token, as authorities over their peasant charges. The remainder of the chapter investigates what planning consisted of in the context of villagization and what effects it produced.

Plans, High-Modernism, and Villagization in West Lake

High-Modernism and the Failure of Villagization

James Scott's account, in *Seeing like a State*, of villagization as a "high-modernist" failure has previously explored these questions and proposed a provocative thesis.[7] Like other high-modernist schemes to improve the human condition, Tanzania's "massive attempt to permanently settle most of the country's population in villages, of which the layouts, housing designs, and local economies were planned, partly or wholly, by officials of the central government" was driven, argues Scott (1998, 223), by an "avant-garde among engineers, planners, technocrats, high-level administrators, architects, scientists, and visionaries" (88). In this lay villagization's downfall: the high-modernist plans dreamed up by this avant-garde proved disastrous. At root, this was because of their high-modernist characteristics, i.e., the "modernist visual aesthetic" (254) they embodied and the valorized orderliness of "administrative regularity, tidiness, and legibility linked to an overall Cartesian order" (237) they gave expression to.[8]

These high-modernist characteristics of plans were implicated in villagization's failure for two reasons. First, "modern (tidy, rectilinear, uniform, concentrated, simplified, mechanized)" (Scott 1998, 254) looks suggested a high degree of functionality and efficiency, but when they were imposed on living social and agricultural systems, they instead turned out to be highly destructive and dysfunctional. The physical remaking of the Tanzanian agronomic and social landscape in the image of the high-modernist plan's "abbreviated visual image of efficiency" (225) produced, Scott thus argues, "environmental and social taxidermy" (228). As "authorities insist on replacing [an] ineffably complex web of activity with formal rules and regulations, they are certain to disrupt the web" (256). Thus, the straitjacket imposed by high-modernist plans strangulated in particular vibrant agricultural systems. Second, the high-modernist qualities of plans were also important in motivating villagization. Their beguiling Cartesian orderliness—suggesting rationality and functionality—had policymakers in its spell and lent conviction to their undertaking. In Scott's account, the distinctive, aesthetic qualities of plans were therefore central in both motivating and dooming villagization.

This section investigates whether these ideas are borne out in the context of a villagization campaign in West Lake Region. Viewed close up, there is little in this campaign to support *Seeing like a State*'s specific story about the implication of planning in villagization's failure. Plans in West Lake did not project a high-modernist aesthetics of orderliness. This makes it hard to argue that such an aesthetics bolstered the resolve of the campaign's organizers. Even more crucially for Scott's argument about what was responsible for the failure of villagization, however, the campaign also thoroughly failed to transform the rural landscape in the image of the—not exactly high-modernist— plans that existed. Villagization in West Lake simply did not squeeze rural Tanzania into the high-modernist disciplinarian straitjacket (or, for that matter, any other specific, "planned" design) that Scott holds responsible for villagization's failure.

This is not to say that "modernity" and "planning" had no significant effect in villagization. But their effects were not rooted in the beguiling nature of high-modernist plans or the imposition of such plans: rather, these effects had to do with planning— quite irrespective of its specific contents or form—being integral to the articulation and production of developmentalist authority. Planning—declaring objectives, setting out targets, drawing up schedules for implementation—was the quintessential set of practices through which officials produced themselves as proactive purveyors of the future. On the flip side, these practices also positioned peasants as deficient recipients for whom such activities had to be performed. Planning yielded constant opportunities to reiterate these positionings of peasants as mired in the past and officials as champions of the future, modernity, and science—a dynamic whose functioning Tania Li (2007, 31) has captured well: "Programs of improvement designed to reduce the distance between trustees and deficient subjects actually reinscribe the boundary that positions them on opposite sides of an unbridgeable divide."

Planning for Villagization in West Lake

This functioning of planning is well illustrated by a villagization campaign launched by West Lake Regional Commissioner Peter Walwa. Walwa, being part of a small cohort of people who cycled through top positions in the party and administration, had arrived in West Lake from his prior posting in Ruvuma in the second half of 1965.[9] When the Arusha Declaration was adopted in early February 1967, he quickly grasped its importance and turned its message into a call for action in his region. By March, Walwa was impressing on his Regional Development Committee the need "to make people exert more effort in their work especially in agriculture"[10] in response to the declaration. Carrying the same message to the Karagwe District Council, Walwa called for a committee to develop a "timetable that will enable all our Councils in this Region to make everybody put all their time to good use."[11] This committee soon canvassed a range of officials for their suggestions, yielding numerous reminders of why officials needed to take charge of planning for peasants.

Thus, the regional game officer put the eradication of witchcraft beliefs on the agenda.[12] The regional agricultural officer emphasized the importance of "following the agricultural calendar" and "reducing the hours of being drunk and increasing the hours of work": overall, it was important to instill in people "an appetite for development, an appetite for increasing what one gets."[13] The end product of this canvassing was Walwa's (1967) *Plan for the Implementation of the Arusha Declaration in the West Lake Region*. Even before its publication, Walwa stressed two key provisions. *Pombe* (local beer) drinking hours were to be restricted to between four and ten o'clock at night—although "it is better to close earlier—maybe at 8 PM."[14] Also, adult education was crucial, as "many people in the villages do not know how to read and write, and are thus unable to understand many issues that concern them such as Economics, Health, Politics etc."[15] The plan's centerpiece, however, was the stipulation that all adults were to cultivate at least two acres, and that people without farms—or with farms that did not meet this minimum acreage—were to be moved to new settlements.

When, after about ten months, promises of an easy life at the planned new settlements had not convinced people of the benefits of moving (Kinyondo 1971, 73–74), Walwa took this as an occasion to explicitly and forcefully claim the authority he wielded in his capacity as planner and strategist of his charges' journey ahead. His April 16, 1968, speech at a town hall meeting at Bukoba Cinema Hall framed this authority in the following terms:

> In every country the holder of the power to declare war is the Head of State and after his declaration, the Government and the leaders of the country make the preparations for war and carry it forward. In all wars there are three steps that must be followed—those being (1) the declaration of war, (2) the preparation for the actual war, and (3) Attacks. Likewise the state of affairs in this country is that TANU as the Head of this country declared a war on 5/2/67—that being the ARUSHA DECLARATION. After the Arusha Declaration the Government made special efforts [*ilijibidisha*] to explain its meaning to the citizens—and what it was that they were supposed to do [*walitakiwa wafanye*]. In every District they made their various work schedule plans and their schedule for the implementation of this Declaration. In this manner also in this Region the Regional Development Committee sat and put together its plan and resolution regarding the work that will be done in the Region as a whole to implement the Arusha Declaration. This was the second step in our war of fighting the enemies of Development.

The resettlement of the underemployed into new villages was the final and third step in Walwa's war: its implementation was to commence within a week. Walwa closed with an admonition that any discussion "should not be to object [*ya kupinga*] but that it should be on problems concerning the settlement of people and the starting of new settlements."[16] There was, in other words, to be no challenge to his authority as a general in the war against ignorance, poverty, and disease.

At least up to this point in the campaign, then, "planning" accomplished primarily two things: it underlined the peasantry's deficiencies (they drank too much, worked too little, believed in witchcraft, failed to follow the agricultural calendar, and were too uneducated to understand things that mattered); and, in a corollary effect, it rendered officials as purveyors of solutions—as they issued decrees to overcome these defects. This positioning was achieved in part through the explicit message that planning documents expounded. But the mere act of engaging in "planning" *for* the population also in a much more immediate sense produced officials as authorities: it was a constitutive practice of their authority.[17]

Physical Planning, Cartesian Aesthetics, and the Shape of Villagization

As Walwa moved to implement villagization, is there evidence that plans also exhibited the aesthetic characteristics and played the particular disciplinarian role that Scott's account attributes to them? There appears to be. In fact, the example Scott produces of a high-modernist Tanzanian plan is a map of one of the villages created in Walwa's campaign (figure 4.1). Upon cursory inspection, this map, identified as "Plan for a[n] ujamaa village: Makazi Mapya, Omulunazi, Rushwa, Tanzania," seems to strongly support Scott's argument. It appears to be just the kind of orderly, Cartesian, high-modernist design that planners might have dreamed up for a village.[18] But upon closer inspection the map does not support either the idea that Tanzanian planners had a Cartesian vision going into the West Lake campaign, or the claim that Tanzania's rural landscape was remade in the image of such a vision.

The first problem with such an interpretation is that—rather than a planning document that would have set out a vision for the new village as part of a planning exercise—the plan is in fact a survey map of the village's evolving land use, drawn by an academic researcher, Jørgen Rald, about one year after the village's inception (*vide* "J. Rald," "per 8/4—1969," and "started 24/4—1968"). It was not a planning document that might have motivated and directed the campaign with its Cartesian vision.

The second problem with interpreting the map as evidence that supports Scott's high-modernism thesis is that—underneath the eye-catching survey grid—it records an actual pattern of land use that is anything but grid-like. Land use (only white areas and the areas marked with tight diagonals are under cultivation) adds up to an organic mosaic of cultivated and uncultivated land, and not a landscape remodeled to fit a contiguous, Cartesian grid.[19] Scott's (1998, 257) argument that the reason for villagization's

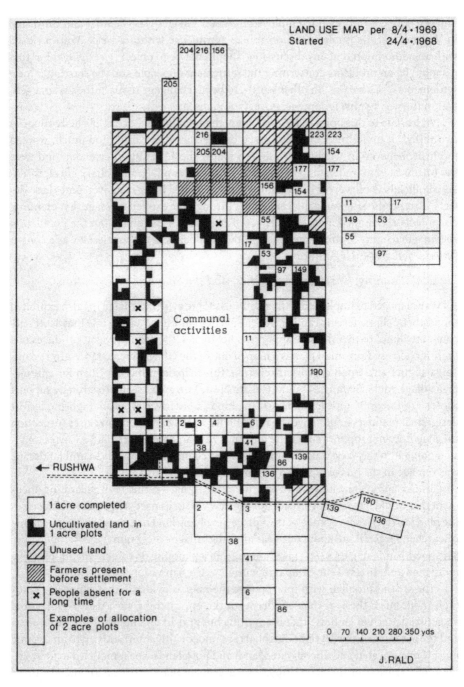

Figure 4.1. Land use map of Omurunazi (Omulunazi) village.

Figure 4.2. Panoramic view of Omurunazi in the village's first months. Courtesy of Jørgen Rald.

failure was the social and environmental taxidermy produced by forcing rural Tanzania into high-modernist grids that aimed "to discipline virtually everything within their ambit" would require that the physical reality of the new villages was in fact effectively disciplined to fit such grids. This did not happen at Omurunazi. A 1968 photograph of the village (figure 4.2) illustrates that the on-the-ground result of villagization at Omurunazi was not what Scott's description of villagized Tanzania as a high-modernist, Cartesian taxidermy might lead one to expect.

Indeed, this absence of orderliness is not especially surprising when the planning process behind the village's establishment is examined. It betrays no investment in visions of orderliness codified in high-modernist plans on the part of the campaign's implementers. Neither Walwa's May 1967 *Plan for the Implementation of the Arusha Declaration in the West Lake Region* nor the reports that were produced in its preparation set out a comprehensive and specifically disciplinarian vision for new settlements. In fact, their layouts did not receive consideration until November 1967 when the Regional Development Committee produced a sketch "plan of an ujamaa village" (figure 4.3).[20] While this plan roughly indicates a few key elements—such as a garden (*"bustani"*), a communal field (*"shamba la ushirika"*), and a large storage/silo (*"ghala kubwa"*)—that would be expected in the new villages, it did not put forth a specific design to be implemented as drawn. Nor does it give expression to what one might recognize as a high-modernist visual aesthetics.

Only on April 20, 1968, within days of the start of resettlement, was the issue of the physical layout of the new villages taken up again. However, a regional subcommittee on agriculture and settlements only laid down some very broad guidelines regarding the new settlements' desirable size and how land ought to be apportioned: (1) villages should have a center, surrounded by one-acre plots for houses and family farming; (2) a belt of two-acre plots was envisioned at the periphery of the settlements; and (3) each of the new settlements should have at least one hundred families and five hundred acres of land.[21] These points do not appear to have been set down in a layout plan at the time.

When, within days of these guidelines being drawn up, settlers were first moved to Omurunazi, the campaign's planners had therefore only given the most general consideration to the question of village layouts. There would, of course, not really have been time to design a layout for Omurunazi: it was mentioned for the first time as one of eight possible sites for new villages in the Nshamba/Rushwa Subdivision on April 19, 1968, and by April 27, 112 people had already reported to the site.[22] Not even the three regional parameters regarding size and layout had filtered down to the operational level: according to B. Bakula (1971, 28), neither the villagers nor local officials had been given any guidance on a desired layout for the village.

Confronted with the practical matter of getting people settled somehow, the agricultural field officer assigned to Omurunazi therefore took matters into his own hands: in consultation with the settlers, he decided that each household would be allocated one-quarter of an acre for a house and a small garden, to which an additional two-acre plot at the periphery of the settlement would be added later.

Of course, this scheme contravened the regional stipulation that primary plots should be one acre in size. In late April, the regional administration dispatched delegations to the four districts of the region to guide and assist in the implementation of the campaign: they came armed with the regional guidelines regarding plot size. In meetings with the district authorities, these guidelines were now also communicated by means of sketches depicting some key elements that would need to be accommodated in the new villages and a general idea of their layout (figures 4.4 and 4.5).[23]

Although plans for the physical arrangement of the new settlement did then make an entry into the campaign, they do not fit Scott's high-modernism thesis for a number of reasons. With respect to their visual qualities, counting them as beguiling embodiments of a high-modernist aesthetics seems a stretch. They also did not enter into the campaign as blueprint designs that would have set out a specific and comprehensive scheme for later implementation. For one, they were ad hoc visualizations that were drawn up in the midst of the campaign, not documents that predated it and may therefore have inspired or guided it. But irrespective of the timing of their appear-

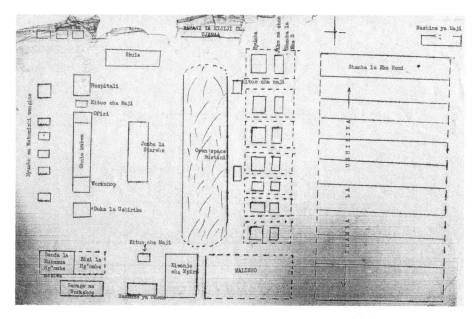

Figure 4.3. *Ramani ya kijiji cha ujamaa* (plan/map of an ujamaa village) from West Lake Region.

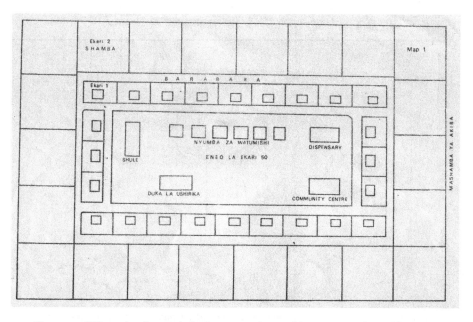

Figure 4.4. Village plan from Bukoba District. It shows a fifty-acre central area (*"eneo la ekari 50"*) containing a cooperative shop (*"duka la ushirika"*), school (*"shule"*), community center, dispensary, and staff houses (*"nyumba za watumishi"*), surrounded by one-acre (*"ekari 1"*) plots with houses and two-acre fields (*"ekari 2 shamba"*).

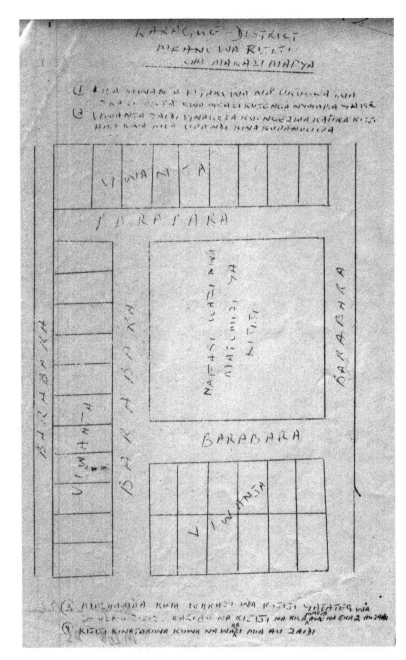

Figure 4.5. *Karagwe District—mfano wa kijiji cha makazi mapya* (Karagwe District—example of a new settlement village). It indicates basic elements such as plots ("*viwanja*"), roads ("*barabara*"), and open space for use of the village ("*nafasi wazi kwa matumizi ya kijiji*") in addition to listing basic stipulations such as the minimum size of villages ("one hundred settlers or more"—presumably meaning households), the need to give each settler a plot for building a house, and the need to have two acres or more of additional land per settler near the village.

ance, they simply did not set out a comprehensive scheme to micromanage land use meant to be implemented as drawn: the Bukoba plan (figure 4.4), for instance, shows only twenty-four plots for houses, mismatched to twenty-two two-acre plots for cultivation, while the new settlements were supposed to accommodate a minimum of one hundred households. In the interpretation of Jørgen Rald, who frequently met with the implementers of the campaign in 1968 and 1969, the sketch "is not a plan, but a suggestion containing the main idea: in the middle a 50 acre space for institutional buildings and around this space for one acre and two acre plots."[24] Instead of setting out a comprehensive, regularized vision for implementation, these plans roughly illustrated some basic ideas: have a village center, give everybody a one-acre plot, and then distribute two-acre plots for additional cultivation. Specific details were clearly left to local implementation.

There is, finally, no sense that the planners of the campaign had much of an investment in specific layouts or aesthetics. That two delegations from the same regional committee came up with evidently quite different designs (figures 4.4 and 4.5) is one indication; another is the afterthought-like nature of these sketches: at least the Karagwe delegation apparently produced its plan (figure 4.5) on the spot when local officials requested a "plan/map for the layout of the new settlements" in a district-level meeting, the minutes of which the sketch is attached to.[25] Not even the few and very basic regional stipulations (one-acre primary plots, two-acre secondary plots, a minimum of one hundred households) that these sketches were meant to visualize were particularly firm in decision-makers' minds: only four days before these parameters were issued, Walwa had given the minimum size of the new settlements as two hundred people.[26] The Karagwe sketch states that the minimum was one hundred settlers. Likewise, the stipulation that primary plots should be one acre in size was apparently followed only in Bukoba and Karagwe, while Ngara District parceled out two-acre plots to its new settlers (Boesen, Madsen, and Moody 1977, 98).

Although these plans are then not evidence that their producers were invested in a specific and comprehensive vision of the physical layout of the new settlements, once guidelines had been issued, they did have an impact on the campaign. But this power of plans had nothing to do with their being embodiments of a particular aesthetics. Irrespective of their contents, they simply functioned as commands that lower-ranking officials could ignore only at their peril.

The effect of the Bukoba plan's (figure 4.4) arrival at Omurunazi illustrates the point. On May 8, 1968, Ihangiro Division's executive officer reported on his visit to the village:

> At Omulunazi-Kashenge the problem is that there are no field officers . . . and the one who is there does not know what he is doing. He has parceled out one quarter of an acre to everyone in order for them to start cultivating, but they were handed [these plots] in a local way [kienyeji], the huts have been built in any random order [ovyo-huko na huko] although he has a plan/map [ramani].[27]

The key issue was that the village had ignored the regional guideline that household plots were to be one acre in size; this could not stand and was to be immediately rectified. Officials knew what was expected of them, whatever the nature of their superiors' command: Bakula (1971, 29) notes that although the criticized field officer's replacement also had ideas that departed from the regional guideline, he "did not press them on the administration because he felt that they would be unacceptable and he regarded it as his duty to implement what had been decided at the regional level."

This scene was repeated elsewhere in Bukoba: on May 3, Kianja Division's executive officer reported on the four new settlements there:

> As bad luck would have it, they [the settlers] had already been given land measured out in a different way from the one shown on the Plan/Map [*Ramani*] that I received enclosed with the minutes of your meeting of 27/4/68. Now! Will it be necessary for the demarcators to go back again and allocate the people anew?

Urgently requesting field officers "for demarcating the plots in accordance with the map that you sent to us,"[28] he anticipated the answer.

Did the regional guidelines then after all effect the imposition of a Cartesian straitjacket? Although Omurunazi was made to comply with the one-acre stipulation for household plots, the resulting village land use pattern, recorded in figure 4.1, shows that this was not their effect: land use did not resemble the kind of contiguous Cartesian grid, unable to accommodate local variability in soils and production requirements, that Scott holds responsible for villagization's failure. (In this regard, Omurunazi's experience was not an exception. Four 1970 land use plans from Karagwe District, for instance, all show similarly "organic" if even sparser land use patterns.[29])

Even if the evolving land use pattern at the villages was not especially regimented, is there nonetheless something to Scott's (1998, 238) general point that villagization was so problematic because its vision of "the modern planned village . . . was essentially a point-by-point negation of existing rural practice"? At least in West Lake's context, the stipulation that primary plots were to be one acre in size and that people should live in nucleated settlements did not imply a radical departure from time-tested local practices. In these respects, the new settlements were broadly in line with existing practices of relatively loosely grouped houses surrounded by rings of cultivation (Rald 1970, 4).[30] Indeed, Bakula (1971, 29) reports that the settlers at Omurunazi were unhappy with the regional directive precisely because "insistence on the one acre plot was seen as a perpetuation of the traditional village layout." By contrast, their *own* initial decision to have a denser settlement pattern featuring one-quarter-of-an-acre plots for houses "was seen as a radical but welcome change from the normal village pattern" (28). If it is the hallmark of high-modernist plans to envision a radical break with longstanding practices, at Omurunazi, at least, it was the settlers and not the planners who were the "high-modernists." Peasants, this also goes to show, do not always position themselves where "planners" and—by likewise casting them as resisters of "modernizing" interventions—Scott's account, too, imagine them to be. Far from always confirming the divide that both narratives—of "conservative" and hence to-be-reformed, and of "resisting" and hence to-be-valorized peasants—affirm, peasants' self-positionings vis-à-vis "modernity" often enough transcend and upend such supposed divides.[31]

In terms of the general picture, Scott of course does have a point: villagization often resulted in settlements that were ecologically and agronomically problematic. But this generally had little to do with their specific layout, grids, or high-modernist aesthetics. Rather, such problems typically arose where permanent settlement per se was at loggerheads with local practices (it was a particular problem for cattle-keepers) and in individual cases where the location of settlements was ill chosen. These problems were rooted not in any high-modernist character of plans and planning, but in the imposition of decisions whose defining characteristic was often that almost no planning or even elementary forethought had gone into them. Such problems, in other words, do not attest to planning's inherent defects—perhaps due to its standardizing nature or high-modernist characteristics. Rather than from such failures *of planning*, they resulted from a failure *to plan*.

Defects of Planning or a Failure to Plan?

The West Lake campaign illustrates this well. If planning input was ad hoc and extremely rudimentary with respect to village layouts, the process of site selection for the new settlements was no different. There was no standardizing, disciplinarian scheme designed on the drawing boards of planners, only a haphazard and chaotic process over which the campaign's implementers exercised very little control. This lack of planning was a significant reason for the problems the new settlements experienced.

This is especially evident with respect to site selection. A background document to Walwa's 1967 plan had listed thirteen places as potential sites for new villages in Bukoba District;[32] when the campaign had just gotten underway a year later, only three of these were still under consideration. At that point, site selection consisted in lower administrative levels hastily compiling lists of options, a process for which Walwa's April 16 Cinema Hall ultimatum to commence resettlement by April 23 had left only one week. Many sites that made it onto such lists never saw any settlers, and several that did were later abandoned.

Having worked with an April 19 list of eight and an April 27 list of nine possible sites,[33] Bukoba District's Ihangiro Division, for instance, saw significant activities at only four: Tukutuku, Kyamnyorwa, Kiteme, and Omurunazi. On May 4, 1968, the delegation that had been dispatched from the regional administration to guide resettlement inspected Kyamnyorwa, which had by then already received 38 settlers, but did not approve of the settlement's situation and "chose a new site for the new settlement that accorded with new regional policies."[34] The delegation also recommended that an alternative be selected for the site at Tukutuku.[35] As it turned out, the delegation's inputs were quickly overtaken by events: a May 11 progress report recorded around 200 people at Tukutuku. At Kyamnyorwa, 107 people were reported to have arrived on May 7, although this group quickly discovered why the regional delegation had had doubts about the site: on May 10, the majority had decided to leave because the site was damp/swampy ("*unyevunyevu*") and mosquito-infested. The only 15 people who remained apparently had their eyes on a nearby site at Kiteme;[36] upon inspecting it, a team of regional and district officials approved a settlement there in early May.[37] A regional meeting on May 28 then substituted Kiteme for Kyamnyorwa in its list of six sites in Bukoba District where villages would be developed, but it also reinstated Tukutuku—despite the regional agricultural officer's assessment that its soils were "not very good."[38] Not that this list would have produced closure: an October report records new settlements at nine sites in Bukoba District: Kyamnyorwa had been revived, and villages had sprung up at two additional sites.[39] Further underlining the minimal extent to which "planning" determined the reality of villagization on the ground, at the end of October, several months into this chaotic process, Omurunazi and Rugazi were the only two of these new settlements in Bukoba that had reached the regional stipulation of a minimum size of one hundred households (there, as elsewhere, population figures belie a reality of very high turnover in the settlements' population that was driven by constant "defections").[40] Two other settlements had around fifty occupied primary plots; the other five were even smaller.[41]

Problems connected to site selection—poor soils at Tukutuku and Kyamnyorwa's swampiness—were not the result of rigid, blueprint planning incapable of taking into account local realities, but of decision-making that took place in a mad rush and lacked even basic planning, coordination, coherence, and control. The same failure to plan was responsible, too, for a number of other problems that arose at the settlements.

With good soils and a water source, Omurunazi apparently escaped some of the more insurmountable liabilities with which several of the other villages were saddled (Boesen, Madsen, and Moody 1977, 100). Nonetheless, it had to contend with serious problems. The most immediate was inadequate food supplies. At the Bukoba Cinema Hall meeting, Walwa had declared that in this and other regards the new settlements would rely on "self-help," i.e., support from relatives and surrounding villages.[42] This "plan" produced predictable results: at Omurunazi, food had run out within the first two weeks (Bakula 1971, 26). At neighboring Rugazi, a food crisis escalated to the point where the agricultural field officer had to lock himself in to avoid being mobbed by the settlers who accused him of starving them (Musoke 1971, 9–10). The schizophrenia exhibited by Walwa's campaign in this regard of course afflicted villagization more generally: while officials claimed expansive authority in development, they then invoked the importance of local initiative and the much-vaunted "self-reliance" to absolve themselves of the responsibility to think such campaigns through and to ensure that at least the most immediately necessary support was forthcoming.

When it finally did commence, official aid to Omurunazi was sporadic and often insufficient.[43] Generally the authorities were unprepared for the task of tiding the new settlements over until agriculture there might be up and running.[44] A July 1969 letter from Bukoba's district executive officer to his regional counterpart conveys a sense of how delicate the situation remained even more than a year after resettlement:

> (a) it would not be good to visit the villages and ask people to declare themselves whether they are hungry and (b) if we were to supply food to one village and refuse it to others, the news will come to the light of day in all villages and this will give us problems. Therefore we will do this work more carefully, remembering every day that these villages should be self-reliant as soon as possible.[45]

Such reminders of the importance of self-reliance notwithstanding, food self-sufficiency would remain long in coming: as late as January 1972—when Omurunazi had considerable land under cultivation and produced significant quantities of food—a report still noted that it was "not enough."[46]

That there would be a need for sustained food aid was in fact eminently predictable. In many parts of the region bananas were the predominant staple, and a long period until a first crop could be harvested from new plantings would be unavoidable. Insufficient planning not only left the villages without food in the interim; it also delayed a first harvest. There were serious problems with getting banana saplings to the new settlements.[47] Moreover, the lack of start-up support forced many settlers to spend much of their time working for farmers in surrounding villages or to return sporadically to their old fields in order to secure sufficient food: as a result, many of the new settlements failed to utilize the planting seasons for annual crops in late 1968 and early 1969.[48]

If such failures to plan and prepare were one cause of problems at the new settlements, another was again the authoritarian and coercive manner in which the settlements were established. Settler "recruitment" essentially amounted to forced deportations of people who had ended up on hastily drawn-up lists.[49] Landlessness was the primary criterion for inclusion, although remarks by Bukoba's area commissioner that the new settlements also served as a dumping ground for "habitual criminals" and "people against whom the local leaders had personal grudges or . . . who did not give beer to these local leaders" (quoted in Musoke 1971, 7) indicate other reasons for selection as well.[50] Those on such lists saw themselves facing arrests and coercive tactics if they were unwilling to move.[51] As an April 19 circular from a local assistant divisional executive officer reminded his subordinates, each landless person over the age of eighteen "should be asked, if he refuses, ordered, and if he absolutely refuses, be made [atimuliwe] to go and stick to a new settlement."[52] Where people did not respond with outright defiance and "defections," they unsurprisingly showed little enthusiasm to be fully engaged with establishing the new settlements in general and communal agriculture in particular.[53] At Omurunazi, Rald records, half the settlers still refused to work at the village a year after its establishment.[54]

Scott (1998, 246) acknowledges that "ingrained authoritarian habits of the bureaucracy and . . . the pell-mell rush of the campaign" magnified the problems of villagization, but also asserts that "to concentrate on such administrative and political short-comings . . . is to miss the point." The fundamental problem was not that villagization needed "more time, more technical skill, and a better 'bedside manner,'" but that it was "fundamentally schematic." In the end, Scott argues, "the origin of these failures can be traced to a deeper level; these were . . . systemic failures and would have occurred under the best assumptions about administrative efficiency and probity" (263). Failure resulted because rural life was forced into compliance with schematic—and hence necessarily deficient—plans that determined sites and layouts: the problem was "by-the-book resettlement," as Scott (246) calls it.

The operational reality of villagization in West Lake shows that there was no book to do resettlement by. Nor do the contents and functioning in the campaign of the few single pages that were provided support the notion that the West Lake campaign was an instance of high-modernist planning. Planning was implicated in producing a deeply problematic campaign not through a sin of high-modernist commission, but through a sin of omission.

There was a sin of commission, too, though: the very act of laying down a however-undefined way ahead for the peasantry (i.e., "planning") was the key practice in which officials' self-positioning on the side of the future, modernity, and rationality crystallized. Vacuous as such planning practices typically were with respect to practical questions or technical considerations, they nonetheless functioned as a practice through which the authority of officials to make decisions for the peasantry was produced. Planning's key sin of commission was that it fortified villagization's "authoritarian habits." Contrary to Scott's assessment that its authoritarian character was not a fundamental reason for villagization's problems, Tanzania's "scheme to improve the human condition"—to borrow Scott's phrase—failed to do so in a very immediate way when it turned its putative beneficiaries into the victims of its coercive actions. With respect to its material failings, too, the popular resentment to which the campaign's authoritarian modality clearly contributed greatly was an important reason why the new settlements tended to be less productive communities than they might otherwise have been.

Planning beyond West Lake

The Physical Planning Machinery

In the rest of the country, physical planning for villagization was typically not very different from West Lake's experience. What little planning there was did not betray a sense of a high-modernist aesthetics driving campaigns. As in West Lake, it also tended to be after-the-fact. Finally, the on-the-ground results of villagization were typically at such variance with what plans set out that Tanzania's rural landscape cannot be said to have been remade in the image of plans.

From 1968 until roughly 1971, at least some attempts were made to provide planning input on the physical layouts and locations of villages in the small number of geographically limited campaigns during this period. To a greater extent than in West Lake, technical planning staff were thus involved in Handeni and Rufiji, and somewhat less intensively in Dodoma, Kigoma, and Singida. But even during this phase, capacity constraints and a lack of interest or willingness by political leaders to await and to be guided by plans did not see planning significantly shape physical realities on the ground.

During the 1973–1975 phase of the rapid and near-simultaneous concentration of rural populations at between seven thousand and eight thousand officially designated sites, physical planning of villages—beyond ad hoc interventions that simply apportioned land to incoming settlers—ceased almost completely.[55] A good measure of the overall very limited role of physical planning in villagization is that by 1990—fourteen years after villagization had been pronounced complete—only "1,123 villages had been surveyed [i.e., had their *boundaries* demarcated], 79 village land use plans had been approved and 96 other plans were at different stages of preparation" (URT 1994, 49–50).

Considering the state's extremely limited resources, the minimal role and effect of planning in a campaign of the scale of villagization was in fact inescapable. In 1968, for instance, the staffing situation at the Division of Surveys and Mapping in the Ministry of Lands, the primary agencies responsible for the physical planning of new villages, was as follows: in the whole country, its technical field staff consisted of twenty-two surveyors, two senior survey assistants, and fourteen, twenty-two, nineteen, and thirty-seven survey assistants of grades I through IV, respectively, with the lower-grade assistants having received only very minimal training (URT 1968). To put this staff position into perspective: a 1971 internal report estimated that it would take a survey team—consisting of at least one surveyor or higher-grade survey assistant plus several supporting staff—one to three months to survey a village's boundaries and another month to demarcate three hundred plots in a village. Actual experience proved this an optimistic estimate: the same study cites the example of the survey work done at Segera village, Handeni District; apparently the surveying of just the boundary of the village lands "took a team of three surveyors from Land Plan and five villagers six months."[56]

These capacity constraints persisted throughout the 1970s: thus, a 1978 report on land planning in Tanzania would still complain about "acute understaffing" and "a number of responsible posts [being] occupied by unqualified personnel" (Sumien 1978, 2). This was a situation that was impossible to remedy in a country with a general scarcity of trained technical personnel. The point is memorably made by the sharp rebuke, likely from the minister of lands, directed at the commissioner for surveys and mapping's idea to give crash courses to personnel from other ministries in order to bolster capacity to undertake land planning:

> Words fail me how to describe folio 13. In short it is like orbiting the outer space and not being in touch with the realities of Tanzania today. . . . If you are short of manpower, are you convinced that Agriculture, Health, Maendeleo [Development], W.D.

& I.D. [Water Development and Irrigation Department], Kijiji [Village Development] have manpower to spare? You are well informed that these organizations complain bitterly of shortage of qualified manpower.[57]

Planning in Handeni: A Best-Case Scenario

In the face of such limitations, physical planning would necessarily be limited in scope and impact. What physical planning amounted to under the best of circumstances is well illustrated by the Handeni campaign. Started in mid-1968 and, next to Rufiji, the earliest centrally initiated, larger-scale villagization drive, it was something of a best-case scenario for planning. In contrast to Rufiji, a campaign enmeshed with a disaster response to floods where any planning was therefore by necessity extremely hasty and rudimentary,[58] technical staff in Handeni might, at least in principle, have had enough of a run-up phase to allow for "proper planning." Unlike in later years, there was also little competition for planners: Handeni could in fact draw on planning capacity from the national level as well as other parts of the country.[59] As in West Lake, the role and efficaciousness of planning were nonetheless very limited.

Starting in May 1968, political authorities in Handeni District had already been drawing up various lists of potential and priority sites before technical planning staff entered the picture in late July of the same year.[60] Facing requests for sixty village plans from the regional commissioner, the Ministry of Lands in Dar es Salaam mounted an extraordinary mission, dispatching three teams—each consisting of a town planner, a surveyor, and support staff—to Handeni for a three-day planning exercise of ten villages in August.[61] The aim was not overly ambitious. As the mission's report noted, the teams were "to go around the proposed site of these ujamaa villages (in many cases there are villages already existing, with community facilities like schools . . . etc.) and find out the feasibility of laying out a village there taking into account the source of water supply, road connections, the general topography, existing community facilities etc."; they would then draw up "quick and rough topographical maps."[62] These, the mission's leader noted, were "conspicuously made simpler (with due regard to topography), for easy demarcation on the ground. The layouts are flexible and slight alterations are permissible accordingly, during the time of demarcation."[63]

While more detailed layouts for the nine sites this mission ended up inspecting (plus one for an additional site) were to be tackled in a follow-up, implementation again quickly took the campaign off the path charted by the planners: by the end of 1968 only eight villages had been surveyed and demarcated—and only three of those were from the list of the ten priority sites that the mission had been sent to inspect four months earlier.[64] By the middle of 1969, only a dozen or so layouts had been completed.[65] Even this meager and piecemeal planning input was only achieved through an extraordinary pooling of personnel from the Ministry of Lands' Town Planning Division, the Surveys and Mapping Division, the Village Settlement Agency, and Land Planning Units of the Ministry of Agriculture's offices in Tanga and Arusha.[66]

As in West Lake, these planning activities largely interfaced with resettlement not by way of setting out blueprints for subsequent implementation. Many sites received new settlers without any prior input by land planners or surveyors, and at only some of them was physical planning undertaken even after the fact.[67] Some sites that had been surveyed were abandoned. Sometimes this was because surveyors had raised concerns, although these were not always taken seriously. In August 1968, they had, for instance, flagged Negero as problematic because of a lack of water.[68] Yet the local ward executive officer demanded "severe steps" ("*hatua kali*") against eighteen people who refused to take part in setting up a village there soon after and the area commissioner ordered a group of eight of them into his office and threatened them with the same "severe steps" if they failed to show.[69] In this case, the authorities seem to have given in eventually: an October 1968 report stated that Negero "no longer carrie[d] any priority rating."[70] But other sites kept being pushed despite similar problems.[71]

Overall, the planners' limited input was evidently not considered at all crucial in shaping the campaign; it was often not awaited, and even where it was provided, it was often ignored. Much of the planning amounted to rough siting and demarcation work—often done after the fact in an attempt to catch up with already existing situations on the ground.[72] This operational reality of planning shows that *Seeing like a State*'s image of the high-modernist state as a united phalanx dominated by "engineers, planners, technocrats, high-level administrators, architects, scientists, and visionaries" (Scott 1998, 88) requires some significant disaggregation, nuancing, and retouching in the Tanzanian case. Contrary to Christophe Bonneuil's notion (2000, 265)—inspired by *Seeing like a State*—that African states' developmental schemes of circa 1930–1970 "put experts in power," Tanzanian villagization clearly indicates that experts and scientists were responsible neither for conceiving this initiative, nor for defining its parameters, nor for giving it specific shape and direction. Politicians' commands, not expert planning, drove the campaign. Villagization and the kind of state power instantiated in it was not rule by experts.

A vignette from Handeni illustrates this very-much-subordinate role of expert planners especially vividly. Shortly after a 1969 presidential visit to Handeni, the commissioner for surveys and mapping wrote to the regional surveyor:

> As you are probably aware the President was not very happy with some of the villages he saw. One criticism was that there was no community nucleus in many of them and the communal facilities which should be at the heart of the village were scattered around. . . . I believe that some instructions were issued for altering the village development. In the case of some layouts this will only mean allocating some of the plots to communal use. In others the background of the planning is obviously complicated, and very likely existing development has been an important factor.[73]

Despite such acknowledged complicating factors on the ground, the commissioner advised his surveyor to rethink the plans for six out of the approximately twelve villages

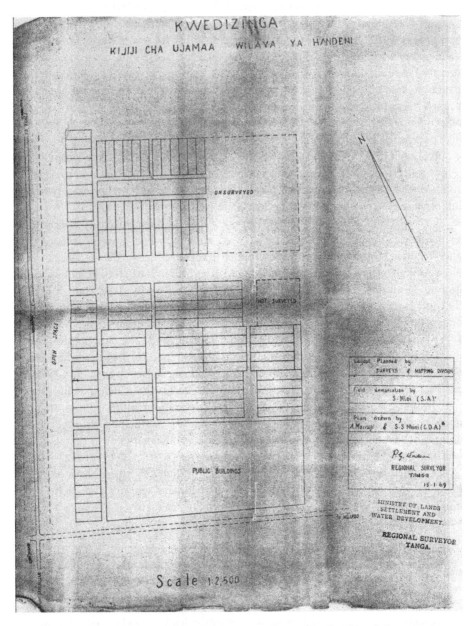

Figure 4.6. Plan for *Kwedizinga kijiji cha ujamaa Wilaya ya Handeni* (Kwedizinga ujamaa village, Handeni District). The plan, dated January 15, 1969, shows an area for "public buildings" on the periphery of the settlement.

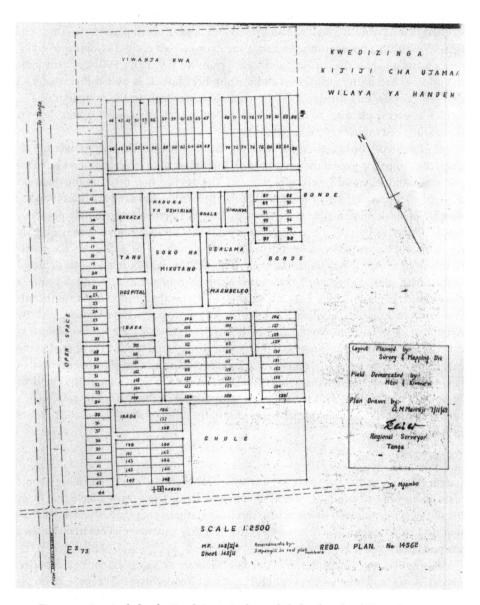

Figure 4.7. A revised plan for Kwedizinga. As demanded, the plan, dated November 7, 1969, shows public-use spaces—*"soko na mikutano"* (market and meetings), *"maduka ya ushirika"* (cooperative shops), and *"TANU"*—at the center of the village.

for which layouts existed at this point. (Referring to direct communications with the president, an earlier letter from the commissioner to all regional surveyors had already stressed that a layout for a village nucleus "MUST appear on all plans for Ujamaa villages."[74]) Within a few months, the Tanga surveyor had ten revised layouts ready. Figures 4.6 and 4.7 show the "before" and "after" plans for Kwedizinga village.[75] The public buildings had been repositioned and the number of plots, as well as their size, had changed considerably. This episode illustrates just how little in the campaign was in fact left to expert planners to decide: the president was clearly ready to overrule even the very limited input they managed to provide.

Can this story be interpreted as showing that high-modernist visions did after all shape the campaign, even if they may have originated not with expert planners but with political authority—and specifically Nyerere? The next section takes up the question of whether Nyerere's desire to have a village center with communal facilities is an indication of his desire for standard, Cartesian designs. Here it is important to point out how little such design decisions in fact affected reality on the ground: even if a highly regimented scheme had been intended, the campaign failed to impose such a straitjacket. In late 1968, Kwedizinga had been "planned" for 132 households—as depicted in the earlier plan (figure 4.6);[76] the revised November 1969 plan showed 148 primary plots (figure 4.7). But neither bore any relation to the on-the-ground reality at the village. In October 1969, the village's population was approximately 50 households.[77] By April 1971, it had fallen to around 35 households.[78] Here as elsewhere the few plans that existed were almost entirely notional documents (this of course also contributed to the ease with which they could be revised).[79] A good overall indication of reality's refusal to fall in line with any such plans is that instead of the 60 to 70 or so villages the Handeni authorities had aimed for at the outset of villagization in the district in 1968/1969, a 1978 post-villagization map officially recorded in the order of 260 villages and hamlets in Handeni.[80]

Visions of Planning

Irrespective of whether they were in fact realized, Nyerere still clearly had at least some ideas about what a "standard village" should look like.[81] Does this indicate that he or his planners were after all invested in a Cartesian aesthetics of regularity, standardization, and orderliness—which, however sketchily it may have been set out in plans, they intended to impose across the country?

Basing Nyerere's inclusion—next to Henri Comte de Saint-Simon, Le Corbusier, Robert Moses, and others—in the pantheon of high-modernists (Scott 1998, 88) on his preference to have communal facilities grouped together in village centers alone would seem to be an overreach. And looking at his broader stance on standardization and central planning, he in fact appears as anything but a champion of a centrally planned, Cartesian order dreamed up in Dar es Salaam. While he did of course insist that every Tanzanian should live in a village, he often also explained that the economy and the physical aspects of such villages ought to be flexible, at least within broad parameters (communal production was the goal; villages should have a locally adaptable economical size; there should be a village center with communal facilities). In Nyerere's mind, villagization did not set out to realize a comprehensively and centrally planned, highly standardized physical or agronomic order. In fact, he quite specifically anticipated many of Scott's arguments about the pitfalls of such a scheme and, conversely, the need to pay attention to local variability and locally rooted, practical knowledge.[82] In this particular regard at least, Nyerere's vision apparently stayed true to some of the lessons he had drawn from the original inspiration behind ujamaa vijijini—which was of course the "organically grown" experience of the Ruvuma Development Association and not a blueprint design sprung from a central planner's drawing board. Thus, it was

> essential to realize that within the unity of Tanzania there is . . . so much diversity that it would be foolish for someone in Dar es Salaam to try to draw up a blueprint for the crop production and social organization which has to be applied to every corner of our large country. . . . It would be absurd to try and settle all these questions from Dar es Salaam, particularly as such variations as those of the type of soil sometimes occur within a very small area. Local initiative and self-reliance are essential. (Nyerere 1968, 348–349)

In general, attempting to centrally micromanage local problems was not sensible because, as Nyerere put it, "Our nation is too large for the people at the center in Dar es Salaam always to understand local problems or to sense their urgency" (Nyerere 1973, 344). Specifically with regard to the optimal size of villages, for instance, no fixed standard could therefore be prescribed because optimal size varied "depending on soil, the appropriate crops or animal husbandry, and the social customs of the people" (Nyerere 1968, 406).[83] If villagization typically failed to take such considerations into account, this was a failure precipitated not by rigid planning that contravened such precepts, but by the chaos of a campaign characterized by a remarkable lack of planning and operational control.

Planners themselves do not appear to have thought about planning in terms of setting out schemes that were to be implemented to the letter. Physical plans in both West Lake and Handeni were largely concerned with providing some guidance on the practical and pressing question of how land was to be apportioned. Neither was it their purpose to dictate a rigid blueprint design for exact implementation, nor were they about giving expression to "a certain aesthetic, what one might call a visual codification of modern rural production and community life" that Scott (1998, 253) imagines Tanzanian "planners carried in their mind's eye."

Thus, the surveyor in charge of drawing up the nine August 1968 plans in Handeni noted that plot size should be varied if land suitable for building was found to be limited. With respect to the plans' "aesthetic" features, he remarked that although "straightforward layouts, with plots arranged in a straight line seems to be ideal from the point of view of demarcation . . . , the limitations and disadvantages of such layouts were explained and appreciated."[84] In implementation, the details of layouts do indeed appear to have been quite flexible: M. Kallabaka (1978), Handeni's district development officer in the early 1970s, notes the example of Suwa village where people were allocated one-quarter-of-an-acre primary plots, in accordance with local preferences for a denser settlement pattern, instead of the more typical one-acre plots. The regional surveyor likewise remarks on settler choices driving layouts, sometimes with—from his perspective—quite undesirable results. In particular, he points to the case of Mkata where settler demand for a plot along the road had led to a ribbon-like settlement.[85] Juma Mwapachu (1979, 121), who headed up villagization in Shinyanga District, remarks about similar villages there—"one long street of houses stretching for miles like the wagons of a locomotive"—and notes that there, too, such patterns were the result "of 'dumping' people at the village site area" and settlers taking "the plots on the main roadside and [building] their houses in the form they wanted. There was no supervision whatsoever in plot allocation and method of building." Scott (1998, 237), who cites Mwapachu's Shinyanga story, asserts that "such linear villages" nonetheless "had a curious logic behind them." But this suggestion ignores that the linear layout along the road was not by design, but a settler-created spontaneous order in the absence of a plan. It was also a settlement pattern that met the explicit disapproval of Nyerere in Shinyanga (Mwapachu 1979, 121), just as it had been criticized by the regional surveyor in Handeni.

A recognition of the need for flexibility and local adaptation was not unique to Handeni (or to postcolonial Tanzania, as Joseph Hodge's [2007] study of colonial experts in British Africa suggests). A 1970 brief on planning for villagization in Dodoma, for instance, emphasized that local customs, systems of pastoral and agricultural production, ecologies, and topography needed to be taken into account in laying out settlements.[86] A 1971 "Study on Physical Planning Aspects of Ujamaa Villages," with apparently quite holistic aspirations for planning, similarly stressed that—in addition to locally variable water needs, drainage, and soil fertility—a key factor that should be considered in designing "layouts which *reflect and enhance* the people's living patterns, culture, and economic activities" should be the "wishes of the people."[87] Shinyanga District's 1975 guidelines for implementing villagization likewise explicitly noted that the "allocation of farms must adhere to the environmental situation obtaining in the local area and [that] the Guideline should not be taken as a biblical implementation plan" (quoted in Mwapachu 1979, 121). In the same vein, a 1975 *Model Village Plan Handbook* (URT 1975, 4)—again rather aspirationally—envisioned giving full consideration to "the social dynamics of rural life, the factors responsible for its growth and the knowledge of the living pattern of its people, their habits, traditions and cultural background." That planning, in these experts' vision, should be made to fit local realities, and not the other way around, is nicely illustrated by this handbook's assessment of two alternative mock layouts for villages (figure 4.8): a "grid iron lay-out imposed on [a] hilly site

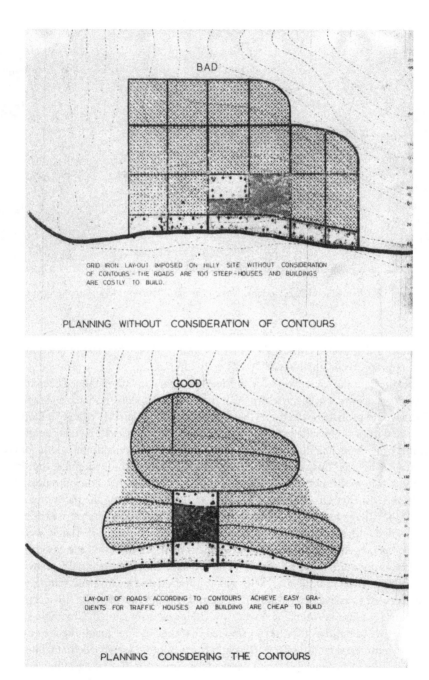

BAD

GRID IRON LAY-OUT IMPOSED ON HILLY SITE WITHOUT CONSIDERATION
OF CONTOURS - THE ROADS ARE TOO STEEP - HOUSES AND BUILDINGS
ARE COSTLY TO BUILD.

PLANNING WITHOUT CONSIDERATION OF CONTOURS

GOOD

LAY-OUT OF ROADS ACCORDING TO CONTOURS ACHIEVE EASY GRA-
DIENTS FOR TRAFFIC HOUSES AND BUILDING ARE CHEAP TO BUILD

PLANNING CONSIDERING THE CONTOURS

Figure 4.8. Two alternative model plans for a hilly site from a *Model Village Plan Handbook* (URT 1975).

Figure 4.9. Chamwino village, Dodoma, December 1971. Courtesy of Tanzania Information Service.

without consideration of contours" receives a "BAD"; conversely, a layout fitted into the local topography is deemed "GOOD" (URT 1975, after 9).

Had the national leadership's and top-level planners' intention indeed been to force the countryside into a neat Cartesian grid, the one place to look for such a vision to be realized would probably have been Chamwino (Buigiri/Bwgiri II) village in Dodoma. Established in 1970, the village soon became a national showcase.[88] Nyerere spent considerable time there. During the hot phase of Operation Dodoma in the middle of 1971, for instance, he was "busy making bricks" with the peasants of Dodoma at the site, as the July 13 *Nationalist* noted; two months later, the September 28 edition reported, he took Prime Minister Olaf Palme of Sweden to Chamwino. Being the focus of such attention, the village had electricity and a presidential lodge (leaders were expected to be associated with an ujamaa village; Chamwino was Nyerere's pick). That it was made to fit a prearranged plan or vision of orderliness no more than was the case in many other places does not, however, appear to have been a concern. Originally planned for 250 families, by the middle of 1971 the site accommodated around 700 families, with more expected to arrive. Since "most of the layed [*sic*] out plots were . . . unacceptable" for various reasons, an August 1971 study on village planning noted, Chamwino's residents started "to build as they liked provided that they did not touch the area demarcated for communal facilities."[89] A December 1971 photograph shows that Chamwino had indeed not been squeezed into a particularly neat Cartesian design (figure 4.9).

The Functioning of Survey Lines

Higher-level decision-makers did not fetishize straight lines or envision villages regimented by them. However, there were nonetheless at least a few instances of grid-like designs being enforced.[90] A confidential report for TANU headquarters documents one such case at Maneromango village in Coast Region:

> The surveyors came and measured the old village. . . . The villagers talked about the surveyors as "watoto," children, who had just come out of training. The lines were drawn straight across the village. Houses were to be removed and rebuilt in straight lines, two plots in a row between the roads. . . . Trees had to be cut mercilessly without any flexibility for the placing of the house within the plot. . . . Time elapsed but in September 1973 the people were urged to demolish their homes and to move voluntarily. Forceful moving started October 1. The whole district staff and all the cars seemed to come out on that day. . . . When people were told, "Move this house two feet" or "Move this house ten feet," it seemed like folly to them. You cannot move a house without breaking it down and to move it a few feet seemed to have no logic.[91]

What made the straight line a protagonist in this story? Former officials whom I asked about such cases suggested two reasons. One—perhaps not in play in this example, as the surveyors appear to have been outsiders—was local politics: local officials often had scores to settle, and enforcing an especially disruptive land reallocation in cases of preexisting settlements showed their political power and provided opportunities for expropriations and destruction of property.

Another suggestion was that some officials might have felt that they were meant to create "towns," characterized not only by a dense settlement pattern but also by straight streets. If this was what the Maneromango surveyors perceived to be their mission, they were—in light of the above—operating on the basis of a mistaken understanding of the intentions of the country's political leadership as well as top-level technical staff's judgment of appropriate designs. That the Maneromango episode caused a scandal over which almost the entire district administrative staff was dismissed strongly suggests that their actions were neither in conformity with the intention of the policy nor an officially sanctioned mode of implementation.[92]

The possibility that these surveyors enforced straight lines because this aesthetics was suggestive of rationality and orderliness cannot be ruled out. But if they perceived the implementation of a grid-like design as an order from their superiors, their actions may have had little to do with any connotations straight lines and right angles might have carried for them. Rather, the episode would demonstrate subordinate officials' readiness to ruthlessly carry out perceived orders whatever their contents. Recalling Omurunazi's field officer who "regarded it as his duty to implement what had been decided at the regional level" (Bakula 1971, 29) despite his misgivings about the regional layout, this seems a plausible interpretation.

But examining how the straight line functioned within the particular local the-ater of the village also suggests another way to make sense of its occasional importance that had little to do with its aesthetic qualities. The survey line was not just a piece of equipment but a central token that established the difference between ordinary villag-ers and officials. In this functioning, it was also an exceedingly thin and fragile line: without it, the surveyors would have been nothing but the *"watoto"* (children) the vil-lagers made them out to be. Ultimately, then, the survey line perhaps had to be defended so uncompromisingly because of its centrality in producing these officials' shaky and thin authority. As Emma Crewe and Elizabeth Harrison (1998, 96) remark, "Experts ef-fectively reinforce themselves as such by the use of language and the creation of tech-niques and tools that have a particular exclusionary mystique attached to them."[93]

How "expert" practices and talk functioned to make and police the distinction between official/expert and peasant is well exemplified by a 1975 collection of four eight-to-thirteen-page group reports on village planning penned by the year's cohort of planning students at the Land Planning Institute of the University of Dar es Salaam (Ardhi Institute 1975). The problems at Lukanga village were due to "laziness, which is due to ignorance" and a "lack of agricultural implements." At Njopeka, "the imple-ments used in farming can be modernized, instead of hoes the villagers could start to use ploughs and tractors." At Binga, "people are conservative. They are not ready to sur-render some of their traditional ways of farming, so agricultural productivity is lower than it could be. . . . Modern agricultural methods must be practiced." Similarly, the salvation of Kisiju lay in "irrigation, modernization, increased acreage, [and] harder work." Summing up, the collection's conclusion underlined that "people are conservative and agriculture could be much expanded if people used ploughs and tractors instead of hoes."

Especially for those removed from the peasantry only by dint of a planning diploma or a surveyor's line, such (hollow) expert discourse functioned as a key practice through which their authority was fabricated; to keep it alive, it had to be performed and de-fended. Reporting from the trenches, perceptive contemporary observers saw this dy-namic everywhere. As Henry Mapolu and Gerard Philippson (1976, 150–151) noted at the time,

> The power of the bureaucracy is largely justified ideologically by the fact that they are the possessors of a type of "knowledge"—i.e. Western technocratic—from which the peasants are radically estranged. They are "experts." The constant display of "knowl-edge" is thus a necessity for the reproduction of the relation of commandism and subservience. . . . New agricultural practices, new implements, etc. are presented from above to the "ignorant" peasants, as steps which are progressive in themselves.

Economic Planning

If physical planning generally neither attempted nor effected the imposition of a grand, disciplinarian scheme, was economic planning perhaps a different story? While during full-scale villagization attempts to draw up economic plans appear to have fallen by the wayside, in the earlier, geographically limited campaigns, there was a push for village-level economic planning.[94] What did this look like and what effects did it produce?

In Handeni, twelve prioritized villages had economic plans drawn up for them in 1969.[95] The standard opening paragraph of the resulting "Five-Year Programmes" conjectured that in 1974, "a family may earn about shs 5000/= per annum as compared to shs 400/00 which is just the National average income or worse still to shs 180/00 which is the local average income in 1968." There followed a list of more detailed projections. At Kwamkono village, for instance, 350 households would have 700 acres of maize and bananas under cultivation in 1970; by 1974 this would have expanded to a total of 2,275 acres.[96]

These plans contained no indication as to the methods and ways in which such highly ambitious targets were to be met. Unsurprisingly, these plans—largely limited to setting targets—remained pipe dreams with no tangible impact: in the middle of 1971, there were 230 people—maybe around eighty households—at Kwamkono, less than a quarter of the plan's projection, and only about one-third of that number had moved permanently to the site. Just under 26 hectares of maize, 1 hectare of cassava, and 2.5 hectares of groundnuts were reported to be under cultivation.[97] This reported 1971 total of roughly seventy-two acres compared rather unfavorably with projections of seven hundred acres for 1970. And the reported figures may well have overstated actual cultivation: at Masaika village in Tanga, for instance, von Freyhold (1971, 27) found that twenty-three acres had been reported but only eleven cultivated in 1970; the next year, forty-three acres were reported while seventeen were actually cultivated.

In their complete detachment from reality and their lack of any concern with concrete and practical "ways and means," these early Handeni plans were broadly representative of economic planning more generally. West Lake's Omurunazi village, for instance, had a four-year plan for 1970/1971–1973/1974 drawn up for it in 1970.[98] This was the product of one of the several planning activities undertaken in West Lake by high-level teams put together by the regional administration and the central government; specially appointed "presidential planning teams," for instance, were sent to West Lake as well as other areas to help get ujamaa villages on their feet economically in 1970 and 1971.[99] The centerpiece of Omurunazi's plan was three tables that projected acreage to be put under various crops over the plan's four years. In 1974, the village would have 1,592 acres under crops. Except for a tractor scheme that was envisioned to plough 175 acres for the village in 1971/1972, there was very little indication as to how this goal was to be met. Despite at least some apparent follow-through on tractor plowing,[100] Omurunazi's targets were quickly revealed to be entirely unrealistic. Whether one believes a January 11, 1972, report that put total land under cultivation at 63 acres or another report's rosier count of 102 acres on February 8, as the latter report frankly admits, achievements lagged massively behind targets. This was true vis-à-vis both the original 1970 plan's projection of more than 800 acres under cultivation in 1972 and the report's own dramatically adjusted target of just 520 acres.[101]

Even in the few prioritized areas of early villagization campaigns, economic planning had far too little concrete bearing and practical impact on rural life to have amounted to a means of comprehensive, centralized control. This was a widely shared experience: as Jannik Boesen (1979, 133) comments on the products of the presidential planning team that worked in West Lake in 1970, "Everyone involved in the exercise must have known that they were utterly unrealistic." Likewise, Henry Mapolu (1973, 131) found another presidential team's plans in Mwanza "most unrealistic and irrelevant." Frances Hill (1979, 108) reports that people in Kondoa District, Dodoma, regarded the plans produced by the presidential planning team there "as either threatening or ludicrous. The Plans made erroneous estimates of both population and land area, set unrealistic targets of economic production, and expected fledgling ujamaa villages to assume a heavy burden of debt. The Area Commissioner, too, knew that these plans were worthless."

Von Freyhold's (1979, 138–139) account of a 1971 visit by a district planning team to Segera village in Handeni suggests especially poignantly the purely ritualistic nature of such planning exercises:

> The list of different crops was read out and villagers were encouraged to mention for each crop how many hectares they would want to plant—and usually the higher figure was entered into the records. . . . The villagers did not take this "auction" very seriously and did not protest when they finally found that they were supposed to plant about 850 hectares in the year. After about two hours the planning team had filled all the columns of the forms and left for Kabuku. "Here they go to spend their night allowance," was one remark by a villager as they left.

The fact that such ritualistic exercises had very little bearing on life and production in the villages does not mean, however, that they had no effects at all. Incessantly engaged in and invoked in speeches and official public discourse, such planning rituals were a key discursive practice in which the positionalities of officials and peasants were performed and fabricated. Practically worthless as they may have been, they nonetheless staged "planning officials" as authoritative guides whose interventions were necessary to point the peasantry toward a better future. "PEASANTS NEED ECONOMIC PLANS—Nyerere," a May 16, 1970, *Nationalist* headline thus had the president insist. Second Vice President Kawawa chimed in when "he told the peasants that they should realise the importance of discarding the habits of working haphazardly and should evolve a planned method of work which would enable them to gauge their progress," the October 3, 1970, *Nationalist* reported. Waxed poetic a January 27, 1970, *Nationalist* editorial,

> Work, to have meaning, must be measured, and measured against set targets: Only then can progress be determined and shortfalls established. And it is targets that spur people to greater feats of production and excellence. The economic plans will

ensure that Ujamaa villagers' efforts are not tittered away in uneconomic ventures and choices.

Conclusion

"Planning" staged state officials as indispensible authorities in the lives of their peasant charges. Of course, as von Freyhold's observations show, neither officials nor peasants appeared to be substantively invested in this, their mutual interpolation in practices of planning. Still, everybody played along. This situation recalls Achille Mbembe's (1992, 4) comment that the postcolonial subject in Africa is constituted in "the common daily rituals that ratify the commandement's own institutionalization (its *recherche hégémo-nique*) in its capacity as a fetish to which the subject is bound . . . and . . . the subject's deployment of a talent for play." With clear echoes in Tanzania, the result of such stagings of authority, diagnoses Mbembe, is the mutual "zombification" and disempower-ment of "subject" and "ruler": planning officials in Tanzania may well have been rati-fied in their authority—but only until their motorcade had turned the corner and their plans had been banished into a desk drawer. Displays of seeming agreement and com-pliance with officials' wishes, common enough in Tanzania to have earned a special designation, the "*Ndiyo, Bwana*" ("Yes, Sir") attitude, were sufficient to underwrite of-ficials' self-validation as authorities, but also refused a more substantive engagement.[102] Officials thus found their authority reduced to commanding the few things they could conceivably control through coercion and compulsion: the location of populations, and, on occasion, the alignment of their houses. Despite being very visible, this was a thin form of rule that barely reached beyond the surface.

Hydén (1975, 34) confesses his puzzlement at "why there is so much talk of plan-ning in spite of its relatively modest role in policy-making in Tanzania." Mwanza's re-gional surveyor, faced with politicians' demands for village surveys, which experience had probably taught him they would rarely practically utilize or even await, may have had the answer: "Survey is a magic wor[d] which is accepted as meaning success—when obviously it is but one stage in a long and complicated series of events leading to the creation of a community."[103] The magical property of planning—irrespective of its particular contents, practical relevance, or actual role in guiding action—consisted in its ability to conjure an aura of future-orientation, control, and rationality around its purveyors. As such, it positioned "planning officials" on the side of modernity and the future, juxtaposed against the peasants' ways of the past. This key element in the as-semblage of officials' authority functioned as a generic and blanket authorizing prac-tice: token rituals of planning, irrespective of their efficaciousness in directing reality on the ground and their aesthetic or other qualities, sufficed to invoke and conjure this broad developmentalist positioning. All states must be "theater states": planning the developed future was a key element in the Tanzanian state's staging of its authority.[104]

5 The World of Officials in the Trenches, Potemkin Villages, and Criticism as Treason

> In the late 1960s abuses by "overzealous" administrators and political authorities upcountry incurred Nyerere's anger. While their acts were often oppressive, he did not apparently get the message about why people with power were using it in such ways, particularly when they were not gaining materially from such acts, or why they thought of themselves and peasants as they did.
>
> —Idrian Resnick, *The Long Transition*

THE KIND OF rule that manifested itself in villagization, the previous chapters have argued, must be traced to its assemblage from a set of thick and historically contingent discursive practices of development and government. This chapter observes how officials in the regions and districts worked within but also *with* the malleable and manipulable terrain of these practices as they negotiated the political incentive structure they faced. These officials were not passive puppets within the determinative structure of discursive practices but active participants in their production as they navigated, enlisted, performed, and thereby also shaped them.

In part, these labors were of course influenced by officials' instrumental calculations aimed at preserving their careers. That this purpose tended to push them in the direction of autocratic practices of rule that were often dysfunctional vis-à-vis their purported developmental goals was conditioned by a political system that incentivized nothing more than pleasing its Philosopher King president.[1] Under pressure to show results, local officials often eschewed careful technical considerations, showed little compunction about antagonizing target populations, and resorted to coercive implementation. The "success"—for their purposes—of this mode of operating was a question of skill—at manipulating information flows, for instance, but also at the deeply contextual task of effective self-positioning that drew on the idioms, practices, and frames of legitimation out of which developmentalist rule was assembled. While the particular angle on villagization this chapter presents then homes in on the role of incentives and officials' "material" interests, it offers a broadened view of what such interests were—beyond the focus in materialist-utilitarian accounts on self-enrichment—and shows that interests and the actions officials took to pursue them were highly contingent on institutional settings as well as the particular field of discursive practices within which officials operated.

One crucial upshot of this chapter's discussion of how officials in the trenches negotiated their thick political universe is that treating "the state" as a unitary agent with "its" interests makes very little sense. Different positions in the state apparatus alone made for dynamics that constantly negated the state's coherence, as central intentions and directions were remolded and often subverted in the hands of their supposed "implementers." These are of course familiar dynamics: Joel Migdal (1988, 2001), for instance, has extensively explored them in analyzing the "triangle of accommodation" that sandwiches mid-level officials between their national-level superiors and society-based local strongmen. While the chapter finds these implementers very much operating as Migdal has described, one aspect of the Tanzanian story fits poorly the image of triangular accommodation: in Tanzania, the "societal" corner of the triangle tended to see very little deference to its interests. While distinctions must again be drawn (parliamentarians, for instance, appeared more willing to speak out for their constituents than did the more powerful, presidentially appointed commissioners), the political center and its implementers tended to unite at least around one issue: vigorously defending the party-state's blanket authority against all challengers and critics. The chapter's latter sections situate this aspect of the Tanzanian story in its broader formative context.

A Political Incentive Structure

Chapter 4 observed Regional Commissioner Walwa casting himself as a developmentalist general directing a war against Tanzanians' underdevelopment. While such framings were crucial components in the constitution of his authority, he of course quite actively drew on them in performing and staking a claim to this authority. That plainly instrumental motivations played into this had been in evidence from the very beginnings of Walwa's West Lake villagization campaign. His *Plan for the Implementation of the Arusha Declaration* (Walwa 1967), for instance, had all the airs of a self-promotional document. Commensurate with this purpose, the plan was "distributed to the national leaders of TANU, various Ministers, and some people in the region," reports Musoke (1971, 3)—who adds for emphasis that "the people referred to here were not the peasants in the villages or workers in the streets." Indeed, the plan's very opening sentence appears to betray who was the key audience for its author: "On February 5, 1967, the Father of our Nation, the Honourable [*Mtukufu*] President of the United Republic of Tanzania, Mwalimu Julius Kambaragwe Nyerere, proclaimed the Arusha Declaration," Walwa declared. To also look its part as a PR production, Walwa had his plan sent to be professionally produced. Lest Nyerere and other political leaders need a reminder just who their loyal lieutenant was, Walwa's regional administrative secretary drew particular attention to an especially important feature when he ordered one thousand copies from the printers: "Inside the Cover you should print Hon. P.C. Walwa's photograph (which is enclosed) & his name. Below the photograph there should be the following words—Uhuru, Usalama na Maendeleo [Freedom, Peace, and Development]."[2]

Presenting himself as the loyal implementer of the president's directives appears to have been a central objective in other initiatives of Walwa's as well. At his posting in Ruvuma, prior to West Lake, this purpose also appears to have driven the purchase—at great, and in the eyes of technical staff in the region, unwarranted, expense—of three Caterpillar tractors: Walwa apparently felt that they would serve as effective showpieces of his impressive work in the region. As Ibbott (1970, 239) relates the story,

> The first of the machines was due to arrive at about the same time as the President's visit and frantic efforts were made to hurry it up to be there before his visit and to find a driver who could operate it. At the Songea showground in front of the platform where the President and his group were seated was deposited a pile of earth. The caterpillar tractor came forward fitted with an earth scoop and rather shakily, with a novice driver, scooped up a load of earth, turned and dropped it into a lorry standing by.

Walwa was of course not alone in his intense concern with his image in the eyes of superiors and the president. James Finucane (1974, 141) reports, for instance, that Mwanza's regional commissioner repeatedly called up the *Nationalist* in Dar es Salaam to "order" the paper to withdraw less-than-flattering stories about rural development initiatives in his region. Officials did not adopt such strategies on a whim: Tanzania's political system incentivized them to do so. The chief local officials, the regional and area commissioners, were especially dependent on remaining in Nyerere's favor. Their appointment, tenure at a particular posting, and ability to retain their position all directly depended on the president.[3] As a result, they quite accurately perceived themselves as "personal representative[s] of the President"—a function one of them likened to that of an "ambassador" (Finucane 1974, 115). An episode Finucane relates from Mwanza Region captures well his appointees' utter vulnerability to Nyerere:

> One Commissioner, after a private meeting with Nyerere in Dar es Salaam, spoke upon his return to the Region of the assurance he had been given that he would be in the Region for a long time so as to get certain projects well underway. Shortly afterwards he was transferred out of the Region, being informed of the move by police radio thirty minutes before it was publicly announced on the mid-day news broadcast. This experience was widely known and discussed amongst political leaders in the Region at the time. (114)

As Resnick (1981, 98) remarks on Nyerere's looming presence, "Certainly, his word was enough to catapult people to the heights or send them to the depths."

In the context of villagization, this general vulnerability to the whims of Nyerere only intensified. In large part specifically to prepare for villagization, the state apparatus was being geared up to even more effectively push central (Nyerere's) commands down to the local level.[4] The primary effect of wide-ranging "decentralization" measures instituted in 1972, for instance, was to create more powerful executive and administrative authorities in the regions, a move closely tied to the purpose of readying the party and government to launch its "frontal attack" on the villagization front.[5] It was no coincidence, therefore, that decentralization saw the installation of a number of powerful and "effective" politicians as regional commissioners: Peter Kisumo, for instance, went to Coast Region. The dramatic reshuffle of the cabinet that went hand in hand with these measures was, in veteran Zanzibari politician Abdul Babu's assessment, likewise designed to strengthen Nyerere's hand with respect to villagization—and was not without problematic effects:

> Historians will probably locate the beginning of the regime's leadership disintegration at the February 1972 unprecedented Cabinet reshuffle which threw out some of the most experienced ministers, including myself (altogether, a total of about one hundred years of combined cabinet experience—a serious manpower loss to the country). In our place were appointed some very junior and inexperienced "technocrats" whose only qualification for such senior appointments was their total and uncritical loyalty to President Nyerere personally. They were all "yes-men," described by Nyerere as the "believers," as in religion (*waumini* in Kiswahili). . . . Nyerere was getting impatient with the slow movement of the people of the new *Ujamaa* villages. (Quoted in Doorbos 1996, 330)[6]

In this context, delivering "results" on the villagization front increasingly became an explicit litmus test for local officials. By 1970, they were listening to a rising chorus that reminded them again and again that the promotion of ujamaa villages was their duty as leaders and, in Nyerere's words as reported in the August 1 and May 19, 1970, *Nationalist,* "true TANU member[s] of modern times" and "good citizens."[7] Direct pressure on particular officials complemented this general atmosphere. In the run-up to Operation Dodoma in 1970, for instance, Nyerere had issued a directive to officials in the region that "in the coming 14 months there should be sufficient progress in the implementation of this policy" of starting ujamaa villages.[8] Over the ensuing months, he would frequently pronounce ujamaa villages to be "the only medicine to cure the frequent famine problems in Dodoma Region."[9] Punitive actions against officials who were perceived to be insufficiently attentive to procuring this "medicine" accompanied such exhortations. Hill (1979, 110) reports:

> In both 1969 and 1970 area commissioners lost their postings for inadequate attention to ujamaa and for misleading President Nyerere about the true state of socialist transformation. . . . The District TANU Chairman was warned about his opposition to ujamaa by President Nyerere during his November 1969 tour of Dodoma. A year later the chairman was removed from office and put under fairly lenient house arrest. The Member of Parliament for Dodoma South opposed ujamaa as openly as had

the District TANU Chairman. He was not allowed to stand for re-election to Parliament and was also put under continual security surveillance. . . . Others whose opposition was less subtle were jailed under preventive detention by the Area Commissioner in late 1970. By early 1971 the new Regional Commissioner and the new Area Commissioner were under intense pressure by Nyerere to make Dodoma both productive and socialist. The Area Commissioner was acutely aware that his two predecessors had been transferred and demoted. The Regional Commissioner, a former Cabinet Minister defeated in the 1970 general election, faced a bleak political future if Dodoma region continued its reputation as a centre of famine but not of ujamaa.

It took considerable spine to remind the president of the practical incompatibility of his demands for dramatic and immediate results with the original spirit of his policy of ujamaa vijijini. In an interview I conducted with a former Singida regional commissioner, he recollected the following conversation with Nyerere in 1970 or 1971:

> COMMISSIONER: "When we met, he was asking me, 'How many villages have you made in Singida?'. . . . I said, 'No, I cannot as yet. I have to do it after some time.' 'What are you waiting for?' 'Until people are prepared and willing to go. If they are not prepared and they are not willing, then I am not going to build ujamaa villages.'"
>
> L. S.: "How did he react?"
>
> COMMISSIONER: "Very badly."

Most people, he surmised, would have avoided such confrontations: "Nyerere, if he had his own idea, he will never tolerate anybody going against it. . . . People feared him."[10]

The incentive structure that officials confronted was the product of a pronouncedly hierarchical and personalistic chain of command that led straight up to the constantly exhorting president. It had a profound impact on their actions. A Mlali (Morogoro District) ward official characterized his situation in 1974 thus:

> Sometimes we acted as if we struggled for survival from the hammer that dangled dangerously above us. The result was a rush, anywhere location, anyhow building in some villages. We had played with time since the policy of villagization was enunciated some years back and now there was no more time. (Quoted in Tuguta 1978, 33–34)

Evidently facing similar pressures, a divisional secretary in Mara Region reminded his subordinates:

> As we were authorized at the Divisional Committee meeting of 22/10/73 to comply with the directive of the honourable President of the United Republic of Tanzania, it is necessary that they [people] be shifted by force. . . . We agree that we shall not pay attention to any problems (whatsoever) during operation Mara except to shift the people. (Quoted in Magoti 1984, 119)

In neighboring Shinyanga, the district development director could then of course not ignore the "progress" Mara's decisive action was producing there:

> There was a competitive attitude. . . . Reports were coming in from Mara Region that they were about to complete their operation when we had not started at all. . . . Who, in such circumstances, would have wished to lag behind? (Mwapachu 1979, 117)

Effects

As previous chapters have argued, pronounced nonchalance and inattentiveness with regard to practical and technical questions in villagization that pervaded all levels of the political system were grounded in a rather blanket and self-assured conviction that state officials fought on the side of modernity and the future. Against the background of this broad framing, officials' solutions required little careful scrutiny or assessment: their superiority vis-à-vis the peasants' outmoded ways was a given. While such framings were a crucial element in making "*Ujamaa* politics . . . tantamount to a deliberate neglect by most party decision-makers of criteria such as efficiency, feasibility, and viability," as Hydén (1980, 112) has put it,[11] the incentive structure Nyerere's appointees had to negotiate amplified the dysfunctionality and authoritarian bent of developmental governing. For local officials in particular, ensuring social, economic, and technical soundness was simply not a priority when the overriding political imperatives pointed in a different direction. In a context in which information from the regions was typically opaque to the center and could be manipulated, there was a systemic tendency to focus on rapid advances in terms of what was readily apprehensible (the number of villages, for instance), to the neglect and detriment of the soundness of interventions and the intended substance—the ujamaa-aspects—of the policy. Part of the dysfunctionality of Tanzania's rural development policies was thus the product of an incentive system that pushed officials toward what Migdal (2001, 87), borrowing Bardach's label, has discussed as "tokenism."

The authoritarianism of officials—their resort to coercive means and their intolerance toward independence, questioning, and criticism—is likewise explicable in part as the result of their need to keep up appearances for their superiors. Independent local initiative simultaneously threatened to steal the limelight from officials and to turn into potential headaches and embarrassments. Always, therefore, tight control was desirable. Criticism was an even greater danger, lest it catch the eye of political superiors: it had to be quashed.

Tanzanian Potemkin villages, set up for the specific purpose of showing them off to a touring Nyerere, and officials' frequent resorting to coercive means were thus in part the unintended and, from the center's perspective, deeply counterproductive result of the incentive structure local officials faced. Nyerere may have been (willfully?) oblivious to his role in creating these dynamics, but the direct pressure he and the center often brought to bear on subordinates clearly aggravated them. This is one reason why conventional understandings of ujamaa/villagization that have tended to credit Nyerere for an attractive, deeply democratic vision while blaming "overzealous" local officials for its coercive and inept implementation are too simplistic.

Expert Advice and Political Commands

Chapter 4 showed that experts and technical staff played only a very secondary role in villagization and that political commands often trumped expert advice even when it was furnished. This resulted in part from officials enacting a rather boundless and blanket developmentalist authority whose underpinnings chapter 4 discussed. In part, however, relegating expert advice to a very much peripheral role was simply the upshot of technical staff's and political officers' strategic behavior shaped by the incentive structures they faced.

A 1965 project of Walwa's to construct a presidential lodge in Songea is a good example of an initiative in which "technical" concerns were overridden by political calculations. Winning kudos with the president was clearly the key intention, even if in this particular case the attempt appears to have fallen flat when, presented with the plan, Nyerere gratefully declined. As is familiar from the stance taken by various experts in chapter 4, in Songea, too, technical staff knew their place: according to Ibbott (1970, 242–243), the regional engineer "felt the project was not possible with the presently available resources" but "in his [the engineer's] job he could not question the move." At the meeting that would decide on the project, Ibbott raised doubts, but "not one of the other members of the committee said a word although I [Ibbott] knew that most were dubious about it and knew that there was no money available." In Ibbott's judgment, an atmosphere suffocating frank discussions prevailed more generally: "The feelings of the Regional Commissioner were seldomly questioned and often people were reluctant to put a point of view until they first knew his. . . . I feel a similar situation exists with the President and those around him."

Like the president's appointees who were fearful of him, lower down the hierarchy, technical staff and political subordinates had to closely mind their political superiors. And so it mattered little that, in Reginald Green's (1995, 92) assessment, technical "officials . . . by and large . . . opposed rapid villagisation as beyond their technical and resource capacity":[12] they often did not speak their minds, and even if they did, they stood little chance of being listened to (compare Nyerere's readiness to put technical staff right by ordering the redrawing of village plans in Handeni).

Potemkin Villages and the Politics of Information

The full extent of the "tokenism" that resulted from subordinate officials' quest to create a facade of results is poignantly illustrated by Handeni's 1968/1969 villagization campaign. It also indicates the degree to which the politics of information unfolding between the center and "the trenches" tended to encase the center in a soothing informational bubble that made realistic assessments of the policy difficult. In early September 1968, right at the start of the campaign, the Handeni area commissioner had made a special assignment of officials to six villages he deemed likely to be visited by Nyerere.[13] Only two weeks later he sent a follow-up letter: "Be reminded that the Honourable President of this Republic will come to this District in order to see villages that have already been started and this is not just piles of timber."[14] Given the pressures on the commissioner— thus duly transmitted down the chain of command to his subordinates—compulsory means and a total lack of concern with substance were all but inevitable, as indeed came to light by accident during one of Nyerere's long-anticipated visits to Handeni in June/July 1969 (see figure 2.3 for a visual impression of the kind of production the president's stop prompted at Kideleko village during that visit):

> One story told at the time was that Julius Nyerere traveled that stretch of road [from Mkata to Handeni via Mazingara] to visit these new settlements and encourage the people in their labors. . . . Things went very well at the first village; there was much building activity, excitement, esprit, and cooperative work going on. At the second village, things were not so well in hand, although some construction had started. The presidential delegation was less pleased. At the third village, house lots were only in the first stages of being laid out, and even less progress had been made. . . . Given this dismal turn of events, someone suggested that they return to the first village, where there was a thriving *hoteli* (tearoom) where they could get some refreshment. Upon returning to the first village, they found virtually no one there, and much of the construction that had been ongoing appeared to have been dismantled or abandoned. President Nyerere was not amused, and the development officer responsible for these 'Potemkin' *ujamaa* villages was dismissed. (Porter 2006, 72)[15]

That the development officer, as well as apparently the area commissioner (Ibbott 1970, 111), lost their jobs over this episode likely only reinforced the very same dynamics that had led to their offense in the first place: the lesson from Nyerere's swift action against them was clearly to underline how crucial it was to stay in his good graces. Given the ambition of his demands, there was little choice about the means—just a greater incentive to keep problematic information out of view. Indeed, the pressure was relentless: within a few days of this incident, the July 29, 1969, *Nationalist* reported, Nyerere closed a Handeni seminar on ujamaa villages with a statement that "praised Handeni District for its fertile land but deplored that there was not even a single shamba [field] of which one could be proud."

The Handeni episode was symptomatic of systemic dynamics. The group of university students reporting on their field trip to Dodoma's new villages in the *Nationalist* of October 5, 1970, made very similar discoveries, for instance. At one village a "few days before the President visited the village, a bull-dozer cut a road to the village. It went further, it pulled down all the scattered 'tembe' huts [traditional buildings], and the wajamaa [villagers] improvised the grass huts—making sure they were clustered together . . . and it was nick-named an Ujamaa village." The second installment of the students' report, on October 7, found that at another village "what was part of the individually held vineyards before and immediately after the President's visit to the place, became communal holdings during the President's visit!" The students, more clairvoyant than those in charge in Tanzania, pinpointed the general trajectory of these dynamics in a prophetic warning: "We are creating a big and dangerous lie to ourselves. And sooner than later, we shall begin to believe this lie."

Creating and believing a lie was the effect of a system in which local information was relatively opaque to superiors to whose whims subordinate officials were defenselessly exposed. Little wonder that Tanzanian officials behaved like their counterparts elsewhere, among whom Migdal (2001, 87) diagnoses a "consuming obsession . . . to prevent the upward flow of information to their supervisors and agency chiefs that would indicate the implementers are not 'handling' the situation." Here is Kigoma's regional surveyor gingerly stepping through such an informational minefield. He had informed the chairman of a presidential planning team working in his region that he did not have the resources to produce all the requested plans for villages; alarmingly, the team's chairman demanded to have this in writing "so that he could take the matter to the President." Reported the surveyor to his commissioner at the ministry: "I have never written a letter to him [the chairman] as I do fear that I may be accusing you to the President. I can write the letter if you feel that there will not be misunderstandings between this division and the politicians."[16] Might Nyerere's planning team have been compromised in its ability to draw up the "expert plans" he felt the peasants needed? The president would be none the wiser.

The Problem with the Local(s)

For local officials it was clearly perilous not to be tightly in control over their domain and the information that flowed from it. Local initiatives, especially when they were truly independent and visible to the center, were thus regarded with a great deal of unease. Local officials' difficulties with the RDA illustrate these dynamics well; they also give a sense of officials' repertoire of strategies through which they sought to manage this problem.

The necessity of managing the center's perceptions is one key reason why the RDA, like any independent initiative, was a constant source of potential headaches (and, apparently, worse) for local officials. For instance, an early Ruvuma regional commissioner had suggested Millinga for the job of Tunduru area commissioner, but Millinga wanted to focus on his work with the RDA instead (Ibbott 1970, 235–236). The commissioner would have none of this and told Millinga "that he had better accept or else his life would be very difficult." After Millinga's next attempt to explain his reasoning, the commissioner, "looking even more worried[,] complained of feeling ill and having pains in his head and chest." Then Millinga informed him that Second Vice President Kawawa had indicated that Millinga's decision would be acceptable to Nyerere: "This changed the whole atmosphere. . . . His [the commissioner's] fear was partly that Ntimbanjayo's [Millinga's] refusal would reflect badly on him in Dar es Salaam."

Managing the center's perceptions was evidently an ever-present concern for local officials. This becomes especially visible in the tensions and anxieties that arose when there was uncertainty (as there often was) regarding what they needed to pander to. The sudden destruction of the RDA provides an excellent example. Clearly, one could no longer be seen to be the association's friend; but, complicating the situation, one also had to be seen as safeguarding its villages' success after their takeover by the state. Official reports from the region struggled to negotiate this set of parameters. On the one hand, they claimed—contrary to fact—that excellent progress was being made in the villages since TANU had taken charge. On the other hand—and also contrary to fact—they made a complete about-face in suddenly painting the RDA's performance prior to the takeover in distinctly negative colors, where only months earlier its work had been hailed (chapter 2). With a lingering degree of uncertainty about what exactly might be expected of them, local officials apparently perceived the aftermath of the RDA's destruction as a minefield, and their nervousness showed.[17] This is well illustrated by an acrimonious dispute that broke out between Songea's area commissioner and Ruvuma Regional Commissioner Makwaia: Did the former harbor RDA sympathies and was he sabotaging the execution of central orders to place TANU branch secretaries in the ex-RDA villages? Did the latter undermine the success of the party's policies by disparaging Matetereka village? Allegations and counterallegations drew TANU's executive secretary at headquarters, Kisumo, and Kawawa into their audience and prompted a regional inquiry.[18] For the regional commissioner, the stakes in being well-aligned with how the wind was blowing—and also thus perceived—appear to have been as high as he likely suspected. As usual, it all came down to the hard-to-predict president. Having fought a running battle with the ex-RDA villages,[19] the commissioner had apparently bet on the wrong horse: shortly after a delegation from Matetereka had complained to Nyerere personally about the commissioner's refusal to give the village the support it had been promised, he was dismissed from his post.[20] Autonomous and visible local initiatives in the main meant potential trouble to local officials, and this was precisely what generations of them made of Matetereka: a village of "troublemakers."[21]

Managing the Local

How a succession of Ruvuma regional commissioners attempted to handle the RDA's presence in their domain gives a good sense of the range of strategies they employed to keep their local realms under control and manage central perceptions. Significant interest in close cooperation with the RDA and drawing its leadership into the state's developmental apparatus in the early phases of Michael Haule's (1963–1964), Peter Walwa's (1964–1965), and Edward Barongo's (1965–1968) tenures could be read as a strategy of "absorption." It simultaneously sought closer control over the association and might have allowed the commissioners to claim the association's successes as their own. Conversely, the consternation that greeted the institutionalization of the RDA's independence from the state in 1965, when a new governing body drawn entirely from the villages and no longer including any official representation was instituted, and the quick souring of relations when newcomer commissioners discovered the RDA's independent streak are testimony to the problems that the failure of this absorption strategy created for officials.

If absorbing the association was not an option, at a minimum officials needed a sense of control over its activities and the flow of information about it. Problematically, the association did not prove pliable. Barongo, for instance, was clearly ill at ease in this situation: at a regional meeting, he demanded to see the association's books,[22] and then—whether out of a sincere concern about what was happening in his own backyard (it could backfire on him) or in an attempt to undercut the association (his life would be less complicated without it)—he accused Millinga of using the RDA for his own material benefit. Although the RDA village managers present at the meeting assured him that there was no such problem (Ibbott 1970, 91), Barongo nonetheless fired off an exasperated call for relief to TANU headquarters and the president. With all the publicity the association was attracting, he was desperate for a measure of control; failing that, with his letter he would at least have washed his hands of any potential troubles in his local kingdom:

> As these schemes have very much spread in Ruvuma Region, and as resulting from the attention of the President to the villages various people come to see their development, . . . the [regional TANU] meeting requests headquarters to deploy a special delegation to come and look into the state of development of the R.D.A. and all new settlements in the region and to give its recommendations. This delegation should have one member who is a specialist in accounting. . . . Because the Honourable President wants a plan [mpango] of the Ruvuma Development Association I have sent to him the complete report about these problems.[23]

If the association could not be absorbed or its activities more closely controlled, diverting the center's attention away from it was another option for avoiding potentially unfavorable comparisons and embarrassments. Thus, Nyerere had to override attempts by both Barongo and Walwa, his predecessor in Ruvuma, to route presidential visits away from the RDA in 1965 and 1966 (Ibbott 1970, 66, 86). Persistent attempts to build up and actively publicize projects such as Mlale and Njoomlole that were more closely associated with the state fall under the same rubric (see chapter 2).

Failing diversions, bad-mouthing the association was also an option. Barongo's and his agricultural officer's feeding Nyerere reports that the RDA villages refused to follow agricultural advice and improperly spaced their tobacco may well have been so motivated. That several such attempts backfired on officials only underlined the problem the association represented: without the RDA, there would have been no public humiliation for Barongo and the agricultural officer when Nyerere personally measured the spacing of Litowa's tobacco and pronounced it unobjectionable.

Life without the association would certainly have been easier for a number of officials. Witness, for instance, the RDA's response to a report by a group of teachers college principals who had been scheduled to spend two days at Litowa to learn about ujamaa in late 1968. The visitors—whose ranks included Martin Chengula, who from mid-1969 was Ruvuma Region's representative on TANU's Central Committee—spent just two hours at the village before escaping to the nearby mission complex at Peramiho and going on a day trip to the shores of Lake Nyasa. Despite the brevity of their visit, their report criticized the school at Litowa for following a curriculum inappropriate for ujamaa and complained about an emerging class society at the village on the basis of having seen some new houses being constructed while some people were still living in old huts. The RDA's outspoken rebuttal, copied—as had been the principals' report—to Nyerere, among others, accused the visitors of "daylight thieving" of the public monies expended on a study trip that they had not taken seriously: "This visit is an example of so much we have to put up with from visitors. Are we to take any notice of what they say when there is no real interest, perhaps even dislike of Ujamaa, and it is said by people with[out?] practical experience?" (reproduced in Ibbott 1970, 269). Such outspokenness gave Walwa, too, ample reason to resent the association. Unlike his direct subordinates, who—in Ruvuma as in West Lake—were easily cowed into sycophancy, the association's people could not, apparently, hold their peace. Here is Ibbott, displeased with Walwa's insistence on the purchase of useless Caterpillar tractors, succumbing to the temptation to engage in some needling:

> I was interested to know the President's views and on his visit to Litowa the next day, while we were discussing with him and his party in our kitchen[,] I brought up the subject of machines. He [Nyerere] laid his hand on Walwa's arm, laughed and said that our friend Walwa couldn't wait, he wanted his big machines now, well he couldn't have them and so on. It probably could have been said with a little more respect for Walwa's feelings! (239)

Dealing with Troublemakers

Views that were critical of flagship initiatives registered as did uncontrollable local activities: for local officials, they were obstacles in the way of producing results as well as perils insofar as they could bring unwanted scrutiny. One therefore did not ask questions about the reasons "troublemakers" might have for their objections and protests; one shut them down with threats, arrests, and—if necessary—violence.

During the Handeni campaign, for instance, alarming news came in from Kwabaya village: a local man had stood up at a meeting and told a "story from the reign of the Germans and the British":

> He said that there came a "liar" [mtu mmoja 'muongo'] by the name of J.K. Nyerere and he [Nyerere] told us that we should join TANU to get Uhuru [freedom, independence] so that we should govern ourselves and so that we would buy "Tembo" beer at the market and so that we should not be paying taxes.

The reporting official's first reaction was to request "steps" against the subversive speaker and, two months later, specifically his arrest (as well as that of four other "troublemakers" at Kwabaya).[24] The detention of these five, as well as seven others from Sindeni village, sparked popular protests. In response, the authorities took 150 people from Kwabaya into temporary custody; 46 remained under arrest for a longer time. Further arrests followed at Sindeni.[25] At Chanika village, people were likewise locked up on several occasions in 1968/1969 because they refused to move to Kitumbi.[26] Nine men from Kwanyanje village were also arrested under tax and compulsory cultivation violation charges, although, as the local divisional executive officer explained, the real issue was that they had started a village at a site "without approval of any committee."[27] A complaint received by TANU headquarters alleged that the executive officer also had at least two houses at Kwanyanje torn down to force people to move.[28]

Similar scenes unfolded in Walwa's West Lake campaign. Already at the Bukoba Cinema Hall meeting, where Walwa had proclaimed his villagization offensive in his "war" for development, he was confronted with pointed opposition. Musoke (1971, 4–5) reports on one man's speech:

> While agreeing that a war had been started, he went on to remind the Regional Commissioner and his fellow delegates that the twentieth century so far had witnessed two great World Wars, both initiated by the Germans. . . . But due to the rash means used by Hitler, the menace he caused to the rest of the world and the losses he inflicted on the German people, everybody now attributes the failure or defeat of Germany to him. He went on to ask if the Regional Commissioner and other leaders . . . were not following this fascist trend and hence risking ultimate failure.

This was quite enough for Walwa who "interrupted and accused the speaker of breeding ill-will" (5) before declaring the discussion closed.

Within a few weeks, however, the speech's sentiment found echoes in the villages. One report from Kamachuma related how a local ringleader, likely the same man who had made the speech at the Cinema Hall meeting, had declared that a group of approximately twenty people scheduled to move had refused to go anywhere—even if they were to be threatened with rifles—because there was a lack of food, housing, and water at the new settlements (and making things worse, there was also a lion).[29] Another report complained about a group that was stirring up trouble at Omurunazi. Alarmingly, in a subversion and mockery of the symbols of the state not uncommon in the repertoire of Tanzanian and African subjects,[30] this group reportedly "had been singing 'TANU breaks/destroys the nation' [*TANU yavunja nchi*]"[31]—this being a subversive take on the lyrics of the party's anthem "TANU Builds the Nation." Likewise, another group, defecting from Rugazi, was observed "singing to themselves rubbish like TANU NEJENGEIZA, instead of singing TANU builds the nation, making it mean that TANU was a tormenter."[32] Upon receiving such reports, the regional administrative secretary wasted no time in instructing the Bukoba area commissioner "to make sure that this sabotage [*uharibifu*] ceases."[33] The area commissioner's telegram to his subordinates was equally unequivocal:

If I hear a leader or anybody in the District talk so as to endanger the plans or activities of the new villages, I will take harsh steps against him [*nitamchukulia hatua kali*], and it will be your first time to lock somebody up. You should explain to everybody in your division that if there is any problem they should immediately fetch you or me, or send for the Honourable Regional Commissioner.[34]

But problems lingered. Two months later, the area commissioner reported to the regional office that "the state of the policy of starting these new villages in Bukoba District is very bad; we are taking a very bad hit, and it is therefore necessary that we watch them [the people] very carefully."[35]

Authority Must Be Defended: The West Lake Affair and Its Resolution in Context

That local officials acted as autocrats with a pronounced intolerance toward open discussion, critique, or opposition is in part explicable by their structural position within the state apparatus. They had to avoid attracting unfavorable attention from superiors, and in particular the president, and they could not afford "obstacles" in the way of producing results. The upshot was authoritarian ways of operating that frequently went against central intentions and guidelines and that—in the context of ujamaa vijijini— ran counter to the spirit of the policy, undermined its chances of success, and prevented problems in implementation from being acknowledged and addressed.

But a severe curtailment of the space for open discussion was a product and feature not just of how local officials operated. At the national level, too, deviation from unquestioning support of the party-state's actions was anathema, even where criticisms appeared perfectly in accordance with official positions. This is well illustrated in the national leadership's adjudication of an open dispute over the conduct of Walwa's villagization campaign that pitted the commissioner against two local MPs in what came to be known as the "West Lake Affair." Surprisingly, given the nature of Walwa's campaign, the national leadership's first priority was to severely sanction Walwa's critics. Why was there such an urgent sense that Walwa's authority, like that of TANU's Central Committee in the context of the RDA's destruction, had to be defended?

In part, the quashing of criticism in West Lake was simply a testimony to Walwa's skill in and capacity for manipulating information and the framing of the situation. But in this latter respect his successful negotiation of the affair also crucially depended on the available frames of legitimation and constructions of authority into which he tapped. Walwa's self-positioning as a purveyor of development was important in this. While vis-à-vis the peasantry this positioning produced an authorizing effect as it invoked the contrast between their conservative incompetence and officials' modernizing leadership, vis-à-vis his fellow politician-critics this framing worked to undergird his authority in interplay with other frames of legitimation. This interlocking is familiar from the destruction of the RDA: the notion that the single party, shaped in the anticolonial struggle, stood for the interests of the whole nation made criticism of any of its actions *a priori* suspicious. But this was also especially true when the target of criticism was a development campaign, which, by definition, had the good of the nation at heart. Development lent itself especially readily to conjuring a neatly segregated political space: development's supporters on one side, and its automatically illegitimate enemies on the other. In a context in which the party constructed its policies, and especially its development campaigns, as a continuation of the anticolonial struggle, now fought against neocolonial enemies, this segregation into friend and enemy was only heightened. These historically contingent framings of legitimacy were thus constitutive of a situation in which the single-party state's development initiatives permitted no criticisms.

Walwa's Campaign in the Spotlight

Already in March 1968, a month before Walwa's resettlement campaign commenced, TANU's National Executive Committee (NEC) had received a report that the MP for Karagwe, Gervazi Kaneno, was obstructing the commissioner's developmental efforts in West Lake. According to the then national executive secretary of TANU Pius Msekwa (1977, 45), Kaneno was reported to be "misleading the people by deliberately misinterpreting some of the words used by Mwalimu [Nyerere] in the policy pamphlet 'Socialism and Rural Development.'" About this, the "NEC was, of course, displeased." Walwa then accused Kaneno and Jeremiah Bakampenja, the MP for Ihangiro, of being obstructionist and anti-TANU in a speech in Parliament (43–44).[36]

In early July, two months into the West Lake villagization campaign, the two MPs shot back and, likewise in Parliament, complained about Walwa and his villagization campaign. (Beholden not just to the party for their nomination but also to their constituents for their election, they were not the only MPs to show a lack of enthusiasm for villagization campaigns instituted by executive officials.[37]) In addition to accusing Walwa of abusing his power for personal gain, they charged that his resettlement campaign had been against the party's policy because it had used force, had lacked planning, and had dumped people in the "wilderness" (*maporini*) without any support. Walwa had also been undermining the MPs' ability to fulfill their political leadership role by prohibiting them from calling meetings and by telling people that they had made a mistake in electing them. Kaneno called Walwa a "Bush-Governor" for his "savage or barbarous behavior" and a "very big dictator" (TANU 1968, 4–13; compare Thoden van Velzen and Sterkenburg 1972, 259).

Walwa rebuked these claims in the assembly. There had been months of planning and informational meetings in the villages. With respect to coercion, he both invoked the higher authority of the party leadership and declared such means to be necessary in dealing with childlike peasants. Had not Nyerere himself stressed the need to have "laws to make it necessary [*kuwalazimisha*] for people to work?" And the second vice president had emphasized the same point (TANU 1968, 16). True, interrupted Kawawa, who was present during the session: after all, every district had minimum acreage bylaws on the books (17). Overall, Walwa added in a long allegorical discourse that likened the birth and building of a nation to the development of a child, Tanzania had now entered the "third phase" of its development: this was the "phase of *Discipline* [in English] for the child" (18): "With the Arusha Declaration, now is the time of *discipline. Yes* [in English]. Now, with any sense, we will prepare [*tutamtandika*] the child, not coddle him [*hatumbembelezi*]" (19). Walwa, the developmental general, was again laying claim to the paternal authority that he was required to exercise in the interest of the development of his underdeveloped, childlike charges.

Criticism as Treason

This éclat sparked a TANU commission of inquiry to look into the political discord in West Lake. In the policy paper the meaning of which Kaneno had allegedly distorted, Nyerere had written, "Viable socialist communities can only be established with willing members; the task of leadership and of Government is not to try and force this kind of development, but to explain, encourage, and participate" (Nyerere 1968, 356). Against the background of such presidential declarations—and given the character, as documented above, of the West Lake campaign—one might assume that Walwa was facing a reckoning. Instead, after ominous rumblings (the *Nationalist* of October 18, 1968: "'Trouble Makers To Be Dealt With' says Nyerere"), TANU's NEC expelled the two MPs from the party and thus from Parliament, having found "at no time, anywhere during the inquiry, . . . evidence suggesting that the people were forced into Ujamaa Villages," as the October 11, 1968, *Nationalist* had reported. How did the MPs end up troublemakers rather than whistleblowers? Why did Walwa's paternal(istic) authority over a childlike population have to be so vigorously defended against their criticism?

Walwa's well-executed information management campaign, aimed in particular at the commission of inquiry's fact-finding mission to the region, played an important part. Thus, the commission would "discover" well-rehearsed local testimonies that invoked the right kind of framings. According to Musoke (1971, 8–9), at Rugazi village, for instance, the regional TANU chairman had visited and told the settlers "that the M.P.s for Karagwe and Ihangiro were opposing the whole scheme and were therefore 'colonialists.' He asked them to say this if they should be questioned by the Commission." The village obliged the regional chairman: in Rugazi's letter to the commission (whose final report included about two dozen such letters from various villages, offices of TANU and the government, and other institutions), the village's chairman affirmed Rugazi's commitment to the Arusha Declaration, expressed profuse gratitude to the leadership for the aid rendered to the village, expressed hope for more, and otherwise studiously avoided any mention of trouble or coercion (TANU 1968, 36). Of course, when Musoke (1971, 6) interviewed forty-two settlers at the village, thirty-six of them reported having been forced to move there and two said that they had been locked up by the divisional executive officer and told upon their release that "worse things would happen to them" if they did not move to Rugazi. Interviewees "also stated that, so far as they knew these M.P.s were not against the schemes as such but against the means used" (8–9). But faced with an official inquiry, it was clearly safer for all involved not to cross a powerful figure like the regional commissioner.

Likewise, the fix was in at the commission's hearing before the TANU Regional Executive Committee. H. U. E. Thoden van Velzen and J. J. Sterkenburg (1972, 259) describe the scene outside the meeting:

> Placards which read: "Parliament is a tool for Tanzania, individualism is an enemy to the nation"; "We refute statements by Kaneno and Bakampenja, we must be transferred to the new villages"; "The [Arusha] Declaration is the poor man's weapon, well done Walwa, a staunch leader"; were carried around. Petitions were offered to the commission and accepted notwithstanding the protests of the M.P.s who alleged that TANU leaders had prepared them long before.

As is apparent from these slogans, Walwa's suppression of information and dissenting voices was then only one side of his winning strategy. The other was his ability to present his actions as legitimate and, conversely, position the MPs' criticisms as illegitimate, subversive, even treasonous. This was accomplished by adroitly tapping into readily accessible, mutually reinforcing discourses of authority and legitimacy that produced an almost Manichean divide of the political space: on one side stood the party, the defender of development and the nation; on the other side one could find only enemies of the people.

As had Walwa's self-defense in Parliament, the slogans on display in West Lake again positioned him as a paternal developer; even his charges appreciated the need for his authority: "We must be transferred to the new villages." This positioning on the side of development, on the part of Walwa and the party, put any critics onto dangerous terrain: criticisms of the actions of the purveyors of development were quickly suspect. The West Lake placards explicitly raised this specter: "The [Arusha] Declaration is the poor man's weapon" and "individualism [i.e., the opposite of the official policy of ujamaa] is an enemy to the nation." To the October 11, 1968, *Nationalist,* the MPs' questionable motivations were therefore obvious: their actions were "clearly designed to keep the poor still poor and to make the poor people in the region permanent victims of the terror of feudalism."

Read from one angle, these castings show how the party's self-positioning specifically as a developmentalist vanguard functioned to undergird its claim to a monopoly on legitimate authority: critics were beyond the pale in good part because as critics of the party's actions they quickly ended up being positioned as "enemies of development," and hence of "the people." But this discursive field can be read in the opposite direction as well: a general claim, underpinned by broader discourses of political legitimacy, that the party was the only legitimate voice in Tanzanian politics also shaped the construction of development. That the West Lake Affair was dominated by the question of who was on the side of TANU—rather than whether the MPs' allegations had any substance to them—shows just how salient these broader discourses of legitimacy were in shaping the politics of the country. Walwa knew how to position himself: "I do not give orders from my own head. . . . The orders given are not mine, but those of the state. I protect Tanu constitution and party orders," he told the hearing in West Lake (quoted in Thoden van Velzen and Sterkenburg 1972, 259). On the other hand, the MPs, the commission of inquiry's final report underlined, were "far from Tanu and their aim was to disrupt the policy of Tanu" (260). The question of loyalty to TANU was so important and consequential because it, in and of itself, determined the legitimacy of one's position. It was simply inconceivable that one "could be against TANU, Afro-Shirazi Party [Zanzibar's ruling party], the Government and the President but not against the nation," as the October 29, 1966, *Nationalist* proclaimed when students were protesting the new National Service requirement. As Nyerere put it in a speech in West Lake reported on by the August 29, 1968, *Standard:* "A leader who disagrees with the policy of Tanu and destroys people's unity, cannot be our friend; he is our enemy and we must take necessary steps" (quoted in Thoden van Velzen and Sterkenburg 1972, 260).

While this Manichean structuration of the political universe was underpinned by TANU's positioning as the purveyor of development, it also drew on broader discourses of legitimacy. A key one revolved around the party's roots in the anticolonial struggle. For Nyerere, this origin provided the argument for why alternative parties were unnecessary (and suspect): after all, nationalist, anticolonial parties like TANU were not "factions—but nationalist movements" representing "the interests and aspirations of the whole nation" (Nyerere 1966, 198). This framing also played into the West Lake Affair. In the *Nationalist*'s October 17, 1968, glossing, for instance, the NEC thought about the dispute in the following terms: "For TANU to fit its historical role as the vanguard of the people in their efforts to consolidate the national independence, discipline and democracy must be accepted and observed both by the leaders and the people." As the anticolonial party, TANU remained the champion of the nation's salvation after independence—and thus legitimately demanded the same unqualified allegiance from all as it had during the anticolonial struggle. Those who refused to give it were traitors to the nation—or so Nyerere would suggest when, according to the March 25, 1971, *Nationalist,* he "criticized people who were unwilling to live in Ujamaa villages [and] compared them with people who did not want Uhuru [Independence]." The branding of the West Lake MPs as "colonialists" thus effectively tapped into this specific idiom of political legitimacy (as had the accusations, in a different context, that the RDA was serving foreign and neocolonial interests).

As, especially from 1968 on, the party's policies were increasingly couched in a hardening language of a "struggle for socialism," and internal and external events were filtered through this lens as well as the prism of "the party versus its neocolonial enemies," this division of the political universe into friend and enemy only sharpened.[38]

In the context of the West Lake Affair, the martial idiom of a struggle against the enemies of socialism was for instance reflected in a warning issued by Nyerere during a tour of the region and reported in the August 27, 1968, *Nationalist*:

> Those who oppose the equality of man, those who want to exploit others, are enemies of the Arusha Declaration. But nothing is going to deter us in our struggle to bring about equality and the leaders have no option because it has been resolved by TANU. Those who oppose us will have to be taught but if they resist it would be imperative for us to find a medicine for them.

Such talk about class enemies, echoed as well in the commission of inquiry's denunciation of the MPs as obstacles in the path toward a socialist society and defenders of vested interests and local class distinctions (Thoden van Velzen and Sterkenburg 1972, 260), in fact resonated with special force in West Lake, where TANU had long fought the local "feudalistic" *nyarubanja* land-tenure system.[39] Branding Bakampenja a perpetrator of "the terror of feudalism" who, because he had "a shamba [field] in Tukutuku, near the Ujamaa Village," saw "the Ujamaa Village as a threat to his feudalistic ambitions," the October 11, 1968, *Nationalist* invoked this local context. In West Lake's particular setting, a broad discourse in which critics were easily cast as class enemies thus found an especially ready application and contributed to a local situation in which, as S. Kinyondo (1971, 46) comments, "the Party tends to suspect people are against them and is really very sensitive even to a constructive and open discussion."[40]

It is clear, then, in this context, that development in Tanzania did not operate entirely in the way of the "anti-politics machine" that James Ferguson (1994, 267) has influentially argued it to be.[41] Of course, in Tanzania, too, the constant invocation of expertise—for instance in practices of planning—did function as a claim that questions in development were (1) susceptible to technical solutions, (2) hence also definitively and authoritatively "solved" by the interventions of "experts," and (3) by implication beyond further discussion once such solutions had been implemented. But not everything in development in Tanzania was thus "rendered technical" and, by means of this "anti-political" move, repositioned onto a nonpolitical terrain devoid of any recognition of the existence of divergent interests, political economy, and struggle. As is especially evident in its framing as a struggle for socialism, development in Tanzania was also quite explicitly a very highly political undertaking. So much so, in fact, that it quickly brought forth that most quintessentially political idiom of "friend and enemy"—as the motives of critics were readily impugned with accusations of selfishness and anti-egalitarianism.

Conclusion

The October 21, 1968, *Nationalist* glossed the central issue in the West Lake Affair thus: "It is one thing to criticise. It is another thing to oppose. We believe in the concept of criticism and self-criticism. . . . But we have nothing to do with the concept of Opposition." If the West Lake Affair demonstrated anything, however, it was that the line between legitimate criticism and illegitimate opposition was prone to being drawn so as to dramatically shrink the space for the former. Although he refers to post-independence Ghana, Robert Price (1974, 190) describes well the overall effect of this: in Tanzania, too, there prevailed a generalized "bias . . . against institutionalization of the principle that public criticism of government policy is a legitimate activity. Those in authority come to perceive any criticism of their policies or actions as direct threats to their status as rulers, that is, as big men, since two of the defining characteristics of such status are, on the one hand, a monopoly of responsibility for public affairs, and, on the other hand, deference to that responsibility on the part of those without authority." The results of such practices of authority and concomitant modes of governing were plain to see in Tanzanian villagization: the lack of interest in careful analysis and planning once those in authority had made a decision, the self-censorship and repression of critical views and even frank assessments, and the blanket insistence of leaders on their authority over both peasants and subordinate officials.

The modality of governing this book has traced was the effect of the complex interplay in a distinctive assemblage of a historically contingent set of practices. That development was such a central preoccupation of government presented fertile ground for a configuration of governing around a paternalistic, unassailable, self-valorizing, and self-validating authority. But this particular elaboration of developmental governing was not somehow automatic or inherent in development as such: it was worked out in historically specific discursive framings and practices that in their complex assemblage shaped and constituted one another. These ranged from particular constructions of peasants and—juxtaposed with them—officials that took shape within a distinctive framing of developmentalist time and practices of planning; cultures of authority encapsulated in idioms of generational hierarchies; particular constructions of political legitimacy centered in the notion of a national-movement party (still) defined in opposition to its (neo)colonial enemies; a specific coloring of development as "socialist," which heightened a martial distinction between friends and enemies; and a positioning of subordinate officials within Tanzania's state apparatus that incentivized sycophantic yes-manship up the chain of command and ferocious intolerance of criticism in the opposite direction. If the political universe they inhabited was thus "structured," observing officials like Regional Commissioner Walwa negotiate it also clearly shows them not as mere puppets in a grand structural orchestration, but as agents who actively and skillfully engaged and shaped the possibilities for self-positioning within this terrain of developmental government in Nyerere's Tanzania.

It was in the immediate aftermath of the West Lake Affair that Nyerere found himself pondering the subject of "Freedom and Development." In light of how the Affair was resolved, his words in that October 1968 paper were already beginning to ring hollow: "Everyone must be allowed to speak freely, and everyone must be listened to. It does not matter how unpopular a man's ideas, or how mistaken the majority think him. . . . Every Tanzanian . . . , every Member of Parliament, . . . must have the freedom to speak without fear of intimidation" (Nyerere 1973, 62–63). Even if this nod to freedom was given some substance by the demotion in late 1968 of Walwa's West Lake administrative secretary to the post of town clerk and Walwa's transferral to Kilimanjaro (he was retired from political service shortly after),[42] overall the West Lake Affair only contributed to an atmosphere in which the freedom to speak freely that Nyerere heralded would hardly extend beyond his private study. In the end, the president was not ready to circumscribe his own or the party-state's blanket prerogative to command. Indeed, if the practices of developmental governing that emerged in Tanzania—and of which Nyerere was a key shaper and practitioner—added up to anything, it was precisely to a glaring violation of the president's own proclamation that "no one person has the right to say, 'I am the people.' No Tanzanian has the right to say 'I know what is good for Tanzania and the others must do it'" (70).

6 The Brave Parsimonious World of Materialist-Utilitarian Analysis

> If the "searchlight" function of the proposed theory and the absence of equally
> sweeping counterhypotheses inhibit the discovery of inconvenient facts, empirical
> regularities may be perceived where none exist. The initial universalist presumption
> that a single theory *might* bear on all the cases thus dances dangerously close to a
> self-fulfilling prophecy.
>
> —David Woodruff, "Commerce and Demolition in Tsarist and Soviet Russia"

AT THE CLOSE of this account that has stressed actors', motivations', and actions' constitution within the thick matrices of discursive practices, it is time to revisit a far more straightforward and parsimonious story about Tanzania. As materialist-utilitarian analyses—pervasive in political science and beyond—would have it, Tanzania's experience with rural development is well captured as a tale of politicians who, as slaves to their own narrowly defined material interests and those of their well-connected, urban clients, diverted public policy to serve these private ends. "Development" policies failed to produce benefits for the majority of Tanzanian peasants because this was simply not their objective. Why not succinctly summarize the Tanzanian experience thus?

This chapter's first point is that the empirical record does not bear out the materialist-utilitarian storyline on the count of either its portrayal of the outcomes of policy or the motivations behind it. This challenge of materialist-utilitarian accounts' empirical narrative is not just an academic quibble. Their misreading of the Tanzanian experience lends apparent empirical support to a theory of the state that conceptualizes it as little more than a collection of maximizers of private, self-regarding interests.[1] In the 1980s and 1990s, this reading of the African state in particular as inevitably and invariably self-seeking greatly contributed to a general skepticism about whether it was an institution that could ever be entrusted with more than the most minimal role in the economy. Although the resulting "free market" agenda was not necessarily wholly endorsed by all exponents of materialist-utilitarian arguments (see, for instance, Robert Bates's programmatically entitled 1989 *Beyond the Miracle of the Market*), this conceptualization of the state thus functioned as a political twin to neoclassical economic arguments: in combination, they acted as the intellectual foundation of an antistatism that manifested itself in the drive to "roll back the state" and "free the market" under structural adjustment programs. That the historical record does not offer unequivocal support for this theory of the state challenges its claim to universality—as well as the generic antistatist policy prescriptions feeding off it even today.[2]

Secondly, this chapter examines how materialist-utilitarian accounts work with evidence. A forensic analysis of how one canonical text, Bates's *Markets and States in Tropical Africa,* employs Tanzanian evidence to make its argument raises some bigger questions about method, explanation, and practices of inquiry. The chapter shows that *Markets and States'* practice and style of argumentation is rooted in an ontology of political action that assumes a tight link between "interests"—construed as universal, narrowly materialist, and self-seeking—and "outcomes." This assumption has important effects on the empirical narrative Bates produces. Going in one direction, it tints the lenses through which Bates's account apprehends the outcomes it observes: they tend to be portrayed as tightly functional to the material interests that supposedly lie behind their production. Going in the opposite direction, the assumption of a tight link between interests and outcomes sanctions the adoption of a strategy whereby supposedly causal interests are not in fact observed but "inferred" from the very outcomes they are said to causally determine. The narrow ontology of human action that holds this materialist-utilitarian research practice together militates against a more open and probing reading of empirical evidence and the assemblage of such evidence into a narrative that might do anything but support the paradigm.

The antidote to these problems that this book has been seeking to practice has two central components. The first is replacing the *assumption* that actions are driven by narrowly material self-interest with an *empirical inquiry* into actors' varied motivations—and their broader situatedness, which shapes them, their "interests," and their repertoires of actions. The second is understanding "outcomes" as typically messy and multidimensional assemblages that are far more than a straightforward reflection of interests and intentions. The kind of explanatory account yielded by this type of inquiry is a programmatically unparsimonious engagement, eschewing a model of hard causality, of the many dimensions that go into shaping the crooked timber of human history.[3] The lack, in such an account, of a neat model of politics and actors, and of universally applicable laws covering general phenomena, will disappoint those social scientists who perceive the uncovering of such laws as the only true purpose of science. But if this book's foray into Tanzania's experience in rural development has shown anything, it is that explaining this history requires, to borrow John Gaddis's (2001, 312) phrase, "a web-like, or ecological, sense of reality." The many interlocking dimensions of such a reality cannot be segregated out as "variables" that act in contextually and temporally invariant ways.[4] Nor is such a reality one of "cases" of historically invariant general phenomena that could thus be subsumed under "covering laws." Nothing of value is gained from pretending otherwise; indeed, much is often lost. In the end, Gaddis reminds us, one can only "build universally applicable generalizations about necessarily simple matters. . . . Because life is complicated, so is history" (302).

Politics of Interests

Materialist-utilitarian analyses of Tanzania's experience with rural development come in two sets of vocabularies. "Dar Marxist" accounts and those leaning on this perspective understand the state's interventions in agriculture and elsewhere as part of an emergent "bureaucratic bourgeoisie's" struggle to outrun a "commercial bourgeoisie" in the race for the position of dominant class.[5] Agricultural policies are an extension of this struggle, as is the exploitation of peasants that results from them. Claims Issa Shivji (2010, 120) retrospectively, "The various villagisation programmes since independence became top-down centrist projects, allowing more intense exploitation and the siphoning off of surplus generated in the agrarian sector."

Though couched in the ostensibly more social "scientific" vocabulary of interest-group politics and rational choice, New Political Economy accounts—in their ascendency in the 1980s and 1990s—in fact made very similar arguments. Bates's *Markets and States in Tropical Africa,* a canonical application of the rational choice approach and the "economics of politics" to African and comparative politics, is a central text in this literature.[6] It features Tanzania as one of several cases adduced to show that the politically unconnected rural poor typically suffer at the hands of development policies designed to serve the interests of political elites and their largely urban, well-connected clients. Argues Bates (1981, 121), "Owners and workers in industrial firms, economic and political elites, privileged farmers and the managers of public bureaucracies—these constitute the development coalition in contemporary Africa. It is they who reap the benefits of the policy choices made in formulating development programs."[7] In the Tanzania-specific literature, Michael Lofchie (1989, 191) is the most prominent proponent of this argument, claiming that "the agricultural policies of the Tanzanian government were framed and implemented by politicians whose political and economic base was exclusively urban. Tanzania's agricultural policies thus provide one of Africa's clearest examples of a system designed to transfer economic resources from the countryside to the city."[8]

Differences in vocabulary aside, in both class-analytical and New Political Economy accounts self-regarding material interests drive policy, and its outcomes are thereby explained as well. This book has rendered a portrait of Tanzanian rural development interventions that points to the importance in their messy production of many other dimensions than just such self-seeking material and political calculations. However, material-utilitarian accounts not only fail to see the importance of dimensions beyond generic self-seeking interest in the production of policy and its outcomes; they also paint a highly questionable picture with respect even to those dimensions of the story that they do focus their attention on: policy's distributional impact and policymakers' intentions in this material regard. While Tanzanian policy did not produce many beneficial results for the agricultural sector and peasants, this was not a failure that primarily resulted from "exploitation" in either intent or effect. In terms of intentions, agricultural and rural development policy was typically pro-rural and antiprivilege; and in terms of distributional outcomes, the overall picture is not one in which politicians and well-connected groups amassed outsized benefits at the expense of the rural majority.

Combating Exploitation in Tanzania: Mere Rhetoric?

In terms of their broad thrust, the Tanzanian state's policies are thus hard to reconcile with the storyline of materialist-utilitarian accounts. Indeed, government policy under Nyerere exhibited a veritable penchant for curbing elite enrichment and promoting egalitarian goals. Thus, Henry Bienen (1970, 147) observes about the 1960s that "there is less open tolerance among national leaders in Tanzania than in the United States for what might be called in America normal patronage politics." Likewise, Ali Mazrui (1991, 64) notes the Tanzanian government's "heroic effort" in its struggle from the mid-1960s well into the 1980s against the exploitation of regular Tanzanians and especially peasants at the hands of state and other elites: "It is even arguable," he writes, "that Tanzania has tried harder in this particular field than any other African country," notwithstanding that such efforts often did not quite succeed. This preoccupation with fighting inequalities especially between the rural poor and privileged urban populations was manifested, on the one hand, in the attention given the rural sector—for instance in the massive resources expended on ujamaa and villagization—and, on the other, in efforts to curb the privileges and the ability to acquire wealth, especially of civil servants and politicians.[9]

The general flavor of the government's stance on these matters is well captured in Nyerere's drive to institute a culture of frugality in public life. Having been served orange juice at a reception during a 1965 state visit to China, Nyerere banned the use of (imported and expensive) alcoholic beverages at State House receptions: in a national radio address entitled "Frugality," he told Tanzanians that Chinese "Government officials too, use cars only when it is really necessary for their job—and then the cars are small and cheap ones. . . . Some of the things we have done in the recent past, like buying big cars for the Regional Commissioners, were bad mistakes of this kind. They must not be repeated" (Nyerere 1966, 332–333). The colonial governor's Mercedes-Benz that Nyerere had been using was retired to a museum.

In line with this emerging focus, party and higher government officials took drastic pay cuts in 1966.[10] In 1967, the Arusha Declaration explicitly warned that "if we are not careful we might get to the position where the real exploitation in Tanzania is that of the town dwellers exploiting the peasants" (Nyerere 1968, 242–243). To forestall such a development, a set of stringent Leadership Conditions were imposed on all party members holding official positions: they were barred from owning houses for rental purposes, owning shares in companies, having more than one income (their official one), and taking on directorship positions in businesses. While the Arusha Declaration did herald sweeping nationalizations that considerably expanded the state's involvement in the economy, it thus combined such measures with "a whole series of limitations on the freedom of state employees to benefit personally from their positions" (Coulson 1982, 183). Many politicians' reception of these conditions—a large number resigned their positions—bears testimony to their stringency.[11] Indeed, Lionel Cliffe (1991, 107) suggests that the mid-1967 resignation from his positions and self-imposed exile to Britain of Oscar Kambona, among a handful of the most powerful politicians in the country, had its roots in his opposition to the Leadership Conditions.[12]

In 1970, the Prevention of Corruption Ordinance (Amendment) Bill provided that officials of the government, party, and parastatals could at any point be called upon to declare their assets and account for how those assets had come into their possession. In an effective reversal of the dictum "innocent until proven guilty," officials who failed to give a satisfactory account faced up to five years in prison.[13] In 1971, TANU's party guidelines *Mwongozo* again renewed this emphasis on curbing government and party officials' privileges. In 1973, Nyerere suspended Parliament when it voted down a bill that would have made the tax code sharply more progressive; the bill was subsequently passed (Barkan 1979b, 75). In 1983, Nyerere's contention—voiced already before independence—that "corruption in a country should be treated in almost the same way you treat treason"[14] ushered in a National Economic Sabotage campaign that targeted illegal trading and racketeering, as well as other exploitative and corrupt practices (Bryceson 1993, 24–27).

These quite draconian measures showed significant results. The privileges of the urban higher and middle salariat, for instance, were dramatically eroded. Post-tax differentials between highest and lowest salaries and wages collapsed precipitously from a ratio of 33:1 in 1967, to 15:1 in 1974, and to 5:1 in 1981 (Mukandala 1983, 13). Absolute salary levels for government officials, compared to those in other African nations, were also very low: for those subsisting on official salaries, what Joel Barkan (1979a, 23) refers to as Tanzania's "harsh egalitarian ethic" had, by the late 1970s, produced conditions that can only be described as austere. While an entire economy of extralegal and illicit activities sprang up in response,[15] this takes away neither from the overall effects of these policies nor from the intentions they embodied. "It is," writes Rwekaza Mukandala (1983, 19), "very difficult to subscribe to the view that civil servants have become part of a bureaucratic bourgeoisie": "even if one considers the money acquired illegally, such cash, given the requirements of the leadership code, has either been squandered in consumption, stashed away in pillows and mattresses, or buried underground in playyards and chicken sheds. . . . Either way, a negative move for class reproduction."

Finally, to the extent to which the comparative economic well-being of urban and rural populations can be attributed to policy, it might also offer some clues regarding the existence of a bias against the rural sector. While comparing sectoral income trends is fraught with methodological and data problems,[16] Frank Ellis (1984, 36) suggests that "average non-farm incomes were subject to a steep real decline over this [1970–1980] period, and . . . the magnitude of their fall was probably greater than that of farm incomes." Coulson (1982, 199) cautiously concurs: "To summarize a complex situation: rural producers, urban workers, and upper income earners were all worse off at the end of the 1970s than they had been at the beginning. It is possible that rural producers took a somewhat smaller decline in their living standards than urban workers, though the statistics on which such a statement is based are unreliable." Vali Jamal and John Weeks (1993, 55) conclude more assertively that "the evidence indicates that in Tanzania there has been a dramatic shift in income from urban to rural areas, contradicting the view of a universal and permanent 'bias' towards urban development."[17] Contrary to Bates's diagnosis of a clear urban bias in the effects of policy, and Lofchie's (1989, 194–195) similar assertion that "Tanzania's urban dwellers have been immeasurably better off than their rural counterparts," the available evidence thus suggests that the rural sector did not fare worse than the urban areas.[18]

Making Tanzania a Case in Point:
Markets and States and the Tanzanian Evidence

Tanzania's persistent and quite effective antiprivilege efforts are hard to square with the image of a state bent on fortifying the position of politicians and the well-connected few. How, then, do materialist-utilitarian accounts arrive at this argument?

Marxist-inspired accounts typically did not overly concern themselves with collecting and weighing systematic evidence regarding their core tenet that class interests lay behind the state's actions—and that the result of these actions was, therefore, exploitation. Close scrutiny of evidence was neither the style nor, perhaps, the point. Shivji's essays, for instance, were in good part polemical interventions about undeniably existing privileges in society. Aspects of these arguments—dispelling a naive assumption that the nationalist postcolonial state was necessarily benevolent, and shedding light on the increasingly undemocratic drift of Tanzanian socialism—were important political interventions. But these analyses' readiness to find exploitation behind every state action also betrayed certain "holier than thou" tendencies.[19] The fact that officials earned a salary at all seemed to inevitably lead to the assessment that, therefore, the state's very *raison d'être* was its self-aggrandizement. What might have constituted counterevidence is not clear, as even interventions such as the Arusha Declaration with its Leadership Conditions, the 1971 *Mwongozo* guidelines, and the policy of ujamaa/villagization—all specifically aimed at curbing power-holders' and privileged classes' pursuit of their self-interests—were swiftly interpreted as mere rhetorical disguises behind the cover of which the bureaucratic bourgeoisie consolidated its self-serving control over surpluses.

Even from a sympathetic vantage point, close observers of the Tanzanian scene have therefore rightly criticized the formulaic nature of many such accounts.[20] Manfred Bienefeld (1986, 6), for instance, comments on "Marxist analyses that identify—or invent—endless numbers of 'petit [sic] bourgeoisies' to explain any and every twist and turn in public policy." With the analysis driven by an ontology that saw the political world populated by struggling classes, systematic evaluation of evidence was typically dispensed with.

The New Political Economy literature, couched in the language of rational choice, at least struck a very different posture. Its supposedly rigorous and evidence-based approach promised to shed class analysis's sins.[21] That it produced a very similar misreading of the Tanzanian experience suggests that skepticism of such claims is warranted.

How does this literature draw on evidence? And how do its research practices contribute to producing a misconstrual of the Tanzanian experience? The following close-up analysis of how Bates's *Markets and States* works with Tanzanian evidence to make the country's experience a case that supports its argument aims to shed light on these questions.

Contending that "the basic problem of farming in the developing countries is improper incentives for farmers," Bates's (1981, 2) analysis focuses chiefly on those agricultural policies that directly affect incentives, that is, prices. Given its broad explanatory goal—finding the reasons behind "shortfalls in agricultural production" and, more generally, the failure of "agricultural development" in sub-Saharan Africa—this narrow focus, shared by much of the New Political Economy literature,[22] leads to a neglect of the main thrust of Tanzania's efforts in rural development, the policy of ujamaa and villagization. But notwithstanding that the book thus adopts too narrow a purview when it comes to policy, what is its evidence on the formation and effect of policy and how is the evidence woven into an explanatory narrative?

Resource Flows between Sectors: Which Way Does the Bias Run?

One of the key pieces of evidence *Markets and States* presents on Tanzania concerns resource flows between different sectors in the country: "With less than 10 percent of its population in towns, its urban centers nonetheless secured 30 percent of the public expenditures under the state's first and second development plans," Bates (1981, 18) claims. This apparently disproportionate allocation of resources to urban centers is adduced as evidence that politically well-connected urban populations were favored.

Bates's source, a study by Edmund Clark (1978, 96), in fact states that 21—not 30—percent of "regional and ministerial spending" under Tanzania's First (1964–1969) and Second (1969–1974) Five-Year Plans were scheduled to go to towns. The 30 percent figure Bates picks up is not planned *expenditure,* but Clark's estimate of "development and consumption benefits" going to towns under the Second Five-Year Plan (the estimate for the First Plan is 29 percent). Although there are serious conceptual and data problems with Clark's "benefits" measure,[23] Bates might argue that this higher number is in fact a better indicator of bias than the lower planned expenditure figures: output is more important than input. Irrespective of whether one picks the higher number (30 and 29 percent of benefits) or the lower number (21 percent of planned spending going to towns), read together with the fact that only 10 percent of the population resided in towns, either seems to suggest a clear bias against the rural areas.

Until, that is, one reads these figures in their necessary context. In order to say something meaningful about a bias in resource flows, it is, in the first instance, imperative to look not just at the destination but also at the source of money. While the urban sector may have received a disproportionate share of expenditures per capita, it also *contributed* an even more disproportionate share: in terms of direct and indirect taxation, urban and rural areas contributed roughly 50 percent each to direct and indirect tax revenues (Clark 1978, 199; Huang 1976, 75). Towns thus paid in considerably more than twice what they received back in terms of planned spending (21 percent)—and close to twice what they received even in terms of Clark's "benefits" measure (29 and 30 percent).[24]

Reading Bates's suggestive numbers in context thus reverses the picture of bias: rather than against the rural sector, it appears to have been in favor of it. A study of 1965–1974 resource flows concurs with this inverted picture: "It seems that the rural areas have enjoyed a substantial surplus of benefits over taxes rendered in almost all years" (Amey 1978, 128). While no overall financial statistics are available for the post-1974 period of intense villagization-related activities, with these activities ongoing, the rural areas almost certainly received even greater attention from 1974 on.[25] (Villagization is generally hard to fit into Bates's logic. The very reordering of dispersed populations into nucleated villages stood to systematically reverse the peasantry's political and spatial marginalization and its institutional disorganization, the very conditions that, according to Bates, afford the state the opportunity to ignore and exploit the smallholder sector. And indeed, villagization in fact did create a rising tide of demands for resources and services—in the face of which Coulson [1977, 94] has wondered, "Why should the Government create impossible demands for services which it must have known it could not fulfill?")

In the end, however, a bias in resource flows is not simply a matter of calculating inflows to the two sectors versus outflows from them. In Tanzania, money whose origin can be traced to either the urban or the rural sector only accounted for about 6 percent of planned expenditures under the 1964–1969 and the 1969–1974 development plans—with far larger proportions coming from foreign aid (45 percent) and foreign borrowing (10 percent).[26] This already heavy reliance on outside financing only increased further in the second half of the 1970s.[27] Inevitably, any determination of "bias" is therefore not just a question of objective inflow versus outflow calculations but one that involves normative dimensions: what do standards of "fairness" demand? It is also a question that involves quite intractable problems of assessment: what proportion of a particular expenditure's benefits accrues to which sector? Finally, it is a question that involves difficult issues of practicality: are expenditures of a certain type even feasible in particular locations? For instance, does fairness demand that a hospital be located in the rural areas? Would such a location be a workable and efficient choice? And is a hospital located in town, but serving the surrounding rural areas, in fact symptomatic of an antirural bias? None of these questions have straightforward answers.

But, bearing in mind these caveats, to the extent to which statements about biases are meaningful, the evidence suggests a pro-rural, not a pro-urban bias. Thus, writes

Thoden van Velzen (1975, 180–181), "the government of Tanzania is channelling more wealth into the rural hinterland than it gets back, or will ever get back, from direct or indirect forms of revenue." Indeed, "at the national level, the planning agencies and the various Ministries consciously strive to protect the interests of the peasants, and the abolition of the poll tax [in 1968/1969] testifies to the seriousness of their intentions. Thus . . . the relationship between centre and periphery cannot be meaningfully characterized as 'exploitative.'"

Bates's account arrives at the opposite conclusion by reading a (misquoted) number out of context and without the necessary careful judgment. Read thus, that number is suggestive just of what we already know about politics: outcomes serve the material interests of the powerful. Investigating what policymakers' decision calculus may have actually been can thus safely be dispensed with: their motivations can be read straight off the supposedly self-serving outcomes of their actions.

Exploitative Marketing Interventions: The Case of Coffee

A second passage about Tanzania homes in on interventions in the marketing of agriculture produce. Bates's broader argument is that government control—achieved through channeling produce through official marketing authorities that determined producer prices—served to extract resources from the agricultural sector. High marketing margins and correspondingly low producer prices are the symptoms of this: they indicate the presence of "rents," some of which "the bureaucrats surrender to the governments in the form of taxes; some they consume themselves; and the remainder they use to build up cadres supportive of governments in power" (Bates 1981, 121). *Markets and States* thus makes two connected claims about the state's interventionism in agricultural marketing: (1) it produced results (high marketing margins) that amounted to the exploitation of farmers for the benefit of state officials and well-connected elites, and (2) this result also explains why the state became so interventionist—or at least why it persisted in its interventionism.[28] Exploitation was interventionism's effect and purpose.

The Tanzanian coffee sector, suggests the book, yields a clear example of this scheme. The evidence adduced is that in 1975/1976 a local instant coffee factory could procure Robusta coffee beans from the official coffee marketing authority at TSh 6.32 per kilo, substantially below the "price on the world market" of TSh 14.84. The suggestion is that growers, locked into an exploitative marketing arrangement, could have done substantially better had their crop been sold at the world market price (Bates 1981, 23).

The problem with this suggestive factoid is that the counterfactual on which Bates's argument rides would have been impossible to realize. The world market price was available only for the restrictive quota allotted to Tanzania under producer countries' International Coffee Agreement. Selling to a domestic processor was a way of disposing of excess supply that was internationally unmarketable.[29] But why was the processor not simply charged a higher price? It is unclear whether it could have been: if within its local market the processor could not have operated with a higher purchasing price, the alternative to "subsidizing" might have been no sale at all.[30] In its particular context, the factory's low procurement price may thus well have served producers' interests.

Furthermore, Bates's numbers—showing that the factory bought from the marketing agency at 43 percent of the world market price—might invite the impression that producer prices must have been impaired by a similar magnitude. While it cannot be definitively determined by how much the low procurement price offered to the factory in fact lowered the price paid to producers,[31] the producer price suffered considerably less than one might be led to expect by reading about the factory's low 1975/1976 procurement cost of 43 percent of the world market price. That year, growers received considerably more than 69 percent of the world market price for Robusta from the marketing agency (over the six seasons from 1971/1972 to 1976/1977 producers' share for both coffee varieties averaged 67 percent).[32]

Even if these shares are less suggestive of exploitation than the figures Bates presents, producers still lost on average a third of the value of their crop to the marketing authority. *Markets and States* considers only one reason why this might have been so: margins fed the state bureaucracy and connected interests. But this conclusion overlooks a host of other reasons for a wedge between international and producer prices.[33] Rationed demand in international markets and a consequent need to sell oversupply into lower-price domestic channels is one such reason. Unavoidable costs—transport, marketing, and basic processing—between farm gate (producer price) and port (final sale price) are another: also taking into account the vast array of services that the coffee authority was supposed to perform for growers especially in the area of agricultural extension, Frank Ellis and Ellen Hanak (1980, 24) conclude on this count that "the performance of the [coffee] marketing authority has been reasonably satisfactory given the rate of inflation, especially in transport costs, over the decade" from 1969 to 1979. Finally, it is not necessarily warranted to count even the remaining portions of marketing margins that were in fact "taxes" over and above unavoidable costs as exploitation and patronage resources: some such taxes (a roasting subsidy to keep a local processor alive?) may well have been in the public (and farmers') interest.

With regard to Tanzania's coffee sector, *Markets and States* highlights a set of numbers that appears to offer unequivocal support for its argument. Upon closer inspection, however, the numbers are again not quite the smoking gun of exploitation that Bates makes them out to be.

Exploitative Marketing Interventions: The General Case

A final passage that anchors *Markets and States'* argument in Tanzanian evidence again homes in on a "tendency to use marketing channels to appropriate revenues generated by the production of cash crops," claiming that "this has been thoroughly documented in Tanzania, where investigations in 1966 . . . and 1970 . . . disclosed rapidly inflating marketing costs on the part of cooperatives, and specified the number and the emoluments of their staffs as major causes of this trend" (Bates 1981, 28).

This claim can be scrutinized from two angles. First, did margins in fact amount to an appropriation of resources from farmers? Second, if they did, did this effect in fact supply the motivation for the state's interventions in marketing?

As I have argued in the case of coffee, marketing margins cannot automatically be read as being due to resource appropriation. The two reports Bates cites do not in fact point the finger quite as readily as does Bates: although both note theft and payroll expansions as part of the problem with cooperative marketing, neither suggests that these were the main or the only reason for large margins in the 1960s.[34] Furthermore, and more critically with respect to Bates's argument, neither suggests that such "appropriations" were the motivation behind the expansion of cooperative and official marketing. Both reports also led to quite dramatic measures to combat the problem of graft and unwarranted payroll expansions: far from finding graft a convenient political resource, the government showed no inclination to tolerate it.[35]

The 1966 *Report of the Presidential Special Committee of Enquiry into Co-operative Movement and Marketing Boards* had found widespread skill problems and misappropriations at the level of cooperatives and their unions that functioned as the two lowest tiers in the marketing system. It called for greater supervision and attention to skills—to be secured through greater government control and supervision over the system (URT 1966b).[36] High-ranking and well-connected casualties show that the ensuing reforms had considerable bite. Notes John Saul (1975a, 218) on the 1967/1968 fundamental restructuring of the Victoria Federation of Cooperative Unions, one of the most important cooperative organizations: "The General Manager (the brother of a prominent Minister) and a variety of other key personnel were, in effect, sacked, and salary structures, perquisites, [and] employment rosters were, ostensibly, rationalized."

Despite these reform efforts, following the report by Herbert Kriesel et al. (1970), the minister of agriculture again voiced his concern in late 1971 that the cooperatives were in fact acting very much like the exploitative middlemen they had been meant to replace, and in 1972–1974 the government followed up with a series of remedial actions. Hydén (1976, 17) comments, "In some cases, very drastic measures have been taken. One union committee after another has been dissolved. In the case of Mwanza [Region], where theft has been particularly common, a total of 1,833 committee men and primary society secretaries were dismissed at once in May 1974." Eventually, the middle-tier cooperative unions, often deemed to be the most problematic part of the system as they could be effectively monitored neither locally by members nor centrally by government, were circumvented entirely and (restructured) national purchasing authorities procured produce directly from the cooperatives.[37]

In essence, a series of moves to centralize and reform the marketing system in Tanzania amounted to vested-interest-busting. This does not fit with the notion that the state intended or was content to feed clientelistic networks. With respect to the results of these efforts, Hydén (1973, 198) judges that the government's "interventions in almost all unions in the country in order to ensure that mismanagement and misappropriation is eliminated or at least reduced . . . have had their effect." Sometimes, clearly, the effect of these efforts was counterproductive: the 1975/1976 replacement of deemed-to-be-corrupt primary cooperative societies with village authorities as the primary purchasers of produce, for instance, likely resulted in increased theft, in good part because, unlike the cooperatives, most villages did not have bank accounts and cash transactions proved more vulnerable to theft as well as highway robbery (Bryceson 1993, 70–71). But while it is thus clear that reform efforts did not eliminate the problem of corruption, this does not take away from the fact that they sought to tackle it, not condone or enable it.

While graft and appropriation then contributed to high margins, they were also clearly not the only culprits. A key problem was inefficiencies that served no one—and thus cannot be counted as rents in a game of exploitative politics. To illustrate: in 1973, the marketing system was restructured. So-called crop authorities, each specializing in one or a few crops, would now purchase their crop(s) directly at the local level (until then cooperatives and their unions had aggregated produce and sold it on to more generalist marketing boards). The crop authorities also took on a greatly expanded list of tasks for their respective crops, ranging from financing to extension services and the development of processing industries. This resulted in major new overhead costs, complex logistical tasks that overwhelmed agencies suffering from acute shortages of well-trained staff, and efficiency costs in the marketing system. Each of the ten new crop authorities, for instance, now had to be equipped with its own separate storage facilities and lorry fleet—which would henceforth "specialize" in collecting different crops at often different harvest times.[38] Producer prices would eventually suffer as they had to absorb at least part of these costs. But it is hard to see who would have benefited from this wasteful restructuring, besides perhaps foreign manufacturers whose order books were filled with the purchase of numerous new vehicles that the authorities soon proved unable even to maintain.[39] Lest a conspiracy of nefarious Tanzanian interests be suspected behind these ill-advised reforms: the recommendation had come from the international management consultancy McKinsey & Co., an actor that presumably had little stake in maintaining Tanzanian clientelistic networks.[40]

To be sure, certain variants of marketing inefficiencies created both such deadweight losses and benefits to certain constituents. The case of maize marketing is a good and—given the importance of the crop as the country's key staple crop—highly significant example. But at least in this case, the beneficiaries of government-induced inefficiencies were not the members of Bates's development coalition, but largely disadvantaged maize farmers in the marginalized periphery of the south and southwest of the country. Into 1973, the central crop purchasers had set prices at which they would buy from the cooperative system after it had aggregated the produce; cooperatives and their unions would deduct their costs before paying producers the remainder. Then this pricing system was changed: there would now be a set price paid at the *local* purchasing point anywhere in the country. The intention was twofold: first, it was hoped that the new pricing policy would overcome the problem of the cooperative level inflating costs and thereby depressing farmers' earnings; secondly, paying the same price everywhere in the country would also level the playing field in favor of peripheral areas disadvantaged by their poor and costly access to markets.

In this second respect, the policy worked as intended: now effectively subsidized, Ruvuma, Iringa, Mbeya, and Rukwa Regions, relatively far and difficult to reach from the major market of Dar es Salaam, saw an impressive increase in their share of nationally marketed maize from a mere 17 percent in 1973/1974 to 87 percent in 1981/1982 (Bryceson 1992, 86).[41] Pan-territorial pricing was thus a major boon to peripheral farmers (it did confer benefits). But the resulting geographical shift in purchasing also caused greatly increased collection and transportation costs in the system (a deadweight loss), amplified further by the 1979 oil price shock (85–86). Pricing policy ignored this—for a while. Between 1973 and 1976, the price for maize that the marketing authorities paid to peasant producers was in fact raised significantly;[42] then nominal increases slowed significantly over the next five years into 1981—and, given high inflation, real producer prices declined.[43] But not even this partial easing of the pressure on its margins saved the official purchaser of maize and other staple food crops from accumulating, by March 1981, debts of 530 percent of its annual domestic purchases of crops (Msambichaka, Ndulu, and Amanti 1983, 62).[44] In the end, producer prices suffered greatly: although these ratios were extreme and likely influenced by the 1978/1979 Tanzania-Uganda war's effect on the area, by the 1979/1980 and 1980/1981 seasons, maize farmers in some Lake Region villages in northwestern Tanzania were able to sell their crop in parallel markets for respectively three and five times what official channels were offering (148).[45] Ironically, a key reason for such poor official prices was a set of eventually unsustainable marketing and pricing policies that was supposed to secure *better* prices for farmers, especially those in disadvantaged, peripheral regions.

Why, in the face of persistent problems and failures, did the government persist in its interventions instead of letting private agents produce efficient outcomes? The answer is that agriculture—especially in settings, such as Tanzania's, characterized by poor information, high transport costs, and many marginal producers—poses challenges that private actors are unlikely to solve, at least not if the solution is supposed to afford small farmers decent opportunities. Policymakers sought to deliver what they had reason to believe free markets would fail to provide: they sought to expand access to input and output markets for peripheral producers; capture and feed back to producers marketing and basic processing profits that would otherwise accrue to deemed-to-be-exploitative middlemen; and provide price stability and predictability for farmers who would otherwise face often violent and very difficult-to-handle swings in inter- and intraseasonal prices.[46] Research emanating from the University of Dar es Salaam consistently seemed to provide rationales for such actions. For instance, a number of case studies demonstrated that when marketing was in private hands, producers' shares of final sales were often very low—so low, in fact, that they seemed firm proof of "exploitative" marketing practices by powerful traders: bringing marketing under government and/or cooperative control would surely improve the situation.[47] The fact that in 1960s

Tanzania many traders were of Indian descent only amplified suspicions that private marketing exploited farmers.[48]

There seemed to be, in other words, good reasons for interventions. Indeed, the moribund state of many parts of the African smallholder sector following the 1980s and 1990s rollback of interventionist marketing regimes confirms that the earlier skepticism about markets' ability to deliver for small farmers was far from baseless.[49] Even during the heyday of the "free market" enthusiasm of the 1980s and early 1990s, a long-serving World Bank agronomist would thus still argue that it was the government's job to "ensure that input and output prices do not discriminate against small producers, that they remain reasonably stable over time, and that they provide sufficient incentives so that new production initiatives can be fostered" (Donaldson 1991, 186).

There is a different story to be told about marketing policy in Tanzania than *Markets and States'* tale of the state elite's drive to enrich itself and its cronies. Tanzanian policymakers persisted in interventions not because this served their private purposes, but because they saw no attractive alternative. They also did not simply keep a problematic system in place, letting it conveniently generate rents for politicians and their clients. Instead, they constantly sought to improve it, often enough seeking specifically to curtail corruption. That Tanzania's thus evolving interventionist regime still did not serve farmers well therefore shows neither that this was primarily because it benefited others ("exploitation"), nor that behind ostensibly pro-farmer intentions lurked ulterior and nefarious motives. Interventionism in marketing proved problematic not because it was designed or maintained to bleed the agricultural sector for "rents," but largely because, pro-farmer intentions notwithstanding, far too frequent,[50] often ill-conceived, and—given the limitations in organizational capacity and skills—overly ambitious interventions and reforms imposed what often amounted to deadweight losses on the sector.[51]

Explaining Problems in *Markets and States*

Howard Stein and Ernest Wilson (1993, 1048) have called rational choice analysis "a premise in search of a history." The fact that this search so often appears to succeed, the above analysis suggests, is rooted in a research practice that reads history through the prism of this premise's impoverished ontology of politics. *Markets and States* detects expanding official marketing operations and high margins. Since the interests of the powerful determine "outcomes," high margins must have served those interests, and been a gain for politicians and their allies. Indeed, they were precisely what politicians must have sought all along. Lionel Cliffe (1991, 106) remarks on the Marxist forerunners of Bates's rational choice account of Tanzania that that literature "sees 'class analysis' as a mechanical exercise in which the 'explanation' of an official policy is that, since it emanates from the state, and since the state has a ruling class, then the [policy, i.e., the Arusha Declaration] must be the project of a certain class." Save for its different vocabulary, this is *Markets and States'* logic of inquiry as well. It too is founded in the materialist-utilitarian paradigm, which tells the analyst that a series of questions can be safely ignored: Were high margins really due to powerful groups skimming surpluses off the top—and can the observed outcome in fact be interpreted as directly functional to the material interests of the powerful? What, in fact, were the interests of the powerful? And did policy have the effects it did because policymakers intended them?

In short-circuiting these questions, *Markets and States* is not an outlier. "Political economy work on India's economic policy," notes Ashutosh Varshney (1994, xi), likewise exhibits a tendency "to 'read off' the reasons underlying state behavior either from the results of state action, or from the interests of powerful interest groups." More broadly, Jon Elster (2000, 693) argues that "much of applied rational choice theory is a combination of just-so stories and functionalist explanation. One constructs a model in which the observed behavior of agents maximizes their interests as suitably defined, and one assumes that the fit between behavior and interest explains the behavior."

But what is wrong with thus reasoning backward from outcomes to underlying interests and—hence—causes of observed behavior? Practitioners of this approach to research have after all defended it. Notes Bates (1986, 13) on *Markets and States'* method: "I attempted to use [international market prices] to determine what would have prevailed in the absence of government market intervention, and then to infer whose interests prevailed." Indeed, this logic of inquiry not infrequently passes for good methodology: as a book on aid and developmental failures in Tanzania proclaims, "I propose in this study that the interests of actors on both sides of the aid process have to be determined not by what their professed policies say, or by what specific pundits judge actors' interests to be, but by what their *actions may have shown their interests to have been.* The analysis of the book, therefore, will *infer* interests of the principal actors from actions and *thereby explain* behaviour" (Rugumamu 1997, 4; emphases added).

Outcomes through the Prism of the Paradigm

A first problem with reading history backward from outcomes to "inferred" interests and causes in *Markets and States'* account of Tanzania is the book's presentation of outcomes. "Data" that is biased in favor of presenting the strongest case for the book's argument and suggestive of a picture that is not actually borne out by the full evidence is one problem.[52] Interpretation is another: Bates's reading of a wedge between international and producer prices as resource appropriation by elites ignores other reasons for marketing margins: legitimate marketing costs, for instance, or the fact that high margins in fact were a reflection of subsidies to disadvantaged farmers, as in the case of pan-territorial maize pricing.

These problems may be just glitches. But something systematic seems to be at work as well. Similar problems of a "tendentious reading of the empirical record" that Donald Green and Ian Shapiro (1994, 43) have found to be widespread in the rational choice literature underline this suspicion. One might conjecture that the particular kind of evidence favored in Bates's account, as it is in the broader literature, must bear some of the blame: supposedly "hard" numbers perhaps suggest that they can only tell the one story they are presented to support.[53] But thin and uncontextualized "data," especially of the hard quantitative kind, can often tell many a story, not just the one that fits the thesis. The *valence* of outcomes such as low producer prices, therefore, needs to be carefully analyzed and interpreted, and the temptation—perhaps amplified by the nature of quantitative evidence—to dispense with careful interrogation suppressed. This would be a first important step toward overcoming an apparent general tendency in this kind of work to recognize in outcomes only what an ontology in which politics is a game of self-interested material gains maximizers tells the analyst to look for: with this hammer in hand, everything in Tanzania looks like a nail.

Interests: Variable or Parameter?

Beyond thus slanting the book's portrayal of outcomes, this ontology also severely limits *Markets and States'* consideration of possible "causes" to agents' self-regarding interests and the instrumental calculations that turn them into actions. Whether this framework is in principle too limiting has been much debated. Detractors have argued that self-seeking interests are only one slice of the array of human motivations, prompting the defenders' rejoinder (which underestimates considerable complications) that any kind of motivation can in principle be described as an interest.[54] Similarly, the assumption of instrumental rationality has been questioned, on account of both its practical possibility (can people really perform the required calculus?) and its realism (do people instead act noninstrumentally, for instance out of habit and routines or for expressive purposes?).[55]

But the question of whether altruistic interests or "bounded rationality" can *theoretically* be accommodated within a rational choice framework is not really the key issue: the constraint that typically binds is not the paradigm's *potential* malleability, but its *typical operationalization* in the practice of empirical research. Here, the supposed variable "interest" tends to be turned into a fixed parameter: invariably, interests are exhaustively described as the desire to maximize one's own material resources—and perhaps political influence, either for its own sake or as just another means to securing wealth.[56]

Bates (1993, 1078) has claimed that this is a justifiable move: "I often do cite the desire for wealth and income in attempting to explain political behavior; but, given the subject on which I tend to focus—the politics of economic policy—it would have been absurd not to have done so." Indeed; but to make this desire out to be the only driver of policy is no less absurd. With respect to the Tanzanian story, doing so creates a palpably unrealistic image of the motivations of policymakers.

Any amount of empirical work on motivations will quickly discover a whole world beyond the materialist-utilitarian paradigm. But what makes the paradigm so attractive and convenient is precisely that—if not in theory, then certainly in practice—it denies that this empirical work needs to be done. As Bienefeld (1986, 11) remarks on *Markets and States:* if bureaucrats' "behaviour is not governed by some self-evident, narrow self-interest, then choices become far more complex and uncertain and the problem of politics arises in a more realistic manner." By force, analysis is more complicated, and its conclusions less satisfyingly parsimonious and certain.

Revealing Preferences When Many Roads Lead to Rome

Instead of empirically investigating motivations, the strategy is, as we have seen, to infer them from outcomes that are supposed to "reveal" them. Bates et al. (2000, 698) remark in their major intervention on social science methodology, "Because it is so difficult to judge intentions, rational choice theorists tend to rely instead on revealed preferences and behavior."[57] We can look at an outcome such as high marketing margins and pretty much know what interests must have lain behind its production.

The problem with this strategy is not just that it often starts with a tendentious or at least very partial reading of outcomes. The methodological assumption itself that outcomes can unambiguously reveal preferences or intentions is deeply problematic. It ignores that in any reasonably complex situation any number of interests may potentially have gone into producing a particular outcome: if many roads leading to Rome, the traveler's arrival there tells us very little about from whence she started.[58] Any scenario in which an outcome or behavior may have its roots in more than one possible preference or intention creates a problem for inferring preferences from outcomes. Likewise, any disturbance to a tight nexus between intention and outcome spells trouble: if agents miscalculate, operate in a fundamentally unpredictable environment, or make calculations—for instance of a strategic nature—that may not be obvious to the observer, outcomes are often not "as intended" or do not point to the interest pursued. They do not, therefore, straightforwardly point to the preferences and intentions that in fact underlie an action. (The "instrumentalist" argument that for a theory to be successful it does not have to present a realistic picture of its causal processes as long as reality behaves "as if" the theory were true is not a coherent defense against this charge.[59])

The more complex the phenomenon to be explained and the looser the nexus between action and outcome the more serious this problem becomes. Take for instance as multi-dimensional and complex a phenomenon as "the policy of villagization." On the one hand, the "outcome" it produced was itself extremely multi-facetted and of course open-ended (in important ways, in Tanzania, too, it is still, forty years later, "too early to tell"). On the other, the notion that one is looking at some singular, coherent phenomenon called "the policy" is substantially a fiction: a vast array of decisions and actions made up this very amorphous entity. There was of course also no one single agency behind it. The notion of a unitary state as the actor whose interests might have driven the policy is especially problematic. Even in terms of their narrowly defined material interests, officials' differential situatedness within the state's hierarchies alone made for very heterogeneous incentives that often enough divided "the state" against itself. Nyerere may have attempted to set an agenda. But what his "implementing" regional commissioners, facing their own incentives, made of that agenda was neither determined, nor adequately anticipated, nor even effectively monitored by the president. With uncertainty, double-guessing, and strategic actions all around, what does the "policy outcome" reveal or reflect? Nyerere did not get what he wanted, and neither did his regional commissioners (for one, they frequently enough lost their job when the president looked into their best attempts to please him). With the "policy outcome" not immediately functional to any of the interests (and broader motivations) that went into its production, there is no conceivable way in which one may infer those interests from it.

Complex phenomena involving a multitude of actors and dimensions require a fine-grained analysis that reads the story forward from the participants' standpoints as it unfolds uncertainly. Such objects of analysis are not susceptible to being reduced to some "revealed" generic underlying interests—especially not those attributed to some supposedly unitary, aggregate actor such as the state.[60]

Beyond Materialist-Utilitarian Analysis

As difficult, uncertain, and unparsimonious an exercise as it may well be, empirically and directly engaging interests, intentions, reasoning, and calculations is not something that explanations of political actions can do without, even—perhaps especially—when they aspire to work within an explanatory framework of (rationally) choosing actors. In actual empirical engagement, however, political actors are likely to reveal themselves not just as wealth- and influence-maximizing instrumental calculators, but as people who also act from an array of other motivations: out of a sense of right and duty—to others, rules, history; out of habit; ideological commitment; vindictiveness; hubris; an unwillingness to surrender; miscalculation; prejudice.

On whatever basis they act, they do so within a social and historical context of material and discursive realms of possibilities and repertoires of practices. The particular, parsimonious world of *homo economicus* is just one field of such practices, and its role in explanation must therefore be, as Elster (2000, 694) has put it, "suitably modest." In short, "action can be intelligible," as Margaret Somers (1992, 607) argues in calling for "social science history,"

> only if we recognize the one or many ontological and public narratives in which actors identify themselves. Rather than deriving from interests, narrative identities are constituted by a person's temporally and spatially specific "place" in culturally constructed stories that comprise (breakable) rules, (variable) practices, binding (and unbinding) institutions, and the multiple stories of family, nation, or economic life.

Understanding how and why people act in politics must engage their situatedness—the realm of what is imaginable and practicable to them—in which their motivations and modes of reasoning and acting are grounded. Understanding how and why people act in politics demands that history be read from the standpoint of its agents—and thus not backward from outcomes to underlying causes, but forward, as it flows toward an unpredictable future that always exceeds intention.

Epilogue

This book has sought to practice an alternative to the kind of analysis that finds all answers regarding the character of rule, the shape of governing, and the effects they produce in some generic and readily apprehensible self-serving interests of actors, be they individuals or collectivities such as "the state" or "the ruling class." I have aimed instead to understand actors, their interests, and their actions as constituted in "thick" discursive practices, while making room for contingency and nonfunctionality in history's making.

Approached from this perspective, the "authoritarian" shape that governing took in Tanzania emerges as the effect of a historically specific assemblage of discourses and practices that produced political elites as a distinctive kind of authority. What this analysis then more broadly suggests is that the phenomenon of "authoritarianism" has to be understood as inextricably embodied in the specific practices that make it up. This is in contrast to typical treatments of this "-ism" as arising out of some sui generis authoritarian impulse, as a simple means to the satisfaction of rulers' hunger for "power" or wealth, or as a function of the state's institutional form.[1] Tanzania's particular manifestation of authoritarianism was constituted in a thick Rousseauian project of governing that sought to rule in the "true" interest of all.[2] But as such a project always flirts with enthroning the general will, known only to the enlightened legislator, over the wills of the unenlightened, it runs the danger of succumbing to the temptations of pedagogical tutelage.

Of course, officials at various levels did navigate, enlist, and shape—often in very much "interested" ways—the framings and practices from which this form of government was assembled in Tanzania. But this means neither that the terrain they maneuvered in can therefore be reduced to their interests, nor that paying close attention to this terrain can be dispensed with. The frames of developmentalist temporality, the authorizing practices of planning, the representations of officials and peasants that were assembled within such framings and practices: these were never *just* instruments in the hands of "interested" actors—and even as instruments, they always also shaped their wielders and the repertoires of actions open to them. It is not just our circumstances, but the very possibilities and shapes of our agency that are never quite of our own choosing.

The particular constellation in Nyerere's Tanzania of practices of governing that rendered state officials as unquestionable and indispensible authorities responsible for bringing development to the masses is of course of a particular time and place. Today, both governing and development have been significantly reconfigured. Centrally, the subjects of state officials' developmental authority have been rethought and repositioned as the self-propelling agents of their own advancement—potential entrepreneurs empowered by the newly "liberated" market, the tether that bound them to the developmentalist state replaced by a loose (and at times ephemeral) connection mediated through multiparty democracy.[3]

In Aili Tripp's (1997, 74) telling, Tanzanians—cudgeled for many years by an authoritarian state—wished for nothing more: "The focus of popular demands was not on extracting goods from the state but, rather, on getting the state to extricate itself from society," she writes about the 1980s and 1990s. Hard-fought as this battle to get out from under the state's yoke may initially have been, a new generation of political leaders certainly warmed to the idea eventually. Not only did the rise of the "free market" as a new modality of governing make for the convenient byproduct of ideologically freeing the political class from the obligations of solidarity; it also opened up new spaces, previously blocked by leadership conditions and the moral discourse of socialism, for politicians and the well-connected to pursue their own ends far more effectively than they had ever been able to do in the previous era. The free market may indeed have rolled back the state's official activities in the economy. But in so doing it set the stage for the privatization of gains by the political class. Hence the historical irony of the apotheosis of Bates's "exploitative" state in Dar es Salaam's millennial real estate market: this state was realized under the very free-market regime that was supposed to rein in this until-then largely imaginary villain.[4] As Timothy Mitchell (2002, 277) observes about parallel developments in Egypt, "The 'free market' program in Egypt was better seen as a multi-layered political readjustment of rents, subsidies, and the control of resources." Tanzanian trends therefore fit into a global picture of deregulation, privatization, increasingly regressive effective taxation systems, and—when push came to shove—the protection of the outsized gains accrued to the select few under this system by way of bailouts: socialism for capitalists, and capitalism for everyone else.

In Tanzania, popular narratives and expressions chart such trends.[5] Nyerere's (1962–1985) reign as the "Father of the Nation" at the helm of the "Party of the Revolution" (*Chama cha Mapinduzi*, CCM, TANU's post-1977 successor) had given way to a new era: the next president, Ali Hassan Mwinyi (1985–1995), was simply "*Mzee Ruksa*," Mr. Permission, and the same ruling party's acronym seemed more reflective of reality when it read "*Chukua Chako Mapema*": "Take Yours Early" (Heilman and Ndumbaro 2002, 16–17).

These, then, are aspects of the new configuration of government that typically comes under the label "the neoliberal condition" and whose practices David Harvey (2005) interprets as a war of the rich and well-connected on a growing global underclass of the "dejected," to borrow Ferguson's (1999) evocative expression. Occasionally celebratory accounts of the escape from under the state have thus given way to the somber lamentation that large swaths of African populations are effectively cut out of the bargains to be made in the new free markets altogether—as they subsist in a rural scramble for livelihoods and the urban informal sector.[6]

Yet, Ferguson (2010, 166) asks, can anything more be said about these new realities than that "the rich are benefiting and the poor are getting screwed"? Since a wholesale return to the developmentalist state broadly of the Tanzanian variety is neither desirable nor generally on the horizon, Ferguson's advice to examine the present constellation for progressive openings is well taken. Indeed, it is worth pausing to ask what is *gained* in the neoliberal assemblage vis-à-vis the configuration of development and government that this book has observed in Nyerere's Tanzania. Here, a celebratory valorization of the newly won "freedom from" the state's authority to direct its subjects' lives—institutionally expressed in electoral democracy—is not infrequently critiqued as substantively less than meaningful, especially in many African settings. Yet, even if multiparty democracy has typically not resulted in very much "voice" and agenda-setting power for its sometimes only putatively democratically empowered citizens, even a degree of electoral accountability can perhaps at least amount to greater popular checks on government, and hence a safeguard for "freedom from."[7]

A small victory it may be, but perhaps not an insignificant one. Looking back, one may for instance wonder with the RDA school's former headmaster where the association's villages "might . . . have been today if they had just left us alone" (quoted in Ibbott 2000, 88). Indeed, in the 2000s, Ntimbanjayo Millinga felt that the checks that multipartyism facilitated were a crucial protection that made it possible to attempt a revival of some old ideas: a new Ruvuma Development Association (new acronym: RUDA) that sought to build several community-based ventures—a pottery project with Scottish support, irrigated rice cultivation, an independent school—along lines and including a set of people that can be traced back to the RDA's earlier endeavors.[8]

How much will be made of such perhaps enlarged spaces for action and organization of course crucially depends on local resources and capacity—and hence also on enabling supports that the local may receive from the "outside." However, here the figure of the "responsibilized" potential-entrepreneur subject of neoliberalism has served often enough as an absolution from obligations of solidarity and equity that are crucial for mobilizing such supports: "handouts" (or a workable health care system) are undeserved and unaffordable; they undercut incentives and breed a mentality of entitlement and sloth.

At the same time, if that figure of the potential entrepreneur were to be inserted into a vision of society not of "each for him/herself," but cognizant of the old liberal insight that "freedom from" requires resources and supports to concretize its potential as "freedom to," the picture may be less dire. On a guardedly hopeful note, Ferguson (2010, 173–181) points out that recent years have in fact seen at least some states reengage in this area to a perhaps greater extent than laments about the neoliberal condition might lead one to expect. A groundswell of interest in cash-transfer programs, either in the form of direct income support or as an alternative mechanism to older forms of support such as in-kind food aid, is one instance of this. In essence, while such programs do enlist "markets" and "choosing agents," they also seek to augment the functioning for the poor of this neoliberal constellation. The result, surmises Ferguson, is at the same time "'pro-poor,' redistributive, and neoliberal" (178). Basic Income Grants for instance—the idea of dispersing minimal cash payments to all citizens that has long been debated in South Africa—could thus be read as aiming to provide capacitating supports that might help turn citizens' empty freedom from into substantive freedoms to. If the market is such an inhospitable place for the poor in good part because it only caters to customers (i.e., those with purchasing power), such schemes may indeed present a remedy insofar as they enable the poor to take advantage of what markets have to offer. In freeing up resources that may then be deployed as capital in income-generating activities, such programs—while working within a scheme that valorizes "greater productivity, enterprise, and risk-taking" (178)—may help to make these dimensions of neoliberalism work for the poor.

As Ferguson argues, there is much to be said in favor of such schemes, not least that they defer to the poor's own choices. But it is equally important to acknowledge that they will only take the poor so far. Leaving aside what possibilities beyond barely coping may exist for the ever-growing informal sector populated by Africa's urban poor, what can the rural poor expect to achieve, even if they are thus supported as individual microentrepreneurs in ways more or less comfortably compatible with the neoliberal assemblage? In rural Africa especially, markets have persistently failed to create arenas in which small agricultural producers have many opportunities for gainful participation (Bryceson 2002; Ellis 2006); and it is highly doubtful whether this would in any meaningful way be remedied by marginally enhancing rural people's purchasing power. Small producers are failed by crop purchasing arrangements, for many reasons: growing to grade, sorting, and packaging are difficult to do, and, with the demise of typically state-sponsored cooperatives and marketing boards, there is little support left in these areas. Likewise, free markets—when they are thin, populated by only a few players, and riddled with informational asymmetries and risks—tend to purchase from small producers at exploitative prices or, often enough, not at all; nor are credit, extension services, crop research, and inputs regularly provided when each small farmer must be treated as an individual customer.

In the face of such challenges, support channeled to *individuals* runs into serious limitations.[9] On the one hand, remedies aimed at a *structural* level—looking to a more broadly interventionist stance on the part of states as regulators, coordinators, and absorbers of risk—are required.[10] This, of course, implies a significant departure from neoliberalism's natural comfort zone—albeit, framed right, perhaps one that is not necessarily anathema to it. On the other hand, thinking beyond supports aimed at individuals also raises the question of *organization*. In the RDA, it was, after all, not "individual entrepreneurs" who were responsible for solving the villages' food self-sufficiency problem, building communal infrastructure, and establishing small industries. The members' local-level organization—connected as it was to the state as well as foreign NGOs and supporters—was a critical ingredient in all of these efforts.[11]

What about this issue of organization, then? Has it not in large part been solved through the rise of the ubiquitous NGO sector? In certain respects, organizations of this nongovernmental type have of course been a natural fit in the neoliberal constellation. Presumed to be nimbler, more efficient, and more in touch with local realities than the state, they have taken on many of the functions formerly within the state's domain. One sees this in the "NGO-ization" of Kenya's health care and education systems; the ever expanding and internationalizing food-aid system; and vaccination campaigns planned, financed, and carried out by the Gates Foundation.[12] All this looks more decentralized, more marketlike, less statelike; and such trends have then often been celebrated not just because they presumably enhance efficiency, but also because they appear to be more hospitable to the freedoms that statist development tended to diminish. This, at least, is part of the narrative of the "new development" through nonstate channels, packaged as "participatory" and directed at "empowerment."

Here, the Tanzanian experience cautions against too Whiggish a celebration of this newest iteration of development. Indeed, if the "new" discovery of participation and empowerment in development traced its lineage, it would discover a long history reaching back to, among others, Nyerere and John Stuart Mill before him. But this history should then be read as a cautionary tale about the ease with which emancipatory motivations may usher in oppressive actions, or, as Li (2007, 279) puts it, "with which vanguard-activists can drift from conceptualizing utopias to prescribing and enforcing . . . programs upon designated groups."

Of course, the deployment of the coercive apparatus of Tanzania's state in pursuit of development was the product of a broad configuration of governing and authority that is in many respects of a bygone age.[13] But meaningful empowerment and participation are undercut not only by the overt coercion Tanzania witnessed in the guise of villagization. Combine the not-atypical developer's sense of authority—underpinned by the interlocking hierarchies of "expertise," origin, resources, and class—with a suitably disenfranchising construction of the beneficiary "stakeholders" in development, and philosophies of participation, even empowerment, are quickly translated into practices that allow for little challenge of the developers, serving merely to reiterate familiar developmental hierarchies in new forms and through new technologies of government.[14] Discursive practices of expertise in particular still subtly but profoundly render and reaffirm hierarchies of authority—and often in no less blanket a fashion or more "deservedly" so than they did in the case of "planning officials" in Tanzania. One can observe that these dynamics are alive and well for instance in Crewe and Harrison's (1998, 104) vignette from a project seeking to promote improved cooking stoves in a number of "developing" countries: "When a [local] potter showed his brand-new design for a sawdust burning stove to a British engineer, the latter asked: 'Do you make any other traditional stoves?' In contrast, when formally educated engineers or scientists develop technology, then the stoves are automatically described as improved or modern."

One does not get Tanzanian villagization that way, but one may still get an authority that makes of the "participation" of stakeholders in development nothing more than their contribution of resources and free labor, and that effectively reduces their "choice" to either taking or leaving a perhaps technologically inappropriate and at any rate not top-priority borehole for a water source (Botchway 2001). Such dimensions of the "new" participatory development are enabled by a lack of accountability of the developers to their charges and rooted in part in their vestedness in their own agendas and incentives. But a degree of paternalistic self-aggrandizement of the expert—still dressed up in still often largely ritualistic paraphernalia of "plans" and "modern expertise"—is also an important part of this picture.[15] As critical analyses of the practices of participatory development have shown, in this regard Tanzania's history often comes uncomfortably close to prophecy. Particular as many of its dimensions certainly are, it therefore is a history that also rhymes with other stories.

Notes

Introduction

1. *"Malalamiko ya Kupewa Kijiji,"* March 18, 1976 (NZC 9/MMT/U30/3/Vol. II). Translations from Kiswahili are my own. See the note on archival sources in the reference section regarding how I indicate the location of archival records.

2. While at certain points in his 1977/1978 lectures Foucault (2007, 108, 364) suggests a tight delimitation of the applicability of the term "governmentality" to the particular domain of post-sixteenth-century Europe and the emergence of the modern state concerned with the government of populations, at other points the reading is much broader (e.g., Foucault 2007, 247). There, "governmentality" denotes an analytical framework with which to think about power. This latter reading predominates in Foucault's subsequent work (Senellart 2007, 388–390). Compare also Dean (2010) and Walters (2012).

3. Dean (2010, 30) remarks on the kind of study of government, an "analytics," that governmentality research aims to produce: "An *analytics* is a type of study concerned with an analysis of the specific conditions under which particular entities emerge, exist and change. It is thus distinguished from most theoretical approaches in that it seeks to attend to, rather than efface, the singularity of ways of governing and conducting ourselves" (emphasis original).

4. Compare Reckwitz's (2002) distinction between textualist, mentalist, and practice-theoretical approaches to culturalist inquiry.

5. Rouse (2007, 644) quotes Charles Taylor on this point: "The vocabulary of a given social dimension is grounded in the shape of social practice in this dimension; that is, the vocabulary would not make sense, could not be applied sensibly, where this range of practices did not prevail. And yet this range of practices could not exist without the prevalence of this or some related vocabulary."

6. Reckwitz (2002, 249–250) defines a practice as "a routinized type of behaviour which consists of several elements, interconnected to one another: forms of bodily activities, forms of mental activities, 'things' and their use, a background knowledge in the form of understanding, know-how, states of emotion and motivational knowledge. A practice . . . forms so to speak a 'block' whose existence necessarily depends on the existence and specific interconnectedness of these elements."

7. Compare Green's (2010b) observations about the centrality of form in the staging of government—involving for instance office designs, rituals of waiting, and guest books—in contemporary Tanzania.

8. Compare especially the contributions to Sachs (1992) and Rahnema and Bawtree (1997). See also Escobar (1995). Ferguson's (1994) account of the effect in Lesotho of development discourse's ordering the world into "primordial" and "national" economies is far more grounded in a specific context, but also tends toward a structuralist theorization of discourse and its workings.

9. This understanding of discourse aligns closely with how practice theory thinks about the question of structure and agency. Notes Rouse (2007, 645): "The relevant social structures and cultural backgrounds are understood dynamically . . . through the continuing reproduction in practice." Reckwitz (2002, 255) similarly stresses the emergent and hence temporary nature of "structural" dimensions of practices, whose essential instability is rooted in "everyday crises of routines, in constellations of interpretative indeterminacy and of the inadequacy of knowledge with which the agent, carrying out a practice, is confronted in the face of a 'situation.'"

10. Power is thus not a determinative structure or force; it is a "mode of action that does not act directly or immediately on others" but an "action upon an action, on possible or actual future or present actions," meaning that "the one over whom power is exercised . . . is recognized and maintained to the very end as a subject who acts" (Foucault 2000, 340).

11. Such is the shape of the kind of explanation sought in a "genealogical" mode to inquiry. In his useful exposition, Walters (2012, 18) identifies the "shift from the study of objects to the practices that produce those objects as their effects" as the essence of this approach: genealogy "engage[s] all objects—and subjects—as effects, as products, . . . as emergent within contingent historical processes."

12. O'Malley, Weir, and Shearing's (1997, 512) observation that a "tendency to separate out programmes from the processes of their 'messy' implementation" leads to a "silencing of the constitutive role of contestation" in much of the early governmentality literature is apropos here: "While it is inescapable that we engage in a degree of hypostatization, idealization and reification of rationalities and programmes in order even to talk of them, the cumulative effect of the problematic features of governmentality work arguably create an insular and *episodic* vision of rule" (emphasis original).

13. Among accounts that to a greater or lesser extent focus on discursive dimensions in development, there are of course also far more contextually rooted treatments: see, for instance, Pigg (1992), Mosse (2005), Li (2007), and Smith (2008).

14. Although he argues strongly against a reading of the political effects of development as the result of some "kind of conspiracy," Ferguson (1994, 256) also sometimes appears to drift in the direction of such a functionalist reading—for instance when he guardedly ventures with respect to the tenacity of development in the face of its "failures" that "it is perhaps reasonable to suggest that it may even be because development projects turn out to have such [political] uses, even if they are in some sense unforeseen, that they continue to attract so much interest and support." Compare, by contrast, his critique of "etatization" arguments (267–271).

15. Although the measure has significant limitations, average income—or per capita gross domestic product (GDP)—is generally assumed to say something meaningful about people's material well-being. Important conceptual shortcomings are the measure's neglect of distribution, nonmonetized economic activity (e.g., subsistence production), and nonmonetized benefits or harms produced by economic activity (externalities). Different methods of calculating GDP at times also yield vastly different readings. For all these reasons, GDP data must thus be approached with care. Figure 1.1 shows data from Maddison's (2009) widely used series that reports internationally comparable GDP figures at purchasing power parity (PPP).

16. Coulson (1982, 188), for instance, has called a reported mid-1970s growth spurt in subsistence crops "extremely improbable," basing this assessment on the rapid growth, at the same time, of food imports and noting that reported figures were based on "impressionistic estimates of production made by agricultural officers" who may have been "reluctant to admit that there was a crisis in subsistence production." Another observer with several years of experience in the Ministry of Development Planning likewise describes that institution's data collection methods in the 1970s as "impressionistic, if not ritualistic" (Amey 1978, 231). The problem is compounded by very significant subsistence production that is in principle hard to record; but even marketed crops are hard to monitor: especially food crops have at times been heavily traded on black markets, as farmers sought to circumvent the unfavorable prices offered by the official marketing boards (Lofchie 1993).

17. Mwase and Ndulu's (2008) study is a recent example. It largely attributes overall growth performance to national policy-regimes, neglecting a broader picture that includes the historical legacy of particular positions in the international division of labor; natural endowments; and climatic and economic shocks. For example: being an importer of both oil and capital goods has perennially counted against Tanzania, argue Green, Rwegasira, and van Arkadie (1980), and made it especially difficult to navigate the oil price shock of 1979 and the generally difficult global economic climate of that time. Likewise, Hydén (1980, 146) argues that drought caused the significant decline in Tanzania's grain

production in 1973/1974 and 1974/1975—although Briggs (1979), Coulson (1992, 260), and Lofchie (1978) disagree and argue that villagization was the main culprit.

18. Bates (1981, 121) argues that it is "owners and workers in industrial firms, economic and political elites, privileged farmers and managers of public bureaucracies . . . who reap the benefits of the policy choices made in formulating development programs." While he sometimes does allow that public-spirited motivations may have lain at the roots of interventionist policies, he explains at least their persistence by reference to the increasingly entrenched material interests of politicians and a narrow coalition of well-connected clients: "Policy choices, made to serve a new vision of the public good, have created a network of self-interest which has proved more enduring than the faith which that vision initially inspired" (Bates 1981, 105; see also 96–97; compare also Lofchie 1994a, 1994b).

19. By contrast to Lofchie's and Bates's formulations, Michael Lipton, the originator of the concept, rejects the linking of the fact of typically high spending on urban areas to exploitative political agendas (as well as the anti-interventionist push that often came with the assertion of such a link). "In the early 1980s," Lipton (1993, 255–256) comments, "I was alarmed at attempts to recruit my work to the flag of Reaganomic characterizations of 'the State,' and of price 'distortions' for which it was alleged to bear the sole and independent responsibility. . . . It is not my fault that the expression 'urban bias' is still persistently misused as part of the polemic of pricism and state minimalism." For critical perspectives on the urban bias literature see Byres (1979), Varshney (1993), and Karshenas (1996/1997). See also chapter 6.

20. Saul (1979, chap. 8) provides an excellent overview of the Dar Marxists. See also the contributions to Othman (1980). For a retrospective take on villagization, see Shivji (1992).

21. See, for instance, Coulson (1975, 1982), Raikes (1975), Thoden van Velzen (1975, 1977), von Freyhold (1979), and Musti de Gennaro (1981).

22. Some of these contributions do make room for a few leaders with sincerely egalitarian aspirations; generally, however, these are found to be quickly subverted by the broader bureaucratic class.

23. Compare Grindle and Thomas (1991, 20–22, 24–27) on class analytic and public choice approaches to policy choice. Foundational texts in the Africa-specific literature include Callaghy (1984), Sandbrook (1985), Joseph (1987), and Fatton (1992); Bayart, Ellis, and Hibou (1999) offer a variant of such arguments.

24. Compare Grindle and Thomas's (1991) critique of this assumption and their argument that policy space is both contingent and malleable.

25. To pick just one example: concerted policy efforts precipitated a dramatic collapse of the post-tax differentials between the highest and lowest salaries and wages in the country from a ratio of 33:1 in 1967, to 15:1 in 1974, and to 5:1 in 1981 (Mukandala 1983, 13); this does not fit with the image of a state bent on facilitating the self-enrichment of officials and their well-connected, urban clients.

26. Li's (2007, 9) remark that "if profit were the issue, no international donor or agricultural department would have invested in the rugged hills of Central Sulawesi" is for instance likewise directed against a literature that seeks to explain development schemes in Indonesia predominantly with reference to the self-seeking material motivations of powerful actors.

27. Because peasants have no incentive to embrace progress and the economic pain and loss of autonomy that would accompany it, argues Hydén (1980), progress has to be imposed—whether through capitalist development or the actions of a socialist state. But peasants' ability to autonomously provide for their own subsistence enables them to repel or co-opt any but the most forceful attempts to shake them out of their "peasant mode of production." And so it was again with ujamaa.

28. Mitchell (1991, 94) has made the general point that the state and society ought to be conceptualized not as preformed, freestanding entities but as the "effect of practices that make such structures [as the state and society] appear to exist." Compare Migdal's (2001) call for an anthropology of the state and Gupta's (1995) and Sharma and Gupta's (2006) outlines of an ethnographic approach to studying it, all stressing a focus on the practices that shape the state and its malleable boundaries

vis-à-vis society. Gupta's (2012) analysis of some of the Indian state's constitutive practices seeks to put these programmatic considerations into practice.

29. In the second half of the 1960s, the two party-owned and controlled papers, the *Nationalist* and the Swahili-language *Uhuru,* the independent *Standard,* and the popular tabloid *Ngurumo* were the four major dailies. In early 1970, the *Standard* (and the weekly *Sunday News*) were taken over by the government. In early 1972, the *Standard* and the *Nationalist* were merged into the government-controlled *Daily News.* See Konde (1984), Sturmer (1998), and Ivaska (2011, 28–34) on the Tanzanian press.

30. Sturmer's (1998, 110, 117–118) figures put the *Nationalist*'s print run in the 1960s at ten thousand, about half of which was sold in the capital Dar es Salaam, the predominant market for all papers. With the four dailies' print runs ranging from eight thousand to fourteen thousand in 1965 and from roughly ten thousand to twenty thousand in 1967, Sturmer cites estimates of a readership of about three times these print runs.

31. Mkapa was the editor of both papers from 1966 and became the editor of the *Daily News* after the *Nationalist*'s merger with the *Standard* (Konde 1984, 25–26); compare also Tordoff and Mazrui (1972, 437–438) on Mkapa as an editor.

32. Other high-ranking officials also contributed to the papers: for instance, Edward Barongo, like Kisumo an important figure in this book's account, contributed pieces to the August 9, 1965, *Standard,* the May 22, 1969, *Nationalist,* and the September 29, 1972, *Daily News.*

33. "Ministerial Circular No. 3 of 1969," November 12, 1969 (TNA 640/KI/C10/17).

34. See, for instance, the special reports of a group of students and their university lecturers on villagization in Dodoma and the responses in letters to the editor discussed in chapter 3. More broadly, as Konde (1984, 105–140) illustrates, the official papers were not government mouthpieces to the point of never engaging in critical journalism.

1. The Ruvuma Development Association

1. Compare Ferguson's (1994, xiv) definition of development as a "problematic," which "imposes questions, not answers," and Cooper and Packard's (1997, 7) treatment of it as a "framing device."

2. Also compare Bose's (1997, 53–57) argument that it was only after independence that development in India lost sight of such substantive goals—as national planning instead increasingly focused on means, such as capital, industrialization, and growth.

3. See, for instance, Escobar (1995), Rahnema (1997), Shrestha (1995), and various contributions to Sachs (1992) for this position; Agrawal (1996) and Ferguson (1999, 243–254) for critiques.

4. Compare, for instance, Young (2004) on Africa, Gupta (1998) on India, and Li (2007) on Indonesia.

5. See especially Rahnema (1992) and Cooke and Kothari (2001).

6. Picking up on such arguments, Bose (1997, 53) observes that "development became an instrument of the state's legitimacy" in postcolonial India. Ferguson (1994) offers a more subtle reading: development and the expansion of a particular form of bureaucratic, state power are co-constitutive—but not necessarily by way of development's supplying a presumably instrumentally deployed legitimating cover for that expansion.

7. Compare Ferguson (1997) on the confluence of ideas about evolutionary change, modernization, and development, and Fabian (1983) on related temporalizing constructions of difference.

8. Compare also Hodge (2007) on the nature of colonial development knowledge.

9. On development in colonial Tanganyika, see, for instance, Hodgson (2001), Hydén (1980), McCarthy (1982), and Pearce (1982).

10. See Brokensha (1970), von Freyhold (1976), and Giblin (1990) on the striking continuities from

colonial times. The cumulative total of districts that had passed agricultural bylaws rose from seven in 1964 to twenty-seven in 1967, and reached forty-three (out of a total of sixty, some of which were urban centers) in 1968. During the period from 1964 to 1966, the average penalty was 2 months in prison; it rose to 3.6 months in 1967, 4.2 months in 1968, and 6 months in 1969—to decline again to 2 months by 1976 (McHenry 1979, 83–84); compare Sumra (1991) and Havnevik (1993) on such policies in the 1970s and 1980s.

11. Minutes of the Regional Development Committee meeting of April 6, 1962 (TNA 513/P4/9/I).

12. Note attached to the minutes of the Regional Development Committee meeting of December 20, 1962; emphases original (TNA 513/P4/9/I).

13. Minutes of the Regional Development Committee meeting of December 20, 1962 (TNA 513/P4/9/I).

14. See Bernstein and Byres's (2001) review of thinking about the "peasant question." Compare also Mitchell (2002).

15. See Ross, Worsley, and Clayton (1965), URT (1966a), Nellis (1972), Newiger (1968), Cliffe and Cunningham (1973), McHenry (1979, 13–27), and Coulson (1977, 1982) on the development and evolution of the settlement program.

16. On the Groundnut Scheme, see, for instance, Hogendorn and Scott (1981) and Coulson (1982, 502).

17. "Address by the President, M.J.K Nyerere, to Parliament—12th May, 1964" (Tanganyika 1964, x). Half of this number were to be settled in massive schemes that were supposed to exploit the agricultural potential of the Kilombero plains.

18. According to Millinga (interview with Millinga, conducted with Edwards, Dar es Salaam, October 2000), Nyerere had voiced his concern about "an army of young independence fighters" who would soon be left without a purpose. A 1962 regional "Memorandum—Southern Region Development Plan" (TNA 967.824) explicitly translates such concerns into the goal of reversing a trend of "urban overcrowding": "One of the urgent problems in the Southern Region is the re-distribution of population from urban and other over-crowded areas to the sparsely populated but productive areas of the Region." This plan already listed "Litowa-type schemes" as one promising outlet. A series of deportations of thousands of unemployed young men from Dar es Salaam to the (rural) Kilombero area immediately after independence reflects similar worries (Sadleir 1999, 266; Burton 2007).

19. Interview with Millinga, conducted with Edwards, Dar es Salaam, October 2000; Ibbott (1970, 21–22).

20. According to some estimates, more than five hundred spontaneous farming schemes had sprung up as self-help nation-building enterprises that often saw the pioneering move of groups of young men from urbanized centers and small towns into the rural areas (Cliffe and Cunningham 1973, 132–133). In 1966, the Rural Settlement Agency had a list of over four hundred such schemes that had failed (Ibbott 1970, 81). The vast majority of these schemes, many of them started by local groups of the TYL, collapsed within a year of their inception (Cunningham 1966, 47–48).

21. Interview with Millinga, conducted with Edwards, Dar es Salaam, October 2000; Ibbott 1970, 23–24. See Edwards (2003) for the importance of the Peramiho mission to the local economy. Brain's report on a visit to the RDA (Syracuse University 1966) likewise notes the professional backgrounds—work on sisal estates and stints with the King's African Rifles—of key members of Liweta, one of the villages that would later join together with Litowa under the Ruvuma Development Association.

22. Ibbott (1970, 76); the Daily News, January 24, 1975.

23. A large number of Kivukoni students—especially from its first class of thirty-nine—went on to have distinguished political careers; the college's 1967 annual report lists nine MPs (four from the first class, Millinga among them), two regional commissioners, and twelve area commissioners among its graduates (various annual reports, in possession of the author, courtesy of Griff Cunningham). Kivukoni, opened in July 1961, had been modeled on and supported by Ruskin College, Oxford, and was administered by a governing council whose chairman was Tanzania's second-in-command, Rashidi

Kawawa. The Tanganyika Education Trust Fund, under the executive leadership of Joan Wicken, Nyerere's longtime personal assistant, played an important role in establishing and running the college (Wicken 1969; Cunningham 1969; Harris 1968).

24. Ibbott had been trained as a quantity surveyor. Before moving to Litowa, he had worked in Southern Rhodesia for ten years: from 1952 until 1958 he was at the St. Faith's Mission Farm at Rusape (Chater 1962); he then moved to the Nyafaru Development Company.

25. Ibbott's (1970) 298-page unpublished account of the association is a key source to which most of what has been published on the RDA can be traced.

26. Interview with Millinga, conducted with Edwards, Dar es Salaam, October 2000; "Appeal for Funds—The Songea Development Association Southern Region Tanganyika," in possession of the author, courtesy of Griff Cunningham.

27. "Appeal for Funds—The Songea Development Association Southern Region Tanganyika," December 1962, in possession of the author, courtesy of Griff Cunningham.

28. Litowa's early constitution had stipulated that up to three-quarters of any profits would be paid out to individual members. However, when monetary surpluses actually arose a few years later, they were largely plowed back into communal ventures and services ("Appeal for Funds—The Songea Development Association Southern Region Tanganyika," December 1962; letter from Cunningham to Belkin, January 24, 1969, in possession of the author, courtesy of Griff Cunningham; Ndonde 1975b, 364, 366–367).

29. Brain's report on a visit to the RDA (Syracuse University 1966) notes that the origin of another key RDA village, Liweta, can, just like Litowa's, be traced back to a group of pioneers who started a farm in 1961/1962 in response to Nyerere's call to develop the land; this group began making informal connections to Litowa in late 1963. Edwards (1998, 13–14) documents how Matetereka, another RDA village, sought the Litowans' advice and became an RDA member.

30. "Appeal for Funds—The Songea Development Association Southern Region Tanganyika," in possession of the author, courtesy of Griff Cunningham; "A Plan for the Development of an Independent Progressive Rural Society in Line with Christian Principles, the African Cultural Background and the Thoughts of the Nation's Leader," n.d., but likely from the first half of 1963 (East Africana Collection, University of Dar es Salaam); "Ujamaa: An Outlining of the Principles for a Plan for the Introduction of African Socialism into the Ruvuma Region of Tanganyika," reproduced in Ibbott (1970). The latter document was the product of a collaborative effort of a committee of six (including Ibbott and Millinga) on the occasion of a seminar on ujamaa organized by the Songea TANU organization.

31. Ruvuma Development Association Newsletters, September and December 1964, and March 1965 (East Africana Collection, University of Dar es Salaam).

32. The new governing body was made up of the members of SERA and two members from each of the villages. It in turn elected an executive committee that was responsible for the running of the everyday business of the association.

33. Ruvuma Development Association Newsletter, June 1965 (East Africana Collection, University of Dar es Salaam).

34. Besides Litowa, the most prominent members were Liweta, Matetereka, and—before it broke with the RDA—Njoomlole ("Come and See"). Among the other members were Ligoma, Njalamatata, Mtakanini, Chimate (later baptized Mapinduzi, "Revolution"), Mhepai, Luhira Goliama (merged with Litowa in late 1964), Kakong'o (which later left the association), Mtiputipu, Luegu, Nalunya, Msichela, and Furaha ("Joy"), which seems to have faltered. In 1969, many of the newest members were still very small: some villages started with a group of just five families.

35. Ruvuma Development Association Newsletters, March and June 1965 (East Africana Collection, University of Dar es Salaam).

36. This venture proved especially popular, not only at Litowa (Lewin 1973, 193–194; Ibbott 1970, 193).

37. Ruvuma Development Association Newsletter, March 1966 (East Africana Collection, University of Dar es Salaam).

38. On the school, nurseries, and the RDA's philosophy on education, see Ibbott (1970), Toroka (1973), Wenner (1970), and Lewin (1973).

39. In Kate Wenner's (1970, 49–61) telling—in 1966/1967 she worked at Litowa as a volunteer—visible benefits (healthier children) and much internal discussions about responsibility were crucial in making the operation of the nursery self-sustaining without close involvement on her part.

40. Compare also Brain (1977, 242–243); Wenner's (1970) account sheds light on the not-always-easy everyday gender relations at Litowa and conveys a sense of the support women provided for one another in the close-knit village community.

41. Wenner (1970, 195) notes this falling out with the mission and the name change; she indicates that other members had likewise adopted new names upon joining Litowa.

42. The document, entitled "Ujamaa: An Outlining of the Principles for a Plan for the Introduction of African Socialism into the Ruvuma Region of Tanganyika," was written to inform the region's political establishment's discussions of the idea of ujamaa; Ibbott contributed a write-up of "the thoughts on development that we had discussed together at Litowa" (Ibbott 1970, 44).

43. Thus, an early RDA document states, "We believe that because the development will have largely been done by the people themselves a spirit can be created which would be impossible from development imposed from above" ("A Plan for the Development of an Independent Progressive Rural Society in Line with Christian Principles, the African Cultural Background and the Thoughts of the Nation's Leader." n.d., but likely from the first half of 1963 [East Africana Collection, University of Dar es Salaam]). Retrospectively, Ibbott (1970, 158–159) argued, "Neither can the real needs and solutions be seen nor programmes be adequately put into effect" by "officials and experts visiting a village, talking, and then going off again." Lewin (1973, 189) judges that, for these reasons, this mode of governing made the difference between the successful village of Matetereka and many other settlements that had sprung up and failed: "Many [such] groups were controlled incompetently from outside. Many failed to start with a realistic idea of the problems they wished to attack and, on the basis, [*sic*] of this understanding, to formulate a strategy to carry out this attack."

44. Most cash receipts were plowed back into communal ventures, but some cash income was apparently distributed (letter from Cunningham to Belkin, January 24, 1969, in possession of the author, courtesy of Griff Cunningham; Ndonde 1975b, 364, 366–367). Brain's 1966 report on a visit to the RDA (Syracuse University 1966) likewise notes cash deductions as a sanction at Liweta.

45. Ibbott to Nyerere, October 31, 1969, in possession of the author, courtesy of Ralph Ibbott.

46. The first, 1965 parliamentary elections held under this system saw quite a few (TANU-sanctioned) challengers defeat incumbent politicians (Cliffe 1967), but this initial space for competition and accountability quickly diminished (see chapter 5).

47. "Appeal for Funds—The Songea Development Association Southern Region Tanganyika," in possession of the author, courtesy of Griff Cunningham.

48. "A Plan for the Development of an Independent Progressive Rural Society in Line with Christian Principles, the African Cultural Background and the Thoughts of the Nation's Leader," n.d., but likely from the first half of 1963 (East Africana Collection, University of Dar es Salaam).

49. "Appeal for Funds—The Songea Development Association Southern Region Tanganyika," in possession of the author, courtesy of Griff Cunningham.

50. Interview with Cunningham, New York, February 13, 2002.

51. See Ibbott (1970, 66–70) on this visit.

52. The RDA subsequently drew repeatedly on this connection in the ministry (Ibbott 1970, 79, 88, 94, 121–122, 167).

53. A June 24, 1968, letter from an assistant of the agricultural principal secretary to the regional agricultural officer in Iringa corroborates Ibbott's (1970, 96) point; regarding the RDA, it notes, "You

will see that I am not requesting you to take any active part in this group's affairs, as the success so far achieved in developing these rural communities, has been due to a great extent to the fact that the people have been encouraged to do things voluntarily and on a self-help basis and there has been no Government 'pressure.' I am attaching a copy of a de-classified confidential letter addressed to the regional agricultural officer, Songea which sets out our own position and indicates the part you are expected to play" (TNA 640/A/ASS/RUV/D).

54. Interview with Millinga, conducted with Edwards, Dar es Salaam, October 2000. Compare also Brain (1977), Cunningham (1966, 51), and Ibbott (1970, 78).

55. Ruvuma Development Association Newsletters, March 1964 and March 1965 (East Africana Collection, University of Dar es Salaam). In late 1968, there was a grant of TSh 38,000 for the school at Litowa from TANU headquarters (*Nationalist*, December 3, 1968). Litowa also received TSh 61,415.50 for a bridge and TSh 14,852.50 for constructing the approach ramps, TSh 3,129 for wool spinning equipment, TSh 2,789 for roofing, around TSh 10,000 for seeds and fertilizer, and TSh 2,700 for six heads of cattle; Liweta was supported with TSh 36,000 for a bridge, TSh 5,000 for a grain storage, and TSh 2,700 for six heads of cattle; and Matetereka received TSh 7,000 for a grain-storage ("*Songea—Taarifa ya Matumizi 31.8.1972 ya Fedha za RDF—Songea*," enclosed in a file on "District Development Minutes" [Songea District Office D3/9/1/Vol. III]; "*Ripoti za Mwaka kuhusu Shuguli za Chama: kwa Kipindi cha Mwaka Mzima wa 1968*" [NZC 4/THQ R20/18]).

56. Betts's connection through the Fabian Colonial Bureau to Nyerere and Wicken reached back to 1956 when he had assisted Nyerere in drafting a London speech calling for independence (Jennings 1998, 143, 152). He visited the RDA on several occasions (Ibbott 1970, 76).

57. In Mlale's case, the Irish Freedom from Hunger Campaign provided large amounts of capital, but two million shillings still came from government coffers (reports in a Ministry of Agriculture file [TNA 640/P/SCH/V/RUV]; Ibbott 1966, 5).

58. Ibbott (1970, 61–62) suggests that Mlale's very poor sales were in part due to settlers' selling tobacco through back channels in order to circumvent any fees that management might levy.

59. Various correspondences between the scheme's manager and the commissioner for village settlement schemes (TNAD 411/VS/C200/3/4).

60. On these ideas and vocabularies compare Korten (1980), Uphoff (1983, 1992), Esman and Uphoff (1984), and Uphoff, Esman, and Krishna (1998).

61. In this respect, the RDA's experience points beyond Putnam's (1993) overly static, "history as destiny" conception of social capital, while at the same time underscoring its importance as a factor in development; compare Evans (1996) and Barker and Cwikowski (1999, 18–19).

62. The so-called Ross Report (Ross, Worsley, and Clayton 1965) and an internal government report (URT 1966a) were the first official reviews. Newiger (1968) reviews most schemes in his report written in late 1965. An in-depth government-commissioned review of the schemes was carried out by the Syracuse University Village Settlement Project between early 1965 and 1966; it comprises forty-three detailed reports compiled by eight researchers associated with the project (Syracuse University 1966). Several of them later published work that drew on this research; see, for instance, Nellis (1972), Myers (1973), and Brain (1977).

63. The Ross Report (Ross, Worsley, and Clayton 1965, chap. 12) severely criticized the managerial staff of the schemes, for instance commenting on assistant managers, "The best of them, and even some managers themselves, are not accustomed to making accurate, regular quantitative estimates of an economic kind." It concluded, "We recognize that such [competent] people are not easy to come by, but they are essential if the country's resources are not to be squandered."

64. See Kawawa (1966) and Bomani (1966) for this announcement and the government's reasoning. A review conducted in August and September of 1967 by René Dumont urged the speeding up of this process in light of continuing mismanagement (URT 1969, 8–10, 33–35).

65. Interview with Millinga, conducted with Edwards, Dar es Salaam, October 2000.

66. On the background of the Arusha Declaration, see in particular Hartmann (1991a, 1985) and Coulson (1982, 176–183).

67. Under the subheading "Let Us Pay Heed to the Peasant," the declaration states, "There are two possible ways of dividing the people in our country. We can put the capitalists and feudalists on one side, and the farmers and workers on the other. But we can also divide the people into urban dwellers on one side and those who live in the rural areas on the other. If we are not careful we might get to the position where the real exploitation in Tanzania is that of the town dwellers exploiting the peasants" (Nyerere 1968, 242–243).

68. Nyerere's first major written exposition of this notion, in his 1962 paper "*Ujamaa*—The Basis of African Socialism," had described it as a "state of mind" that would forestall exploitative relations in the newly emerging nation (Nyerere 1966). Now, this earlier emphasis on utilizing the fruits of the nation's labor "for the good of all" was crucially augmented with a stress on "working together," i.e., the organization of production.

69. Both Ibbott (1966) and Cunningham (1966) wrote on the RDA for *Mbioni*, the journal of Kivukoni College. Nyerere specifically requested to see the report drafted by Betts and Cunningham on a follow-up to the April seminar on rural development in September 1966 (Jennings 2008, 152–153). Shortly after, TANU's Research Department solicited copies of any available written documents on its activities from the RDA (Ibbott 1970, 85–86). In January 1967, Nyerere had sent Joan Wicken to Litowa to collect ideas for the March 1967 post-Arusha paper "Education for Self-Reliance" (Ibbott 1970, 88): "Many of the ideas in 'Education for Self-Reliance' originated at Litowa, and not the other way around," notes Coulson (1984, 13). Nyerere occasionally explicitly acknowledged these connections. The 1967 "Socialism and Rural Development," for instance, proposed that "although it must be stressed that no one model should be imposed on any village," "the experience of existing ujamaa villages, such as those now operating within the Ruvuma Development Association, could be helpful" in drawing up "a model constitution for [ujamaa] villages" (Nyerere 1968, 365). The RDA is also referred to elsewhere, for instance in Nyerere's January 21, 1968, paper "Implementation of Rural Socialism" (Nyerere 1973, 7).

70. By contrast, in his 1962 "President's Inaugural Address," Nyerere (1966, 183–184) had still stressed easier provision of services, economies of scale, and the need for more capital-intensive production: "If our people are going to continue living scattered over a wide area . . . we shall not be able to provide ourselves with the things we need to develop our land and to raise our standard of living. We shall not be able to use tractors; we shall not be able to provide schools for our children; we shall not be able to build hospitals, or have clean drinking water."

71. Cunningham's "Memorandum on Organisation of Ujamaa Village Implementation in 2nd Five Year Development Plan," in possession of the author, courtesy of Griff Cunningham.

72. The January 10, 1969, *Nationalist* reported that a first course for village leaders would take about thirty people and last for about four months. Three courses for village leaders eventually took place; a group of graduates from the Teachers Training College at Morogoro had also been selected to receive training (Ibbott 1970, 112–113).

73. The *Nationalist* reported extensively on these seminars: see the issues of June 11 and 27; July 2, 3, 5, 16, 19, and 29; August 2, 6, and 21; and September 1, 1969. RDA speakers are often noted; see also Edwards (1998, 15) and Ibbott (1970, 105, 118–119).

74. "*Mpango wa Semina Kuhusu Vijiji vya Ujamaa*," September 29, 1969 (TNA 513/D3/14/V); *Nationalist*, September 25, October 3 and 20, and November 21, 1969; January 5, and March 4 and 20, 1970. After the RDA's destruction in late September 1969, the seminars were run by Kisumo's Ministry of Regional Administration and Rural Development.

75. Fifteen political education students from Kivukoni College went to RDA villages, for instance ("*Wanafunzi 15 Kwa Vijiji vya Ujamaa*," August 13, 1969 [NZC 9/MMT/V.20/15]; *Nationalist*, August 16, 1969).

2. Culture Clash

1. The ministry was formed through a merger in mid-1968 of the Ministry of Regional Administration with the Ministry of Local Government and Rural Development, itself only created in 1967; Kisumo had been in charge of the latter almost from its beginnings (*Sunday News,* January 21, 1968; *Nationalist,* March 7 and August 31, 1968).

2. In addition to these seventeen representatives, the committee included the president, the second vice president, and a handful of other important officials.

3. The *Nationalist* carried the announcement on July 30, 1969. The other two villages were Mbambara in Tanga, which had been advised by the RDA, and Njoomlole, which had earlier been associated with the RDA but had by then cut its ties (see below). Mbambara's chairman B. Kilonso attended the RDA's first leadership training program from November 1966 until May 1967 (Ibbott 1970, 105). The "best village in Tanga Region" in 1970, Mbambara's fortunes were apparently declining toward the mid-1970s (Mapolu 1973; Coulson 1982, 243–244).

4. *"Kumbukumbu za Mkutano wa Kamati Kuu Uliofanyika D'Salaam Tarehe 20th September, 1969 na Kuendelea 24/9/1969"* (NZC 3/115).

5. Rajabu Diwani, a high-ranking party official responsible for culture and youth; Pius Msekwa, the party's national executive secretary; and Thomas Musa rounded out the delegation (*"Taarifa ya Kazi za Chama Mwaka 1969"* [NZC 4/THQ/R20/18]).

6. In a similar vein, Musti de Gennaro (1979, 4) remarks that the RDA challenged "the elitist conception of people as passive recipient[s] of directives descending from the top." This chapter's discussion seeks to give this observation the close attention it deserves.

7. Coulson (1984, 19) suggests that "officials probably realised—consciously or subconsciously—that if the RDA type of village became the norm there would be no place for them."

8. There was a dispute over a third tractor; Liweta appears to have received a new one (*"Mhutasari wa Matatizo ya Njoomlole kwa Ufupi,"* n.d. [NZC 9/MMT/T50s/II]; interview with Millinga, conducted with Edwards, Dar es Salaam, October 2000). A report on the best villages in the country notes that Litowa derived substantial income, thirty-two thousand shillings for July 1971 to July 1972, from a timber business (URT 1972). On January 25, 1975, the *Daily News* reported that "last year" Litowa had earned sixty thousand shillings from "timber works."

9. Matetereka, for instance, pushed an apparently reluctant regional commissioner hard to eventually receive a grain mill, a water pump, and construction materials for a dispensary and a school (*"Development Kijiji cha Ujamaa Matetereka"* [Songea District Office D3/16]; *"Taarifa ya Kujenga Taifa Mwezi Januari 1970"* [TNA573/FU/K/II/II]). The village finally appealed directly to Nyerere, who ordered the regional commissioner to deliver what had been requested (Edwards 1998, 18–21).

10. In the two years following the disbanding, the ex-RDA villages received: several hundred chickens for several of the villages; a new tractor for Liweta; land surveys at Liweta and Matetereka; a grain mill, a water pump, and construction materials for a dispensary and a school at Matetereka; and several cattle dips and other construction projects (*"Taarifa ya Mwaka 1970 Mkoa wa Ruvuma"* [TNA 597/FA/D10/11]; *"Songea—Taarifa ya Matumizi 31.8.1972 ya Fedha za RDF—Songea"* [Songea District Office D3/9/1/Vol. III]; *"Taarifa ya Mapato na Matumizi ya No. 3 A/c. Fedha za kazi za maendeleo 1968—31st Dec. 1970"* [Songea District Office D30/5B]; URT [1971]; miscellaneous reports by the Ministry of Agriculture contained in TNA 640/A/AR/R/RUV; *"Development Kijiji cha Ujamaa Matetereka"* [Songea District Office D3/16]; *"Taarifa ya Kujenga Taifa Mwezi Januari 1970"* [TNA573/FU/K/II/II]).

11. Originally from Bukoba, Barongo had served as district secretary and, from 1957, provincial secretary of TANU in that area before becoming TANU's provincial chairman in 1958; he was also elected as an MP in 1960. After independence, he became deputy secretary general of TANU and was

appointed regional commissioner in the Northern Region and parliamentary secretary in the Ministry of Agriculture. After his 1965 defeat in the parliamentary elections for Ihangiro constituency at the hands of Jeremiah Bakampenja, one of the MPs dismissed in the West Lake Affair (see chapter 5), he succeeded Peter Walwa as regional commissioner in Ruvuma (Hydén 1967; 1969, 127–129; Bienen 1970, 25, 136–137).

12. Barongo remained connected to the crop past Ruvuma. During his brief subsequent tenure as regional commissioner in Morogoro Region, he presided over the opening of a tobacco processing plant about which he wrote a glowing report for the May 22, 1969, *Nationalist*. By 1972 he had become the executive chairman of the newly created Tobacco Authority of Tanzania (*Daily News,* September 28, 1972) in which position he was afforded the opportunity to report on the good work he had done for tobacco in Songea in his earlier career (*Daily News,* September 29, 1972).

13. Interview with Millinga, conducted with Edwards, Dar es Salaam, October 2000.

14. Ibbott to Nyerere, October 31, 1969, in possession of the author, courtesy of Ralph Ibbott.

15. Millinga made at least three successful recommendations to Nyerere from the second half of 1968 (Ibbott 1970, 110–111).

16. When the ministry was created out of its two predecessors in mid-1968, there was no Ujamaa Division (*Nationalist,* August 31, 1968).

17. Joan Wicken, correspondence with the author, April 29, 2002.

18. *"Kumbukumbu za Mkutano wa Kamati Kuu Uliofanyika D'Salaam Tarehe 20th September, 1969 na Kuendelea 24/9/1969"* (NZC 3/115).

19. *"Taarifa ya Kazi za Chama Mwaka 1969"* (NZC 4/THQ R20/18).

20. See Jennings (1998, 155). Brain (1977, 244) likewise comments on the "official adoption of the policy of *Ujamaa* villages": it was "in theory very like the RDA villages. . . . To those who had been concerned in settlement in Tanzania and were now outside the country these seemed exciting developments, and it was hoped that the RDA villages would be able to form a model for the new *Ujamaa* villages."

21. The composition of this group is not certain. According to the July 30, 1969, *Nationalist*, Rajabu Diwani, A. S. Masasi, A. Biseko, and A. Matope had initially been scheduled to go to Litowa, although, according the official minutes of the Central Committee meeting of July 29, 1969, Matope was supposed to go to Njoomlole, and Martin Chengula (Ruvuma's representative on the Central Committee who had been part of the visiting party of college principals) was supposed to be the fourth member of the Litowa group (*"Kumbukumbu za Mkutano wa Kamati Kuu Uliofanyika katika Ofisi ya TANU Handeni. Tarehe 29/7/69"* [NZC 5/1618]). However, neither Diwani nor Masasi were reported to have arrived in Ruvuma (*"Taarifa ya Kazi za Chama Mwaka 1969"* [NZC 4/THQ/R20/18]). Ibbott (1970, 121) reports that "Bisekwa" [*sic:* Biseko?] was the "most outspoken of those staying at Litowa."

22. The author was the headmaster of the Ujamaa Cadre School at Litowa that had been established by Millinga's Ujamaa Department.

23. The Litowa school was apparently not the only school in the country that failed to instill in its pupils sufficient respect for officials. Notes Honeybone (1985, 41–42), once the vice principal of the University of Dar es Salaam, "I recall when the Principal, Cranford Pratt, and I were invited to State House in the very early days of the College for an informal discussion on the concern felt by some Ministers at the rudeness shown to them on various formal visits to secondary schools."

24. See the headmaster's description of education at Litowa (Toroka 1973); see also Ibbott (1970, 94, 164–190, 241–242) and Wenner (1970).

25. Joan Wicken, correspondence with the author, April 29, 2002.

26. Ibbott to Nyerere, October 31, 1969, in possession of the author, courtesy of Ralph Ibbott.

27. Millinga identifies Nyerere, his brother Joseph Nyerere, and Selemani Mhigiri as the RDA's only supporters at the meeting (Edwards 1998, 17).

28. In his October 1969 letter to Nyerere, Ibbott notes specifically that Martin Chengula, Ruvuma's representative on the CC, had sensed a plot against him that involved Litowa's bull, Simba: perhaps ridiculous at the surface, noted Ibbott, such fears appeared to be quite genuine and real.

29. According to Edwards (1998, 31), Matetereka's longtime chairman was thus accused by a local government official in 1971 and again in 1991; after the second incident, "the allegation of witchcraft spread further: 'Nothing can be done in Matetereka. If you do anything, you will get sick!' Apparently, this rumour was even repeated recently [in the 1990s] by a Government Minister." Brain (1981, 12), commenting more generally on the corrosive nature of witchcraft accusations, notes "that people . . . may say that the entire successful village is a group of witches, as I [was] told was the case with the original *ujamaa* village of the Ruvuma Development Association [Litowa]."

30. See Brain (1981) for very similar arguments about the specific Tanzanian context and Thompson (1985) for a fascinating case study of a village politician and his encounter with witchcraft that also illustrates such dynamics. Smith (2008) has explored the intricate interconnection of development and witchcraft in Kenya.

31. The wording of the paper's September 25 coverage and the wording of the (secret) minutes of the prior day's Central Committee meeting were quite similar, for instance.

32. Although it had in its early days been tightly bound into the state apparatus—under its first (1963) constitution the Ruvuma regional commissioner was the association's chairman and its governing body included representatives from various ministerial and government departments—these formal ties had lost practical relevance by mid-1964 and were severed de jure in 1965 with the adoption of a new constitution that established the association as an independent organization.

33. Ibbott for instance acted as treasurer of the Regional Development Fund in 1964/1965 (Ibbott 1970, 73–74) and Millinga had received a personal invitation from the regional commissioner to join the body in late 1964 (letter from P. C. Walwa to Millinga, November 16, 1964 [File D30/2 "Regional Development Committee (Songea) 1964–8/1965" at the regional office, Songea]). Ibbott and Millinga were also members of the Songea District Council, and Millinga chaired it in 1964 (Ibbott 1970, 45, 73–74; Minutes of Songea District Council meeting of June 1964 [TNA 511/NA/34]).

34. Likewise, Edwards (1998, 16), whose informant on the proceedings was Millinga, reports that at the September 1969 Central Committee meeting, the school was singled out for teaching its students to work against the party.

35. Joan Wicken, correspondence with the author, April 29, 2002.

36. Compare especially Cliffe (1967) and Brennan (2005) on the establishment of one-party democracy and the short history of opposition parties in Tanzania.

37. Edwards (1998, 44), citing personal communications with Joan Wicken and Ralph Ibbott.

38. Musti de Gennaro (1979, 2) notes the rumor without indicating whether it circulated before or after the RDA's destruction. The "Kambona Affair" reached a fever pitch in October 1969, just after the RDA's destruction, when allegations of a coup attempt resulted in the institution of a treason trial (Tordoff and Mazrui 1972, 440; Mwakikagile 2007, 356–374). Kambona hailed from Ruvuma and served as the association's ceremonial president in its early days.

39. "*Kuagana na Bw. Ralph Ibbott—Mshauri wa Litowa Ujamaa Village*" (NZC 3/109).

40. Joan Wicken, correspondence with the author, April 29, 2002.

41. Regional Commissioner Klerruu's 1969 annual report from Mtwara Region, to the west of Ruvuma and also sharing a border with Mozambique, for instance, noted the assassination and connected it to increased vigilance and efforts to support FRELIMO in his region ("Taarifa ya Mwaka 1969" [TNA 584/A3/41]).

42. Letters of July 22 and August 16, 1968, from K. Johansen, for principal secretary of agriculture, Dar es Salaam, to ESTABS (TNA 640/A/ASS/RUV/D).

43. The trope of self-reliance had a central place in Tanzanian discourse on development and socialism and played in a number of registers. Thus, individual Tanzanians and village collectivities

were called upon to be self-reliant—as much as national self-reliance was counterposed against (neo) colonial dependency. The notion could then be invoked to deflect demands for public provisions (a village could be told to be self-reliant) as well as to make such demands (the nation's self-reliance implied collective obligations). Compare especially Lal (2012) and chapter 4 for a case of the concept's invocation in officials' attempts to deflect popular demands and deny responsibility.

44. Compare also Sadleir (1999, 284) on this and related vocabulary.

45. Compare also Burgess (2005) on Zanzibar.

46. See Ranger's (1983) classic argument about the "invention" of such traditions under indirect rule; Iliffe (1979) for a general treatment of Tanzania; Hodgson (2001) for the case of Tanzanian Maasai with a focus on gender; and Spear (2003) for a treatment that highlights the complexities and many-sidedness of the workings of indirect rule in Tanzania.

47. Joan Wicken, correspondence with the author, April 29, 2002.

48. Ibbott to Nyerere, October 31, 1969, in possession of the author, courtesy of Ralph Ibbott.

49. Ibbott to Nyerere, October 31, 1969, in possession of the author, courtesy of Ralph Ibbott.

50. A detailed report and three-year plan (n.d.) were sent to the regional commissioner, the area commissioner, and, unusually, Second Vice President Kawawa, while Nyerere was ignored—hinting perhaps at certain political alignments (TNA 640/P/SCH/V). A five-year plan dated June 7, 1965, and addressed to the Songea District Development Council came with a request for TSh 469,450 in aid (TNA 511/D2/1). Copies of Njoomlole's 1967 constitution are in the files of the Ministry of Agriculture (TNA 640/P/SCH/V/RUV) and a collection of personal files of Rajabu Diwani, a member of the Central Committee, at the party headquarters (NZC 5/924).

51. As early as March 1968, Kisumo referred to such a "general line" that was being worked out by his ministry (Nationalist, March 11, 1968). Guidelines dealing with organizational aspects of ujamaa villages were sent out to all local authorities shortly after (Nationalist, June 29, 1968).

52. Njoomlole's constitution is, for instance, referred to in an early 1970 Karagwe District report on village development ("Taarifa ya Kazi za Wajumbe Katika Kijiji cha Kiruruma," n.d., but stamped February 4, 1970 [TNAM M20B/D34]). TANU headquarters sent a sample constitution modeled on Njoomlole's to all regional commissioners on July 12, 1969 (TNA 562/UV/1/1); on September 6, 1969, the commissioner for development in Kisumo's ministry also sent out such a document (TNA 562/UV/1/1).

53. The Nationalist repeatedly singled out as especially praiseworthy the contributions to the July 1969 Central Committee seminar of "Mr. J. Mhagama, a peasant [and local MP] from Njoomlole uja-maa village" (Nationalist, July 5, 1969; see also July 3 and 16). The paper also ran reports on the village's activities on August 5, 1969; July 8, 1970 (in the context of its being declared the best ujamaa village in Ruvuma Region); and November 2, 1970.

54. Kawawa, who had been born near Njoomlole, and Kisumo are believed to have been behind large financial support to the village (Ibbott to Nyerere, October 31, 1969, in possession of the author, courtesy of Ralph Ibbott; interview with Millinga, conducted with Edwards, Dar es Salaam, October 2000). An August 1969 document records a tractor, cars, fifty thousand shillings in financing, and a grain mill going to Njoomlole. The "Benefactor" is indicated as "Govt." (TNA 562/UV/1/1). That none of these items, with the exception of the milling machine (ten thousand shillings), appears to have come from the predominant and typical source of such funding, the Regional Development Fund, is a strong indication that the village had powerful supporters outside the region ("Taarifa ya Mwaka 1970 Mkoa wa Ruvuma" [TNA 597/FA/D10/11]; "Ripoti za Mwaka kuhusu Shuguli za Chama: kwa Kipindi cha Mwaka Mzima wa 1968" [NZC 4/THQ/R20/18]; "Songea—Taarifa ya Matumizi 31.8.1972 ya Fedha za RDF—Songea" [Songea District Office D3/9/1/Vol. III]; "Taarifa ya Mapato na Matumizi ya No. 3 A/c. Fedha za kazi za maendeleo 1968—31st Dec. 1970" [Songea District Office D30/5B]).

55. This crisis, which erupted in 1970, is documented in about a dozen pieces of correspondence collected in a report compiled by Millinga, whose department had been asked to look into the mat-

ter ("*Mhutasari wa Matatizo ya Njoomlole kwa Ufupi,*" n.d. [NZC 9/MMT/T50s/II]). It saw interventions by the area and regional commissioners and a delegation from TANU headquarters—none of which apparently resolved the issue. Through all this, commented Millinga, "Njoomlole regresses instead of growing and people outside Njoomlole have a demonstration that they should rather start other villages than join with it."

56. Various planning documents and reports connected to the scheme in a Ministry of Agriculture file (TNA 640/P/SCH/V/RUV).

57. It had been felt that Mlale and two neighboring schemes might require relocation because of their proximity to the sensitive border with Mozambique (various reports in a file from the Ministry of Agriculture [TNA 640/P/SCH/V/RUV]).

58. "*Kumbukumbu za Mkutano wa Kamati Kuu Uliofanyika D'Salaam Tarehe 20th September, 1969 na Kuendelea 24/9/1969*" (NZC 3/115); *Nationalist,* September 22, 23, 24, and 25, 1969.

59. Ibbott to Nyerere, October 31, 1969, in possession of the author, courtesy of Ralph Ibbott.

60. "*Mhutasari wa Matatizo ya Njoomlole kwa Ufupi,*" n.d. (NZC 9/MMT/T50s/II).

61. "*Taarifa ya 1/2 Mwaka ya Chama Julai—Disemba 1969*" (NZC 4/THQ R20/18).

62. Interview with Millinga, conducted with Edwards, Dar es Salaam, October 2000; Musti de Gennaro (1979, 21). Edwards (2003, 170) notes two of the smaller villages that did survive; one more is noted in 1978 reports contained in a file on villages in Songea District (TNAD PMO15/PM/UV/V96).

63. See URT (1972, i) and Mapolu (1973) for these selections; for a general background and some selection criteria used in these competitions see McHenry (1979, 94–97). A few years later Matetereka, too, won the honor (Ergas 1980, 410).

64. The school's new headmaster, for instance, caused severe strains when he refused to allow the long-established communal use of "the school's property" ("*Mhutasari wa Matatizo ya Njoomlole kwa Ufupi,*" n.d. [NZC 9/MMT/T50s/II]).

65. In the 1980s, Matetereka was declared the sixth best village in the country, best village in the region, and twice the best village in the district (Edwards 1998, 34, 38).

66. Ndonde (1975a, 176) remarks on "the confusion brought about by the influx of non-wajamaa to Litowa during Operation Tanzania" in early 1974. By 1976 Litowa had ceased to be an ujamaa village (Musti de Gennaro 1981, 131). Matetereka negotiated this influx more successfully, albeit with great difficulty (Edwards 1998, 29–38).

67. See chapter 3. Ndonde (1975a, 167–168) notes that villagization heralded the widespread destruction of existing ujamaa activities—as ujamaa fields were parceled out to new settlers and as some practicing ujamaa groups were forced to resettle; compare Barker (1974, 459), Mesaki (1975), von Freyhold (1976, 142; 1979, 58–59, 102), de Vries and Fortmann (1979, 143), and Hill (1979, 107–109).

3. Chronicle of a Failure Foretold

1. Confidential memorandum "Implementing Ujamaa," in possession of the author, courtesy of Griff Cunningham. Griff Cunningham was a member of this group, as were Lionel Cliffe and Andrew Coulson.

2. Confidential memorandum "Points for Discussion at Inter-Ministerial Meeting on Implementing Ujamaa," in possession of the author, courtesy of Griff Cunningham.

3. Confidential memorandum "Implementing Ujamaa," in possession of the author, courtesy of Griff Cunningham.

4. All documents in possession of the author, courtesy of Griff Cunningham.

5. Cunningham recollects that an official from the Ministry of Development Planning, Brian van Arkadie, acted as the messenger to a mid-1968 meeting of the group (interview with Cunningham, New York, February 13, 2002).

6. Wrote Nyerere (1973, 59) in "Freedom and Development": "Freedom from hunger, sickness and poverty depends upon an increase in the wealth and the knowledge available in a community; for a group of people can only consume and use the wealth they have already produced."

7. Nyerere was very familiar with Mill's thought: as a student in 1944, he had, for instance, written a major essay entitled "The Freedom of Women" that drew heavily on Mill (Mwakikagile 2007, 79, 571).

8. The *Nationalist* of April 10, 18, and 25, 1968, reported on these visits.

9. Kami (1981, 17) reports that by the late 1970s a compromise seemed to have been reached: "There are temporary huts in the valley, where farmers can reside during the farming and harvesting seasons. However, the huts are restricted to remain as mere temporary only, by the government." Compare also Havnevik (1993, 223–224) for the existence of a not quite enforceable policy to keep people in the new villages. There appears to have been a general pattern of tolerating a loosening of the newly imposed settlement pattern when its agricultural costs became clear (compare Edwards [2003, 170] on Ruvuma).

10. Four months later, there was a plan for construction projects, a land-clearing program, and a cash-crop development program involving various ministries (various folios, Ministry of Agriculture [TNA 640/P/SCH/V/RUF]).

11. The *Nationalist* of November 27, 1969, reported on another speech by Kawawa: "Crime was one of the problems facing the nation at present, but the masses could easily surmount it if they lived in ujamaa villages." In similarly broad terms, he also advertised ujamaa villages as "the main bases of [the] struggle" "to eradicate all weakness inflicted on our nation by those who oppressed and exploited us" (*Nationalist*, October 3, 1970). The vice chairman of Tanzania's official women's organization supplied more reasons: "Nothing would make many longstanding problems affecting women in this country completely disappear like the spreading of Ujamaa villages" (*Nationalist*, July 11, 1970). McHenry (1979, 120–121) cites a series of similar messages.

12. See Mesaki (1999, 209–210) on witchcraft fears in post-villagization Rufiji. Compare Barker (1974, 457–458) for Mbeya; Omari (1976, 134) for Kibondo; van Bergen (1981, 124) for Dodoma; Mesaki (1994, 54–56) for Sukumaland; Mombeshora (1994, 84) for Ubena; and Brain (1981, 11) for a general treatment.

13. "*Ripoti Kuhusu Maendeleo ya Ujenzi wa Ujamaa Katika Vijiji Vya Vya [sic] Ujamaa Vya Rufiji*," January 4, 1971 (NZC 3/115). The report indirectly attacks Kisumo for putting such stress on the need to get things done, which, the report suggests, has only "put these people into the difficulty they are now in."

14. In March 1970, only ten out of twenty-eight settlements listed in a table compiled by the administrative officer of Rufiji District had a piped water supply or a spring (Yoshida 1974, 104–105).

15. People had coped with the dual environmental constraint of droughts and flooding through a system of mobile settlement and flexible regimes of subsistence that relied on agriculture and fishing in the plains and included the option of labor migration as far as Dar es Salaam. As resettlement undercut this system, the area's food self-sufficiency and agricultural output deteriorated, with the worst effects in the upstream areas: there resettlement implied moving not just out of the floodplains but to the opposite river bank. On this and other aftereffects of resettlement in Rufiji, see Angwazi and Ndulu (1973), Sandberg (1973), Turok (1975), Bantje (1979, 1980), and Havnevik (1983, 1993).

16. As Angwazi and Ndulu (1973, 2–3) note, people eventually adapted to the secular decline of agriculture with intensified out-migration to urban centers and by shifting into alternative activities such as charcoal making, petty trading, and fishing.

17. Compare the *Daily News* of August 12, 1972, for another Nyerere speech and the August 21 paper for a speech by Vice President Jumbe.

18. Thus the January 3, 1968, *Standard* (quoted in Ingle 1970, 81–82) reported on Nyerere's appearance at a conference for officials of the Ministry of Local Government and Rural Development, "Look-

ing at the Minister . . . President Nyerere said: 'So Bwana [Mister], let us have some bylaws to check this laziness.'"

19. "Interview with Nyerere: Tanzania July 7, 1974—Saba Saba Twenty Years After" in *African Development, Special Tanzania Supplement,* July 1974.

20. A 1974 confidential BRALUP report "Villagisation in the Coast Region" for TANU headquarters by Marja-Liisa Swantz (NZC 5/1235) critically comments on the widespread notion in Coast Region "that 'people have to be told,' that 'people have to be taught, people have to be made to understand.'" Boesen, Madsen, and Moody (1977, 155) comment on state officials' "attitudes towards ordinary villagers as ignorant, unskilled, subordinate people to whom it was useless to listen." Examples of such official/peasant dynamics are many, including a videotaped case of the local agricultural officer at Mbambara in Tanga; for the impressions of the team that filmed Mbambara's life see Tanzania Year 16 Project (1975). Resnick (1981, 117–118, 251–253) reports on several village meetings that also bear vivid testimony to such dynamics. See Mshana (1992), Swantz (1995), and Swantz and Tripp (1996) for perceptive case studies that observe such tendencies more recently.

21. 1974 confidential BRALUP report "Villagisation in the Coast Region" for TANU headquarters by Marja-Liisa Swantz (NZC 5/1235) for Coast Region; Mesaki (1975) for Kisarawe District; Havnevik (1993, 223) for Rufiji District; compare Mesaki (1999, 210–211) for the persistence of such official attitudes in Rufiji that made coercive measures palatable into the 1990s.

22. *"Taarifa ya Uhamiaji Vijijini Vya Maendeleo Mkoani Pwani 1974,"* October 26, 1974 (NZC 3/118). Such enforcement actions were often carried out by the People's Militia, created in early 1971 for national defense purposes (*Nationalist,* February 22 and March 8, 1971). Von Freyhold (1979, 56) notes that the militia was composed of "government staff . . . and frustrated rural youth who longed for jobs and status and to whom free uniforms and meals and the excitement of para-military campaigns were a welcome break in their wretched life in the villages."

23. *"Malalamiko ya Kupewa Kijiji . . . ,"* March 18, 1976, and attached *"Malalamiko ya Kuvunjiwa Nyumba . . . ,"* December 1, 1975 (NZC 9/MMT/U30/3/Vol. II).

24. Mesaki (1975, 92) documents that the district authorities in Kisarawe as well as the regional commissioner faced intense lobbying from "people who have relatives in the affected areas but residing in Dar es Salaam [who] formed an opposition group to fight for their relatives to stay where they are." Sitari (1983, 20) likewise contends that the "process passed off relatively peacefully in Bagamoyo District."

25. As Shivji (1986, 6) has noted, "Law becomes simply and without mediation the instrument of control and power. . . . Legislation is about enabling the state and state organs to exert unquestionable power rather than about individual rights." In the context of villagization, for instance, there "was total disregard of the existing customary land tenure system. . . . Villagisation was not preceded by any enabling legislation nor was any existing piece of legislation cited or applied to enable such an exercise" (URT 1994, 43). Only in 1973 did an act finally "g[i]ve the President unrestricted discretionary powers to declare any part of Tanzania a 'specified area'" in which the minister of regional administration was then "empowered to make regulations to control virtually any land use" (43).

26. Kisumo's remarks, quoted in the minutes of a regional meeting (*"Kumbukumbu ya Mkutano wa Pamoja wa R.D.C. na Halmashauri kuu ya TANU ya Mkoa wa Dodoma Uliofanyika Tarehe 28.3.70"* [TNA 640/AF/P/UV/DR]).

27. The November 27, 1969, *Nationalist* reported on an a speech by Kawawa—engaging in some interesting arithmetical acrobatics regarding land, people, and cattle pertinent to Dodoma's situation—that is another good example of the often mindless repetition of this mantra: "Ujamaa villages were very desirable . . . because cattle needed more land," the second vice president suggested. "If they [the people] stayed together there would be more land left for their cattle."

28. Compare Scott (1998, 245) for the same observation. Attention was almost exclusively directed to the most superficial countables: even the records of the Ministry of Agriculture are largely con-

cerned with the number of people moved to how many villages (TNA 640/AF/P/UV/DR). Hill (1979, 106–107) interprets Operation Dodoma as a crucial moment in the subtle but profound shift in emphasis from promoting an intangible—ujamaa vijijini (i.e., ujamaa in the villages) to a single-minded focus on establishing (countable) villages.

29. "Operation Dodoma—A Brief Evaluation" (NZC 5/1300). With villagization in Dodoma District completed, Mpwapwa and Kondoa districts were still lagging behind. According to the report, the plan for Dodoma District had been to set up seventy-two villages (26,315 families) in 1971, fifty-one villages (26,407 families) in 1972, and nineteen villages (18,000 families) in 1973. An earlier report was likewise heavily invested in its numbers, although they were slightly different ("*Taarifa ya Kazi za Chama kwa Kipindi Kinachoanzia Mwezi Mei, 1972 Hadi Machi, 1973 Mkoa wa Dodoma*" [NZC 3/107]).

30. "*Mpango wa Kijiji cha Ujamaa cha Nkulabi*" (TNAD A98); see chapter 4 on such plans and their general disconnect from the realities of the villages concerned.

31. Rigby (1969, 44–46) and Luttrell (1971, 10–11) raised these concerns at the time. See also Mascarenhas (1973).

32. Figures for December 1968, December 1969, and June 1971 from Ellman (1975, 321), who sources *The Economic Survey 1970–1*; for July 1969 from the *Nationalist* of July 15, 1968; for June 1975 and February 1977 from Havnevik (1993, 206); for October 1976 from Hirst (1978); all other figures from Coulson (1982, 241), who sources *The Economic Survey 1973–4*. National population figures from the IMF, International Financial Statistics.

33. Mara accounted for another fourteen villages, with the other regions boasting fewer than eight villages each.

34. In late 1971, Klerruu was fatally shot by a farmer in Iringa; upon his earlier transferral there, he had again produced a remarkable and rapid increase in the number of registered villages. The *Daily News* of September 14, 15, and 19 and October 3, 1972, covered the trial of the farmer, who was sentenced to hang.

35. A letter of January 11, 1969, from the Mtwara regional surveyor to the commissioner of the Surveys and Mapping Division in the Ministry of Lands, for instance, remarks that the idea of planning settlements had been "dropped" in Mtwara and "no requests for planning Ujamaa villages have ever been made to this office" (Confidential File C55 "Ujamaa Villages," Ministry of Lands, Division of Surveying and Mapping, Dar es Salaam). That the number of registered villages in Mtwara rose to around 1,100 by late 1972 and then dropped to 466 by 1976 (Hirst 1978) likewise suggests that only later developments consolidated a settlement pattern that had remained quite dispersed during this early period.

36. Klerruu's 1969 annual report makes several references to the region's frontline situation: for instance, it notes Eduardo Mondlane's February 1969 assassination in Dar es Salaam and increased support for FRELIMO ("Taarifa ya Mwaka 1969" [TNA 584/A3/41]). Already on July 18, 1968, the *Nationalist* had reported that Second Vice President Kawawa had announced the creation of twenty-six "Defense Ujamaa Villages" in Mtwara, as well as eighteen such villages in Ruvuma.

37. Accordingly, villages were to be organized into Sections ("*Kikundi*") of ten people, which would be combined into Platoons and Companies ("*Kombania*"). This somewhat exceptional situation likely heightened some of the martial and gendered characteristics that Lal (2010), largely basing her argument on Mtwara material, attributes to ujamaa and villagization more generally.

38. Thomas (1982, 182) comments on statistics from 1973: "Many of these villages were notional (that is, associations of scattered households often interspersed with non-member households) rather than discrete and nucleated settlements." Compare von Freyhold (1979, 43–44) on Tanga. Klerruu, who had established this pattern in Mtwara, appears to have continued with it at his subsequent postings: the three regions with the largest percentage drops in the number of registered villages between the early 1970s and 1976—Mtwara, from 1,100 in late 1972 to 466 in 1976; Lindi, from 626 in 1972 to 257 in 1976;

and Iringa, from 659 in 1973 to 464 in 1976—had all recorded earlier rapid increases in the number of registered villages under, or immediately following, a stint by Klerruu as regional commissioner.

39. Mmbaga (1976/1977) reports on 1973 struggles in Itobo Ward, Tabora Region, over which existing settlements would be declared official village sites. Edwards (2003, 170–171) observes the importance of existing infrastructure and ujamaa activities for determining who did, and who did not, have to move in Songea District; there, significant differences in the disruptiveness of resettlement between the largely Christian west and the predominantly Muslim east are in part explained by the fact that while churches were apparently treated as infrastructure that was worth preserving, mosques were not. Magoti (1984, 122) reports from Mara, "The progressive farmers, having built good, modern and permanent houses, persuaded the other peasants to come and settle in their fields, so as to save their good houses from destruction. . . . This had a very negative effect on productivity because the progressive farmers then became beggars of land." For similar dynamics involving large landholders, see von Freyhold (1976, 142; 1979, 44–46) and McHenry (1979, 145).

40. Letters of complaint from the group at Suwa-Kweikona dated October 25, 1968 [sic:1969] and October 26, 1969 (TNA 513/D3/14/V); Kallabaka (1978, 57–58).

41. Dodoma's example is instructive. Mascarenhas (1977, 27–28) estimates that of the 163 villages in Dodoma District, 93 were started on sites without prior settlement clusters and that approximately 25 percent of the people of Dodoma District moved distances greater than 5 miles. Thiele's (1986, 247) study of three Dodoma villages found that 18, 22, and 37 percent of their early 1980s population, respectively, had lived at these sites prior to villagization and that the mean distance moved in two of these villages was 2.2 and 3.9 kilometers, respectively; the greatest reported distance any interviewee had moved was 16.7 kilometers.

42. Preceded by an unusually long run-up phase, villagization in Kigoma was envisioned to take place in four annual phases starting in 1972 ("*Taarifa ya Maendeleo ya Shughuli Mbali Mbali za Chama. Mkoa wa Kigoma. Mei Hadi Septemba, 1972*" [NZC 3/111]). As it turned out, "Operation Kigoma" quickly moved beyond its established parameters. See McHenry (1974), Omari (1976), van Bergen (1981, 222–233), and, on Oxfam's involvement, Jennings (2008). The first noted resettlements in Chunya seem to have been related to a World Bank credit of sixty-five million shillings for tobacco development that was channeled into "tobacco villages" there as well as into Tabora and Kigoma (*Nationalist*, August 2, 1971; *Daily News*, September 25, 28, and 29, 1972). A full-scale "Operation Chunya," reported to have started in May 1972, more broadly aimed "to combat famine" (*Daily News*, October 3, 1972).

43. See Barker (1979, 111), Boesen (1979, 137), Ellis and Hanak (1980, 10), and Thomas (1982, 182). Maro and Mlay (1982, 180) observe, "Since 1975 there has been very little redistribution of population through villagization. The Villages and Ujamaa Villages Act of 1975 provided for the demarcation and registration of villages without necessarily redistributing the population."

44. Thomas (1985, 147, 149–150) estimates that in Iringa District the average distance households moved between 1967 and 1974 was 4.94 kilometers; in 1976, registered villages typically consisted of several, sometimes far-flung population clusters; see also Kikula (1997). Sitari's (1983) study of Bagamoyo shows that few village sites were new, that in cases of larger preexisting settlements slightly more than half the people had lived there before villagization, and that most moves were less than 5 kilometers. Kjaerby (1989, 37) reports a broadly similar picture from Hanang District, Arusha Region. Mascarenhas (1977) and Thiele (1982, 1986) put the mean distance moved in Dodoma at around 3 kilometers, the percentage of people moved around 70–75 percent, and the percentage of new sites among the registered villages at slightly more than half.

45. While Hydén (1980, 146) doubts that there was such an effect, most commentators come to the conclusion that villagization must have had serious costs not only, but certainly also, in terms of agricultural production (Lofchie 1978, 460; 1989, 117; Briggs 1979; Coulson 1982, 259–262; Kitching 1982, 108–110; Raikes 1986, 128).

46. As in Rufiji (see above), previously sporadic food-deficit conditions became a permanent state of affairs in many of Dodoma's new villages, for instance (Thiele 1982, 88). See chapters 4 and 5 on West Lake.

47. See especially Boesen, Madsen, and Moody (1977), Bernstein (1981), Coulson (1982), and McCall (1985).

48. Because of the latter issue, villagization also contributed to a concentration of cattle ownership in the hands of those who could afford to maintain and staff byres outside the villages. Overall, villagization in Dodoma resulted in increased dependence on government aid, a rise in wage-labor relations between and within villages, and—similar to Rufiji—a shift into nonagricultural production (e.g., charcoal making), especially in villages close to the urban center of Dodoma, although a few resettlement sites apparently escaped such detrimental effects by dint of lucky site selection. In one of three villages that Thiele studied in depth, for instance, large areas of fertile *nyika* soil ensured a boost to agricultural productivity—for as long, at least, as these soils had not been exhausted (Thiele 1982, 1986).

49. "*Taarifa ya Kamati ya Pamoja ya Chama na Serikali ya Kukagua Marekebisho ya Vijiji,*" March 10, 1981 (TNA 640/KI/D10/26). See also Boesen (1979, 128), de Vries and Fortmann (1979), and Hydén (1980, 145).

50. See, for instance, Boesen and Raikes (1976), Boesen, Madsen, and Moody (1977), de Vries (1978), and von Freyhold (1979).

51. Von Freyhold (1979, 87) documents severely limited capacity at the village level in this specific respect in Tanga in the early 1970s.

52. File on "Cooperative and Ujamaa Development" (TNAM 1/C20/9).

53. "Operation Dodoma—A Brief Evaluation" (NZC 5/1300).

54. Von Freyhold (1976, 142; 1979, 58–59, 102) and Barker (1974, 459) make similar observations in Tanga and Mbeya.

55. See Ergas (1980, 395, 410)—although a largely unenforced legal requirement to maintain a communally managed field of at least one hundred acres in each village seems to have been issued as late as 1980 (Sumra 1991, 242).

56. McHenry (1979, 137–145), drawing on reports by University of Dar es Salaam students from 1975, offers a broad review of the use of force during this period. Jennings (1998, 36–39) cites internal reports by Oxfam and other development agencies that document the use of force and especially the burning down of houses, sometimes with human casualties. See Mwapachu (1979, 119) for Geita, Shinyanga, and Maswa Districts; Matango (1975) for Mara Region; de Vries and Fortmann (1979) for Iringa Region; Parkipuny (1979) for Maasailand; Mesaki (1975) for Coast Region; Thiele (1982, 42) for Dodoma; and Bugengo and Mutangira (1976) for West Lake Region. Coulson (1982, 250–252) quotes relevant passages from several of these accounts.

57. "*Taarifa ya Juma Kuhusu Vijiji Vipya,*" May 8, 1968 (TNAM 19/WLD3/26). See chapter 5.

58. This history can be reconstructed from Kami (1981, 66), Havnevik (1993, 222–223), and the 1974 confidential BRALUP report "Villagisation in the Coast Region" for TANU headquarters by Marja-Liisa Swantz (NZC 5/1235).

59. McHenry (1979, 124–133) presents an overview of various forms of material inducements; see also Boesen (1979, 134–136) on West Lake and von Freyhold (1979, 45–50) on Tanga. Nyerere's Presidential Circular No. 1 of 1969 (Nyerere 1975, 28) had of course already stressed in March 1969 that "we have to give them [ujamaa villages] priority in all our credit, servicing and extension services."

60. In Iringa, for instance, struggles over land that were often the inevitable byproduct of chaotic resettlement to sites of previously existing settlements apparently became especially prevalent after a 1971 announcement by Nyerere that explicitly opened the way to land redistribution in the name of ujamaa/villagization (Awiti 1975, 418–419); it was also in Iringa that Regional Commissioner Klerruu was shot by a large farmer later that year (see note 34, above). Compare Kjaerby (1989, 40–44) on the

equalizing effects of villagization on land distribution in Hanang District. On the other hand, Edwards (2003, 184) documents the persistence of very large individual holdings based on claims to pre-villagization customary rights in Songea District. See Raikes (1975, 45) and Sender (1974) on opening up land for resettlement that had been reserved for conservation.

61. Almost identical speeches by the village chairman, retelling the story and indicating the village's profuse gratitude for this honor and for all the other things the government had done for it, are, for instance, reported on the occasions of Second Vice President Kawawa's visit to the village in April 1970 and Minister Sijaona's visit in September of the same year ("*Makamu wa Pili wa Rais, Bwana Rashidi Mfaume Kawawa,*" April 8, 1970 [TNAM 19/WLD3/26A]; report of September 22, 1970 [TNAM 19/ZM/BK/T/D30/46]).

62. Various folios in two files on the village, "*Kijiji cha Ujamaa—Rugazi*" (TNAM 19/ZM/BK/T/D30/46) and "*Kijiji cha Ujamaa—Rugaze—Tarafa Kianya*" (TNAM 19/WLD3/26A).

63. These efforts are documented in a file "*Development Kijiji cha Ujamaa Matetereka*" (Songea District Office D3/16) and a report "*Taarifa ya Kujenga Taifa Mwezi Januari 1970*" (TNA573/FU/K/II/II).

64. Collier, Radwan, and Wange (1986) offer a broad assessment based on a sample of six hundred households in twenty villages that notes achievements especially in health provision and education. Maro (1991) gives a sympathetic review of achievements in the provision of safe water, education, and health facilities—not, however, without also documenting serious problems. Compare also Kitching (1982, 105–106) and Coulson (1982, 216–218).

65. See especially Tschannerl (1976); compare Coward (1976) and Coulson (1982, 217–218).

4. Planning the Future

1. Headlines in the *Nationalist* of April 24 and January 9, 1968, November 9 and August 5, 1969, and August 7, 1967.

2. For a full discussion, see Schneider (2006).

3. The campaign's pitch would periodically sharpen and soften during a lifetime that extended at least into the mid-1970s. According to Talle (1999, 116), the issue of Maasai dress was again on the political agenda "more recently" (in the early 1990s?). However, Swantz (1995, 230) notes that "contemporary" rules to wear trousers under the lubega have "in the course of time been forgotten" and Hodgson (2001, 150) shows that "authentic" Maasai have in recent years become acceptable—and valued—as tourist attractions as well as security guards.

4. Hodgson (2001, 149) notes that political leaders, including Sokoine, were publicly cursed and that there were plans to complain directly to Nyerere. Since Mwakang'ata did not like to arrest offenders outright, the March 14, 1968, *Nationalist* reported, he had police take them to town for an explanation of the policy and a reprimand before releasing them. On December 17, 1968, the paper noted that students wearing the lubega had been banned from schools. Aud Talle (1999, 114, 116) states that the government also threatened to deny improperly dressed Maasai medical care and sanctioned their being denied access to bars, restaurants, and public transport.

5. Compare Mitchell (2000, xvi): "Modernizing approaches . . . must gather all the different histories of colonialism into a singular narrative of the coming of modernity. They can deal with the non-modern only as the absence of modernity, only as forms that lack the discipline, rationality, and abstraction of the modern order of things—and therefore, since they are defined by what they are not, as essentially similar to non-modern forms everywhere else."

6. Examples are legion; the *Nationalist* reported on numerous such speeches by top politicians: e.g., March 3, 1969 (Kisumo); March 14, 1969, and January 5, 1970 (Kawawa); and March 10, 1970 (Nyerere).

7. The remainder of this chapter draws heavily on Schneider (2007).

8. With respect to other cases, Scott argues that what made such schemes high-modernist—and hence harmful—was (also) their excessive reliance on generalizing "scientific" knowledge that is incapable of dealing with specific contexts. Scott (1998, 288; see also 298, 316) thus argues "that a substantial part of the problem lies in the systematic and necessary limitations of scientific work whenever the ultimate purpose of the work is practical adoption by a diverse set of practitioners working in a large variety of conditions." At times, he aims this critique at what he makes out to be essential qualities of scientific knowledge—describing it as inherently and irretrievably imperialist, exclusionary, and dangerously limited (340); at other times, he points the finger at how scientific knowledge may be drawn upon in an irresponsible manner that neglects *ceteris paribus* warnings (304). In the case of Tanzanian villagization, however, Scott stresses a different reading of high modernism: "Plans were not scientific or rational in any meaningful sense of those terms. What these planners carried in their mind's eye was a certain aesthetic, what one might call a visual codification of modern rural production and community life" (253).

9. Walwa had gotten his political start as TANU district chairman in Kwimba two years before independence. From July 1961, he attended Kivukoni College among the first batch of thirty-nine students that also included Millinga of the RDA. Before becoming Ruvuma's regional commissioner in 1964, he held a variety of other posts, including provincial secretary for Tanga, regional commissioner of the Northern Region, junior minister of agriculture in 1962, and junior minister of defense in 1963. He served as regional commissioner in West Lake until his transfer to Kilimanjaro in December 1968; he was dismissed from that post in early 1969 (Maguire 1969, 297–300, 326, 350; Ibbott 1970, 58, 244; Bienen 1970, 133–138; *Nationalist,* November 19 and December 2, 1968).

10. "*Mkutano wa Viongozi wa Wizara Zote Mkoa wa Magharibi,*" March 23, 1967 (TNAM 19/WLC 5/23/Vol. II and WLD3/23).

11. "*Hotabu ya Mheshimiwa Bwana P. C. Walwa, RC, West Lake—Wakati wa Kufungua Halmashauri ya Karagwe 23/3/67*" (TNAM 19/WLD3/23).

12. Report, May 18, 1967 (TNAM 19/WLD3/23).

13. "*Kumbukumbu juu ya Kilimo na Kujitegemea,*" n.d., but filed between documents dated April 14 and 21, 1967 (TNAM 19/WLD3/23).

14. Walwa's letter of May 31, 1967 (TNAM 19/WLD3/23).

15. "*Utimizaji wa Azimio la Arusha Utengenezaji wa Sheria za Kilimo Na Pombe,*" May 31, 1967 (TNAM 19/WLC 5/23/III).

16. "*Mkutano wa RC na Watumishi wa Serikali Wakuu wa Wizara Mkoani na Wilayani Viongozi na Watumishi wa Tanu Bukoba Cinema Hall 16/4/1968*" (TNAM 19/WLD3/25).

17. Compare Gupta's (2012) examination of writing as a constitutive state practice in the contemporary Indian context.

18. Scott (1998, 243) reproduces Boesen, Madsen, and Moody's (1977, 78) map, itself a reproduction, with slight modifications, of Rald's (1970) original.

19. This is unlikely to have changed substantially in the years after the survey was conducted: the map shows 244 primary, household plots; however, after a period from early 1969 into early 1970 when several reports claimed around six hundred people at the site (and when Rald's map was produced), Omurunazi's population declined and then remained relatively stable at only around three hundred people into at least 1976; i.e., there were unlikely more than perhaps seventy-five to one hundred households (population statistics from Jørgen Rald's "Progress Report on Land Use Survey of Omurunazi Ujamaa Vjijijini [*sic*]—Ihangiro—Bukoba. 20 May 1969," partial copy in [TNAM 19/D3/26], complete copy in possession of the author, courtesy of Jørgen Rald; Mugezi 1977; and various official reports [TNAM 19/BDC/D30/5/Vol. II/517; 19/D3/26; D3/34/Vol. III; 19/D3/34/Vol. IV; 19/WLD3/26; 19/WLD3/25; 19/ZM/K/M/2]).

20. The plan was likely produced for the November 30, 1967, meeting of the West Lake Regional Development Committee; it is archived with the minutes (TNAM 19/BTC/WEL12/Vol. II).

21. *"Kumbukumbu ya Mkutano wa Kamati Ndogo ya Kilimo na Makazi,"* April 20, 1968 (TNAM 19/WLD 3/25).

22. *"Taarifa ya Week Kuhusu Vijiji Vipya,"* April 27, 1968 (TNAM 19/WLD3/26).

23. The Bukoba plan is reproduced in Rald (1970, map 1), who notes this provenance (4). Both the divisional executive officer of Bukoba's Kianja Division (*"Ripoti Juu Ya Vijiji Vipya,"* May 3, 1968 [TNAM 19/WLD3/26]) and his colleague in Ihangiro Division (*"Taarifa ya Juma Kuhusu Vijiji Vipya,"* May 8, 1968 [TNAM 19/WLD3/26]) mention such a plan/map. The Karagwe plan is attached to the minutes of a district-level meeting (*"Muhtasari wa Mkutano wa Halmashauri ya Kilimo na Makazi Mapya Uliofanyika Tarahe 22/4/68 Katika Office ya Mkuu wa Wilaya Karagwe"* [TNAM 20B/D3]).

24. Jørgen Rald, correspondence with the author, April 19, 2001.

25. *"Muhtasari wa Mkutano wa Halmashauri ya Kilimo na Makazi Mapya Uliofanyika Tarahe 22/4/68 Katika Office ya Mkuu wa Wilaya Karagwe"* (TNAM 20B/D3).

26. *"Mkutano wa RC na Watumishi wa Serikali Wakuu wa Wizara Mkoani na Wilayani Viongozi na Watumishi wa Tanu Bukoba Cinema Hall 16/4/1968"* (TNAM 19/WLD3/25).

27. *"Taarifa ya Juma Kuhusu Vijiji Vipya,"* May 8, 1968 (TNAM 19/WLD3/26). The referred-to plan/map is almost certainly the one shown in figure 4.4: Rald recalls that this plan arrived at Omurunazi in the first week of May (Jørgen Rald, correspondence with the author, April 19, 2001).

28. *"Ripoti Juu Ya Vijiji Vipya,"* May 3, 1968 (TNAM 19/WLD3/26).

29. The maps, less professionally drawn than Rald's, show the villages at Kibimba, Kiruruma, Bukangara (TNAM 20B/D3A), and Rukuraijo (TNAM 19/D3/28/II); Moody (1972) reviews the development of several of these villages.

30. Boesen, Madsen, and Moody (1977, 92) likewise note that villages in Bukoba and Karagwe District were typically "nucleated" with between fifty and three hundred homes. The size of the primary plots at the new settlements seems to have been in line with what typically existed in the area, although the principle of one acre per household at least initially resulted in a more equal land distribution than what might typically have been found elsewhere (Boesen, Madsen, and Moody 1977, 93, 98–101).

31. Compare Ferguson's (1999) critique of the postdevelopment literature for ignoring the popular attractiveness of the kind of modernities connected to development. Li (2007, 164) likewise finds that in a resettlement project in Indonesia the "program accurately read the desire of isolated highlanders to be integrated into the Indonesian mainstream." The problem was not that "modernity" was forced onto them, but that the project "failed to deliver the goods."

32. *"Kumbukumbu juu ya Kilimo na Kujitegemea,"* n.d., but filed between documents dated April 14 and 21, 1967 (TNAM 19/WLD3/23). This list largely copied an ad hoc listing of swaths of uncultivated land produced by the regional agricultural officer.

33. *"Taarifa ya Mpango wa Kujenga Vijiji Vipya Katika Tarafa Ndogo hii 19/4/1968"*; *"Taarifa ya Week Kuhusu Vijiji Vipya,"* April 27, 1968 (TNAM 19/WLD3/26).

34. *"Taarifa ya Ujumbe wa Kamati ya Kilimo na Makazi Mapya ya Mkoa, Wilaya ya Bukoba,"* May 4, 1968 (TNAM 19/WLD3/26).

35. Had these two recommendations been followed, they would have removed two of the only three sites in Bukoba District that were still in play from the original list of thirteen from the time of Walwa's 1967 plan.

36. *"Taarifa Fupi juu ya Maendeleo ya Makazi Mapya 11th May, 1968"* (TNAM 19/WLD3/26).

37. Report, May 12, 1968 (TNAM 19/WLD3/26).

38. *"Mkutano wa Kamati ya Kilimo na Makazi Mapya—Mkoa Tarehe 28/5/68"* (TNAM 19/WLD3/25).

39. Regional Subcommittee for Agriculture and Settlements Report on Bukoba District, October 31, 1968 (TNAM 19/WLD3/25).

40. Such defections were recorded in a number of reports and caused serious concern in the administration (e.g., *"Watoro Katika Vijiji vya Ujamaa,"* October 29, 1968, recording two and nine runaways

from Kiteme and Kyamyorwa, respectively, by name [TNAM 19/D3/26]). Bakula (1971, 30) states that after 350 people had arrived there between April 24 and the middle of May 1968, "great numbers of people withdrew from the Omurunazi settlement scheme." Kinyondo (1971, 73–74) reports that of the fourteen people moved to a new settlement from Katome village, all but two had returned to Katome within three months. From Ngara District, Boesen, Madsen, and Moody (1977, 64) report "busy traffic of people moving in and out" at the four settlements established there throughout their first year.

41. Regional Subcommittee for Agriculture and Settlements Report on Bukoba District, October 31, 1968 (TNAM 19/WLD3/25). A year after its initiation, the campaign had established nineteen new settlements in the region overall, with, according to official counts, just under 3,500 settlers (Rald 1970, 5); on average, and assuming a (small) household size of 3–4 people, the official numbers thus show the villages to be much smaller than the one-hundred-household minimum stipulation. Fifteen new settlements are reported to have survived into the 1970s, six of them in Bukoba District (Boesen, Madsen, and Moody 1977, 64, 98).

42. *"Mkutano wa RC na Watumishi wa Serikali Wakuu wa Wizara Mkoani na Wilayani Viongozi na Watumishi wa Tanu Bukoba Cinema Hall 16/4/1968"* (TNAM 19/WLD3/25).

43. This is reflected in a number of official reports, e.g., *"Katika Kijiji cha Ujamaa Omulunazi 7.10.1968"* (TNAM 19/WLD3/25), as well as a flurry of correspondence on the subject of food dating from October 1968 to July 1969 in TNAM 19/D3/26.

44. In July 1969, for instance, seventy thousand shillings had already been spent on aid to the new settlements that year, while Bukoba District's total annual budget for all development expenditures was only sixty thousand shillings (*"Hali ya Chakula—Kijiji cha Ujamaa Omurunazi—Rushwa,"* July 12, 1969 [TNAM 19/D3/26]).

45. *"Hali ya Chakula—Kijiji cha Ujamaa Omurunazi—Rushwa,"* July 12, 1969 (TNAM 19/D3/26).

46. *"Safari katika Kijiji cha Ujamaa Omulunazi,"* January 11, 1972 (TNAM 19/BDC/D30/5/Vol. II/517). Although the general picture in West Lake was that "after nearly four years the villages remain dependent on government assistance and have made very little progress towards social or economic viability" (Ellman 1975, 333), at least Omurunazi seems to have overcome some of these hurdles eventually: in Boesen, Madsen, and Moody's (1977, 100) assessment, it turned out to be "one of the more successful ujamaa settlements." Mwanahamisi Mtengula, who worked at neighboring Rugazi village as an agricultural trainee in 1972, remembers that, at this point, people at Rugazi and Omurunazi had stopped going back to their old fields and there was sufficient food. Both villages also boasted dispensaries and other amenities (interview with Mtengula, Dar es Salaam, October 18, 2000).

47. On October 22, 1968, for instance, Omurunazi's village chairman told a regional team tasked with supporting villages in Bukoba that "in total 4291 holes have been dug out [for banana saplings] of which 3441 have not been planted" (*"Mkutano wa Kamati ya Maendeleo ya Kijiji cha Ujamaa Umulunazi Rushwa 22.10.68 Saa 4.05"* [TNAM 19/D3/26]). A subsequent report by the regional team blames transport problems for the banana saplings' not getting to Omurunazi (*"Barua na. WL. D.3/26/. 31/10/1968"* [TNAM 19/WLD3/25]). Further delaying a first yield, plantings did not benefit from soil enhancement with manure, critical to the successful agricultural system that existed in many parts of the region (Rald 1970, 6).

48. *"Taarifa ya Kazi ya Wanafunzi Kijiji cha Omurunazi,"* June 20, 1970 (TNAM 19/WLD3/26E); Rald 1970, 5–7; Musoke 1971, 10.

49. E.g., a list of fifty-nine people from Bugabo drawn up on April 23, 1968, and attached to the Kiamtwara divisional executive officer's report *"Vijana Watakaohamia Makazi Mapya Toka Bugabo,"* April 24, 1967, and other similar lists in TNAM 19/WLD3/26.

50. Landlessness being the primary criterion for settler selection, the new villages were overwhelmingly comprised of inexperienced and young people (Rald 1970, 3; Bakula 1971, 30).

51. See Musoke (1971, 6–8) on coercion at Rugazi, and Kinyondo (1971, 72, 74) on coercion and threats of arrests at Kitoma village.

52. "*Taarifa ya Mpango wa Kujenga Vijiji Vipya Katika Tarafa Ndogo hii 19/4/1968*" (TNAM 19/WLD3/26).

53. A letter of June 8, 1970, from Omurunazi's village chairman to the regional commissioner complains about people not attending communal work (TNAM 19/D3/26E). A 1972 report by the district ujamaa coordinator complains about the same issue ("*Taarifa ya kijiji cha Ujamaa Omurunazi*," February 5, 1972 [TNAM 19/D3/26E]). In early 1970, only twelve people at the (according to official figures) 177-household-strong Kilimilile were reported to be doing work on communal fields ("*Kijiji cha Ujamaa—Kilimilile*," March 13, 1970 [TNAM 19/D3/26]). Compare Rald 1970 (16–17, 19–20).

54. Jørgen Rald, "Progress Report on Land Use Survey of Omurunazi Ujamaa Vjijijini [*sic*]—Ihangiro—Bukoba. 20 May 1969," partial copy in TNAM 19/D3/26; complete copy in possession of the author, courtesy of Jørgen Rald.

55. Kikula (1997, 66) on Mufindi District; Sitari (1983, 42) on Bagamoyo; URT (1994, 48) on Dodoma; Mwapachu (1979, 121) on Shinyanga; de Vries and Fortmann (1979, 131) on Iringa; Boesen, Madsen, and Moody (1977, 171–172) on West Lake.

56. "Study on Physical Planning Aspects of Ujamaa Villages" by the Town Planning Division, Ministry of Lands, August 1971 (TNA 640/KI/DO/26).

57. Minute on folio 13 (Confidential File C55 "Ujamaa Villages," Ministry of Lands, Division of Surveying and Mapping, Dar es Salaam); the folio, in the same file, is a memorandum by the commissioner for surveys and mapping, n.d., probably September–December 1968.

58. As the regional surveyor in charge noted in an account written in 1971, "Once it was determined that a large number of villages (25) would have to be laid out in a very short space of time, established survey methods had to be abandoned. Not only was there no time for sophisticated surveying and planning, but the Division was desperately short of experienced and qualified personnel" (Turok 1975, 404). Kunduchi and Ikwiriri, two of the largest "villages" (they quickly grew into small towns far beyond the size originally envisioned), were thus "laid out . . . with little supervision" by a senior chainman on whom the surveyor comments, "He does not know how to read or write but he is used to the survey instruments" (letter from regional surveyor of Coast Region to commissioner for surveys and mapping, March 4, 1969 [Confidential File C55 "Ujamaa Villages," Ministry of Lands, Division of Surveying and Mapping, Dar es Salaam]).

59. On July 15, 1968, Tanga's regional commissioner remarked that the government had selected Handeni as one of only three priority areas for the formation of ujamaa villages; this, he comments, was "big luck, about which Handeni must be happy" ("*Hotuba ya Kamishna wa Mkoa Tanga Bwana M. R. Kundya*" [TNA 513/D3/14]).

60. Minutes of the District Development Committee meeting of July 15, 1968; "*Mkutano Maalum Juu ya Vijiji*," July 17, 1968; letter from the area commissioner to the regional commissioner, July 23, 1968; minutes of a special meeting on July 19, 1968 (TNA 513/D3/14).

61. Report by Division of Town Planning, July 26, 1968 (Confidential File C55 "Ujamaa Villages," Ministry of Lands, Division of Surveying and Mapping, Dar es Salaam); report by C. K. Jayarajan, August 9, 1968 (TNA 513/D3/14).

62. "Safari Report by C. K. Jayarajan, J. D. Msele, J. Kasege 4–8/8/68," September 3, 1968 (TNA 513/D3/14II).

63. Report by C. K. Jayarajan, August 9, 1968 (TNA 513/D3/14).

64. Minutes of a Subcommittee Meeting, August 23, 1968 (TNA 513/D3/14); report by the regional surveyor, January 4, 1969 (TNA 513/D3/14/II). Work at one of the prioritized sites was postponed pending the arrival of the team's lead officer, who would be on loan from Tabora Region; another site was officially dropped, possibly because water supply problems had been identified; scheduled planning at the other sites was apparently overtaken by implementation that took the campaign in a different direction (reports by the regional surveyor of August 29 [TNA 513/D3/14] and October 2, 1968

[TNA 513/D3/14II]; "Safari Report by C. K. Jayarajan, J. D. Msele, J. Kasege 4–8/8/68," September 3, 1968 [TNA 513/D3/14II]).

65. A letter of July, 13, 1969, from C. K. Jayajaran to the area commissioner refers to thirteen completed layouts (TNA 513/D3/14/IV).

66. Reports by the regional surveyor, October 2, 1968; December 3, 1968; January 4, 1969; letter from the regional surveyor to the regional commissioner, January 1, 1969; "Safari Report for Handeni District by J. W. Kasege, C. K. Jayarajan, J. D. Msele (14–23/9)," September 27, 1968 (TNA 513/D3/14/ II); Ministry of Agriculture Land Planning Unit Arusha Monthly Report, January 7, 1969 (TNA 481 A3/2/Vol. III).

67. Officials for instance pushed sites at Kwabaya, Kiva, and Kilimilang'ombe, none of which had seen any survey work; all three were apparently later abandoned in the face of local resistance (various reports [TNA 513/D3/14; TNA 513/D3/14/II]). Tanga's regional surveyor had resigned himself to playing second fiddle: "It is understood that the people in the Mkata, Manga, Kwamsisi, Suwa and Kwamkono areas [none of which was among the nine villages sited by the town planners in August] are to begin building their new villages immediately without the assistance of either the Town Planning or Surveys and Mapping Division" (report by the regional surveyor, August 29, 1968 [TNA 513/ D3/14]).

68. "Safari Report by C. K. Jayarajan, J. D. Msele, J. Kasege 4–8/8/68," September 3, 1968 (TNA 513/ D3/14II).

69. *Mtendaji wa Mtaa Negero* to area commissioner, September 12, 1968; area commissioner to *mtendaji wa Mtaa Negero*, September 13, 1968 (TNA 513/D3/14).

70. Report by the regional surveyor, October 2, 1968 (TNA 513/D3/14/II).

71. For example, water supply problems also existed at Mkata, one of the villages that received more sustained attention from the authorities: in 1969, the village chairman told the people to go back to their original homesteads because of a lack of water (letter from a branch official to the district office, September 10, 1969 [TNA 513/D3/14/V]). One of the village's two supplies had dried up and the other provided only undrinkable water ("Safari Notes—Handeni District—11/9–12/9/69" by the regional director of agriculture, September 16, 1969 [TNA 513/D3/14/IV]).

72. Reports by the regional surveyor, October 2 and December 3, 1968, and January 4, 1969 (TNA 513/D3/14/II).

73. Commissioner for surveys and mapping to regional commissioner, June 24, 1969 (TNA 513/ D3/14/III).

74. Confidential File C55 "Ujamaa Villages," Ministry of Lands, Division of Surveying and Mapping, Dar es Salaam.

75. Figure 4.6 in TNA 562 D3/17/1B; figure 4.7 in the archives of the Surveys and Mapping Division of the Ministry of Lands, Dar es Salaam.

76. A December 3, 1968, report by the regional surveyor states that "132 plots were provided" at Kwedizinga (TNA 513/D3/14/II).

77. Forty-eight men, forty-nine women, and eighty children were recorded ("*Taarifa ya Mwezi September 1969*" by the ujamaa villages cooperative officer Tanga, October 16, 1969 [TNA 562/UV/1/1]).

78. Thirty-seven men, thirty-four women, and fifty-five children were reported ("Tanga Region— 'Ujamaa Village' Monthly Report for April 1971" by the Ministry of Agriculture's regional office in Tanga, May 25, 1971 [TNA 542/D30/14]).

79. Segera village, also in Handeni, had, for instance, been "planned and surveyed for 263 plots (263 families)," but in mid-1971 only "110 plots [were] occupied by 297 people" ("Study on Physical Planning Aspects of Ujamaa Villages" by the Town Planning Division, Ministry of Lands, August 1971 [TNA 640/KI/DO/26]). From Dodoma, Thiele (1982, 46–48) reports the opposite: where officials tried to impose an (often ad hoc) layout on residential areas in the new settlements in the early phases of

the establishment of a new village, such "plans" could often not even accommodate the immediate influx of people and were made entirely obsolete by the steady stream of new arrivals that stretched over two or three years.

80. "*Ramani ya Vijiji vya Mkoa wa Tanga*" by the Surveys and Mapping Division, Ministry of Lands (TNA Map G8434 T32 T3 1978).

81. Scott (1998, 237) suggests that "Nyerere and his planners" had "a visual idea of just how a modern village should look."

82. In his February 29, 1968, lecture "The Intellectual Needs Society," Nyerere (1973, 27) for instance almost literally anticipated Scott's (1998, 228–229, 288) comments on the 1940s Groundnut Scheme: "The assumption that uneducated local elders know nothing can lead to disastrous results. In Tanganyika, for example, £36 million was spent by our colonial masters on what was called the Groundnut Scheme—and now we import peanut butter! One of the contributory reasons for this expensive failure was that the 'experts'—that is to say, the educated fellows—found the average rainfall over a ten year period in the relevant area, and planned accordingly. They assumed that, because the local farmers were illiterate, they could give no information about the regularity of the rains, year by year, or month by month."

83. Nyerere generally abstained from sketching in more than quite broad terms how ujamaa communities should work. His September 1967 "Socialism and Rural Development" stressed, for instance, that while the Ministry for Local Government and Rural Development might "draw up a model constitution for the villages at different stages, . . . it must be stressed that no one model should be imposed on any village. Any model which is drawn up should just be a guide" (Nyerere 1968, 365).

84. "Safari Report by C. K. Jayarajan, J. D. Msele, J. Kasege 4–8/8/68," September 3, 1968 (TNA 513/D3/14II).

85. Report by the regional surveyor, December 3, 1968 (TNA 513/D3/14/II).

86. "Brief Planning and Laying Out of Ujamaa Villages in Dodoma Region," n.d., but filed between documents from the first half of 1970 (Confidential File C55 "Ujamaa Villages," Ministry of Lands, Division of Surveying and Mapping, Dar es Salaam).

87. "Study on Physical Planning Aspects of Ujamaa Villages" by the Town Planning Division, Ministry of Lands, August 1971 (TNA 640/KI/DO/26); emphasis added. In terms of "aesthetic" considerations, the study explicitly criticizes the grid iron layout of a plan for Segera village in Handeni as "too rigid" and "uninteresting" (the village's reality did not, at any rate, reflect this plan; see above).

88. Compare Hill (1979, 111), van Bergen (1981, 11–120), and the October 5, 1970, *Nationalist* on the village.

89. "Study on Physical Planning Aspects of Ujamaa Villages" by the Town Planning Division, Ministry of Lands, August 1971 (TNA 640/KI/DO/26).

90. Boesen and Raikes (1976, 15) and Boesen, Madsen, and Moody (1977, 130) note such instances from West Lake; de Vries and Fortmann (1979, 135) from Iringa.

91. 1974 confidential BRALUP report "Villagisation in the Coast Region" for TANU headquarters by Marja-Liisa Swantz (NZC 5/1235).

92. 1974 confidential BRALUP report "Villagisation in the Coast Region" for TANU headquarters by Marja-Liisa Swantz (NZC 5/1235).

93. Fisher and Arce (2000, 80) make a related observation about the functioning of microscopes in the sleeping sickness campaigns of the 1920s and 1930s in western Tanganyika, where they proved quite useless with respect to their technical purpose: "The role of the microscope becomes more significant as a symbol of legitimacy within the 'hierarchy of credibilities.' This political legitimacy was more important than questioning the performance of the instrument *per se*."

94. As von Freyhold (1979, 185) reports from Tanga, in 1972, "visits of planning teams and planning of production targets stopped." The 1974/1975 initiative to draw up more holistic "Regional In-

tegrated Development Plans" by outsourcing the task to at least fifteen expatriate teams—one region per donor country—did not result in a qualitative change for the better: Armstrong's (1984) scathing assessment characterizes these plans as purely ritualistic.

95. *"Mipango ya Maendeleo—Vijiji vya Ujamaa Handeni,"* February 18, 1969 (TNA 562 D3/17/1A).

96. *"Vijiji vya Ujamaa—*A 5 Year Programme (Kwamkono)" (TNA 513/D3/14/II).

97. Report by the regional director of agriculture, May 25, 1971 (TNA 542/D30/14).

98. *"Habari wa Mipango ya Uchumi 1970/71–1973/74"* (TNAM 19 WLD3/26E). At the end of 1970, there existed economic plans for a number of villages (TNAM 19 D3/34/Vol. III). Boesen, Madsen, and Moody (1977, 69–79) review the plan for Ntobeye village, Ngara District, in particular detail.

99. These teams were typically composed of five officials and headed by members of TANU's Central Committee. Boesen, Madsen, and Moody (1977, 69) note the arrival in early 1970 of an "Economic Planning Team for West Lake Ujamaa villages" staffed by various high-ranking officials from other regions. Moody (1972) mentions five plans drawn up by a regional planning team. Whether either of these was the "presidential planning team" on whose work in West Lake the December 15, 1970, *Nationalist* reported is not clear. Several such presidential teams were dispatched to Mtwara, Rufiji, Tanga, Tabora, and Sumbawanga in early 1970 (*"Kumbukumbu za Mkutano wa Kamati Kuu Uliofanyika Dar es Salaam Tarahe 24/1/70"* [NZC 3/115]). West Lake, Dodoma, and Kigoma were later added (*Nationalist,* December 15, 1970). They worked extremely rapidly: in the short period between August and mid-December 1970, the Kigoma team, for instance, drew up thirty village plans for villages in Kibondo District (*"Safari ya Mkoa wa Kigoma—A.S. Kaduri"* [TNA 523/D30/61]).

100. An undated tractor plan is contained in TNAM 19 D3/34/Vol. III; there also existed another, dated July 18, 1972 (TNAM 19 D3/34/Vol. IV).

101. *"Safari katika Kijiji cha Ujamaa Omulunazi,"* January 11, 1972 (TNAM 19 File BDC/D30/5/Vol. II/517); *"Taarifa ya 1971 Vijiji vya Ujamaa,"* Febuary 8, 1972 (TNAM 19 D3/34/Vol. III). In its annual report of April 1972, the Ministry of Agriculture reports larger numbers ("Agricultural Annual Report for Ujamaa Villages—West Lake Region 1971," April 9, 1972 [TNAM 19 D3/34/Vol. IV]).

102. Compare Boesen, Madsen, and Moody (1977, 166) and Caplan (1992) for Tanzania, and Michener (1998, 2113) on the existence of the same phenomenon in many other settings.

103. Letter from the Mwanza regional surveyor to the commissioner for surveys and mapping, January 13, 1969 (Confidential File C55 "Ujamaa Villages," Ministry of Lands, Division of Surveying and Mapping, Dar es Salaam).

104. Geertz (1980) famously analyzes the Balinese state as a theater state. Compare Cruise O'Brien (1991), Mbembe (1991, 1992), and Migdal (2001) on the performative aspects of the state.

5. The World of Officials in the Trenches, Potemkin Villages, and Criticism as Treason

1. Pratt (1972, 237), who ascribes an extremely central role in the politics of the country to Nyerere, explicitly likens the president to Rousseau's legislator: "Nyerere hoped, as Rousseau had hoped for his legislator, that, by example, by leadership and by teaching, but without coercion, he could lead his people to adopt institutions which would then bolster and reinforce rather than undermine and corrupt the social values which featured in his vision of a just society. As Nyerere came to see his role in terms such as these, he sought to exercise a much more direct leadership both within his Government and his Party. From then on, Presidential leadership played a much more prominent role and the genuinely collegiate element became less in the operations of both the Cabinet and of the National Executive Committee."

2. Letter, June 10, 1967 (TNAM 19/WLC5/23/III). For unknown reasons, the picture did not make it into the version of the plan printed by Dar es Salaam Printers Limited, although another chance

might have offered itself in the printing of a second edition by Bukoba Printers: Rald and Rald (1975) cite such an edition.

3. See Bienen (1970, 76–77, 129–132, 146–147) and Cliffe and Saul (1972) on the commissioners. Since independence, their appointment by the president personally had been a de facto reality even before it became legally enshrined in 1965.

4. In mid-1971, for instance, the new post of district ujamaa coordinator was created (*Nationalist*, July 12, 1971). In early 1972 this position was further fortified when it evolved into that of development directors who were appointed to the districts and regions where they would oversee the various technical ministries' activities; these positions also came with quite extensive and expanded budgetary and supervisory powers (*Nationalist*, March 29, 1972; Finucane 1974, 181; Hydén 1975, 35).

5. In his May 1972 address entitled "Decentralization," Nyerere (1973, 348) explained these measures with reference to "TANU accepting enlarged responsibility for initiating ujamaa villages and other co-operative activities." Compare also McHenry (1979, 74–79) and Finucane (1974).

6. Two months after Babu's dismissal in February 1972, Sheik Karume was murdered. Babu was arrested and thrown into prison for six years without trial—ostensibly for his own protection from the Zanzibaris (Doornbos 1996, 331–332; Saul 2005, 151).

7. The paper frequently reported similar statements by the top-leadership, for instance on September 1 and October 1, 1969, and March 30 and 31, 1970. McHenry (1979, 123) cites examples from 1973 and 1974.

8. Nyerere's directive was issued on the occasion of his tour of Dodoma on March 11, 1970; it is referred to and quoted in the minutes of a regional meeting held two weeks later ("*Kumbukumbu ya Mkutano wa Pamoja wa R.D.C. na Halmashauri kuu ya TANU ya Mkoa wa Dodoma Uliofanyika Tarehe 28.3.70*" [TNA 640/AF/P/UV/DR]).

9. This statement of Nyerere's at the annual conference for regional commissioners held in Dodoma was reported in the July 6, 1970, *Nationalist;* the paper picked up on similar statements at rallies in Mpwapwa on July 15 and 17.

10. Interview with former regional commissioner Kapilima, conducted in Dar es Salaam, August 8, 2006.

11. Compare Leys (1969, 271–272), Raikes (1972, 8–9), and various contributions to Coulson (1979) for similar assessments.

12. See also Green, Rwegasira, and van Arkadie's (1980, 93) assessment that the 1973 decision to go ahead with rapid and countrywide villagization was "on the whole against technical advice, especially that of agricultural and local Government officials."

13. Letter, September 3, 1968 (TNA 513/D3/14/I).

14. Letter, September 17, 1968 (TNA 513/D3/14/II).

15. Ibbott (1970, 111) notes that convicts from a local prison had been brought in to boost numbers at Handeni ujamaa villages on the occasion of a presidential visit in 1969.

16. Kigoma regional surveyor to commissioner for surveys and mapping, March 23, 1971 (Confidential File C55 "Ujamaa Villages," Ministry of Lands, Division of Surveying and Mapping, Dar es Salaam).

17. Ibbott (1970, 124) comments on the atmosphere in Songea after the association's destruction: "Everyone was worried at putting a foot wrong."

18. Letters from Area Commissioner Mhagama to Regional Commissioner Makwaia: "*Hotuba Matetereka*," May 12, 1970; "*Katibu wa Mkoa Kutembelea Matetereka*," July 8, 1970; "*Katibu wa Mkoa Kutembelea Matetereka*," July 16, 1970; letters from Makwaia to Mhagama: "*Katibu wa Mkoa Kutembelea Matetereka*," July 15, 1970; "*Katibu wa Mkoa Kutembelea Matetereka*," August 8, 1970; letter from regional TANU chairwoman to TANU executive secretary: "*Barua za Makitabu Kuhusu Hotuba ya Matetereka*," July 20, 1970 (NZC 9/MMT/V.20/15).

19. According to Edwards (1998, 20) and Ibbott (1970, 125), Makwaia even approached Kawawa for

a detention order against at least three RDA leaders (Lukas Mayemba of Matetereka, and Ngairo and Ndonde, both of Litowa), and possibly Millinga as well; however, Kawawa was not prepared to seek Nyerere's necessary approval.

20. Edwards (1998, 21) reports Matetereka's leaders' perception that these events were linked; the *Nationalist* of February 18, 1972, reported Makwaia's dismissal.

21. Musti de Gennaro (1981, 134) reports that a regional official referred to the village in this way in 1979. See chapter 2 on officials' 1971 and 1991 witchcraft accusations against the village.

22. Barongo's letter of complaint to TANU headquarters following the meeting states that "there are no bookkeeping accounts that have been shown," emphasizes that "this matter refers to the use of money," and notes that Millinga "flung all the books of the RDA in front of the meeting" (appended to the minutes of the TANU Central Committee meeting of November 30, 1967, *"Mkutano wa Kamati Kuu Alhamisi 30/11/67—Agenda"* [NZC 3/114]).

23. Barongo's letter, appended to the minutes of the TANU Central Committee meeting of November 30, 1967 (*"Mkutano wa Kamati Kuu Alhamisi 30/11/67—Agenda"* [NZC 3/114]).

24. *"Mgomo wa Vijiji vya Ujamaa vya 1. Vikomba 2. Kilimilang'ombe' by Divisional Executive Officer Chanika,"* August 2, 1968 (TNA 513/D3/14); *"Watu Wachochezi, Wachafuzi na Wavunjaji wa Mipango ya Maendeleo ya Kijiji Kwabaya,"* October 4, 1968 (TNA 513/D3/14/II). The same official repeatedly identified by name the main "troublemakers" *(wachafuzi)* at local meetings (e.g., *"Report ya Mgomo wa Vijiji vya Ujamaa Kideleko na Kutokueleana K-cha Kiva,"* August 9, 1968 [TNA 513/D3/14]).

25. *"Taarifa Kuhusu Vijiji vya Ujamaa, Handeni,"* October 13, 1968 (TNA 513/D3/14/II). See also Kallabaka (1978, 50).

26. *"Taarifa Kuhusu Vijiji vya Ujamaa, Handeni,"* October 13, 1968 (TNA 513/D3/14/II); *"Report ya Watu Wanaojijengea Vijiji vyao bila Uamuzi wa Kamati Yeyote,"* September 5, 1969 (TNA 513/D3/14/ IV). Compare von Freyhold (1979, 143, 187) and Kallabaka (1978, 50–51).

27. *"Report ya Watu Wanaojijengea vijiji vyao bila uamuzi wa kamati yeyote,"* September 5, 1969 (TNA 513/D3/14/IV).

28. "Memo" to TANU headquarters, n.d., received on September 4, 1969 (TNA 513 D3/14/IV).

29. *"Vijana Waliotoroka Kwenye Makao Mapya,"* n.d., received by regional headquarters on May 15, 1968 (TNAM 19/WLD3/26). This report and *"Matatizo Juu ya Uhamiaji Katika Makazi Mapya,"* May 3, 1968 (TNAM 19/WLD3/26), identify a "Daniel(i) Angelo" of Ilogero village as the ringleader of local opposition. Musoke (1970, 15) identifies the speaker at the Cinema Hall meeting as "Super Angelo." In October 1968, Daniel Angelo and three others had apparently again "absconded" from their designated village (this time Rugazi), and were sought by the Kianja divisional executive officer for questioning (*"Watoro Katika Makazi Mapya—Rugaze,"* October 18, 1968 [TNAM 19/ WLD3/26A]).

30. Compare Caplan (1992, 111–112) on often vulgar and sexually explicit subversions of state authority in songs on Mafia Island.

31. *"Taarifa ya Juma Kuhusu Vijiji Vipya,"* May 8, 1968 (TNAM 19/WLD3/26).

32. *"Matatizo Juu ya Uhamiaji Katika Makazi Mapya,"* May 3, 1968 (TNAM 19/WLD3/26).

33. *"Makazi Mapya,"* May 8, 1968 (TNAM 19/WLD3/26).

34. *"Wahamiaji Toka Kamachumu,"* May 8, 1968 (TNAM 19/WLD3/26).

35. Letter, July 29, 1968 (TNAM 19/WLD3/26).

36. Bakampenja had won his seat in the 1965 parliamentary elections by defeating the powerful Edward Barongo, then sent to Ruvuma as regional commissioner. See Hydén (1967, 53–76) on the two MPs as candidates.

37. See various contrubtions to Cliffe (1967) on the processes of selecting, nominating, and electing candidates for Parliament in Tanzania's one-party democracy. McHenry (1979, 144) cites a case from Maswa District (Shinyanga) where, "because many people were against shifting," the local MP "argued that he was a true representative of the people, and because of that, he found it useless to in-

volve himself." MPs in Dodoma seemed similarly reluctant to push villagization (Hill 1979, 110); Millinga's lack of support for Barongo's compulsory tobacco campaign fits the same pattern.

38. Compare Shivji's (2012) charting of Tanzania's post-independence history. Internally, an army mutiny and the revolution in Zanzibar in 1964 had early on forcefully brought home the vulnerability of the regime (e.g., Bienen 1972; Coulson 1982, 123–133, 140–141; Sadleir 1999, 267–273). In July 1967, Oscar Kambona, by many estimates the only potential rival to Nyerere in Tanzania, fled the country; subsequent allegations of a coup attempt culminated in a treason trial (Bienen 1970, 437; Tordoff and Mazrui 1972, 440; Mwakikagile 2007, 356–374). Externally, the falling out with Britain over Rhodesia, with West Germany over the Hallstein Doctrine (Tanzania had recognized the GDR), and with the United States over its foreign policy epitomized by the Vietnam War led to a heightened sense of Tanzania's exposure to an "imperialist" world beyond its borders. Katanga, Rhodesia, Mozambique, Biafra, and coups in African nations—often suspected or known to have been executed with "imperialist" support—demonstrated that the threat was all too real (Pratt 1976, 134–152; Coulson 1982, 142–143, 299–311). The February 1971 TANU guidelines (*Mwongozo*) then marked, in Cliffe and Saul's (1973, 297) assessment, "a significant sharpening in the 'official' outlook and in the Tanzanian analysis of internal and external forces . . . , a heightened awareness of the dangers of imperialism, of the need for a tighter control over the economy and for the increased centrality of the party's role, and of the prime importance of rising mass consciousness (to be crystallized, in part, around the development of a novel 'people's militia')." The late 1971 fatal shooting of Regional Commissioner Klerruu (McHenry 1979, 160–161; Coulson 1982, 248–249), a driving force behind villagization, would reinforce these "lessons" in the particular context of rural development.

39. Although the system covered only around 10 percent of cultivated land and most of the remaining tenants had stopped paying rent by the late 1960s, TANU continued its longstanding agitation against its remnants, including through an apparently ineffectual 1968 ban (Hydén 1969, 161–163, 166–168; 1977, 190–194; 1980, 82–85; Kinyondo 1971, 54; Rald and Rald 1975, 39–40; Bienen 1970, 106–109).

40. The issue of "feudalism" also evoked the specter of the "traditionalist" (Tanzanian) African National Congress (ANC), which, before being banned with the declaration of "one-party democracy" in early 1963, had been a relatively strong, albeit geographically confined, challenger to TANU. West Lake, and especially in the area of Bugabo and Kamachumu where villagization had provoked anti-TANU songs in 1968 (see above), had remained a key point of ANC and oppositional stirrings (Maguire 1969, 349–352; Bienen 1970, 102–106; Hydén 1967, 59–61; 1969, 133–137; 1977, 136–137, 189; Kinyondo 1971, 4, 40–46, 53; van Bergen 1981, 202–205; Brennan 2005, 260).

41. Compare for instance Li's (2007, 7, 10–11) treatment, drawing heavily on Ferguson's argument in this respect, of development in Indonesia.

42. See the November 19 and December 2, 1968, *Nationalist* and Cliffe (1973, 199–200) on the development of these two officials' careers. Joan Wicken recollects that the immediate issue that prompted Walwa's eventual dismissal was that he expropriated some expatriate landholdings at his new posting (interview with Joan Wicken, Keighley, July 31, 2002). Samoff (1974, 67) reports that Walwa single-handedly suspended the provisions of a new law regulating opening hours for bars and that local officials appealed this to higher authorities; this may have been another strike against him. After the end of his career as a regional commissioner, he was made chairman of the national licensing authority.

6. The Brave Parsimonious World of Materialist-Utilitarian Analysis

1. Compare Evans (1995) on the "neo-utilitarian" theory of the state.

2. For two recent, much-publicized examples of prescriptions based on a general skepticism of African states, see Calderisi (2006) and Dambisa (2009).

3. Compare Hirschman's (1984) call "against parsimony."

4. Compare, for instance, Brown and Langer's (2011) argument that correlates of conflict are not time-invariant, a point that virtually the entire "econometrics of conflict" literature ignores.

5. Saul (1979, chap. 8) for an overview; Shivji (1973, 1976, 1992), Othman (1980), Coulson (1982, 1975), Thoden van Velzen (1977, 1975), von Freyhold (1979), and Musti de Gennaro (1981) draw on this framing to varying degrees.

6. Stein and Wilson (1993, 1035) call Bates "the most prominent representative of this [rational choice] paradigm in African studies, and perhaps the most widely cited social scientist working on Africa today." "No scholar," they write, "has done more than Robert Bates to employ this framework and to crusade for it through explicitly methodological pieces" (1033). In their overviews of the comparative politics literature, Lichbach (1997) and Migdal (2001, 243–245) likewise review Bates's work as the paradigmatic exponent of the rationalist research tradition in comparative politics.

7. The suggestion, in the last paragraph of *Markets and States,* that "the dominant interests may be persuaded to forsake the pursuit of unilateral short-run advantage, and instead to employ strategies that evoke cooperation by sharing joint gains" (Bates 1981, 132), acts, as Bienefeld (1986, 11) has put it, "like a sudden self-destruct mechanism . . . undermining the entire argument that has gone before."

8. See also Putterman (1980) and Rugumamu (1997). Lofchie (1994a) finds that the pre-1985 Tanzanian policies are well explained by Bates's model (politicians had no stake in agriculture and so felt free to bleed it), but then argues that post-1985 reforms can only be explained by the force of new ideas in the face of economic crisis. This begs the question of why before the mid-1980s only interests seemed to matter.

9. Compare Brennan (2012) on the "anti-exploitation" ethos and discourse of the late 1960s and 1970s.

10. Coulson (1982, 181–182) reviews them. The memorandum detailing these reductions is reproduced as appendix A of a report by the International Labour Office (1967).

11. Compare Tripp (1997, 174–175) and Pratt (1976, 236–242). Samoff (1974) traces the reception in Kilimanjaro, where politicians slowly came to terms with the new conditions by either divesting or resigning from office. The key area in which they defended their privileges was educational access for their children.

12. Compare also Mwakikagile (2007, 357, 369) on a disagreement between Kambona and Nyerere over the Arusha Declaration and Kambona's retrospective reasoning against its communalist implications.

13. See Mazrui (1991, 71–72): the police were authorized to search any person or premise for evidence of corruption.

14. Nyerere's speech during the debate on the budget, May 17, 1960, quoted in Mazrui (1991, 69).

15. See Tripp (1997, 176–185) for an excellent overview.

16. Ellis (1988, 80–81) issues a strong caveat: "The results of these exercises are inconclusive, and depend on various assumptions concerning the relative rate of inflation between rural and urban areas, the meaningfulness of agricultural GDP figures, and the extent of parallel market and unofficial transactions in both sectors. . . . Intersectoral income comparisons, increasingly, have little statistical validity or analytical relevance. In particular such interpretations ignore the complex channels of familial and barter transactions between urban and rural households." Compare also Bryceson (1993, 105): "The distinction between urban and rural populations was, in the face of urban crisis and urban-rural ties, considerably overemphasized."

17. Compare also Bryceson (1992, 94–95). The neglect in most structural adjustment programs in the 1980s and early 1990s of the very real hardship of urban populations is one of the problematic results of the blanket, and not universally warranted, assumption that there was an urban bias: compare Walton and Seddon (1994) and Nugent (1995, 27–28).

18. Lofchie (1994a, 165) notes the urban plight of the early 1980s, but only to assert, without docu-

mentation, that this constituted a reversal of the fortunes of "those who had once benefited from urban bias."

19. Compare Tordoff and Mazrui's (1972) article "The Left and the Super-Left in Tanzania."

20. Compare Saul (1973) and Cliffe (1991, 106).

21. Leys (1996, 102) has commented, "The NPE [New Political Economy] seems to have something particularly valuable to offer (in addition to the appeal of its seeming rigour, esoteric knowledge, and so on): namely, a way of talking about some of the core issues dealt with in Marxist theory, without professional penalties."

22. Compare, for instance, Krueger (1992) and the case study volumes connected to that volume.

23. Conceptually, it is hard to attribute benefits: how, for instance, should a processing plant built by rural construction workers, with imported components, close to an urban center, but vital for the viability of rural tobacco-growers be accounted for? Clark (1978, 96) constructs two indices that attempt to make this attribution: his "Consumption Index" yields the following benefits under the First and the Second Five-Year Plans, respectively: urban: 24 and 23 percent; rural: 46 and 40 percent; national: 26 and 36 percent. Bates picks the larger figures (30 and 29 percent) for benefits going to urban areas yielded by Clark's second index, the "Development and Consumption Index." It should also be noted that spending planned did not necessarily mean money spent: the Second Plan only had the idea of ujamaa villages inserted into it at the very last minute, which makes it very likely that it seriously underprojected expenses connected to the, at the time, still-unforeseen massive villagization drive.

24. Clark's (1978, 200) contention that the urban areas drew more benefits from public investment (45 percent) than they contributed to public financing (34 percent) is based on debatable measures of the incidence of investments and burdens of financing that greatly inflate spending on urban areas beyond what ministerial spending of 21 percent indicates and, conversely, considerably deflate the contribution of urban areas below the 50 percent indicated by their contribution to direct and indirect taxes (96, 199).

25. For instance, Semboja and Therkildsen (1994, 809) show large and increasing donor funding for education, health, and water supplies during the second half of the 1970s: these three items saw massive spending in the rural areas as villagization strove for a school, dispensary, and water supply in every village. Compare also Kleemeier (1984).

26. Tax revenues, the only revenue source attributable to sectors, contributed only 17 percent to government financing of the first two development plans, and government financing in turn only accounted for 36 percent of the two Five-Year Plans' total budgets (Clark 1978, 197, 195): therefore, only 6 percent of the budget is attributable to one or the other sector.

27. Kleemeier (1984) documents that in the late 1970s considerably more than half of the total development budget came from foreign loans and aid, with large portions going into services in the rural areas. As Svendsen (1986, 70) shows, foreign development assistance rose from one-third of the total development budget in 1970–1972 to more than half of the development budget by the end of the 1970s. See also Coulson (1982, 299–316) for a comprehensive overview.

28. Bates (1981, 96–97, 105) notes the possibility that policies might have created their own vested interests—which then explain the persistence of policies, but not nessarily their inception.

29. According to Clark's (1968, 174) survey of East African coffee policies, delivered to a forum that included, among others, Tanzania's minister of agriculture, governments faced not a problem of how to expand, but of how to curb, production of the crop. The question was, "How can coffee-producing capacity in East Africa be reduced to the level at which the entire crop can be sold, at the least cost to the East African economies?" The answer: "The simplest way . . . is to widen the differential between export prices and producer prices." In a paper originally presented in 1966, Helleiner (1979, 190–191) similarly argued that pricing policy was in fact too generous to coffee producers because it resulted in production much in excess of the quota. Compare also Ellis and Hanak (1980, 27). In later work,

Bates (1986, 12–13) notes that coffee exporters operated under quotas that necessitated policies aimed at reducing production and disposing of surpluses.

30. Ellis and Hanak (1980, 27) remark that a roasting subsidy benefiting local processors and paid for by producers "was introduced in the 1960s in order to encourage domestic coffee consumption under the conditions then prevailing of concern about production exceeding quotas under successive International Coffee Agreements." The subsidy was dramatically reduced after 1976, when export constraints appear to have lessened.

31. It is not clear whether growers in fact bore all or most of the cost of low procurement prices for the processor. While a roasting subsidy was deducted from the price they received, crop authorities generally took on massive debts during the second half of the 1970s. This debt effectively narrowed the gap between producer and purchaser prices—supporting the former and/or lowering the latter. Had producer prices eventually been lowered sufficiently to eliminate these debts, producers would of course have borne all costs in the end. But instead of being paid back, large amounts of accumulated debts were in fact either directly taken over by the state in the early 1980s or reduced through public subsidies—thereby socializing their impact (Ellis 1982, 265–270, 276–277; 1983, 230–235; Bryceson 1993, 78).

32. Bates's (1981, 141) appendix lists 1971/1972 through 1976/1977 producer prices of 75, 69, 57, 66, 58, and 46 percent, respectively, of the price achieved by the crop authority at auction for mild Arabica coffee, the predominant variety in Tanzania. Growers of Robusta, the variety sold to the factory, did better: Ellis and Hanak (1980, 16) report combined producer shares for mild Arabica and Robusta of 79, 72, 61, 72, 69, and 48 percent for the 1971/1972 through 1976/1977 seasons (the inclusion of Robusta thus lifts producers' shares above Bates's shares for Arabica only in every year). It is worth noting that in 1976/1977, when producers' *share* sank to just 48 percent, the *price* they received was also three and a half times the 1974/1975 price: international prices had spiked and producers' share fell in accordance with the logic of a price stabilization scheme (see next note).

33. That crop authorities typically attempted to stabilize producer prices also had important implications for margins. Over time, price-stabilization schemes have a tendency to run at a loss, especially if producers have any opportunity to circumvent official marketing channels (more likely in the case of food crops than export crops). This is in part because such schemes' operators tend to be swamped by supply in years when they offer a "good" price compared to prevailing market conditions (forcing them into large losses), while producers will have an incentive to withhold supplies from official purchasers in years when they offer less favorable prices (i.e., in such years the purchasers' profits will be small). Over time, this pressures margins or debts higher—but not because of misappropriations or inefficiencies. Compare Jayne and Jones (1997, 1519) and de Fontenay and Leung (2002) on this and other technical problems arising in price stablization.

34. See URT (1966b) and Kriesel et al. (1970), who offer some instructive local examples of cost breakdowns in the late 1960s; however, broad generalizations are hard to make in a situation of very considerable local variability (Ellis 1983).

35. Compare Mushi (1974, 171–176) on serious concerns among top-ranking politicians about misappropriations in the cooperative sector as early as 1964/1965.

36. On the 1966 report, Saul (1975b, 209) remarks, "The most common corrective introduced so far has been increased government controls."

37. Bryceson (1993, 69) notes on the rationale behind these reforms, "It was thought that cooperative clientage practices and financial leaks at the local level could be kept in check." Compare Ellis (1983, 233): "The two main efficiency arguments for the creation of the crop parastatals were (i) to realize potential economies of scale in crop marketing, and (ii) to attain a much greater degree of central control over the financial flows involved in crop marketing."

38. See Ellis 1988 (70–71); Bryceson (1985, 61–68; 1993, 68–73, 78); and Raikes 1986 (124–125).

39. Compare Bryceson (1993, 72–73) on the massive transportation problems of the marketing system.

40. Raikes (1986, 124) notes McKinsey's involvement; the consultancy was very widely involved in redesigning public institutions in Tanzania in the early 1970s. Kleemeier (1984, 190–192) documents this for decentralization and Coulson (1980, 290–294) discusses the highly disruptive and inefficient restructuring, mirroring many of the problems in agricultural marketing under the new crop authorities, of the State Trading Corporation under a McKinsey plan.

41. It should be noted that only 8 and 3 percent, respectively, of total reported maize production was marketed through official channels in 1973/1974 and 1974/1975; in 1977/1978, a year with far better official prices, this proportion was 18 percent (Msambichaka, Ndulu, and Amanti 1983, 25). This may have been a question of greater supply in excess of subsistence demand, but may also be an indication of the extent to which low official prices may have driven farmers to circumvent official marketing channels.

42. In nominal terms, this increase was steady and very large, almost doubling the price over the four years. In real terms (deflated by the non-food retail price index, a somewhat imperfect measure for rural consumers), the increase was smaller and more erratic, but still gave producers 43 percent higher prices in 1976 than in 1973 (Bryceson 1993, 232).

43. A nominal increase of 18 percent from 1976 to 1981 translates into a real decline of 42 percent (Bryceson 1993, 232).

44. This was the result of margins being squeezed from two sides: relatively high producer prices, but also low consumer prices (Bryceson 1993, 74–75).

45. Compare Bryceson (1993, 71, 76–77, 272–273) for typically less dramatic ratios of official and parallel prices in a variety of local markets in the 1980s.

46. Compare, for instance, Timmer (1991) and Dorward et al. (2004) on the rationales for such interventions. Already around the time of independence, these arguments had framed the policy discussions surrounding the establishment of marketing boards in Tanzania (various documents in the file "Establishment of Marketing Boards '61–'63" [TNA 593/AG/1/2]). They would continue to underlie discussions of marketing.

47. Kriesel et al. (1970, 6–7) on this logic. For instance, in a 1971 paper, Livingstone (1979) found producer shares of 30 percent and less and 22 percent and less in two vegetable farming areas; Mascarenhas and Mbilinyi (1969) documented producer shares ranging from 25 to 30 percent in the Dar es Salaam banana market.

48. On Indian traders, see Bryceson (1993, 32–38) and Coulson (1982, 60–69). See Bryceson (1990, 140–144) and Hydén (1976, 10–12) on anti-Indian sentiment as a factor in the move to expand the cooperatives, and Brennan (2012) on race relations in twentieth-century Tanzania.

49. See, for instance, Bryceson (2002), Dorward et al. (2004), and Ellis (2006). Compare the UNDP's (2012) *Africa Human Development Report* on food security and the World Bank's (2007) *World Development Report 2008: Agriculture for Development*.

50. As Chambers (1972, 138) comments, "The fluency with which the Tanzanian government changes its ministries and departments may be a symptom of evasion of the need not for structural change but for means to improve the working of what already exists." Hydén (1975) has identified similar tendencies in Tanzanian policymaking and characterized them as a style of "we must run while others walk."

51. Ellis (1988, 93) comments, "Ever since the mid 1960s the scope of producer price policy in Tanzania has been too ambitious, and beyond the capacity of the state to administer effectively." See URT (1966b), Kriesel et al. (1970), Helleiner (1972), and Bryceson (1990, 1993) on the extreme shortages of trained personnel.

52. Twenty-one, not 30 percent, of planned expenditure was destined for the urban areas. Expenditure alone on urban versus rural areas does not establish a bias in resource flows. No single coffee producer share listed in the book's appendix is as low as the very cheap purchaser's price might lead one to expect—and all six annual Arabica prices shown in the appendix are worse than any of the

Robusta or combined prices (not shown) during those six years. The high world market price for coffee, against which the domestic processor's price looks very low, was not available for the crop sold to the processor.

53. See Woodruff (2005, 217) for parallel points about Ronald Rogowski's heavy reliance on price data and the "radically evacuated vision of the international economy" this produces.

54. Bates (1993, 1078; compare 1983, 134, 140) makes the point that "'rational choice theory' itself places constraints not on the content of preferences but rather on the choices that are made given them."

55. Deontological or altruistic motivations, as well as noninstrumental (e.g., expressive) modes of action/choice, can either not be accommodated in rational choice frameworks at all, or give rise to major complications (Elster 1986, 2000; Abelson 1996; Lane 1996; Taylor 1996).

56. Compare Stein and Wilson (1993, 1042) on the emphasis on material motivations in Bates and his convergence with radical political economy work on this front.

57. The endorsement, two paragraphs prior, of "the use of qualitative materials, fieldwork, and the painstaking reconstruction of events as anticipated, observed, and interpreted by political actors" (Bates et al. 2000, 698) runs fundamentally counter to this embrace of revealed preferences. Compare also Bates's (1993, 1078) statement that the "beliefs and values that enter into a 'rational choice' analysis . . . enter as data derived from observation rather than as assumptions derived from the theory itself. . . . 'Good' uses of the approach can be distinguished from 'bad' by the degree to which the authors are sensitive to the values, beliefs, and expectations that inform the choices that they study." My argument is that it is not such statements but the simultaneously endorsed revealed preference strategy that captures the essence of rational choice research in practice.

58. There is no need to venture beyond the paradigm of rational choice to recognize this problem. Even in some extremely simplified strategic choice settings such as that of the prisoner's dilemma, Sen (1977, 72) has shown, "the revealed preference approach goes off the rails altogether." This is because the outcomes that the interactions of the players' interest-maximizing choices produce suggest that the players have preferences different from the ones they actually hold.

59. This argument invokes Milton Friedman's instrumentalist claim from his essay "The Methodology of Positive Economics": all that matters for a theory's success is whether it successfully predicts that from a set of verifiable conditions a particular observable effect follows. Leaving aside the issue of whether the ability to predict is equivalent to the ability to explain (it is not), a theory that takes preferences and instrumental choices to be its causal variables, but then infers interests instead of observing them, cannot claim instrumentalism as a defense: if interests are not directly observed, the theory is stripped of its antecedent conditions and could not possibly generate predictions. The instrumentalist argument is not a coherent defense of the strategy of revealed preferences (Elster 1999, 1–10, 44–47; 2000, 693; Hausman 1992; Boniface and Sharman 2001, 485).

60. Compare van de Walle (2001, 27), Elster (2000), Stein and Wilson (1993), and Moore (1990). Critiques of Marxist analyses' inattention to the *question* of the existence of classes as collective actors go to this latter point. Likewise, the rational choice account is rare that does not swiftly kick aside its supposed commitment to methodological individualism to talk in terms of the interests of groups and collective actors—perhaps with a gesture toward "collective action problems" or, as in Bates's (1989) work on Kenya, the introduction of "institutions" as intervening variables, but often without much empirical investigation of the precarious existence and coherence of such collectivities.

Epilogue

1. Mamdani (1996) has argued that authoritarianism in postcolonial Africa is a function of the institutional legacy of the colonial state. The idea that authoritarianism can be conceptualized simply

as a means to "power," bereft of particular purpose and sought for its own sake or pursued as a means to self-enrichment, underlies most thinking on the subject.

2. Shivji (2012, 114) notes that Nyerere completed a translation of Plato's *Republic* into Kiswahili shortly before his death in 1999.

3. Compare Smith (2008, 16–17) on Kenya.

4. Compare, for instance, the contributions to Gibbon (1995).

5. Compare, for instance, Kamat's (2008) exploration of the popular nostalgia that the new neoliberal age has spawned in Dar es Salaam's periphery.

6. See Bryceson (2002) and Mueller (2011) on the rural scramble in Tanzania (and Africa) and Kaiser (1996) for an early skeptical assessment of the effects of informality in Tanzania.

7. See Chatterjee (2004) and Postero (2006) on the complex ways in which poor people's politics interact with such political structures, sometimes in unforeseen, unconventional, and empowering ways.

8. Edwards (2000) reviews the early beginning of RUDA.

9. As Mitchell (2002, 172) observes with regard to conceptualizations of Egyptian peasants as "individuals," "To be an individual in such a village economy means to be already situated in a set of coercive relations. For the landless 40 percent it means being positioned as a person living with poverty, malnutrition and a desperate need for work—all of which constitute forms of coercion, invisible to a narrative that focuses on interacting individuals."

10. Compare Botchway (2001) on this broad point. Dorward et al. (2004) present an excellent overview of the malaise of African agriculture and ways forward that would avoid veering between the extremes of "the market" and "the state" as panaceas while acknowledging the importance of structural interventions.

11. Compare Tripp (2003) on promises and limitations of local-level organizations and Moore (2001) on the importance of the question of organization if development's newly fashionable "empowerment" agenda is taken seriously.

12. Compare, for instance, Hearn (1998), Michener (1998), and de Waal (1998) for examples of such developments.

13. Compare, however, the Rwandan state's contemporary drive to reshape the rural landscape that on many levels is acutely reminiscent of Tanzanian villagization (Ansoms 2009).

14. While aiming to say more about "participation" than that it typically fails to be liberational (or that this is somehow its inevitable destiny), Green (2010a, 1241) nonetheless finds at least its key representational effect in contemporary Tanzania to be "the consolidation of the hierarchical relationships between central and local governments, between ordinary citizens and the administrative elite and between the poor and the national project of development." More generally, Cooke and Kothari (2001) have thus wondered whether participation has become "the new tyranny."

15. See, for instance, Reddy and Heuty (2008) on "technocratic pretensions" and the fetishization of quantification and targets in the context of the UNDP's Millenium Development Goals.

References

The sources of all archival materials are given in notes. The following abbreviations are used:

TNA   Tanzania National Archives, Headquarters in Dar es Salaam
TNAM Tanzania National Archives, Mwanza Branch Office
TNAD Tanzania National Archives, Dodoma Branch Office
NZC   *Nyaraka za Chama,* the TANU/CCM Party Archives in Dodoma

The first number after the archive's acronym is the accession number of the material; it is followed by the number of the file containing the document cited. As indicated in notes, other archival and primary materials were accessed at the regional and district offices in Songea (Ruvuma) and at the Ministry of Lands in Dar es Salaam. The East Africana Collection at the University of Dar es Salaam and the collection housed at the Ardhi (Land Planning) Institute at the university were also consulted. Some other documents are contained in private collections. Compare Schneider (2003) on the Tanzania National Archives system.

Abelson, Robert P. 1996. "The Secret Existence of Expressive Behaviour." In *The Rational Choice Controversy: Economic Models of Politics Reconsidered,* edited by Jeffrey Friedman, 25–36. New Haven, CT: Yale University Press.

Agrawal, Arun. 1996. "Poststructuralist Approaches to Development." *Peace & Change* 21 (4): 464–477.

Amey, Alan B. 1978. "Rural-Non-Rural Relations in Tanzania, 1965–1974: An Analysis of Intersectoral Resource Flows." Master's thesis, University of East Anglia.

Angwazi, Joseph, and Benno Ndulu. 1973. *Evaluation of Operation Rufiji 1968.* Dar es Salaam: Bureau of Resource Assessment and Land Use Planning.

Ansoms, An. 2009. "Re-engineering Rural Society: The Visions and Ambitions of the Rwandan Elite." *African Affairs* 108 (431): 289–309.

Ardhi Institute. 1975. *Village Master Plan Report.* Dar es Salaam.

Awiti, A. 1975. "The Development of Ujamaa in Ismani." In *Rural Cooperation in Tanzania,* edited by Lionel Cliffe, Peter Lawrence, William Luttrell, Shem Migot-Adholla, and John S. Saul, 418–425. Dar es Salaam: Tanzania Publishing House.

Bakula, B. B. 1971. "The Effect of Traditionalism on Rural Development: The Omurunazi Ujamaa Village, Bukoba." In *Building Ujamaa Villages in Tanzania,* edited by J. H. Proctor, 15–32. Dar es Salaam: Tanzania Publishing House.

Bantje, Han. 1979. *The Rufiji Agricultural System: Impact of Rainfall, Floods, and Settlement.* Dar es Salaam: Bureau of Resource Assessment and Land Use Planning.

——. 1980. *Floods and Famine: A Study of Food Shortages in Rufiji District.* Dar es Salaam: Bureau of Resource Assessment and Land Use Planning.

Barkan, Joel D. 1979a. "Comparing Politics and Public Policy in Kenya and Tanzania." In *Politics and Public Policy in Kenya and Tanzania,* edited by Joel D. Barkan and John J. Okumu, 3–40. New York: Praeger.

——. 1979b. "Legislators, Elections, Political Linkage." In *Politics and Public Policy in Kenya and Tanzania,* edited by Joel D. Barkan and John J. Okumu, 64–92. New York: Praeger.

Barker, Jonathan S. 1974. "Ujamaa in Cash-Crop Areas of Tanzania: Some Problems and Reflections." *Journal of African Studies* 1 (4): 441–463.

———. 1979. "The Debate on Rural Socialism in Tanzania." In *Towards Socialism in Tanzania*, edited by Bismarck U. Mwansasu and Cranford Pratt, 95–124. Toronto: University of Toronto Press.

Barker, Jonathan S., and Anne-Marie Cwikowski. 1999. *Street-Level Democracy: Political Settings at the Margins of Global Power*. Toronto: Between the Lines.

Bates, Robert H. 1981. *Markets and States in Tropical Africa: The Political Basis of Agricultural Policies*. Berkeley: University of California Press.

———. 1983. *Essays on the Political Economy of Rural Africa*. Cambridge: Cambridge University Press.

———. 1986. "The Politics of Agricultural Policy—A Reply." *IDS Bulletin* 17 (1): 12–15.

———. 1989. *Beyond the Miracle of the Market: The Political Economy of Agrarian Development in Kenya*. Cambridge: Cambridge University Press.

———. 1993. "A Reply." *World Development* 21 (6): 1077–1081.

Bates, Robert H., Avner Greif, Margaret Levi, Jean-Laurent Rosenthal, and Barry Weingast. 2000. "Analytic Narratives by Bates, Greif, Levi, Rosenthal, and Weingast: A Review and Response." *American Political Science Review* 94 (3): 685–702.

Bayart, Jean-François, Stephen Ellis, and Béatrice Hibou. 1999. *The Criminalization of the State in Africa*. Oxford: International African Institute in association with James Currey.

Bennett, Andrew, and Alexander George. 2001. "Case Studies and Process Tracing in History and Political Science: Similar Strokes for Different Foci." In *Bridges and Boundaries: Historians, Political Scientists and the Study of International Relations*, edited by Colin Elman and Miriam Fendius Elman, 137–166. Cambridge, MA: MIT Press.

Bernstein, Henry. 1981. "Notes on State and Peasantry: The Tanzanian Case." *Review of African Political Economy* 21: 44–62.

Bienefeld, Manfred. 1986. "Analysing the Politics of African State Policy: Some Thoughts on Robert Bates' Work." *IDS Bulletin* 17 (1): 5–11.

Bienen, Henry. 1970. *Tanzania: Party Transformation and Economic Development*. Princeton, NJ: Princeton University Press.

———. 1972. "National Security in Tanzania After the Mutiny." In *Socialism in Tanzania*, Vol. 1, *Politics*, edited by Lionel Cliffe and John S. Saul, 216–225. Dar es Salaam: East African Publishing House.

Binamu, I. G. 1969. "Wataalamu kutoka nchi za nje na ujenzi wa vijiji vya ujamaa Tanzania." *Ujamaa—Gazeti la Wajenga Taifa* [Swahili-language journal of Kivukoni College] 13: 44–57.

Boesen, Jannik. 1979. "Tanzania: From Ujamaa to Villagization." In *Towards Socialism in Tanzania*, edited by Bismarck U. Mwansasu and Cranford Pratt, 125–144. Toronto: University of Toronto Press.

Boesen, Jannik, Birgit Storgaard Madsen, and Tony Moody. 1977. *Ujamaa: Socialism From Above*. Uppsala, Sweden: Scandinavian Institute of African Studies.

Boesen, Jannik, and Philip L. Raikes. 1976. "Political Economy and Planning in Tanzania." Project Papers (West Lake Tanzania), 76.6. Copenhagen: Centre for Development Research.

Bomani, Paul. 1966. "Planning for Rural Development." *Mbioni: The Journal of Kivukoni College* 2 (11): 16–27.

Boniface, Dexter, and Jason C. Sharman. 2001. "An Analytic Revolution in Comparative Politics?" *Comparative Politics* 33 (4): 475–493.

Bonneuil, Christophe. 2000. "Development as Experiment: Science and State Building in Late Colonial and Postcolonial Africa, 1930–1970." *Osiris* 15 (1): 258–281.

Bose, Sugata. 1997. "Instruments and Idioms of Colonial and National Development: India's Historical Experience in Comparative Perspective." In *International Development and the Social Sciences: Essays on the History and Politics of Knowledge,* edited by Frederick Cooper and Randall Packard, 45–63. Berkeley: University of California Press.

Botchway, Karl. 2001. "Paradox of Empowerment: Reflections on a Case Study from Northern Ghana." *World Development* 29 (1): 135–153.

Brain, James L. 1977. "Is Transformation Possible? Styles of Settlement in Post-Independence Tanzania." *African Affairs* 76 (303): 231–245.

———. 1981. *Witchcraft and Development: University of Dar es Salaam Inaugural Lecture Series No. 31.* Dar es Salaam: Dar es Salaam University Press.

Brennan, James R. 2005. "The Short History of Political Opposition and Multi-Party Democracy in Tanganyika, 1958–1964." In *In Search of a Nation: Histories of Authority and Dissidence in Tanzania,* edited by Gregory H. Maddox and James L. Giblin, 250–276. Oxford: James Currey.

———. 2006. "Blood Enemies: Exploitation and Urban Citizenship in the Nationalist Political Thought of Tanzania, 1958–1975." *Journal of African History* 47 (3): 387–411.

———. 2008. "Destroying Mumiani: Cause, Context and Violence in Late Colonial Dar es Salaam." *Journal of Eastern African Studies* 2 (1): 95–111.

———. 2012. *Taifa: Making Nation and Race in Urban Tanzania.* Athens: Ohio University Press.

Briggs, John. 1979. "Villagisation and the 1974–6 Economic Crisis in Tanzania." *Journal of Modern African Studies* 17 (4): 695–702.

Brokensha, David. 1970. "Handeni Revisited." *African Affairs* 70 (279): 159–168.

Brown, Graham K., and Arnim Langer. 2011. "Riding the Ever-Rolling Stream: Time and the Ontology of Violent Conflict." *World Development* 39 (2): 188–198.

Bryceson, Deborah Fahy. 1985. "The Organization of Tanzanian Grain Marketing: Switching Roles of the Cooperative and the Parastatal." In *Marketing Boards in Tropical Africa,* edited by Kwame Arhin, Paul Hesp, and Laurens van der Laan, 53–78. London: KPI.

———. 1990. *Food Insecurity and the Social Division of Labor in Tanzania, 1919–85.* New York: St. Martin's Press.

———. 1992. "Urban Bias Revisited: Staple Food Pricing in Tanzania." *European Journal of Development Research* 4 (2): 82–106.

———. 1993. *Liberalizing Tanzania's Food Trade: The Public and Private Faces of Urban Marketing Policy, 1939–1988.* Geneva: United Nations Research Institute for Social Development in association with James Currey/Mkuki Na Nyota/Heinemann.

———. 2002. "The Scramble in Africa: Reorienting Rural Livelihoods." *World Development* 30 (5): 725–739.

Bugengo, James, and J. P. Mutangira. 1976. *The Nyarubanja System and Ujamaa Villages Development in West Lake Region.* Dar es Salaam: Economic Research Bureau, University of Dar es Salaam.

Burgess, Thomas. 2005. "The Young Pioneers and the Rituals of Citizenship in Revolutionary Zanzibar." *Africa Today* 51 (3): 3–29.

Burton, Andrew. 2007. "The Haven of Peace Purged: Tackling the Undesirable and Unproductive Poor in Dar es Salaam, ca. 1950s–1980s." *International Journal of African Historical Studies* 40 (1): 119–151.

Byres, Terence J. 1979. "Of Neo-Populist Pipe-Dreams: Daedalus in the Third World and the Myth of Urban Bias." *Journal of Peasant Studies* 6 (2): 210–244.

Calderisi, Robert. 2006. *The Trouble with Africa: Why Foreign Aid Isn't Working.* New York: Palgrave Macmillan.

Callaghy, Thomas M. 1984. *The State-Society Struggle: Zaire in Comparative Perspective.* New York: Columbia University Press.

Caplan, Pat. 1992. "Socialism From Above: The View From Below." In *The Tanzanian Peasantry: Economy in Crisis,* edited by Peter G. Forster and Sam Maghimbi, 103–123. Aldershot, UK: Avebury.

Carthew, John. 1980. "Life Imitates Art: The Student Expulsion in Dar es Salaam, October 1966, as Dramatic Ritual." *Journal of Modern African Studies* 18 (3): 541–549.

Chambers, Robert. 1972. "Planning for Rural Areas in East Africa: Experience and Prescriptions." *African Review* 1 (3): 130–147.

Chater, Patricia. 1962. *Grass Roots: The Story of St. Faith's Farm in Southern Rhodesia.* London: Hodder and Stoughton.

Chatterjee, Partha. 2004. *The Politics of the Governed: Reflections on Popular Politics in Most of the World.* New York: Columbia University Press.

Clark, Ralph. 1968. "East African Coffee Policies." In *Agricultural Planning in East Africa, Proceedings of a Conference at the University College, Dar es Salaam, April 1967,* edited by Gerald K. Helleiner, 160–177. Nairobi: East African Publishing House.

Clark, W. Edmund. 1978. *Socialist Development and Public Investment in Tanzania, 1964–73.* Toronto: University of Toronto Press.

Cliffe, Lionel, ed. 1967. *One Party Democracy: The 1965 Tanzania General Elections.* Nairobi: East African Publishing House.

———. 1972. "Nationalism and the Reaction to Enforced Agricultural Change in Tanganyika During the Colonial Period." In *Socialism in Tanzania,* Vol. 1, *Politics,* edited by Lionel Cliffe and John S. Saul, 17–24. Dar es Salaam: East African Publishing House.

———. 1973. "The Policy of Ujamaa Vijijini and the Class Struggle in Tanzania." In *Socialism in Tanzania,* Vol. 2, *Policies,* edited by Lionel Cliffe and John S. Saul, 195–215. Dar es Salaam: East African Publishing House.

———. 1991. "Political Struggles around the Adoption and Implementation of the Arusha Declaration." In *Re-Thinking the Arusha Declaration,* edited by Jeannette Hartmann, 105–112. Copenhagen: Axel Nielsen & Søn.

Cliffe, Lionel, and Griffith L. Cunningham. 1973. "Ideology, Organisation and the Settlement Experience in Tanzania." In *Socialism in Tanzania,* Vol. 2, *Policies,* edited by Lionel Cliffe and John S. Saul, 131–140. Dar es Salaam: East African Publishing House.

Cliffe, Lionel, and John S. Saul. 1973. "Introduction." In *Socialism in Tanzania,* Vol. 2, *Policies,* edited by Lionel Cliffe and John S. Saul, 297–303. Dar es Salaam: East African Publishing House.

Collier, Paul, Samir Radwan, and Samuel Wange. 1986. *Labour and Poverty in Rural Tanzania: Ujamaa and Rural Development in the United Republic of Tanzania.* Oxford: Clarendon Press.

Comaroff, John L., and Jean Comaroff. 1997. *Of Revelation and Revolution.* Vol. 2, *The Dialectics of Modernity on a South African Frontier.* Chicago: Chicago University Press.

Cooke, Bill, and Uma Kothari. 2001. *Participation: The New Tyranny?* New York: Zed Books.

Cooper, Frederick. 1997. "Modernizing Bureaucrats, Backward Africans, and the Development Concept." In *International Development and the Social Sciences: Essays on the History and Politics of Knowledge,* edited by Frederick Cooper and Randall Packard, 64–92. Berkeley: University of California Press.

Cooper, Frederick, and Randall Packard. 1997. Introduction to *International Development and the Social Sciences: Essays on the History and Politics of Knowledge,* edited by Frederick Cooper and Randall Packard, 1–41. Berkeley: University of California Press.

Coulson, Andrew. 1975. "Peasants and Bureaucrats." *Review of African Political Economy* 3: 53–58.

———. 1977. "Agricultural Policies in Mainland Tanzania." *Review of African Political Economy* 10: 74–100.

———, ed. 1979. *African Socialism in Practice: The Tanzanian Experience.* Nottingham, UK: Spokesman Books.

———. 1982. *Tanzania: A Political Economy.* Oxford: Clarendon Press.

———. 1984. "The Ruvuma Development Association 1960–1969." *Utafiti: Journal of the Faculty of Arts and Social Science, University of Dar es Salaam* 6 (1): 5–22.

———. 1992. "The Contribution of Economists to Rural Development in Tanzania." In *The Tanzanian Peasantry: Economy in Crisis,* edited by Peter G. Forster and Sam Maghimbi, 190–202. Aldershot, UK: Avebury.

Coward, E. Walter, Jr. 1976. "Indigenous Organization, Bureaucracy and Development: The Case of Irrigation." *Journal of Development Studies* 13 (1): 92–106.

Cowen, Michael, and Robert Shenton. 1995. "The Invention of Development." In *Power of Development,* edited by Jonathan Crush, 27–43. New York: Routledge.

Crewe, Emma, and Elizabeth Harrison. 1998. *Whose Development? An Ethnography of Aid.* London: Zed Books.

Cruikshank, Barbara. 1999. *The Will to Empower: Democratic Citizens and Other Subjects.* Ithaca, NY: Cornell University Press.

Cruise O'Brien, Donal B. 1991. "The Show of State in a Neo-Colonial Twilight: Francophone Africa." In *Rethinking Third World Politics,* edited by James Manor, 145–165. London: Longman.

Cunningham, Griffith L. 1966. "The Ruvuma Development Association—An Independent Critique." *Mbioni: The Journal of Kivukoni College* 3 (2): 44–55.

———. 1969. "Kivukoni College—The First Eight Years." *Mbioni: The Journal of Kivukoni College* 5 (8): 3–32.

Dambisa, Moyo. 2009. *Dead Aid: Why Aid Is Not Working and How There Is a Better Way for Africa.* New York: Farrar, Straus and Giroux.

Dean, Mitchell. 2010. *Governmentality: Power and Rule in Modern Society.* 2nd ed. London: SAGE.

de Fontenay, Patrick, and Suiwah Leung. 2002. "Managing Commodity Price Fluctuations in Vietnam's Coffee Industry." Working Paper 02-4, Asia Pacific School of Economics and Government, Australian National University.

de Vries, James. 1978. "Agricultural Extension and Development Ujamaa Villages and the Problems of Institutional Change." *Community Development Journal* 13 (1): 11–20.

de Vries, James, and Louise Fortmann. 1979. "Large-Scale-Villagization: Operation Sogeza in Iringa Region." In *African Socialism in Practice: The Tanzanian Experience,* edited by Andrew Coulson, 128–135. Nottingham, UK: Spokesman Books.

de Waal, Alex. 1998. *Famine Crimes: Politics and the Disaster Relief Industry in Africa*. Bloomington: Indiana University Press.

Donaldson, Graham. 1991. "Government-Sponsored Rural Development: Experience of the World Bank." In *Agriculture and the State: Growth, Employment, and Poverty in Developing Countries*, edited by C. Peter Timmer, 156–190. Ithaca, NY: Cornell University Press.

Doornbos, Martin R. 1996. "A.M. Babu: 'The Outline.'" *Review of African Political Economy* 69: 324–333.

Dorward, Andrew, Jonathan Kydd, Jamie Morrison, and Ian Urey. 2004. "A Policy Agenda for Pro-Poor Agricultural Growth." *World Development* 32 (1): 73–89.

Edwards, David M. 1998. *Matetereka: Tanzania's Last Ujamaa Village*. Edinburgh: Centre of African Studies, University of Edinburgh.

———. 2000. "Mwalimu Nyerere, African Socialism and the Revival of the Ruvuma Development Association." In *Nyerere: Student, Teacher, Humanist, Statesman*, edited by Tom Molony and Kenneth King, 101–117. Edinburgh: Centre of African Studies, University of Edinburgh.

———. 2003. "Settlement, Livelihoods and Identity in Southern Tanzania: A Comparative History of the Ngoni and Ndendeuli." PhD diss., University of Edinburgh.

Ellis, Frank. 1982. "Agricultural Price Policy in Tanzania." *World Development* 10 (4): 263–283.

———. 1983. "Agricultural Marketing and Peasant-State Transfers in Tanzania." *Journal of Peasant Studies* 10 (4): 214–242.

———. 1984. "Relative Agricultural Prices and the Urban Bias Model: A Comparative Analysis of Tanzania and Fiji." *Journal of Development Studies* 2 (3): 28–52.

———. 1988. "Tanzania." In *Agricultural Pricing Policy in Africa: Four Country Case Studies*, edited by Charles Harvey, 67–104. London: Macmillan.

———. 2006. "Agrarian Change and Rising Vulnerability in Rural Sub-Saharan Africa." *New Political Economy* 11 (3): 387–396.

Ellis, Frank, and Ellen Hanak. 1980. "An Economic Analysis of the Coffee Industry in Tanzania 1969/70–1978/79: Towards a Higher and More Stable Producer Price." Dar es Salaam: Economic Research Bureau, University of Dar es Salaam.

Ellman, Antony. 1975. "Development of the Ujamaa Policy in Tanzania." In *Rural Cooperation in Tanzania*, edited by Lionel Cliffe, Peter Lawrence, William Luttrell, Shem Migot-Adholla, and John S. Saul, 312–345. Dar es Salaam: Tanzania Publishing House.

Elster, Jon. 1986. *Rational Choice*. Oxford: Basil Blackwell.

———. 1999. *Alchemies of the Mind*. Cambridge: Cambridge University Press.

———. 2000. "Rational Choice History: A Case of Excessive Ambition." *American Political Science Review* 94 (3): 685–695.

Ergas, Zaki. 1980. "Why Did the Ujamaa Village Policy Fail?—Towards a Global Analysis." *Journal of Modern African Studies* 18 (3): 387–410.

Escobar, Arturo. 1995. *Encountering Development: The Making and Unmaking of the Third World*. Princeton, NJ: Princeton University Press.

Esman, Milton J., and Norman Thomas Uphoff. 1984. *Local Organizations: Intermediaries in Rural Development*. Ithaca, NY: Cornell University Press.

Evans, Peter B. 1995. *Embedded Autonomy: States and Industrial Transformation*. Princeton, NJ: Princeton University Press.

———. 1996. "Government Action, Social Capital and Development: Reviewing the Evidence on Synergy." *World Development* 24 (6): 1119–1132.

Fabian, Johannes. 1983. *Time and the Other: How Anthropology Makes Its Object*. New York: Columbia University Press.

Fafchamps, Marcel, and Ruth Vargas Hill. 2008. "Price Transmission and Trader Entry in Domestic Commodity Markets." *Economic Development and Cultural Change* 56 (4): 729–766.

Fatton, Robert. 1992. *Predatory Rule: State and Civil Society in Africa*. Boulder, CO: Lynne Rienner.

Feierman, Steven. 1990. *Peasant Intellectuals: Anthropology and History in Tanzania*. Madison, WI: University of Wisconsin Press.

Ferguson, James. 1994. *The Anti-Politics Machine: "Development," Depoliticization, and Bureaucratic Power in Lesotho*. Minneapolis: University of Minnesota Press.

———. 1997. "Anthropology and Its Evil Twin: 'Development' in the Constitution of a Discipline." In *International Development and the Social Sciences: Essays on the History and Politics of Knowledge*, edited by Frederick Cooper and Randall Packard, 150–175. Berkeley: University of California Press.

———. 1999. *Expectations of Modernity: Myths and Meanings of Urban Life on the Zambian Copperbelt*. Berkeley: University of California Press.

———. 2010. "The Uses of Neoliberalism." *Antipode* 41 (S1): 166–184.

Finnemore, Martha. 1997. "Redefining Development at the World Bank." In *International Development and the Social Sciences: Essays on the History and Politics of Knowledge*, edited by Frederick Cooper and Randall Packard, 203–227. Berkeley: University of California Press.

Finucane, James R. 1974. *Rural Development and Bureaucracy in Tanzania: The Case of Mwanza Region*. Uppsala, Sweden: Scandinavian Institute of African Studies.

Fisher, Eleanor, and Alberto Arce. 2000. "The Spectacle of Modernity: Blood, Microscopes and Mirrors in Colonial Tanganyika." In *Anthropology, Development and Modernities: Exploring Discourses, Counter-Tendencies and Violence*, edited by Alberto Arce and Norman Long, 73–98. London: Routledge.

Foucault, Michel. 1998. *The Essential Works of Foucault, 1954–1984*. Vol. 2, *Aesthetics, Method, and Epistemology*. New York: New Press.

———. 2000. *The Essential Works of Foucault, 1954–1984*. Vol. 3, *Power*. New York: New Press.

———. 2007. *Security, Territory, Population: Lectures at the Collège de France, 1977–1978*. Edited by Michel Senellart. Translated by Graham Burchell. New York: Palgrave Macmillan.

Gaddis, John Lewis. 2001. "In Defense of Particular Generalization: Rewriting Cold War History, Rethinking International Relations Theory." In *Bridges and Boundaries: Historians, Political Scientists and the Study of International Relations*, edited by Colin Elman and Miriam Fendius Elman, 301–326. Cambridge, MA: MIT Press.

Geertz, Clifford. 1980. *Negara: The Theatre State in Nineteenth-Century Bali*. Princeton, NJ: Princeton University Press.

Geschiere, Peter. 1997. *The Modernity of Witchcraft: Politics and the Occult in Postcolonial Africa*. Charlottesville: University of Virginia Press.

Gibbon, Peter, ed. 1995. *Liberalised Development in Tanzania*. Uppsala, Sweden: Nordiska Afrikainstitutet.

Giblin, James L. 1990. "Peasant Self-Sufficiency in Tanzania: Pre-Colonial Legacy or Colonial Imposition?" In *Sustainable Agriculture in Africa*, edited by Elizabeth Ann McDougall, 257–272. Trenton, NJ: Africa World Press.

———. 2005. *A History of the Excluded: Making Family a Refuge from State in Twentieth-Century Tanzania.* Athens: Ohio University Press.

Green, Donald P., and Ian Shapiro. 1994. *Pathologies of Rational Choice Theory: A Critique of Applications in Political Science.* New Haven, CT: Yale University Press.

Green, Maia. 2010a. "Making Development Agents: Participation as Boundary Object in International Development." *Journal of Development Studies* 46 (7): 1240–1263.

———. 2010b. "After *Ujamaa*? Cultures of Governance and the Representation of Power in Tanzania." *Social Analysis* 54 (1): 15–34.

Green, Reginald Herbold. 1995. "Vision of Human-Centred Development: A Study in Moral Economy." In *Mwalimu: The Influence of Nyerere,* edited by Colin Legum and Geoffrey R. V. Mmari, 80–107. London: Britain-Tanzania Society in association with James Currey.

Green, Reginald Herbold, Delphin Rwegasira, and Brian van Arkadie. 1980. *Economic Shocks and National Policy Making: Tanzania in the 1970s.* The Hague: Institute of Social Studies.

Grindle, Merilee S., and John W. Thomas. 1991. *Public Choices and Policy Change: The Political Economy of Reform in Developing Countries.* Baltimore, MD: Johns Hopkins University Press.

Gupta, Akhil. 1995. "Blurred Boundaries: The Discourse of Corruption, the Culture of Politics, and the Imagined States." *American Ethnologist* 22 (2): 375–402.

———. 1998. *Postcolonial Developments: Agriculture in the Making of Modern India.* Durham, NC: Duke University Press.

———. 2012. *Red Tape: Bureaucracy, Structural Violence, and Poverty in India.* Durham, NC: Duke University Press.

Harris, Bell. 1968. "An Ideological Institute for Tanzania?" In *Tanzania: Revolution by Education,* edited by Idrian N. Resnick, 153–162. Arusha, Tanzania: Longmans of Tanzania.

Hartmann, Jeannette. 1985. "The Arusha Declaration Revisited." *African Review* 12 (1): 1–11.

———, ed. 1991a. *Re-Thinking the Arusha Declaration.* Copenhagen: Axel Nielsen & Søn.

———. 1991b. "The Two Arusha Declarations." In *Re-Thinking the Arusha Declaration,* edited by Jeannette Hartmann, 113–124. Copenhagen: Axel Nielsen & Søn.

Harvey, David. 2005. *A Brief History of Neoliberalism.* New York: Oxford University Press.

Hausman, Daniel M. 1992. *Essays on Philosophy and Economic Methodology.* Cambridge: Cambridge University Press.

Havnevik, Kjell J. 1983. *Analysis of Rural Production and Incomes, Rufiji District, Tanzania.* Bergen, Norway: Department of Research and Action Programme (DERAP).

———. 1993. *Tanzania: The Limits to Development from Above.* Uppsala, Sweden: Nordic Africa Institute.

Hearn, Julie. 1998. "The 'NGO-isation' of Kenyan Society: USAID & the Restructuring of Health Care." *Review of African Political Economy* 75: 89–100.

Heilman, Bruce, and Laurean Ndumbaro. 2002. "Corruption, Politics, and Social Values in Tanzania: An Evaluation of the Mkapa Administration's Anti-Corruption Efforts." *African Journal of Political Science* 7 (1): 1–19.

Helleiner, Gerald K. 1972. "Socialism and Economic Development in Tanzania." *Journal of Development Studies* 8 (2): 183–205.

———. 1979. "Agricultural Export Pricing Strategy for Tanzania." In *Papers on the Political Economy of Tanzania,* edited by Kwan S. Kim, Robert B. Mabele, and Michael J. Schultheis, 189–192. Nairobi: Heinemann Educational.

Hill, Frances. 1979. "Operation Dodoma 1969–71." In *African Socialism in Practice: The Tanzanian Experience*, edited by Andrew Coulson, 106–113. Nottingham, UK: Spokesman Books.

Hirschman, Albert O. 1984. "Against Parsimony: Three Ways of Complicating Some Categories of Economic Discourse." *AEA Papers and Proceedings* 74 (2): 89–96.

Hirst, M. 1978. "Recent Villagization in Tanzania." *Geography* 63 (2): 122–125.

Hodge, Joseph Morgan. 2007. *Triumph of the Expert: Agrarian Doctrines of Development and the Legacies of British Colonialism*. Athens: Ohio University Press.

Hodgson, Dorothy Louise. 2001. *Once Intrepid Warriors: Gender, Ethnicity, and the Cultural Politics of Maasai Development*. Bloomington: Indiana University Press.

Hogendorn, Jan S., and K. M. Scott. 1981. "The East African Groundnut Scheme: Lessons of a Large-Scale Agricultural Failure." *African Economic History* 10: 81–115.

Honeybone, Reg. 1985. "University Visitor Extraordinary." In *The Nyerere Years: Some Personal Impressions by His Friends*, 40–44. London: Britain-Tanzania Society.

Huang, Yukon. 1976. "Distribution of the Tax Burden in Tanzania." *Economic Journal* 86 (341): 73–86.

Hydén, Göran. 1967. "Buhaya: Selection and Election Processes in Bukoba and Karagwe Districts." In *One Party Democracy: The 1965 Tanzania General Elections*, edited by Lionel Cliffe, 53–76. Nairobi: East African Publishing House.

———. 1969. *Political Development in Rural Tanzania: TANU Yajenga Nchi*. Nairobi: East African Publishing House.

———. 1973. *Efficiency versus Distribution in East African Cooperatives: A Study in Organizational Conflicts*. Nairobi: East African Literature Bureau.

———. 1975. *"We Must Run While Others Walk": Policy-Making for Socialist Development in the Tanzania-Type of Polities*. Dar es Salaam: Economic Research Bureau, University of Dar es Salaam.

———. 1976. "The Politics of Cooperatives in Tanzania." In *Cooperatives in Tanzania: Problems of Organisation Building*, edited by Göran Hydén, 7–20. Dar es Salaam: Tanzania Publishing House.

———. 1977. "Political Engineering and Social Change: A Case Study of Bukoba District, Tanzania." In *Government and Rural Development in East Africa: Essays on Political Penetration*, edited by Lionel Cliffe, James S. Coleman, and Martin R. Doornbos, 183–200. The Hague: Martinus Nijhoff.

———. 1980. *Beyond Ujamaa in Tanzania: Underdevelopment and an Uncaptured Peasantry*. Berkeley: University of California Press.

Ibbott, Ralph. 1966. "Ruvuma Development Association." *Mbioni: The Journal of Kivukoni College* 3 (2): 3–43.

———. 1970. "The Origin, Growth & Disbanding of the Ruvuma Development Association 1960–1969." Unpublished manuscript.

———. 2000. "Julius Nyerere and Ujamaa Vijijini." In *Nyerere: Student, Teacher, Humanist, Statesman*, edited by Tom Molony and Kenneth King, 81–88. Edinburgh: Centre of African Studies, University of Edinburgh.

Iliffe, John. 1979. *A Modern History of Tanganyika*. Cambridge: Cambridge University Press.

Ingle, Clyde R. 1970. "Compulsion and Rural Development in Tanzania." *Canadian Journal of African Studies* 4 (1): 77–100.

———. 1972. *From Village to State in Tanzania: The Politics of Rural Development*. Ithaca, NY: Cornell University Press.

International Labour Office. United Nations Development Programme. 1967. *Report to the Government of the United Republic of Tanzania on Wages, Incomes and Prices Policy.* Dar es Salaam: Government Printer.

Ivaska, Andrew M. 2005. "Of Students, 'Nizers', and a Struggle for Youth: Tanzania's 1966 National Service Crisis." *Africa Today* 51 (3): 83–107.

———. 2011. *Cultured States: Youth, Gender, and Modern Style in 1960s Dar es Salaam.* Durham, NC: Duke University Press.

Jamal, Vali, and John Weeks. 1993. *Africa Misunderstood, or, Whatever Happened to the Rural-Urban Gap?* London: Macmillan.

Jayne, T. S., and Stephen Jones. 1997. "Food Marketing and Pricing in Eastern and Southern Africa: A Survey." *World Development* 25 (9): 1505–1527.

Jennings, Michael. 1998. "Surrogates of the State: Oxfam and Development in Tanzania, 1961–1979." PhD diss., School of Oriental and African Studies, University of London.

———. 2008. *Surrogates of the State: NGOs, Development, and Ujamaa in Tanzania.* Bloomfield, CT: Kumarian Press.

Joseph, Richard A. 1987. *Democracy and Prebendal Politics in Nigeria: The Rise and Fall of the Second Republic.* Cambridge: Cambridge University Press.

Kaiser, Paul J. 1996. "Structural Adjustment and the Fragile Nation: The Demise of Social Unity in Tanzania." *Journal of Modern African Studies* 34 (2): 227–237.

Kallabaka, M. W. J. 1978. "The March Towards Ujamaa: Ten Years After Evaluation of the Ujamaa Programme at the Local Community Level." Master's thesis, University of Dar es Salaam.

Kamat, Vinay. 2008. "This is Not Our Culture! Discourse of Nostalgia and Narratives of Health Concerns in Post-Socialist Tanzania." *Africa: Journal of the International African Institute* 78 (3): 359–383.

Kami, J. M. 1981. "A Physical Development Study of the Lower Rufiji Valley Settlements." Diploma thesis, Ardhi Institute, University of Dar es Salaam.

Karshenas, Massoud. 1996/1997. "Dynamic Economies and the Critique of Urban Bias." *Journal of Peasant Studies* 24 (1 & 2): 60–102.

Kawawa, Rashidi M. 1966. "New Approaches to Rural Development." *Mbioni: The Journal of Kivukoni College* 2 (11): 4–15.

Kikula, Idris S. 1997. *Policy Implications on Environment: The Case of Villagisation in Tanzania.* Uppsala, Sweden: Nordiska Afrikainstitutet.

Kinyondo, S. 1971. "The Building of Socialism in Tanzania—Katoma Traditional Village: A Case Study of Problems and Possibilities of Transforming a Traditional Village into an Ujamaa Village." Bachelor's thesis, University of Dar es Salaam.

Kitching, Gavin N. 1982. *Development and Underdevelopment in Historical Perspective: Populism, Nationalism and Industrialization.* London: Methuen.

Kjaerby, Finn. 1989. *Villagization and the Crisis: Agricultural Production in Hanang District, Northern Tanzania.* Copenhagen: Centre of Development Research.

Kjekshus, Helge. 1977. *Ecology Control and Economic Development in East African History: The Case of Tanganyika, 1850–1950.* Berkeley: University of California Press.

Kleemeier, Lizz. 1984. "Domestic Policies Versus Poverty-Oriented Foreign Assistance in Tanzania." *Journal of Development Studies* 20 (2): 171–201.

Klerruu, Wilbert A. 1968. *Maongozi na utaratibu wa kutekeleza Azimio la Arusha katika Mkoa wa Mtwara* [Guide and Plan for the Implementation of the Arusha Declaration in Mtwara Region]. Dar es Salaam: Government Printer.

Konde, Hadji S. 1984. *Press Freedom in Tanzania*. Dar es Salaam: Eastern Africa Publications.

Korten, David C. 1980. "Community Organization and Rural Development: A Learning Process Approach." *Public Administration Review* 40 (4): 480–511.

Koselleck, Reinhart. 1985. *Futures Past: On the Semantics of Historical Time*. Cambridge, MA: MIT Press.

Kriesel, Herbert C., Charles K. Laurent, Carl Halpern, and Henry E. Larzelere. 1970. *Agricultural Marketing in Tanzania: Background Research and Policy Proposals*. East Lansing: Michigan State University.

Krueger, Anne O. 1992. *The Political Economy of Agricultural Pricing Policy*. Vol. 5, *A Synthesis of the Political Economy in Developing Countries*. Baltimore, MD: Johns Hopkins University Press.

Lal, Priya. 2010. "Militants, Mothers, and the National Family: *Ujamaa*, Gender, and Rural Development in Postcolonial Tanzania." *Journal of African History* 51 (1): 1–20.

———. 2012. "Self-Reliance and the State: The Multiple Meanings of Development in Early Post-Colonial Tanzania." *Africa: Journal of the International African Institute* 82 (2): 212–234.

Lane, Robert E. 1996. "What Rational Choice Explains." In *The Rational Choice Controversy: Economic Models of Politics Reconsidered*, edited by Jeffrey Friedman, 107–126. New Haven, CT: Yale University Press.

Latour, Bruno. 2005. *Reassembling the Social: An Introduction to Actor-Network-Theory*. Oxford: Oxford University Press.

Lewin, Roger. 1973. "Matetereka." In *Socialism in Tanzania*, Vol. 2, *Policies*, edited by Lionel Cliffe and John S. Saul, 189–194. Dar es Salaam: East African Publishing House.

Leys, Colin. 1969. *Politics and Change in Developing Countries: Studies in the Theory and Practice of Development*. Cambridge: Cambridge University Press.

———. 1996. *The Rise and Fall of Development Theory*. Bloomington: Indiana University Press.

Lichbach, Mark Irving. 1997. "Social Theory and Comparative Politics." In *Comparative Politics: Rationality, Culture, and Structure*, edited by Mark Irving Lichbach and Alan S. Zuckerman, 239–276. Cambridge: Cambridge University Press.

Lipton, Michael. 1993. "Urban Bias: Of Consequences, Classes and Causality." In *Beyond Urban Bias*, edited by Ashutosh Varshney, 229–258. London: Frank Cass.

Li, Tania Murray. 2007. *The Will to Improve: Governmentality, Development, and the Practice of Politics*. Durham, NC: Duke University Press.

Livingstone, Ian. 1979. "Some Requirements for Agricultural Planning in Tanzania." In *Papers on the Political Economy of Tanzania*, edited by Kwan S. Kim, Robert B. Mabele, and Michael J. Schultheis, 29–40. Nairobi: Heinemann Educational.

Lofchie, Michael. 1978. "Agrarian Crisis and Economic Liberalization in Tanzania." *Journal of Modern African Studies* 16 (3): 451–475.

———. 1989. *The Policy Factor: Agricultural Performance in Kenya and Tanzania*. Boulder, CO: Lynne Rienner.

———. 1993. "Trading Places: Economic Policy in Kenya and Tanzania." In *Hemmed In: Responses to Africa's Economic Decline*, edited by Thomas M. Callaghy and John Ravenhill, 398–462. New York: Columbia University Press.

———. 1994a. "The Politics of Agricultural Policy." In *Beyond Capitalism vs. Socialism in Kenya & Tanzania*, edited by Joel D. Barkan, 129–173. Boulder, CO: Lynne Rienner.

———. 1994b. "The New Political Economy of Africa." In *Political Development and the New Realism in Sub-Saharan Africa*, edited by David E. Apter and Carl G. Rosberg, 145–183. Charlottesville: University of Virginia Press.

Loxley, J., and A. Seuchi. 1975. "Financing Ujamaa—State Resources and Co-operative Development." In *Rural Cooperation in Tanzania*, edited by Lionel Cliffe, Peter Lawrence, William Luttrell, Shem Migot-Adholla, and John S. Saul, 538–554. Dar es Salaam: Tanzania Publishing House.

Ludden, David. 1992. "India's Development Regime." In *Colonialism and Culture*, edited by Nicholas Dirks, 247–287. Ann Arbor: Michigan University Press.

Luttrell, William L. 1971. *Villagisation, Co-operative Production, and Rural Cadres: Strategies and Tactics in Tanzanian Socialist Rural Development.* Dar es Salaam: Economic Research Bureau, University of Dar es Salaam.

Maddison, Angus. 2009. "Statistics on World Population, GDP and Per Capita GDP, 1–2006 AD." http://www.ggdc.net/Maddison/Historical_Statistics/horizontal-file_03–2009.xls.

Magoti, Charles K. 1984. *Peasant Participation and Rural Productivity in Tanzania: The Case of Mara Cotton Producers 1955–1977.* Hamburg: German Institute for Global and Area Studies.

Maguire, G. Andrew. 1969. *Toward "Uhuru" in Tanzania: The Politics of Participation.* London: Cambridge University Press.

Mamdani, Mahmood. 1996. *Citizen and Subject: Contemporary Africa and the Legacy of Late Colonialism.* Princeton, NJ: Princeton University Press.

Mapolu, Henry. 1973. "The Social and Economic Organization of Ujamaa Villages." Master's thesis, University of Dar es Salaam.

Mapolu, Henry, and Gerard Philippson. 1976. "Agricultural Co-operation and the Development of the Productive Forces: Some Lessons from Tanzania." *African Review* 6 (2): 65–107.

Maro, Paulo S. 1991. "The Arusha Declaration and the Social Services." In *Re-Thinking the Arusha Declaration*, edited by Jeannette Hartmann, 348–360. Copenhagen: Axel Nielsen & Søn.

Maro, Paulo S., and W. F. I. Mlay. 1982. "Population Redistribution in Tanzania." In *Redistribution of Population in Africa*, edited by John Innes Clarke and Leszek A. Kosiński, 176–181. London: Heinemann Educational.

Mascarenhas, Adolfo C. 1973. *Environment and Spatial Problems of Food Supply and Nutrition in Tanzania.* Dar es Salaam: Bureau of Resource Assessment and Land Use Planning.

———. 1977. *Settlement and Population Redistribution in Dodoma.* Dar es Salaam: Bureau of Resource Assessment and Land Use Planning.

Mascarenhas, Adolfo C., and S. M. Mbilinyi. 1969. *Bananas and the Dar es Salaam Market.* Dar es Salaam: Economic Research Bureau, University of Dar es Salaam.

Matango, Reuben R. 1975. "Operation Mara: Paradox of Democracy." *Maji Maji* [Journal of the University of Dar es Salaam Branch of the TANU Youth League] 20: 17–29.

Mazrui, Ali. 1991. "Building Socialism Without a Vanguard Party." In *Re-Thinking the Arusha Declaration*, edited by Jeannette Hartmann, 63–82. Copenhagen: Axel Nielsen & Søn.

Mbembe, Achille. 1991. "Power and Obscenity in the Post-Colonial Period: The Case of Cameroon." In *Rethinking Third World Politics*, edited by James Manor, 166–182. London: Longman.

———. 1992. "The Banality of Power and the Aesthetics of Vulgarity in the Postcolony." *Public Culture* 4 (2): 1–30.

McCall, Michael. 1985. "Environmental and Agricultural Impacts of Tanzania's Villagization Programme." In *Population and Development Projects in Africa*, edited by John Innes

Clarke, Mustafa Khogali, and Leszek A. Kosiński, 123–140. Cambridge: Cambridge University Press.

McCarthy, Dennis M. P. 1982. *Colonial Bureaucracy and Creating Underdevelopment: Tanganyika, 1919–1940*. Ames: Iowa State University Press.

McHenry, Dean E. 1974. "Concentration and Ujamaa Villages: A Note on Resettlement Efforts in Kigoma Region." *Taamuli: A Political Science Forum* 5 (1): 54–59.

———. 1979. *Tanzania's Ujamaa Villages: The Implementation of a Rural Development Strategy*. Berkeley: Institute of International Studies, University of California.

Mesaki, Simeon. 1975. "Operation Pwani: Kisarawe District—Implementation Problems and Prospects." Master's thesis, University of Dar es Salaam.

———. 1994. "Witch-Killing in Sukumaland." In *Witchcraft in Contemporary Tanzania*, edited by Ray Abrahams, 47–60. Cambridge: African Studies Centre, University of Cambridge.

———. 1999. "Near and Yet So Poor: Explaining Underdevelopment in the Coast Region of Tanzania." In *Agrarian Economy, State and Society in Contemporary Tanzania*, edited by Peter G. Forster and Sam Maghimbi, 200–213. Aldershot, UK: Ashgate.

Michener, Victoria. 1998. "The Participatory Approach: Contradiction and Co-option in Burkina Faso." *World Development* 26 (12): 2105–2118.

Migdal, Joel S. 1988. *Strong Societies and Weak States: State-Society Relations and State Capabilities in the Third World*. Princeton, NJ: Princeton University Press.

———. 2001. *State in Society: Studying How States and Societies Transform and Constitute One Another*. Cambridge: Cambridge University Press.

Mitchell, Timothy. 1991. "The Limits of the State: Beyond Statist Approaches and Their Critics." *American Political Science Review* 85 (1): 77–96.

———. 2000. Introduction to *Questions of Modernity*, edited by Timothy Mitchell, xi–xxvii. Minneapolis: University of Minnesota Press.

———. 2002. *Rule of Experts: Egypt, Techno-Politics, Modernity*. Berkeley: University of California Press.

Mmbaga, F. E. 1976/1977. "Villagization and Decentralization in Itobo Ward—Nzega District." Bachelor's thesis, University of Dar es Salaam.

Mombeshora, Solomon. 1994. "Witches, Witchcraft and the Question of Order: A View from a Bena Village in the Southern Highlands." In *Witchcraft in Contemporary Tanzania*, edited by Ray Abrahams, 71–86. Cambridge: African Studies Centre, University of Cambridge.

Moody, Tony. 1972. "A Comparative Study of Six Ujamaa Villages in Karagwe District—West Lake Region." IDR Paper 72.13. Copenhagen: Institute for Development Research.

Moore, John E. 1979. "The Villagisation Process and Rural Development in the Mwanza Region of Tanzania." *Geografiska Annaler* 61 (B): 65–80.

Moore, Mick. 1990. "The Rational Choice Paradigm and the Allocation of Agricultural Development Resources." *Development and Change* 21 (2): 225–246.

———. 2001. "Empowerment at Last?" *Journal of International Development* 13 (3): 321–329.

Mosse, David. 2005. *Cultivating Development: An Ethnography of Aid Policy and Practice*. New York: Pluto Press.

Msambichaka, Lucian A., Benno J. Ndulu, and H. K. R. Amanti. 1983. *Agricultural Development in Tanzania: Policy Evolution, Performance and Evaluation; The First Two Decades of Independence*. Göttingen, Germany: Friedrich-Ebert Stiftung and Göttinger Tageblatt.

Msekwa, Pius. 1977. *Towards Party Supremacy.* Kampala: East African Publications.

Mshana, Rogate R. 1992. *Insisting Upon People's Knowledge to Resist Developmentalism: Peasant Communities as Producers of Knowledge for Social Transformation in Tanzania.* Frankfurt: Verlag für Interkulturelle Kommunikation.

Mueller, Bernd E. T. 2011. "The Agrarian Question in Tanzania: Using New Evidence to Reconcile an Old Debate." *Review of African Political Economy* 38 (127): 23–42.

Mugezi, P. 1977. "Location of New Villages in Bukoba and Muleba Districts." Diploma thesis, Ardhi Institute, University of Dar es Salaam.

Mukandala, Rwekaza S. 1983. "Bureaucracy and Socialism in Tanzania: The Case of the Civil Service." *African Review* 10 (2): 1–21.

Mushi, Samuel S. 1974. "Revolution by Evolution: The Tanzanian Road to Socialism." PhD diss., Yale University.

———. 1981. "Ujamaa Planning and the Politics of Allocation in Tanzania: The Case of Morogoro District." In *Approaches to Rural Transformation in East Africa,* edited by H. W. O. Okoth-Ogendo, 134–163. Nairobi: Bookwise.

Musoke, I. K. S. 1970. "The Establishment of Ujamaa Villages in Bukoba: Rugazi (Nyerere) Village—A Case Study." Bachelor's thesis, University of Dar es Salaam.

———. 1971. "Building Socialism in Bukoba: The Establishment of Rugazi (Nyerere) Ujamaa Village." In *Building Ujamaa Villages in Tanzania,* edited by J. H. Proctor, 1–14. Dar es Salaam: Tanzania Publishing House.

Musti de Gennaro, Bruno. 1979. "Ten Years After: A Comment on the Ruvuma Development Association." Paper presented at an Economic Research Bureau Seminar, University of Dar es Salaam, October 16, 1979.

———. 1981. "Ujamaa: The Aggrandizement of the State." In *The Political Economy of Rural Development: Peasants, International Capital, and the State; Case Studies in Colombia, Mexico, Tanzania, and Bangladesh,* edited by Rosemary Galli, 111–155. Albany: State University of New York Press.

Mwakikagile, Godfrey. 2007. *Nyerere and Africa: End of an Era.* Dar es Salaam: New Africa Press.

Mwapachu, Juma V. 1979. "Operation Planned Villages in Rural Tanzania: A Revolutionary Strategy for Development." In *African Socialism in Practice: The Tanzanian Experience,* edited by Andrew Coulson, 114–127. Nottingham, UK: Spokesman Books.

Mwase, Nkunde, and Benno J. Ndulu. 2008. "Tanzania: Explaining Four Decades of Episodic Growth." In *The Political Economy of Economic Growth in Africa 1960–2000,* Vol. 2, edited by Benno J. Ndulu, Stephen A. O'Connell, Jean-Paul Azam, Robert H. Bates, Augustin K. Fosu, Jan Willem Gunning, and Dominique Njinkeu, 426–470. Cambridge: Cambridge University Press.

Myers, Robert B. 1973. "The Structure and Performance of a Commercial Farm Settlement: An Economic Analysis of One of Tanzania's Village Settlement Schemes." PhD diss., Syracuse University.

Ndonde, Emil C. 1975a. "Educational Methods for Self-Reliant Development." In *Agricultural Extension in Ujamaa Village Development,* edited by Hermann Hänsel, James de Vries, and Phillip C. Ndedya, 164–179. Papers and proceedings of a workshop held at the University of Dar es Salaam, Morogoro, September 22–27, 1975.

———. 1975b. "Litowa—Interview with E. Ndonde." In *Rural Cooperation in Tanzania,* edited by Lionel Cliffe, Peter Lawrence, William Luttrell, Shem Migot-Adholla, and John S. Saul, 360–369. Dar es Salaam: Tanzania Publishing House.

Nellis, John R. 1972. *A Theory of Ideology: The Tanzanian Example.* Nairobi: Oxford University Press.

Newiger, Nikolaus. 1968. "Village Settlement Schemes: The Problems of Co-operative Farming." In *Smallholder Farming and Smallholder Development in Tanzania: Ten Case Studies,* edited by Hans Ruthenberg, 251–273. London: C. Hurst.

Nugent, Paul. 1995. *Big Men, Small Boys and Politics in Ghana: Power, Ideology and the Burden of History, 1982–1994.* London: Pinter.

Nyerere, Julius K. 1966. *Freedom and Unity: Uhuru na Umoja; A Selection from Writings and Speeches 1952–65.* London: Oxford University Press.

———. 1968. *Freedom and Socialism: Uhuru na Ujamaa; A Selection from Writings and Speeches 1965–1967.* New York: Oxford University Press.

———. 1973. *Freedom and Development: Uhuru na Maendeleo; A Selection from Writings and Speeches 1968–1973.* New York: Oxford University Press.

———. 1975. "Presidential Circular No. 1 of 1969: The Development of Ujamaa Villages." In *Rural Cooperation in Tanzania,* edited by Lionel Cliffe, Peter Lawrence, William Luttrell, Shem Migot-Adholla, and John S. Saul, 27–36. Dar es Salaam: Tanzania Publishing House.

O'Malley, Pat, Lorna Weir, and Clifford Shearing. 1997. "Governmentality, Criticism, Politics." *Economy and Society* 26 (4): 501–517.

Omari, Cuthberg K. 1976. *Strategy for Rural Development: Tanzania Experience.* Kampala: East African Literature Bureau.

Othman, Haroub, ed. 1980. *The State in Tanzania: Who Controls It and Whose Interest Does It Serve?* Dar es Salaam: Dar es Salaam University Press.

Parkipuny, Ole M. L. 1979. "Some Crucial Aspects of the Maasai Predicament." In *African Socialism in Practice: The Tanzanian Experience,* edited by Andrew Coulson, 136–157. Nottingham, UK: Spokesman Books.

Pearce, Robert D. 1982. *The Turning Point in Africa: British Colonial Policy 1938–48.* London: Frank Cass.

Pigg, Stacey Leigh. 1992. "Inventing Social Categories through Place: Social Representations and Development in Nepal." *Comparative Studies in Society and History* 34: 491–513.

Porter, Philip Wayland. 2006. *Challenging Nature: Local Knowledge, Agroscience, and Food Security in Tanga Region, Tanzania.* University of Chicago Geography Research Papers 246. Chicago: University of Chicago Press.

Postero, Nancy Grey. 2006. *Now We Are Citizens: Indigenous Politics in Postmulticultural Bolivia.* Stanford: Stanford University Press.

Pratt, Cranford. 1972. "The Cabinet and Presidential Leadership in Tanzania in 1960–66." In *Socialism in Tanzania,* Vol. 1, *Politics,* edited by Lionel Cliffe and John S. Saul, 226–240. Dar es Salaam: East African Publishing House.

———. 1976. *The Critical Phase in Tanzania, 1945–1968: Nyerere and the Emergence of a Socialist Strategy.* Cambridge: Cambridge University Press.

Price, Robert. 1974. "Politics and Culture in Contemporary Ghana: The Big-Man Small-Boy Syndrome." *Journal of African Studies* 1 (2): 173–204.

Putnam, Robert D. 1993. *Making Democracy Work: Civic Traditions in Modern Italy.* Princeton, NJ: Princeton University Press.

Putterman, Louis G. 1980. "The Producer's Organizational Choice: Theory and the Case of the Tanzanian Villages." PhD diss., Yale University.

Rahnema, Majid. 1992. "Participation." In *The Development Dictionary: A Guide to Knowledge as Power,* edited by Wolfgang Sachs, 116–131. London: Zed Books.

———. 1997. "Towards Post-Development: Searching for Signposts, a New Language and New Paradigm." In *The Post-Development Reader,* edited by Majid Rahnema and Victoria Bawtree, 377–403. London: Zed Books.

Rahnema, Majid, and Victoria Bawtree, eds. 1997. *The Post-Development Reader.* London: Zed Books.

Raikes, Philip. 1972. "Village Planning for Ujamaa." *Taamuli: A Political Science Forum* 3 (1): 3–26.

———. 1975. "Ujamaa and Rural Socialism." *Review of African Political Economy* 3: 33–52.

———. 1986. "Eating the Carrot and Wielding the Stick: The Agricultural Sector in Tanzania." In *Tanzania: Crisis and Struggle for Survival,* edited by Jannik Boesen, Kjell J. Havnevik, Juhani Koponen, and Rie Odgaard, 105–142. Uppsala, Sweden: Scandinavian Institute of African Studies.

Rald, Jørgen. 1970. *Ujamaa—Problems of Implementation (Experience from West Lake).* Dar es Salaam: Bureau of Resource Assessment and Land Use Planning.

Rald, Jørgen, and Karen Rald. 1975. *Rural Organization in Bukoba District, Tanzania.* Uppsala, Sweden: Scandinavian Institute of African Studies.

Ranger, Terence. 1983. "The Invention of Tradition in Colonial Africa." In *The Invention of Tradition,* edited by Eric Hobsbawm and Terence Ranger, 211–262. Cambridge: Cambridge University Press.

Reckwitz, Andreas. 2002. "Toward a Theory of Social Practices: A Development in Cultural Theorizing." *European Journal of Social Theory* 5 (2): 243–263.

Reddy, Sanjay, and Antoine Heuty. 2008. "Global Development Goals: The Folly of Technocratic Pretensions." *Development Policy Review* 26 (1): 5–28.

Resnick, Idrian N. 1981. *The Long Transition: Building Socialism in Tanzania.* New York: Monthly Review Press.

Rigby, Peter. 1969. "Pastoralism and Prejudice: Ideology and Rural Development in East Africa." In *Society and Social Change in Eastern Africa,* edited by Peter Rigby, 42–52. Kampala: Makerere Institute of Social Research.

———. 1977. "Local Participation in National Politics: Ugogo, Tanzania." *Africa: Journal of the International African Institute* 47 (1): 87–108.

Ross, C. R., P. M. Worsley, and G. Clayton. 1965. "Report of the British Economic Mission on the Tanzania Five-Year Development Plan." Unpublished report.

Rouse, Joseph. 2007. "Practice Theory." In *Handbook of the Philosophy of Science,* edited by Stephen P. Turner and Mark W. Risjord, 639–681. Dordrecht: Elsevier.

Rugumamu, Severine Mushambampale. 1997. *Lethal Aid: The Illusion of Socialism and Self-Reliance in Tanzania.* Trenton, NJ: Africa World Press.

Sachs, Wolfgang, ed. 1992. *The Development Dictionary: A Guide to Knowledge as Power.* London: Zed Books.

Sadleir, Randal. 1999. *Tanzania: Journey to Republic.* London: Radcliffe.

Samoff, Joel. 1974. *Tanzania: Local Politics and the Structure of Power.* Madison: University of Wisconsin Press.

Sandberg, Audun. 1973. "Ujamaa and Control of Environment." Paper presented at the Annual Social Science Conference of East African Universities, Dar es Salaam, December 1973.

Sandbrook, Richard. 1985. *The Politics of Africa's Economic Stagnation.* Cambridge: Cambridge University Press.

Sanger, Clyde. 1969. *Half a Loaf: Canada's Semi-Role Among Developing Countries.* Toronto: Ryerson.

Saul, John S. 1973. "African Socialism in One Country: Tanzania." In *Essays on the Political Economy of Africa*, edited by John S. Saul and Giovanni Arrighi, 237–312. New York: Monthly Review Press.

———. 1975a. "The Reorganization of the Victoria Federation of Cooperative Unions." In *Rural Cooperation in Tanzania*, edited by Lionel Cliffe, Peter Lawrence, William Luttrell, Shem Migot-Adholla, and John S. Saul, 212–220. Dar es Salaam: Tanzania Publishing House.

———. 1975b. "The Role of the Cooperative Movement." In *Rural Cooperation in Tanzania*, edited by Lionel Cliffe, Peter Lawrence, William Luttrell, Shem Migot-Adholla, and John S. Saul, 206–211. Dar es Salaam: Tanzania Publishing House.

———. 1979. *The State and Revolution in East Africa*. New York: Monthly Review Press.

———. 2005. *The Next Liberation Struggle: Capitalism, Socialism, and Democracy in Southern Africa*. Toronto: Between the Lines.

Schatzberg, Michael. 2001. *Political Legitimacy in Middle Africa: Father, Family, Food*. Bloomington: Indiana University Press.

Schneider, Leander. 2003. "The Tanzania National Archives." *History in Africa* 30: 447–454.

———. 2004. "Freedom and Unfreedom in Rural Development: Julius Nyerere, Ujamaa Vijijini, and Villagization." *Canadian Journal of African Studies* 38 (2): 344–393.

———. 2006. "The Maasai's New Clothes: A Developmentalist Modernity and Its Exclusions." *Africa Today* 53 (1): 100–131.

———. 2007. "High on Modernity? Explaining the Failings of Tanzanian Villagization." *African Studies* 66 (1): 9–38.

Scott, James C. 1985. *Weapons of the Weak: Everyday Forms of Peasant Resistance*. New Haven, CT: Yale University Press.

———. 1998. *Seeing like a State: How Certain Schemes to Improve the Human Condition Have Failed*. New Haven, CT: Yale University Press.

Semboja, Joseph, and Ole Therkildsen. 1994. *Service Provision under Stress in East Africa: The State, NGOs & People's Organizations in Kenya, Tanzania & Uganda*. Copenhagen: Centre for Development Research in association with James Currey.

Sen, Amartya K. 1977. "Rational Fools: A Critique of the Behavioral Foundations of Economic Theory." *Philosophy & Public Affairs* 6 (4): 317–344.

———. 1999. *Development as Freedom*. New York: Knopf.

Sender, John. 1974. *Some Preliminary Notes on the Political Economy of Rural Development in Tanzania*. Economic Research Bureau, University of Dar es Salaam.

Senellart, Michel. 2007. "Course Context." In *Security, Territory, Population: Lectures at the Collège de France, 1977–1978*, by Michel Foucault, edited by Michel Senellart, translated by Graham Burchell, 369–401. New York: Palgrave Macmillan.

Sharma, Aradhana, and Akhil Gupta. 2006. "Introduction: Rethinking Theories of the State in an Age of Globalization." In *The Anthropology of the State: A Reader*, edited by Aradhana Sharma and Akhil Gupta, 1–41. Oxford: Blackwell.

Shivji, Issa G. 1973. "Tanzania: The Silent Class Struggle." In *Socialism in Tanzania*, Vol. 2, *Policies*, edited by Lionel Cliffe and John S. Saul, 304–330. Dar es Salaam: East African Publishing House.

———. 1978–1981. "The State of the Constitution and the Constitution of the State in Tanzania." *Eastern Africa Law Review* 11–14: 1–34.

———. 1986. "Introduction: The Transformation of the State and the Working People." In *The State and the Working People in Tanzania*, edited by Issa G. Shivji, 1–15. Dakar: CODESRIA.

———. 1992. "The Roots of an Agrarian Crisis in Tanzania: A Theoretical Perspective." In *The Tanzanian Peasantry: Economy in Crisis,* edited by Peter G. Forster and Sam Maghimbi, 124–150. Aldershot, UK: Avebury.

———. 2010. "The Village in Mwalimu's Thought and Political Practice." In *Africa's Liberation: The Legacy of Nyerere,* edited by Chambi Chachage and Annar Cassam, 120–133. Kampala, Uganda: Pambazuka Press.

———. 2012. "Nationalism and Pan-Africanism: Decisive Moments in Nyerere's Intellectual and Political Thought." *Review of African Political Economy* 39 (131): 103–116.

Shrestha, Nanda. 1995. "Becoming a Development Category." In *Power of Development,* edited by Jonathan Crush, 266–277. New York: Routledge.

Sitari, Taimi. 1983. "Settlement Changes in the Bagamoyo District of Tanzania as a Consequence of Villagization." *Fennia* 161 (1): 1–90.

Smith, James Howard. 2008. *Bewitching Development: Witchcraft and the Reinvention of Development in Neoliberal Kenya.* Chicago: University of Chicago Press.

Smith, William Edgett. 1981. *Nyerere of Tanzania.* Harare: Zimbabwe Publishing House.

Somers, Margaret. 1992. "Narrativity, Narrative Identity, and Social Action: Rethinking English Working-Class Formation." *Social Science History* 16 (4): 591–630.

Spear, Thomas. 2003. "Neo-Traditionalism and the Limits of Invention in British Colonial Africa." *Journal of African History* 44 (1): 3–27.

Stein, Howard, and Ernest Wilson. 1993. "The Political Economy of Robert Bates: A Critical Reading of Rational Choice in Africa." *World Development* 21 (6): 1035–1053.

Sturmer, Martin. 1998. *The Media History of Tanzania.* Ndanda: Ndanda Mission Press.

Sumien, T. 1978. *Training Programme for Operational Physical Planners, Ardhi Institute, Dar es Salaam.* New York: UN Office of Technical Cooperation.

Sumra, Suliman. 1991. "Education, Production and Social Change in Rural Tanzania." In *Re-Thinking the Arusha Declaration,* edited by Jeannette Hartmann, 240–247. Copenhagen: Axel Nielsen & Søn.

Svendsen, Knud Erik. 1986. "The Creation of Macroeconomic Imbalances and a Structural Crisis." In *Tanzania: Crisis and Struggle for Survival,* edited by Jannik Boesen, Kjell J. Havnevik, Juhani Koponen, and Rie Odgaard, 59–78. Uppsala, Sweden: Scandinavian Institute of African Studies.

Swantz, Marja-Liisa. 1995. "Conflicts Between the Systems of Knowledge of the Pastoralists and Developmentalists: The Case of Parakuyo Maasai in Bagamoyo District." In *The Tanzanian Peasantry: Further Studies,* edited by Peter G. Forster and Sam Maghimbi, 218–255. Aldershot, UK: Avebury.

Swantz, Marja-Liisa, and Aili Marie Tripp. 1996. "Development for 'Big Fish' or for 'Small Fish'? A Case Study of Contrasts in Tanzania's Fishery Sector." In *Decolonizing Knowledge: From Development to Dialogue,* edited by Frédérique Apffel-Marglin and Stephen A. Marglin, 43–66. Oxford: Clarendon.

Syracuse University. 1966. *Syracuse University Village Settlement Project—Report Nos. 1–43.* Mimeograph.

Talle, Aud. 1999. "Pastoralists at the Border: Maasai Poverty and the Development Discourse in Tanzania." In *The Poor Are Not Us: Poverty and Pastoralism in Eastern Africa,* edited by David M. Anderson and Vigdis Broch-Due, 106–124. Oxford: James Currey.

Tanganyika. 1964. *Tanganyika Five-Year Plan for Economic and Social Development, 1st July, 1964–30th June, 1969.* Vol. 1, *General Analysis.* Dar es Salaam: Government Printer.

TANU (Tanganyika African National Union). 1968. *Taarifa ya tume maalum iliyokwenda*

Mkoa wa Ziwa Magharibi kusikiliza matatizo juu ya wabunge wa mkoa huo na mkuu wa mkoa huo. Dar es Salaam: Government Printer.

———. 1972. *Mwongozo wa TANU.* Dar es Salaam: Printpak.

———. 1973. *Maendeleo ni kazi.* Dar es Salaam: Government Printer.

Tanzania Year 16. 1975. "Postscript to Mbambara 1972." In *Rural Cooperation in Tanzania,* edited by Lionel Cliffe, Peter Lawrence, William Luttrell, Shem Migot-Adholla, and John S. Saul, 392–395. Dar es Salaam: Tanzania Publishing House.

Taylor, Michael. 1996. "When Rationality Fails." In *The Rational Choice Controversy: Economic Models of Politics Reconsidered,* edited by Jeffrey Friedman, 223–234. New Haven, CT: Yale University Press.

Thiele, Graham. 1982. "Development Plans and the Economics of Household and Village in Dodoma Region, Tanzania." PhD diss., Cambridge University.

———. 1986. "The Tanzanian Villagisation Programme: Its Impact on Household Production in Dodoma." *Canadian Journal of African Studies* 20 (2): 243–258.

Thoden van Velzen, H. U. E. 1975. "Controllers in Rural Tanzania." In *Town and Country in Central and Eastern Africa,* edited by David Parkin. Oxford: Oxford University Press.

———. 1977. "Staff, Kulaks and Peasants: A Study of a Political Field." In *Government and Rural Development in East Africa: Essays on Political Penetration,* edited by Lionel Cliffe, James S. Coleman, and Martin R. Doornbos, 223–250. The Hague: Martinus Nijhoff.

Thoden van Velzen, H. U. E., and J. J. Sterkenburg. 1972. "The Party Supreme." In *Socialism in Tanzania,* Vol. 1, *Politics,* edited by Lionel Cliffe and John S. Saul, 257–264. Dar es Salaam: East African Publishing House.

Thomas, Ian D. 1982. "Villagization in Tanzania: Planning Potential and Practical Problems." In *Redistribution of Population in Africa,* edited by John Innes Clarke and Leszek A. Kosiński, 182–190. London: Heinemann Educational.

———. 1985. "Development and Population Redistribution: Measuring Recent Population Redistribution in Tanzania." In *Population and Development Projects in Africa,* edited by John Innes Clarke, Mustafa Khogali, and Leszek A. Kosiński, 141–152. Cambridge: Cambridge University Press.

Timmer, C. Peter. 1991. "The Role of the State in Agricultural Development." In *Agriculture and the State: Growth, Employment, and Poverty in Developing Countries,* edited by C. Peter Timmer, 1–28. Ithaca, NY: Cornell University Press.

Tordoff, William, and Ali A. Mazrui. 1972. "The Left and the Super-Left in Tanzania." *Journal of Modern African Studies* 10 (3): 427–445.

Toroka, Suleman R. 1973. "Education for Self-Reliance: The Litowa Experiment." In *Socialism in Tanzania,* Vol. 2, *Policies,* edited by Lionel Cliffe and John S. Saul, 264–270. Dar es Salaam: East African Publishing House.

Tripp, Aili Marie. 1997. *Changing the Rules: The Politics of Liberalization and the Urban Informal Economy in Tanzania.* Berkeley: University of California Press.

———. 2003. "Forging Developmental Synergies Between States and Associations." In *Beyond Structural Adjustment: The Institutional Context of African Development,* edited by Nicolas van de Walle, Nicole Ball, and Vijaya Ramachandran, 131–158. New York: Palgrave Macmillan.

Tschannerl, Gerhard. 1976. "Rural Water Supply in Tanzania: Is 'Politics' or 'Technique' in Command?" *African Review* 6 (2): 108–166.

Tuguta, M. Y. 1978. "Rural Spatial Reorganization: The Case of Mlali." Master's thesis, University of Dar es Salaam.

Turok, Ben Turok. 1975. "The Problem of Agency in Tanzania's Rural Development: The Rufiji Ujamaa Scheme." In *Rural Cooperation in Tanzania*, edited by Lionel Cliffe, Peter Lawrence, William Luttrell, Shem Migot-Adholla, and John S. Saul, 396–417. Dar es Salaam: Tanzania Publishing House.

UNDP (United Nations Development Programme). 2012. *Africa Human Development Report 2012: Towards a Food Secure Future*. New York: United Nations Publications.

Uphoff, Norman Thomas. 1983. *Rural Development and Local Organization in Asia: South East Asia*. Delhi: Macmillan.

———. 1992. *Learning From Gal Oya: Possibilities for Participatory Development and Post-Newtonian Social Science*. Ithaca, NY: Cornell University Press.

Uphoff, Norman Thomas, Milton J. Esman, and Anirudh Krishna. 1998. *Reasons for Success: Learning From Instructive Experiences in Rural Development*. West Hartford, CT: Kumarian.

URT (United Republic of Tanzania). 1966a. *The Rural Settlement Commission—A Report on the Village Settlement Programme from the Inception of the Rural Settlement Commission to 31st December, 1965*. Ministry of Lands, Settlement and Water Development. Dar es Salaam: Survey Division.

———. 1966b. *Report of the Presidential Special Committee of Enquiry into Co-operative Movement and Marketing Boards*. Dar es Salaam: Government Printer.

———. 1967. *Wages, Incomes, Rural Development, Investment and Price Policy*. Dar es Salaam: Government Printer.

———. 1968. *Annual Report of the Surveys and Mapping Division*. Ministry of Lands, Settlement and Water Development. Dar es Salaam: Government Printer.

———. 1969. *Tanzania Second Five-Year Plan for Economic and Social Development, 1st July, 1969–30th June, 1974*. Vol. 1, *General Analysis*. Dar es Salaam: Government Printer.

———. 1971. *Annual Report on Livestock Industry, Ruvuma Region*. Ministry of Agriculture.

———. 1972. *Vijiji vya ujamaa vilivyoshinda*. Office of the Prime Minister and Second Vice President. Dar es Salaam: Printpak.

———. 1975. *Model Village Plan Handbook*. Ministry of Lands, Housing and Urban Development.

———. 1980. *Report on Village Survey 1979*. Ujamaa and Cooperative Development Department, Office of the Prime Minister. Dodoma: Government Printer.

———. 1994. *Report of the Presidential Commission of Inquiry into Land Matters*. Vol. 1, *Land Policy and Land Tenure Structure*. Uddevalla, Sweden: Bohusläningens Boktryckeri.

van Bergen, Jan P. 1981. *Development and Religion in Tanzania: Sociological Soundings in Christian Participation in Rural Transformation*. Madras/Leiden, the Netherlands: Christian Literature Society.

van de Walle, Nicolas. 2001. *African Economies and the Politics of Permanent Crisis, 1979–1999*. New York: Cambridge University Press.

Varshney, Ashutosh, ed. 1993. *Beyond Urban Bias*. London: Frank Cass.

———. 1994. *Democracy, Development, and the Countryside: Urban-Rural Struggles in India*. Cambridge: Cambridge University Press.

von Freyhold, Michaela. 1971. "Rural Development through Ujamaa Vijijini (Some Considerations Based on Experiences in Tanga). Vol. 3, Case Studies for Tanga Coast." Unpublished typescript, University of Dar es Salaam.

———. 1976. "The Problem of Rural Development and the Politics of Ujamaa Vijijini in Handeni." *African Review* 6 (2): 129–142.

———. 1979. *Ujamaa Villages in Tanzania: Analysis of a Social Experiment*. New York: Monthly Review Press.

Walters, William. 2012. *Governmentality: Critical Encounters*. New York: Routledge.

Walton, John, and David Seddon. 1994. *Free Markets & Food Riots: The Politics of Global Adjustment*. Oxford: Blackwell.

Walwa, Peter C. 1967. *Mpango wa kutekeleza Azimo la Arusha Mkoa za Ziwa Magharibi* [Plan for the Implementation of the Arusha Declaration in the West Lake Region]. Dar es Salaam: Dar es Salaam Printer.

Wenner, Kate. 1970. *Shamba Letu*. Boston: Houghton Mifflin.

West, Harry G. 2005. *Kupilikula: Governance and the Invisible Realm in Mozambique*. Chicago: University of Chicago Press.

Wicken, Joan E. 1969. "The Beginnings of Kivukoni College." *Mbioni: The Journal of Kivukoni College* 5 (8): 5–11.

Woodruff, David M. 2005. "Commerce and Demolition in Tsarist and Soviet Russia: Lessons for Theories of Trade Politics and the Philosophy of Social Science." *Review of International Political Economy* 12 (2): 199–225.

World Bank. 2007. *World Development Report 2008: Agriculture for Development*. Washington, DC: World Bank.

Yalan, E. 1963. *Report on the Creation of an Organizational Framework for the Villagization of Tanganyika*. Jerusalem: State of Israel, Ministry of Foreign Affairs.

Yoshida, Masao. 1974. *Agricultural Survey of the Lower Rufiji Plain*. Dar es Salaam: Government Printer.

Young, Crawford. 1994. *The African Colonial State in Comparative Perspective*. New Haven, CT: Yale University Press.

———. 2004. "The End of the Post-Colonial State in Africa? Reflections on Changing African Political Dynamics." *African Affairs* 103: 23–49.

<1/2LINE#>

Index

LEANDER SCHNEIDER holds a PhD in political science from Columbia University. He has done extensive field research in Tanzania, work based on which has appeared in *African Studies,* the *African Studies Review,* and *Africa Today,* among other journals. He currently teaches African and comparative politics and politics of development at Concordia University in Montreal, where he is Associate Professor of Political Science.

Lightning Source UK Ltd.
Milton Keynes UK
UKOW06f1439191014

240264UK00016B/101/P